CATO
SUPREME COURT
REVIEW

2017—2018

CATO SUPREME COURT REVIEW

2017—2018

ROGER PILON
Publisher

ILYA SHAPIRO
Editor in Chief

TREVOR BURRUS
Managing Editor

ROBERT A. LEVY
Associate Editor

CLARK NEILY
Associate Editor

WALTER OLSON
Associate Editor

**ROBERT A. LEVY
CENTER FOR CONSTITUTIONAL STUDIES**

INSTITUTE
Washington, D.C.

THE CATO SUPREME COURT REVIEW (ISBN 978-1-948647-19-9) is published annually at the close of each Supreme Court term by the Cato Institute, 1000 Massachusetts Ave., N.W.,Washington, D.C. 20001-5403.

CORRESPONDENCE. Correspondence regarding subscriptions, changes of address, procurement of back issues, advertising and marketing matters, and so forth, should be addressed to:

Publications Department
The Cato Institute
1000 Massachusetts Ave., N.W.
Washington, D.C. 20001

All other correspondence, including requests to quote or reproduce material, should be addressed to the editor.

CITATIONS: Citation to this volume of the Review should conform to the following style: 2017-2018 Cato Sup. Ct. Rev. (2018).

DISCLAIMER. The views expressed by the authors of the articles are their own and are not attributable to the editor, the editorial board, or the Cato Institute.

INTERNET ADDRESS. Articles from past editions are available to the general public, free of charge, at www.cato.org/pubs/scr.

ISBN 978-1-948647-19-9 (print)
ISBN 978-1-948647-20-5 (digital)

Printed in the United States of America.

Cato Institute
1000 Massachusetts Ave., N.W.
Washington, D.C. 20001
www.cato.org

Published through the generosity of George M. Yeager

Contents

CONTENTS

The First Amendment and The Culture Wars

Federalism and Government Structure

Next Year

The Battle for the Court: Politics vs. Principles

Roger Pilon[*]

The Cato Institute's Robert A. Levy Center for Constitutional Studies is pleased to publish this 17th volume of the *Cato Supreme Court Review*, an annual critique of the Court's most important decisions from the term just ended plus a look at the term ahead, all from a classical liberal, Madisonian perspective, grounded in the nation's first principles, liberty through constitutionally limited government. We release this volume each year at Cato's annual Constitution Day symposium. And each year in this space I discuss briefly a theme that seemed to emerge from the Court's term or from the larger setting in which the term unfolded.

The October 2017 term was noteworthy for a number of decisions, discussed further on by our authors, but barely had it ended when it was overshadowed by Justice Anthony Kennedy's announcement that he would be stepping down from the seat he had held for three decades. The foreboding on the left was immediate. Despite his failure this term to join the Court's four liberals on any of the contentious 5-4 decisions, Kennedy had long been the Court's "swing" vote—a term he disliked—often rescuing the liberals' agenda from the Court's conservatives, and at times advancing it himself. But the left's anger grew only more intense when President Trump nominated the apparently more predictably conservative Judge Brett Kavanaugh for the seat.

In fact, so distraught were Senate Democrats that many, knowing little about Kavanaugh except his billing as a conservative, announced

[*] Vice president for legal affairs at the Cato Institute, founding director of Cato's Center for Constitutional Studies, inaugural holder of Cato's B. Kenneth Simon Chair in Constitutional Studies, and founding publisher of the *Cato Supreme Court Review*.

immediately that they would vote against his confirmation. Editorials and op-eds quickly appeared demanding reams of records bearing little if at all on his qualifications. The aim, plainly, was to stall the hearings until after the mid-term elections—or better still, until after a new Congress had been seated, possibly with a Democratic Senate. Those efforts have come up short: At this writing, Senate Judiciary Committee Chairman Chuck Grassley has just scheduled hearings to begin on September 4, prompting calls for Democrats to boycott them.

Committee Democrats will doubtless ignore those calls, which means that by the time this volume appears we are likely to have endured a repeat of the bitter politicized hearings we witnessed a year ago for then-Judge Neil Gorsuch, about which I wrote at length in this space. But these hearings may be even more politicized because the stakes for the left are higher. Last year a conservative was replacing another conservative, the late Justice Antonin Scalia (although Gorsuch is proving to be as much a classical liberal as a conservative). This time it is that swing-vote seat that is at stake—and liberals fear, not without reason, that Kavanaugh's vote will swing less often their way. At stake, they say, is nothing less than the Court's "balance."

The Politicization of the Law

The anger on the left is due partly, of course, to the perfectly legitimate political gamble Senate Republicans made when they decided to sit on President Obama's nomination of Judge Merrick Garland as the 2016 presidential primaries were already under way. Part of the tit-for-tat behavior that began with the brutal confirmation battle that followed President Reagan's 1987 nomination of Judge Robert Bork, the Republican refusal to act reflected simply how politicized our courts have become—to say nothing of our law. The idea that the Court should be ideologically "balanced," for example, a plea seemingly for "fairness," bespeaks at bottom a conception of law more politics than law, more will than reason—a conception better suited for the legislature than the courtroom. Indeed, it says that there is no objective standard for law, that law *is* politics by another name. No less than Justice Elena Kagan, reflecting on the current battle to confirm Kavanaugh, said it makes the Court look like we are "junior varsity politicians."

To be sure, there are domains of law where "politics"—defined as the assertion of will informed, usually, by reason—properly belongs, where reasonable people can have reasonable differences about where to draw the line in such common-law areas as nuisance, risk, and remedies. So too with various due process matters such as determining "reasonable" searches and seizures. One wants some balance on the courts or legislatures that draw such lines, to say nothing of legislatures authorized to pursue various public ends where differing value judgments are ordinarily in play.

But it is quite another matter where the law is relatively clear and, especially, where background presumptions limiting discretion are manifest, for there is no balancing to be done in such cases. State police power, for example, is meant mainly to secure our rights. Thus, to take a few cases that have made their way to the Court, laws criminalizing interracial marriage, the sale and use of contraceptives, or same-sex sodomy among adults will not withstand rational scrutiny. Whose rights do such laws secure? Those decisions should all have been 9-0 since the states had no justification for the restrictions—as a matter not of policy or politics but of *law*. Where is "balance" appropriate in such cases?

The Blurring of Law and Politics

The failure to distinguish the respective domains of law and politics is at the core of many of our disputes today and the growing battle for the courts. Foreshadowed by Justice Oliver Wendell Holmes's infamous 1905 dissent in *Lochner v. New York*, the main roots of that failure are in progressivism, which rejected the limited-government principles of the Constitution as amended after the Civil War. For Progressives, nearly all was and still is politics—as in their effort in *Lochner* to limit the hours that bakers might work, freedom of contract notwithstanding. They were social engineers pursuing change through *legislation*. Thus, legal relationships defined largely by property and contract principles under the common law came in time to be redefined by statutes overriding those principles in the name of progressive social values. And as Progressives ascended to the courts, animated by those values and the underlying political rationale majoritarian democracy purported to afford, the conflict with judges abiding by the earlier order and its principles was inevitable—as was the tyranny of, at best, the majority, at worst but far more common, special interests more able to work the system to their advantage.

That conflict came to a head during the New Deal, of course, when President Roosevelt, shortly after his landslide reelection in 1936, attempted to pack the Supreme Court with six new justices—a blatant political move that succeeded only because of the famous "switch in time that saved nine." Unlike after the Civil War, when federalism as originally established was changed legitimately by constitutional amendment, the politically cowed New Deal Court began itself, in effect, to rewrite the Constitution, without the legitimacy afforded by an amendment.

In 1937, the Court eviscerated the document's basic substantive principle, the doctrine of enumerated powers, after which the floodgates were opened for Congress to redistribute and regulate at will with the Court looking the other way. But the burgeoning legislation that followed often ran roughshod over our rights, which brought judges back into the picture. To address that problem, the Court in 1938 distinguished "fundamental" from "nonfundamental" rights, plus differing levels of judicial review to match—all written from whole cloth and all enabling judges thereafter to make value and hence political judgments about which rights were and were not "fundamental." Finally, in 1943, the Court declined to check Congress's growing practice of delegating ever more of its lawmaking authority to the executive branch agencies it had created and would continue to create, thus leading to today's gargantuan executive state where most law is written, notwithstanding the Constitution's very first sentence after the Preamble: "*All* legislative Powers herein granted shall be vested *in a Congress*" (emphasis added).

Thus, in brief, were the institutional arrangements for executing the progressive agenda created, however inconsistent with the Constitution, the original understanding of those who wrote and ratified it, and the theory of legitimacy undergirding it. The Court's role in this constitutional inversion was essentially passive and deferential: allowing a vast expansion of congressional power; reducing rights that might impede legislative, executive, and state actions, especially by treating economic liberty as a second-class right; and allowing the growth and scope of the administrative state, thus enabling bureaucratic social and economic planners to order our private affairs better than we, left free to do so ourselves, would ever do—or so both early Progressives and later liberals believed.

But shortly thereafter the Court's passive posture and deference to the political branches and the states were overtaken by the civil rights movement, and not a moment too soon. Coming before the Court was the Civil War's unfinished business, itself a product in part of a passive Court that had eviscerated the Fourteenth Amendment's Privileges or Immunities Clause in the infamous *Slaughterhouse Cases* of 1873. It remains today an embarrassment that a Court now dominated by conservative originalists has failed to correct that mistake. In the 1950s, however, it was liberals who dominated the Court, turning to the amendment's Due Process and Equal Protection Clauses to begin correcting, if not the Court's reading of the amendment, at least the result of that earlier misreading, racial segregation.

With that, however, a funny thing happened. As the Warren and Burger Courts became more active in protecting not only civil rights but other rights as well—concerning criminal procedure, for example—political conservatives began to question the legitimacy of this "judicial activism." They did so first because they sometimes disagreed with the results, but second, and more basic, because judges were overturning democratic decisions, thereby raising what Yale Law's Alexander Bickel famously called a "countermajoritarian difficulty," a question about the legitimacy of judicial review itself. Conservatives, in short, were buying into the far-reaching majoritarianism that underpinned Roosevelt's New Deal constitutional revolution.

Thus emerged the constitutional vision of modern conservatives, at least until rather recently. Reacting to what they saw, sometimes rightly, as liberal judicial activism—judges invoking progressive social values to defeat democratic decisions—conservatives urged judicial restraint and deference to majoritarian rule. The contrast between the two constitutional visions was never more sharply drawn than during the confirmation battle over Bork's 1987 nomination, and the theoretical confusions surrounding that battle have clouded our constitutional debate ever since.

Two Mistaken Constitutional Visions

Truth to tell, both sides had it wrong. Liberals read the Constitution, when they did, as authorizing far-reaching rule by democratic majorities—except when majorities trampled on rights they thought "fundamental," whether constitutionally recognized or not. Conservatives, believing the restoration of the enumerated powers doctrine to be a lost cause, stood also for far-reaching majoritarian rule, especially at the state level; but from fear of judicial activism—liberal judges inventing rights from whole cloth—they urged judges to secure only those rights enumerated *expressly* in the Constitution.

Neither of those readings was consistent with the Framers' vision, especially after the ratification of the Civil War Amendments. Drawing from moral and political theory, history, and their recent experience in the states under the Articles of Confederation, they distrusted majorities almost as much as the king, which is why they wrote a constitution designed to preserve liberty and limit power. Not by accident, therefore, did it conclude with the Tenth Amendment, which makes it clear that Congress's powers are enumerated and therefore limited. And the Ninth Amendment—which together with the Tenth recapitulates the libertarian vision of the Declaration of Independence—makes it equally clear that we "retained" countless unenumerated rights, distinguishing none as "fundamental" or "nonfundamental." Consider finally that the Framers of the Civil War Amendments repaired repeatedly to that vision, made clear by the debates in the 39th Congress and the state ratification conventions, and you end with a vision of a polity animated by individual liberty under limited constitutional government.

It was, again, the Progressives and their progeny who rejected that vision, joined later by modern conservatives: Progressives because they rejected the Constitution itself, especially its plan for limited government (read Woodrow Wilson, among many others); conservatives of the Bork era because they chose to resist what they often saw as judicial activism basically on *political* grounds—more precisely, on an erroneous constitutional vision of wide majoritarianism and limited rights.

Nowhere did Bork more clearly state that vision than in his justly famous 1990 book, *The Tempting of America*. Madison, he wrote, held "that in *wide* areas of life majorities are entitled to rule, if they wish, simply because they are majorities; . . . there are nonetheless *some* things majorities must not do to minorities, *some* areas of life in which the individual must be free of majority rule" (emphasis added). That gets Madison exactly backwards. Madison held that in "wide areas" individuals are entitled to be free simply because they are born so entitled, while in "some" areas majorities are entitled to rule, not because they are inherently so entitled, but because we have authorized them to. That gets the order right: individual liberty first, self-government second, as a means toward securing that liberty.

A Return to Madisonian Constitutionalism

But much has changed on the conservative side since Bork wrote those words. In particular, we have seen a slow revival of true constitutionalism: led by classical liberals and libertarians like those of us here at Cato's Center for Constitutional Studies, together with many in the legal academy; aired and tested at events through organizations like the Federalist Society and the Heritage Foundation; and litigated by the Institute for Justice, the Pacific Legal Foundation, and other free-market public-interest legal groups. Edwin Meese, attorney general under President Reagan, can be credited with bringing a more principled constitutionalism to the fore with his July 1985 ABA speech on originalism, prompting a response by Justice William Brennan a few months later. The debate thus joined, it was dominated early on by conservatives like Bork, but in the years since, libertarians, drawing on philosophical and historical work begun years earlier, have slowly shifted it back to First Principles, especially with an appeal to the natural rights foundations of the Declaration, the Constitution, and the Civil War Amendments.

As is often the case with ideological shifts, this evolution in constitutional thought on the right, whether in debates or in the courts, has been glacial, with fits and starts. Yet a substantial body of writings shows by now that the shift is real—so much so that it is now liberals, looking especially to the courts, who call conservatives "judicial activists." A more accurate term would be "judicial restorationists." Thus, early on, in 1995, in *United States v. Lopez*, the Court revived the doctrine of enumerated powers, which had lain dormant for 58 years. Finding that Congress's power to regulate interstate commerce was not a power to regulate any and everything, Chief Justice William Rehnquist wrote, "We start with first principles. The Constitution creates a Federal Government of enumerated powers." Long forgotten, those words appeared again in 2000 in *United States v. Morrison*, but then escaped the Court's grasp five years later in *Gonzales v. Raich*, the California medical marijuana decision, only to be revived in 2012 in *NFIB v. Sebelius*, the Obamacare decision. We are only at the beginning of that restoration, however, and it has occurred thus far only at the edges, but at least the principle is back in play.

On the rights side, things have been uneven, and truer, unfortunately, to the earlier divide between conservatives and liberals. It is perilous to generalize here, but in general, in recent years, the Court's conservatives have protected enumerated rights rather better than the liberals have in areas like free speech (especially campaign finance), religious liberty, freedom of association (limits on affirmative action, for example), gun rights, property rights, and, unevenly, Fourth Amendment privacy rights. But on "social-issue" rights, which are mostly unenumerated, it is liberals who have generally done better, again if unevenly, as in *Lawrence v. Texas*, the 2003 same-sex sodomy decision, and *Obergefell v. Hodges*, the 2015 same-sex marriage decision that should have been decided easily on equal-protection grounds, from which the rights would have followed by implication. But except for Justice Clarence Thomas, the Court's conservatives treated *Obergefell* as a due-process case. That immersed them in a deeply mistaken discussion of "substantive due process" that included an unbridled attack on *Lochner* by Chief Justice John Roberts.

Fortunately, a number of judges coming along on the lower courts have had less difficulty incorporating in their decisions a truer understanding of the classical theory of rights that underpins and informs the Constitution, especially concerning unenumerated rights to both economic and personal liberty. They understand that one can be a textualist and an originalist and, *as a result,* be compelled to do the work needed to find retained unenumerated rights—a very different undertaking from that of earlier liberal judges who appealed simply to "evolving social values," thus conflating rights and values, two very different moral concepts. Those developments below constitute an important reason for hope, including hope for the confirmation of Judge Kavanaugh. For the generational shift that he and Justice Gorsuch reflect marks also the coming of judges and justices who, from an early age, have been immersed in the right's constitutional ferment.

And why is this important? It is because the Progressives who have dominated our constitutional world for more than a century now have unleashed the modern welfare state and the appetites for public goods and services that today are crushing us—and will crush coming generations even more. Put simply, we are demanding more such goods than we are willing to pay for, so we borrow. The federal debt now exceeds $21 trillion and is growing, having more than doubled over the past decade, and unfunded liabilities vastly exceed that. In fewer than 20 years, our debt-to-GDP ratio has more than doubled, from 33 percent in 2000 to 78 percent today; it is projected to reach 100 percent in 10 years and continue rising thereafter. As history makes clear, this cannot go on.

The Federalist teaches that constitutions are written to discipline not only rulers but the ruled, we the people, but the limits they establish must be respected. Over the past century we took a number of wrong constitutional turns and today are reaping the results. The Court made those wrong turns, but we, ultimately, are responsible for them, because it is we who elect the people who nominate, confirm, and, at times, prevail upon the justices to make such turns. This far down the road, the Court alone cannot reverse the destructive course we have been on, but it can begin. And one place to begin is with the last of the three main steps the Court took that opened the door for the modern executive state. It is time to put teeth into the Constitution's first word: *"All* legislative Powers herein granted shall be vested *in a Congress."*

Fortunately, the records of both Justice Gorsuch and Judge Kavanaugh show them keen to rein in the excesses of the administrative state, to challenge the deference doctrines that have enabled that state to grow, and to return law-making power to Congress, where it should always have been kept. If this new generation can thus require Congress to take responsibility for the massive redistributive and regulatory state it has created and to start reining it in, we may be on the road to addressing the entitlements crisis looming ahead before it overwhelms us. It is time for the least dangerous branch to discipline the most dangerous branch and the executioner it empowered, for which the Constitution, properly understood, is the proper guide.

* * *

Speaking of generational shifts, after publishing 17 volumes of the *Cato Supreme Court Review,* conceiving and creating Cato's Center for Constitutional Studies, which I've directed now for 30 years, and reaching the three-quarters mark on life's big clock, it's time for me to step down and hand the reins over to the next generation, which I'm delighted to do. When I discovered Ilya Shapiro some 11 years ago and invited him to become a senior fellow with the Center and the editor-in-chief of the *Review*, it was with an eye to his becoming my successor. He has exceeded my hopes beyond anything I could have imagined. A prolific author and speaker, Ilya has, among much else, vastly expanded the quantity and quality of the Center's well-regarded amicus brief program and brought great credit to the Center. He will soon be named director of the Center and will be the publisher of next year's *Review*.

Stepping into Ilya's shoes as editor-in-chief of the *Review* will be current managing editor and research fellow, Trevor Burrus. He too is a prolific author and speaker when he is not co-hosting Cato's "Free Thoughts" podcast. Trevor came to us in 2010, first as an intern, then as a one-year legal associate, where we found him a polymath and so could not let him go.

My indebtedness over these years extends to many, but three individuals stand out. The *Review*'s first editor-in-chief, who played a major role in selecting everything from the authors to the Constitution Day speakers to the *Review*'s federalist color scheme, was the Lincoln scholar James Swanson, who left after two years to find the time to write his masterful *New York Times* best seller, *Manhunt*. James got the *Review* off the ground. I was fortunate to find a worthy successor, Mark Moller, who at Cambridge had studied the common law, on which so much of our work rests; alas, four year later we lost Mark to his dream job in the legal academy. It may be no accident that James did his B.A., Mark and Ilya their J.D.s, and I my Ph.D. at the University of Chicago, where "the life of the mind" is understood by all.

Finally, the Center, the Review, and the Constitution Day symposium would likely not have come into being were it not for Cato's co-founder and president emeritus, Ed Crane, who needed no encouragement to see the potential of the proposal for the Center that I put before him exactly 30 years ago, in September 1988. At the time, as I discussed above, two approaches to constitutional interpretation and the role of the courts pursuant to each dominated our jurisprudence, one liberal, the other conservative. A very few of us, like the late Professor Bernard Siegan, had long urged a more Madisonian approach, grounded in the nation's natural rights foundations, but our voices were then only beginning to be heard. We needed an institutional base, which Ed provided at the still young Cato Institute— and the rest, as they say, is history, and a good history it has been.

Introduction

*Ilya Shapiro**

This is the 17th volume of the *Cato Supreme Court Review,* the nation's first in-depth critique of the Supreme Court term just ended, plus a look at the term ahead. We release this journal every year in conjunction with our annual Constitution Day symposium, less than three months after the previous term ends. We're proud of the speed with which we publish this tome and of its accessibility, at least insofar as the Court's opinions allow. I'm particularly proud that this isn't a typical law review, whose submissions' esoteric subject matter is matched only by their pedantic execution and superfluous footnoting. Instead, this is a book of essays on law intended for everyone from lawyers and judges to educated laymen and interested citizens.

And we're happy to confess our biases: We approach our subject from a classical Madisonian perspective, with a focus on individual liberty that is protected and secured by a government of delegated, enumerated, separated, and thus limited powers. We also maintain a strict separation of law and politics. Whether the president is Barack Obama, Donald Trump, or anyone else, just because something is good policy doesn't mean it's constitutional—and vice versa. Moreover, just because being faithful to the text of a statute might produce unfortunate results doesn't mean that judges (or administrative agencies!) should take it upon themselves to rewrite the law—as the new "junior justice," Neil Gorsuch, has already reminded us. Accordingly, just as judges must sometimes overrule the will of the people—as when legislatures act without constitutional authority or trample individual liberties—resolving policy problems caused by poorly conceived or inartfully drafted legislation must be left to the political process.

---

* Senior fellow in constitutional studies, Cato Institute, and editor-in-chief, *Cato Supreme Court Review.*

This was the first full term with the Court back at its "full strength" of nine justices after Justice Antonin Scalia's death, so all eyes were on Justice Gorsuch to see how he would fit in—and how the Court's internal dynamic and voting patterns would shift. While early reports, based on what turns out to be unsubstantiated speculation, spoke of tensions between the newest justice and several of his colleagues, he quickly settled in and ended up writing many thoughtful opinions, including casting a handful of deciding votes and being assigned to write for the majority in several important cases.

Gorsuch's first full term was part of what made this a Supreme Court year for the ages. I don't know if I would necessarily count any of the rulings as ones we'll look back on as setting historic precedents—unlike, say, *District of Columbia v. Heller* (Second Amendment), *Citizens United v. FEC* (campaign finance), *Shelby County v. Holder* (voting rights), and *Obergefell v. Hodges* (same-sex marriage)—but as a whole it was a year where a new court came together. To be sure, there were several "big" cases, like *Murphy v. NCAA* (sports gambling/federalism), *South Dakota v. Wayfair* (state sales tax on e-commerce), and *NIFLA v. Becerra* (compelled speech in crisis pregnancy centers). We cover these cases in this volume, but they won't necessarily roll off layman tongues.

Even *Trump v. Hawaii* (Travel Ban 3.0), while launching millions of Twitter wars, doesn't break new ground given the broad discretion that Congress gives the president on immigration law and the deference courts (rightly) give the executive on matters of national security. Recall that most experts were predicting this wouldn't even be a 5-4 split (that the administration would win more handily)—and it really wasn't, because Justice Stephen Breyer, joined by Justice Elena Kagan, merely filed a technocratic opinion about needing more evidence before really being able to decide, declining to enlist in the judicial #Resistance that only garnered two votes (Justices Sonia Sotomayor and Ruth Bader Ginsburg).

The cases that arguably had the greatest potential for changing the legal landscape, *Masterpiece Cakeshop v. Colorado Civil Rights Commission* (First Amendment challenge to antidiscrimination law) and *Gill v. Whitford* (partisan gerrymandering), fizzled. Instead, the most long-lasting rulings from a practical purpose were *Carpenter v. United States* (police need a warrant to collect cell phone location data) and *Janus v. American Federation of State, County, and Municipal*

Employees (public-sector unions can't charge nonmembers fees). So there was a lot going on, in many fields of law, but it seemed that the Court was really playing second-fiddle to whatever was happening in the political world.

At least that was true until Wednesday, June 27, the last day of the term (and also my birthday). Not only did the Court hand down *Janus*—provoking paroxysmal fits among the "anti-authoritarians" who can't get enough of telling people what to do or think—but, three hours later, Justice Anthony Kennedy announced his retirement.

Kennedy has long been the Court's "swing" vote—though he hates that term—and thus was most often in the majority in those 5-4 cases that split along conventional ideological lines. Well, this term there were 19 such hotly split decisions. Of those 19, 15 featured Kennedy joining the four "conservatives" and *none* had him joining the four "liberals." (Two of them did have Chief Justice John Roberts joining the liberal bloc.) That simply hadn't happened in the 13 years since Justice Samuel Alito replaced Justice Sandra Day O'Connor to put Kennedy in his vaunted role as the man in the middle.

So while it's simplistic to characterize particular terms as liberal, conservative, or anything else—recall that there was even a "libertarian moment" in 2012–14 when Cato went 15-3 and 10-1 in our amicus brief filings—this term gave progressives plenty of heartburn. And now it should only get worse for them. President Trump has followed through on his promise to pick from his fabulous list of terrific judges (they really are the best, believe me). Assuming Senate Majority Leader Mitch McConnell shepherds Judge Brett Kavanaugh through the Senate—neither Susan Collins (R-ME) nor Lisa Murkowski (R-AK) has yet wavered on judicial votes—the confirmation of *Justice* Kavanaugh will mean that the chief justice becomes the median vote.

I don't want to oversell that point. John Roberts will have even more incentive to indulge his minimalist fantasies to lead the Court from the squishy commanding heights, but—incrementalist judicial restraint and all—he is a far surer vote for conservatives (if not necessarily libertarians) than Kennedy ever was. He even agreed with Cato more than any other justice both this and last year!

President Trump, who likely wouldn't have won the election had it not been for the Scalia vacancy, has now ensured that a major part of his legacy will be in the judicial realm. Having appointed an eighth of all federal circuit (appellate) judges in less than 18 months, he will have had back-to-back lifetime appointments to the Supreme Court. And Justices Ginsburg (85), Breyer (80), and Thomas (70 and by some accounts getting restless) aren't getting any younger, so we may see more opportunities—at least if the Republicans keep the Senate this fall. In short, the 2017–2018 term, while rolling out in fits and starts, ended up giving a lot to those who want the law applied as written and see constitutional structure as a way to secure liberty. But we're just getting started.

Moving to more of the statistics I've been sprinkling in, this term the Court somehow beat last year's record for low output by ruling on only 60 cases after argument. Unlike last term, it no longer had the excuse of being limited to eight members (though it did issue one 4-4 affirmance), but did end up dismissing six cases it had taken up, as well as issuing 11 summary reversals. At the same time, the justices perhaps had more work to do behind the scenes, with only 39 percent of decisions on the merits being unanimous (28 of 71).[1] The previous term it was 59 percent, and the preceding five terms registered 48, 41, 66, 49, and 45, respectively (so you see the anomalies that were the mostly eight-justice October Term 2016 and the October Term 2013 that papered over real doctrinal differences). Indeed, this was the lowest rate of unanimous cases since October Term 2008. Some of this can be attributed to lingering controversies held over from the previous deadlocked term, but really we're seeing stark doctrinal differences—even if Justices Roberts and Kennedy facilitated punts on the partisan-gerrymandering cases.

As mentioned earlier, the term produced 19 5-4 decisions—26 percent of the total, a bit high but within modern norms—including one 5-3 ruling that counts for comparison's sake. Again, 15 of those were "conservative" majorities, while another two had the chief justice joining the liberals, and one very interesting one, *Sessions v. Dimaya*, where Gorsuch joined the liberals.[2]

---

[1] The total includes the 11 summary reversals (without oral argument), eight of which were unanimous. All statistics taken from Kedar Bhatia, Final Stat Pack for October Term 2017 and Key Takeaways, SCOTUSblog, June 29, 2018, https://bit.ly/2vKZP2s. For detailed data from previous terms, see Statpack Archive, SCOTUSblog, http://www.scotusblog.com/reference/stat-pack.

[2] See Ilya Shapiro, Surprised by Neil Gorsuch's Ruling? You Weren't Paying Attention, Wash. Examiner, Apr. 17, 2018, https://washex.am/2PeoAMk.

The increased disagreement naturally resulted in more dissenting opinions, 49, whereas in the previous term there were 32 (the yearly average going back to 2005–2006 is 52). Not surprisingly, the total number of all opinions (majority, concurring, and dissenting) was also high—165, up from 139 last term and not far from the 13-year average of 171 despite the lower number of cases. Justice Thomas per usual wrote the most opinions (31, including eight dissents), followed by Justice Sotomayor (23, including nine dissents), Breyer (19), and Gorsuch (17). Justice Thomas also produced the most opinion pages (340), followed by Justices Alito (317) and Sotomayor (311). Justice Kagan wrote the least this term, with nine opinions totaling 133 pages.

The Court reversed or vacated 52 lower-court opinions—74 percent of the 71 total, including the separate cases that were consolidated for argument—which is lower than last term but in line with recent trends. Of the lower courts with a significant number of cases under review, the U.S. Court of Appeals for the Ninth Circuit attained a 2-12 record (86 percent reversal), maintaining its traditional crown as the most-reversed court, followed by the Eleventh Circuit (1-5, 83 percent reversal). State courts also fared poorly, with a 2-6 record (75 percent reversal). But really, whatever court you're appealing from, it's safe to say that getting the Supreme Court to take your case is most of the battle.

Also interesting is *which* justices were in the majority. Chief Justice Roberts edged Justice Kennedy, being in the majority in 93 percent of all cases (and 89 percent of divided cases). Kennedy was 92 percent, while Justice Gorsuch was next at 85 percent. Justice Sotomayor brought up the rear (68 percent and just 49 percent of divided cases).

Chief Justice Roberts also won in 5-4 cases, being in the majority in 17 of the 19 (89 percent). Justices Kennedy and Gorsuch were each in the majority in 16 of those (84 percent), followed by Justices Thomas and Alito at 15 (79 percent). Justice Kagan was in the majority in only 3 of 18 5-4 cases (17 percent). Notably, Justice Gorsuch wrote *five* majority opinions in 5-4 cases—more than any other justice which means that the average strength of the majority in cases he authored was lowest on the Court.

For the first time, Justice Alito became the leading "lone dissenter," writing two of those. Justices Thomas and Gorsuch each wrote one, with Thomas's 13-year average of 2.2 solo dissents per term more than doubling his closest colleague. Chief Justice Roberts and Justice Kagan have still *never* written one of those during their entire tenures (13 and 8 terms, respectively).

More news comes from judicial-agreement rates. Three terms ago, the top six pairs of justices most likely to agree, at least in part, were all from the "liberal bloc." Last term, Justices Thomas and Gorsuch voted the same way in every single case (17 of them once Gorsuch joined the Court), but this term their agreement fell to 56 of 71 cases (81 percent). It was Justices Ginsburg and Sotomayor who were most in accord (68 of 71 cases, or 96 percent), followed by Justices Thomas and Alito (93 percent), Breyer and Kagan (93 percent), Sotomayor and Kagan (91 percent), and Roberts/Kennedy and Breyer/Sotomayor (90 percent). The rest of the pairings were below 90 percent. Justices Alito and Sotomayor and Gorsuch voted together less than anyone else (in 35 of 71 cases, or 49 percent). The next three lowest pairs were Justices Thomas and Sotomayor (51 percent), then Ginsburg/Alito and Breyer/Alito (54 percent each).

My final statistics are more whimsical, relating to the number of questions asked at oral argument. In this post-Scalia world, Justice Sotomayor has solidified her title as most-frequent interlocutor. She asked more than 24 questions per argument, asked the most in 37 percent of the cases (and top-3 in 81 percent of them). Justice Breyer asked just over 21 questions per case, including the most in 27 percent of the cases. Justice Gorsuch has settled into the middle of the pack at just over 15 questions per case. Justice Ginsburg maintained her run as first interrogator (in 54 percent of arguments), followed by Sotomayor (17 percent) and Kennedy (13 percent). Justice Thomas remained silent.

Moving closer to home, Cato filed in 15 merits cases. One of those got dismissed because of legislative developments (*United States v. Microsoft*), leaving 14 opinions. (I'm including in that count two briefs filed by our Project on Criminal Justice but not the one filed in *Trump v. Hawaii* because it was an immigration-policy brief which no Cato lawyer signed.) Improving on last year's 9-4 performance, Cato achieved an 11-3 showing. Perhaps most importantly, we handily beat our biggest rival, the federal government, which amassed an 11-15 record. (It's an inexact comparison, I know, because the government typically appears as a party, not simply as amicus, and almost always participates in oral argument.) Cato also effectively drew votes from across the judicial spectrum, winning 13 votes from Chief Justice Roberts, 12 from Justice Kagan, 11 each from Justices Kennedy and Gorsuch, 9 each from Justices Thomas, Breyer, and Alito, and 7 each from Justices Ginsburg and Sotomayor.

Turning to the *Review*, the volume begins as always with the previous year's B. Kenneth Simon Lecture in Constitutional Thought, which in 2017 was delivered by Professor Philip Hamburger of Columbia Law School. Hamburger, whom I had the pleasure of having as a professor when he was at the University of Chicago, recently founded the New Civil Liberties Alliance, which he describes as "the only civil rights organization entirely devoted to checking the administrative state." It's altogether fitting, then, that his Simon Lecture covered the administrative threat to personal freedom. Hamburger focuses on the systemic threats to individual rights wrought by a virtually unchecked fourth branch of government. Tracing executive power in the Anglo-American legal tradition from England through the present day, he explains how checks and balances have been subverted, leading to a loss of procedural rights that makes the constitutional protection of substantive rights a hollow promise. "Administrative power is a profound threat to civil liberties," Hamburger concludes, enumerating the ways. "In the ongoing struggle, there is a role for everyone, not just lawyers."

Then we move to the 2017–18 term, starting with Josh Blackman's evaluation of the "travel bans"—which he so names because there have been three executive orders, each with different legal and political salience. Blackman, a professor at South Texas College of Law Houston and Cato adjunct scholar, details the fascinating and fast-paced litigation that culminated in *Trump v. Hawaii*. This was an unusual case in that "the president has the statutory and constitutional authority to deny entry to aliens from certain countries based on national-security concerns. Yet the judiciary still moved at warp speed to halt President Donald Trump's signature policy." That's because the ultimate tension here wasn't over the legal issues as such, Blackman argues, but about whether to treat this case as a "normal" one or something different given the identity of the current wielder of executive power. It's a thought-provoking essay.

My colleague Walter Olson then provides a fascinating ride through what could've been the term's biggest cases—*Gill v. Whitford* and *Benisek v. Lamone*—but ultimately became just the latest in a long series of punts on challenges to partisan gerrymandering. (Olson, in addition to his brilliant writings on civil litigation, also happened to have been co-chair of the Maryland Redistricting Reform Commission.) Academics had teed up a tale of "efficiency gaps" and "wasted votes," but still Justice Kennedy apparently didn't find the administrable standard he had long sought for determining when, as a constitutional matter, politicians had employed too many political considerations in drawing district lines. Olson concludes nevertheless that "there are good reasons for states to act on their own to curb the evils of partisan gerrymandering without looking to One First Street."

Trevor Burrus, this journal's managing editor, enlisted superstar legal intern James Knight to help tackle *Carpenter v. United States*, in which a dastardly robber of Radio Shacks and T-Mobile stores was hoisted by his own cell phone ("ironically enough," noted Chief Justice Roberts). The FBI used cell-site location information (CSLI) to place Timothy Carpenter at the crime scenes. To create CSLI, all you need is a cell phone on your person—most readers can relate, I'm sure—that automatically connects with cell towers and can roughly identify your location. But do police need a warrant to access that data, which is stored by your cell phone carrier? The majority said yes, but wasn't clear about why. More interesting, argue Burrus and Knight, are the dissents, especially Justice Gorsuch's. Gorsuch saw *Carpenter* as an opportunity to launch "the opening salvo in what will likely be a career-long attempt to rework the Court's Fourth Amendment jurisprudence."

Lucian Dervan, a law professor at Belmont University, does a deep dive into an overlooked criminal-procedure case, *Class v. United States*. This case looked at a particularly thorny aspect of plea bargaining: what rights does a criminal defendant waive when he pleads guilty? Although the facts are colorful—involving a self-described "constitutional bounty hunter"—the issues the case raises go to the heart of deep concerns with the criminal-justice system. As Dervan puts it, *Class* raises "fundamental questions regarding the operation of the plea-bargaining machine, the psychology of defendant decision-making, and the voluntariness of plea bargaining given our growing understanding of the phenomenon of factually innocent defendants pleading guilty."

Our next essay covers *Masterpiece Cakeshop*, which could've been Justice Kennedy's defining case but ended up as a bookend to his opinion in *Romer v. Evans* (1996), in which the Court struck down a state constitutional amendment preventing political subunits from treating homosexuality as a protected class. *Romer* took no position on whether discrimination against gays and lesbians was always suspect under equal-protection principles—and so it's not as iconic as *Lawrence v. Texas* (2003) or *Obergefell v. Hodges* (2015)—but it effectively ushered in such protections. University of St. Thomas law professor Thomas Berg argues that *Masterpiece* essentially did the same thing for religious objectors.[3] Even as the Court shied away from declaring a First Amendment right not to participate in same-sex weddings, it found that evidence of "hostility" toward religion had prejudiced the enforcement of an antidiscrimination law.

Janus turned out instead to be the biggest First Amendment case, and we have Cleveland State law professor David Forte analyzing the high-profile ruling. Overturning a 40-year precedent that allowed states to authorize public-sector unions to charge nonmembers certain "agency fees"—which can constitute some 80 percent of full union dues—the Court struck a blow for the freedom of association. No longer will workers in the 22 states affected by this decision be forced to support positions they oppose. As Justice Alito described in his majority opinion, Mark Janus "is not a free rider on a bus headed for a destination that he wishes to reach but is more like a person shanghaied for an unwanted voyage." Moreover, the distinction between "chargeable" expenses relating to collective bargaining and "nonchargeable" politics-related expenses is illusory in the public sector, where negotiating for, say, teacher tenure protection rather than merit pay (or vice versa) has real impact on budgets and education policy.

Then we have Robert McNamara and Paul Sherman of the Institute for Justice, two experienced First Amendment advocates both in the courts and the court of public opinion, evaluating *NIFLA v. Becerra*. This case revolves around California's regulation of (pro-life) crisis-pregnancy centers in a way that's different from regulations affecting clinics that offer abortion services: by mandating certain

---

[3] Berg is one of three lawyers to have signed briefs supporting both Jim Obergefell and Jack Phillips (owner of Masterpiece Cakeshop). The other two are University of Virginia law professor Douglas Laycock—his co-counsel and the dean of religious-liberty legal scholars—and me. Cato is the only organization in the entire country to have filed briefs supporting those respective positions.

statements about the availability of state-financed abortions; and for unlicensed centers without doctors on staff, disclosures about the absence of licensed medical professionals. Setting aside the underlying controversy over abortion, this was a case about speech, and, more specifically, First Amendment protection for professional or occupational speech. The authors explain why "*NIFLA* cements the Roberts Court as the most libertarian in our nation's history on free-speech issues."

The dean of Widener University Delaware Law School, Rodney Smolla, examines *Minnesota Voters Alliance v. Mansky*, an intriguing case regarding what voters can wear—or what states can stop them from wearing—to the polls. This was probably the least-controversial free-speech case of the term, but it still raised fraught questions of what kind of speech is so "political" that it disrupts the solemnity of the voting area. I happen to agree with Smolla that the Court, while striking down Minnesota's broad and vague ban on "political" apparel, didn't go far enough—that the passive wearing of slogans or symbols is different than electioneering or obstruction (which are already banned in all states). "American voters are not so squeamish, frail, or fragile as to be intimidated or defrauded by a fellow voter's T-shirt or button," Smolla concludes. "Nor are they . . . driven to fisticuffs or undignified outbursts at the mere sight of the very opposing views to which they have been unrelentingly exposed" during the campaign.

Next we have the attorney general of Arizona, Mark Brnovich, writing on the term's big federalism case, *Murphy v. NCAA. Murphy* involved a 25-year-old federal law that prohibited states from facilitating sports gambling—so it's appropriate that the author not only represented his state in supporting the challenge to this law, but had previously been the director of its department of gaming. It came as no surprise that the Supreme Court, by a wide margin, struck down the law as a sort of "regulation on the cheap," with Congress telling the states to do something it didn't want to itself. Sports-betting policy will now be allowed to develop state-by-state, which is as it should be, but the case has wide-ranging implications beyond that. "On a host of issues, [*Murphy*] promises to produce the kind of federal-state tension on which our federal system thrives," Brnovich explains. "That federalism, in turn, helps secure our liberties."

In *South Dakota v. Wayfair*, the Supreme Court reversed its own long-held rule that only businesses with a physical presence in a state may be subject to that state's sales tax. It remains to be seen what impact this ruling will have on e-commerce, but I'm glad that we have Joseph Bishop-Henchman to unpack it all. Bishop-Henchman is the executive vice president and general counsel of the Tax Foundation and knows more about tax law—from constitutional heights to regulatory nits—than anyone I know. He presents here an engaging history not just of internet sales taxes but of all state taxes that have affected interstate commerce. "*Wayfair* may prove to be the first case where the Supreme Court truly confronted the need to pair, on one hand, constitutional and legal systems that define protections and obligations based on physical presence . . . [and] economic activities that are increasingly borderless, instantaneous, and nonphysical."

Our final article about a decided case looks at *Lucia v. SEC*, which some may view as arcane pedantry but actually goes to the heart of our republican order. If you call an employee of an executive agency a "judge" and give that person broad discretion and decisionmaking authority, is that person a mere clerk or bureaucrat, or more an agency official? As Scalia Law School's Jennifer Mascott details, the answer to that question is both important as a matter of constitutional design and clear from the historical record. Although the Court got the narrow question right—that SEC administrative law judges (ALJs) are "officers of the United States" and thus must be appointed by the commissioners themselves instead of rising through the ranks of the civil service—it left open bigger questions both as to the removal of these ALJs and how to determine whether ALJs in other agencies are similarly subject to executive appointment.

The volume concludes with a look ahead to October Term 2018 by Erin Murphy of Kirkland & Ellis. As of this writing—before the term starts—the Court has taken up 38 cases, a bit low given recent history but actually above where we were at this point last term. The term so far doesn't have any blockbusters to match the top half-dozen cases from last term, but there should still be a little something for everyone. Here are some of the issues: judicial deference to administrative agencies regarding the Endangered Species Act (*Weyerhaeuser Co. v. U.S. Fish & Wildlife Service*); the delegation of legislative authority to the executive (*Gundy v. United States*); the procedural hoops property owners must jump through to vindicate their rights (*Knick v. Township of Scott*); state sovereign immunity (*Franchise Tax Board of California v. Hyatt*—for the third time up at the Court);

the constitutionality of successive prosecutions by state and federal governments (*Gamble v. United States*); and the "incorporation" of the Excessive Fines Clause against the states (*Timbs v. Indiana*). There's something for every legal nerd, really, but the Court may well take up cases of interest to normal people too, such as sexual-orientation discrimination, (more) partisan gerrymandering, the Establishment Clause, and the Second Amendment. "At worst," Murphy concludes, "we will still learn whether you can use your hovercraft in Alaska, what constrains the state from trying to seize your Land Rover, and where to turn if the state mandates public access to your private cemetery."

* * *

This is the 11th, and final, volume of the *Cato Supreme Court Review* under my editorship, and the fourth with Trevor Burrus as managing editor. Trevor, who will now be taking the editorial reins, has been a huge help over the years with both the *Review* and our amicus brief program—this past year was particularly challenging—so I'm delighted to give credit where it's due. I'm also most thankful to our authors, without whom there would literally be nothing to edit or read. We ask leading legal scholars and practitioners to produce thoughtful, insightful, readable commentary of serious length on short deadlines—this term only two cases we covered were decided before June—so I'm grateful that so many agree to my unreasonable demands every year.

My gratitude goes also to my colleagues Bob Levy, Clark Neily, Walter Olson, and Jay Schweikert, who provide valuable counsel and editing in legal areas less familiar to me. Legal associate Matthew Larosiere took over the administrative side of this journal, keeping track of the editing being done by his colleagues Aaron Barnes, Meggan DeWitt, Michael Finch, Nathan Harvey, and Reilly Stephens, plus interns James Knight, Zane Lucow, and Charles Yates, who in turn performed many thankless tasks without complaint. Neither the *Review* nor our Constitution Day symposium would be possible without them.

Finally, thanks to Roger Pilon, who founded Cato's Center for Constitutional Studies 30 years ago and also conceived this journal. Roger is one of the giants of classical-liberal legal thought, having contributed immensely to rights theory and constitutionalism—and the separation of law and policy—with an intellectual openness and integrity that even Cato's harshest critics respect. He's the best mentor I could've had as I grew from baby lawyer to think-tank scholar. It's my honor to succeed him as director of Cato's Robert A. Levy Center for Constitutional Studies and publisher of this journal.

I reiterate our hope that this collection of essays will secure and advance the Madisonian first principles of our Constitution, giving renewed voice to the Framers' fervent wish that we have a government of laws and not of men. In so doing, we hope also to do justice to a rich legal tradition in which judges, politicians, and ordinary citizens alike understand that the Constitution reflects and protects the natural rights of life, liberty, and property, and serves as a bulwark against government abuses. In these uncertain times when the people feel betrayed by the elites—legal, political, corporate, and every other kind—it's more important than ever to remember our proud roots in the Enlightenment tradition.

We hope that you enjoy this 17th volume of the *Cato Supreme Court Review*.

The Administrative Threat to Civil Liberties

*Philip Hamburger**

Administrative power is the greatest threat to civil liberties in our era. Traditionally, the most systematic threats to civil liberties came in attacks on particular groups, and this remains a problem. But increasingly, there are also broader threats, which affect the civil liberties of all Americans, and administrative power is the primary example of this broad sort of danger. No single development in our legal system deprives more Americans of more constitutional rights. It is therefore not an exaggeration to say that it is our greatest threat to civil liberties.

Not an Economic Critique

At the outset, I must emphasize that this is a legal critique of administrative power, not an economic critique. Most complaints about administrative power are economic. It is said to be inefficient, dangerously centralized, burdensome on business, destructive of jobs, stifling for innovation and growth, and so forth. All of this is painfully true, but economic complaints are not the entire critique of administrative power. There are also constitutional objections, and the economic critique does not fully address these.

Indeed, the economic critique tends to protest merely the degree of administrative regulation, and it thereby usually accepts its legitimacy—as long as it is not too heavy-handed on business. It is therefore no wonder that the economic criticism has not stopped the growth of administrative power.

* President, New Civil Liberties Alliance; Maurice and Hilda Friedman Professor of Law, Columbia Law School. This is a slightly revised version of the 16th annual B. Kenneth Simon Lecture in Constitutional Thought, delivered at the Cato Institute on September 18, 2017. To learn more about the administrative threat to civil liberties, read Philip Hamburger, *Administrative Threat* (Encounter 2017).

In contrast, the argument here is a legal challenge: that administrative power violates one constitutional freedom after another. This argument is therefore not merely against administrative "abuses" or against "inefficient" or "burdensome" regulation. Rather than suggest that administrative abuses should be tamed, my point is that all administrative power threatens our constitutional rights.

Legal Obligation

Of course, in objecting to administrative power as unconstitutional, I am not denying that executive power is extensive. Executive power includes not merely the power to execute the laws, but more broadly the power to execute all of the nation's lawful force. It thus includes the power to prosecute offenders in court, to exercise discretion in distributing benefits, to determine the status of immigrants, and so forth. The objection here is not to any of this, but rather to extralegal attempts to impose legal obligation.

What do I mean by extralegal attempts to impose legal obligation? Put simply, whereas the Constitution authorizes the government to bind Americans only through the law (and its enforcement in courts), administrative agencies attempt to bind Americans through other mechanisms—and in this sense administrative power is extralegal.

Post-Benthamite theorists reduce law to a sovereign's command, backed by coercion. But traditionally in America, law was understood to come not merely with coercion, but also with obligation—the obligation to obey the law. Working from underlying ideas about consent, early Americans assumed that a rule could have the obligation of law only if it came from the constitutionally established legislature elected by the people, and that a judicial decision could have legal obligation only if it came from a constitutionally appointed judge exercising independent judgment. The U.S. Constitution therefore places the power to bind Americans in Congress and the courts, not in executive or independent agencies.

Extralegal Power

Nonetheless, the government purports to create legal obligation through executive and other agency edicts. It binds Americans and limits their liberty not merely through acts of Congress and of the courts, but through other mechanisms. In this sense, administrative power is extralegal.

Put another way, administrative power is an evasion of law. Rulers are always tempted to exert more power with less effort. They therefore are rarely content to govern merely through the law, and in their restless desire to escape its pathways, many of them work through other, "extralegal" mechanisms. English kings engaged in binding extralegal governance when they legislated through proclamations, regulations, and interpretations, and when they adjudicated in the Star Chamber and the High Commission. They called this "absolute power."

Much of absolute power was authorized by statute, but regardless of statutory authorization, it was an extralegal mode of binding subjects. American presidents similarly engage in extralegal governance when they legislate through binding agency rules and interpretations, and when they adjudicate through binding agency decisions. As in the past, such power often has statutory authorization, but it remains an extralegal pathway and a threat to constitutional freedom. In particular, it is an evasion of the Constitution's legislative and judicial processes.

The danger of extralegal power (of evasions of constitutional pathways) is thus enduring. Whether in monarchies or republics, there will always be those who seek to avoid the trouble of binding persons merely through acts of the legislature or the courts.

The U.S. Constitution's Response to Extralegal Power

Once one recognizes administrative power as a type of evasion or extralegal power, which runs outside the Constitution's pathways for binding Americans, one can begin to see that the Constitution was drafted to bar this danger. Apologists for federal administrative power say that it is a modern development, which therefore could not have been anticipated by the U.S. Constitution. But early Americans were familiar with English constitutional history, and they therefore knew the danger from absolute or extralegal power.

Seventeenth-century English history centered on the attempts of kings to bind subjects extralegally through "absolute" power, and on the struggle of their subjects to establish constitutional limits on such power. I will not recite the history in detail. Suffice it to say that after James I and Charles I openly ruled extralegally, with what they called their "absolute prerogative," Parliament in 1641 abolished their primary administrative or "prerogative" agencies (the Star Chamber and the High Commission) and then engaged in a civil war to defeat the king and his pretensions. James II repeated some of his namesake's evasions of law and thereby prompted the English Revolution of 1688. And underlying all of these events were English constitutional ideas. Put simply, constitutional ideas developed in England precisely to defeat the extralegal aspects of absolutism. Constitutional law was thus inextricably intertwined with an early version of what would become administrative power.

Many constitutional commentators said kings should rule only through acts of Parliament and the courts, not through other edicts. Some added that, under the English constitution, legislative power was in Parliament, judicial power in the judges, and executive power in the Crown. From this perspective, the English constitution left no room for the Crown to bind subjects extralegally.

Early Americans were familiar with the English experience, including both the danger of extralegal power or "absolute prerogative" and the need for a constitutional response. It is therefore mistaken to say that the U.S. Constitution could not have anticipated administrative power. Extralegal or absolute power was a familiar problem, and Americans were determined to repudiate it even more systematically than had the English.

The term "administrative power" was not yet ordinarily used in England or America, but absolute power was a known quantity. In the U.S. Constitution, therefore, Americans adopted structures and rights that systematically barred this danger.

The Constitution's Structural Barriers

How exactly does the U.S. Constitution bar administrative power? At the very least, the Constitution's structures preclude extralegal or absolute power.

Let's begin with Articles I and III. Article I blocks extralegal lawmaking by placing legislative power exclusively in Congress. Article III prevents extralegal adjudication by placing judicial power exclusively in the courts. The Constitution thus authorizes only two pathways for binding Americans (in the sense of imposing legal obligation on them). There are some jurisdictional exceptions. But generally, the government can impose binding rules only through acts of Congress (or treaties ratified by the Senate), and can impose binding adjudications only through acts of the courts. Other attempts to bind Americans (by rule or adjudication) are unconstitutional.

These are core civil liberties issues, not merely a matter of structure. Binding agency rules deny Americans their freedom under Article I to be subject to only such federal legislation as is enacted by an elected Congress, and administrative rules thereby dilute the constitutional right to vote. Binding agency adjudications deprive Americans of their freedom under Article III to be subject to only such federal judicial decisions as come from a court, with a real judge, a jury, and the full due process of law. Thus, even under Articles I and III, administrative power is a serious assault on civil liberties.

Administrative lawmaking is often justified as delegated power—as if Congress could divest itself of the power the people had delegated to it. But the Constitution expressly bars any such subdelegation.

"Wait a minute!" you may protest. The Constitution contains no nondelegation clause; so how does it bar congressional subdelegation?

The answer comes in the Constitution's first substantive word. The document begins: "All legislative powers herein granted shall be vested in a Congress . . . ." If all legislative powers are in Congress, they cannot be elsewhere. If the grant were merely permissive, not exclusive, there would be no reason for the word "All." That word bars subdelegation.

The Constitution's barrier to subdelegation of legislative power may sound merely technical, but it gives expression to a crucial principle, which underlies the efficacy of the Constitution. The logic is that once the people delegate legislative power to their legislature, any subdelegation would allow the government to evade the structure of government chosen by the people. Alas, this has happened.

I could say more about the Constitution's structure—for example, about waivers, federalism, and the implications for civil liberties. But time is short. So as to structure, I will simply summarize: To be sure, the United States remains a republic, but administrative power creates within it a very different sort of government. The result is a state within the state—an administrative state within the Constitution's United States—which deprives Americans of their freedom to make and unmake their own laws.

Juries and Due Process

Now let's turn to the Constitution's enumerated rights, especially jury rights and due process. The administrative violation of these rights makes especially clear that administrative power is a serious assault on civil liberties.

The Fifth Amendment secures "the due process of law," and in defense of administrative adjudication, it is often suggested that due process is centrally a limit on the courts, not so much on the other parts of government. But guarantees of due process of law developed precisely to bar extralegal adjudications rather than merely set a standard for the courts.

These guarantees evolved primarily to bar any binding adjudication outside the courts. The principle of due process became constitutionally significant already in 14th-century English due process statutes, which barred binding prerogative or administrative adjudication. The principle (stated at the head of the 1368 statute) was this: "None shall be put to answer without due process of law." On this basis, the English asserted due process of law against the High Commission and the Star Chamber, and Americans guaranteed the principle in the Fifth Amendment.

One of the earliest academic commentators on the U.S. Bill of Rights recognized the amendment's implications. When lecturing on the Constitution at the College of William and Mary in the 1790s, St. George Tucker quoted the Fifth Amendment's Due Process Clause and concluded, "Due process of law must then be had before a judicial court, or a judicial magistrate." Similarly, Chancellor James Kent explained that the due process of law "means law, in its regular course of administration, through courts of law." And Justice Joseph Story echoed both Tucker and Kent. So much for administrative adjudication!

Nonetheless, nowadays, the government often imposes fines and other penalties in administrative proceedings. Administrative adjudication thereby repeatedly violates the due process of law.

Like due process, the right to a jury bars administrative and other extralegal adjudication. Juries are available only in the courts, and the right to a jury (in both civil and criminal cases) thus precludes binding adjudication in other tribunals.

Early Americans understood this point. For example, in the decade after American independence, two state legislatures authorized judicial proceedings before justices of the peace. New Jersey authorized *qui tam* forfeiture proceedings with a six-man jury, and New Hampshire authorized small claims actions without a jury. Rather than accept these evasions of regular judicial proceedings, the courts—in the one state in 1780 and in the other in 1786—held the statutes void for violating the right to a jury under their state constitutions.

The U.S. Constitution in 1788 guaranteed juries only in criminal cases, prompting an outcry for it to protect jury rights in civil cases. The Seventh Amendment therefore secured the right to a jury in "Suits at common law." This phrase meant civil suits brought in the common-law system, as opposed to those brought in equity or admiralty. The words thus make clear that the amendment secures juries in all civil cases, other than those in equity and admiralty.

But nowadays the Supreme Court says that the government's interest in congressionally authorized administrative adjudication trumps the right to a jury. In the Court's strange locution, where the government is acting administratively to enforce newly created statutory "public rights," these public rights defeat the private assertion of the Constitution's jury rights. The Court traditionally had used the term "public rights" merely as a label for the lawful spheres of executive action. In *Atlas Roofing Co. v. Occupational Health and Safety Commission* (1977) and other cases, the Court unmoored the phrase from its traditional usage and used it to displace the Seventh Amendment right to a jury in civil cases. But no government power can sweepingly defeat a constitutional right, for the Constitution's rights are limits on government power. In other words, rights trump power.

Understanding this obstacle, the Supreme Court in *Atlas Roofing* recast administrative power as a right—indeed, as a "public right." In effect, it denigrated the constitutional right to a jury as merely private, so that the government's "public" right could defeat the "private" assertion of the constitutional right.

Procedural Rights in General

Administrative adjudications violate not merely jury rights and due process, but almost the full range of procedural rights. To understand this, let's pause to consider how the Constitution's procedural rights were drafted.

First, they are mostly in the passive voice. Rather than actively stating that the courts cannot violate various procedures, the procedural rights are typically recited in the passive voice, thereby limiting government in general, including Congress and the executive.

Second, they are added at the end of the Constitution. The drafters initially planned to rewrite particular articles in the body of the Constitution. In this way, for example, they could have modified

Article III. But if they had simply modified that article, they would have limited only the courts, and that would have been inadequate, as they also had to limit Congress in Article I and the executive in Article II. They therefore ultimately added their amendments at the end of the Constitution—so that the procedural rights could limit all parts of government.

These two drafting techniques—the passive voice and amendments at the end—give the procedural rights their breadth in limiting all parts of government and thus barring all binding adjudication outside the courts, including administrative adjudication.

Nonetheless, agencies impose binding adjudication outside the courts, without judges and juries; they issue summons, subpoenas, warrants, and fines without the due process of law of the courts; they deny equal discovery, as required by due process where agency proceedings are civil in nature; they impose prosecutorial discovery, which is forbidden by due process in cases that are criminal in nature; they even reverse the burdens of proof and persuasion required by due process. Agencies thereby repeatedly deprive Americans of their procedural rights.

Ambidextrous Enforcement and the Transformation of Rights

The seriousness of the administrative evasion of procedural rights has not been sufficiently recognized, but it becomes apparent when one realizes that the government now enjoys ambidextrous enforcement.

The government once could engage in binding adjudication against Americans only through the courts and their judges. Now, it can choose administrative adjudication. Sometimes, Congress alone makes this choice; other times, Congress authorizes an agency (such as the Securities and Exchange Commission) to make the selection. One way or the other, the government can act ambidextrously— either through the courts and their judges, juries, and due process or through administrative adjudication and its faux process.

The evasion thereby changes the very nature of procedural rights. Such rights traditionally were assurances against government. Now they are but one of the choices for government in its exercise of power. Though the government must respect these rights when it proceeds against Americans in court, it can escape them by taking an administrative path.

Procedural rights have thereby been transformed. No longer guarantees for the people, they are now merely options for the government. It is difficult to think of a more serious civil liberties problem for the 21st century.

Loss of Procedural Rights in the Courts

Unfortunately, the loss of procedural rights in administrative tribunals is not the end of the matter, for the deprivation of procedural rights persists in the courts. The result is a double violation of rights—first by agencies, and then by the courts themselves.

Let's start with judicial deference to agency interpretations. When courts defer to agencies—regardless of whether they invoke the *Chevron, Auer,* or *Mead-Skidmore* precedents—the judges are abandoning their office or duty of independent judgment. Indeed, when the government is a party to a case, the doctrines that require judicial deference to agency interpretation are precommitments in favor of the government's legal position, and the effect is systematic judicial bias in violation of the due process of law. Put bluntly, "*Chevron* deference" (to agency interpretations of statutes) is really *Chevron* bias; "*Auer* deference" (to agency interpretations of rules) is really *Auer* bias; and although "*Mead-Skidmore* respect" (for informal agency interpretations) is not as predictable, it is also a form of bias. All such deference grossly violates the most basic due process right to be judged without any judicial precommitment to the other party.

This deference to agency interpretation is bad enough, but it gets worse, for courts also defer to agency fact-finding. When a court reviews an agency adjudication, the judges rely on the agency's fact-finding, as preserved in its administrative record. Such reliance deprives private parties of their right to a jury trial. Juries (like other procedural rights) are a constitutional right in the first instance—not merely later when one gets to court—as was decided already in some of the earliest American constitutional cases. But the reality is that, even after one appeals from an agency to a court, one still does not get a jury trial!

Even worse is the bias in fact-finding. Where the government is a party to a case, the judges are relying on a record that is merely one party's version of the facts. The judges are thus favoring one of the parties.

Court cases involve two types of questions: those of law and those of fact. Accordingly, when there is systematic judicial bias in favor of the government on both the law and the facts, what is left for unbiased judgment?

The judicial bias continues even after courts hold agency acts unlawful. Courts usually hesitate to declare an unlawful agency action void (instead remanding it to the agency). And the *Brand X* doctrine often allows agencies to disregard judicial precedent about the interpretation of statutes.

The administrative assault on the Constitution's procedural rights is thus pervasive. Administrative adjudication denies many of these rights in agency proceedings; and then, in defense of administrative power, the courts add their own assaults on procedural rights. The result is a double violation of such rights, both administrative and judicial.

Equal Voting Rights

The most basic administrative assault on civil liberties concerns equal voting rights. The two preeminent developments in the federal government since the Civil War have been voting rights and the administrative state. It must therefore be asked whether there is a connection.

Federal law was slow to protect equal suffrage. In 1870, the Fifteenth Amendment gave black men the right to vote; in 1920, women acquired this right; and in 1965, equality for blacks began to become a widespread reality.

Interestingly, administrative power tended to expand in the wake of expanded suffrage. In 1887, Congress established the first major federal administrative agency, the Interstate Commerce Commission; in the 1930s, the New Deal created many powerful new agencies; and since the 1960s, federal administrative power has expanded even further.

Of course, it would be a mistake to link administrative power too narrowly to the key dates for equal voting rights. But growing popular participation in representative politics has been accompanied by a shift of legislative power—out of Congress and into administrative agencies.

The explanation is not hard to find. Although equality in voting rights has been widely accepted, the resulting democratization has prompted misgivings. Worried about the rough-and-tumble character of representative politics, and about the tendency of newly enfranchised groups to reject progressive reforms, many Americans sought what they considered a more elevated mode of governance.

Some early progressives were quite candid about this. Woodrow Wilson complained that "the reformer is bewildered" by the need to persuade "a voting majority of several million." Wilson especially worried about the diversity of the nation, which meant that the reformer needed to influence "the mind, not of Americans of the older stocks only, but also of Irishmen, of Germans, [and] of Negroes."

Elaborating this point, he observed, "The bulk of mankind is rigidly unphilosophical, and nowadays the bulk of mankind votes." And "where is this unphilosophical bulk of mankind more multifarious in its composition than in the United States?" Accordingly, "in order to get a footing for new doctrine, one must influence minds cast in every mold of race, minds inheriting every bias of environment, warped by the histories of a score of different nations, warmed or chilled, closed or expanded, by almost every climate of the globe."

Rather than try to persuade such persons, Wilson welcomed administrative governance. The people could still have their republic, but much legislative power would be shifted out of an elected body and into the hands of the right sort of people.

Far from being narrowly a matter of racism, this has been a transfer of legislative power to the knowledge class—meaning not a class defined in Marxist terms, but those persons whose identity or sense of self-worth centers on their knowledge. More than merely the intelligentsia, this class includes all who are more attached to the authority of knowledge than to the authority of local political communities. This is not to say that such people have been particularly knowledgeable, but rather that their sense of affinity with cosmopolitan knowledge, rather than local connectedness, has been the foundation of their influence and identity. And appreciating the authority they have attributed to their knowledge, and distrusting the tumultuous politics of a diverse people, they have gradually moved legislative power out of Congress and into administrative agencies, where it can be exercised in more genteel ways by persons like themselves.

In short, the enfranchised masses have disappointed those who think they know better.

Of course, the removal of legislative power from the representatives of a diverse people has implications for minorities. Leaving aside Wilson's overt racism, the problem is the relocation of lawmaking power a further step away from the people and into the hands of a relatively homogenized class. Even when exercised with solicitude for minorities, it is a sort of power exercised from above—and those who dominate the administrative state have always been, if not white men, then at least members of the knowledge class.

It therefore should be no surprise that administrative power comes with costs for the classes and attachments that are more apt to find expression through representative government. In contrast to the power exercised by elected members of Congress, administrative power comes with little accountability to (let alone sympathy for) local, regional, religious, and other distinctive communities. Individually, administrators may be concerned about all Americans, but their power is structured in a way designed to cut off the political demands with which, in a representative system of government, local and other distinctive communities can protect themselves.

Administrative power thus cannot be understood apart from equal voting rights. The gain in popular suffrage has been accompanied by disdain for the choices made through a representative system and a corresponding shift of legislative power out of Congress.

Although the redistribution of legislative power has gratified the knowledge class, it makes a mockery of the struggle for equal voting rights. It reduces equal voting rights to a sort of bait and switch, and it confirms how severely administrative power threatens civil liberties.

Conclusion

Administrative power is a profound threat to civil liberties:

- It denies us our freedom to be bound only by laws made by our elected legislature.
- It denies us our freedom to be bound only by adjudications held in courts.
- It transforms our constitutional procedural rights from guarantees for the people into mere options for government.
- And this massive violation of procedural rights happens not only in administrative proceedings, but also in the courts themselves—thus corrupting judicial proceedings and making administrative power one of the most shameful episodes in the history of the federal judiciary.

- Although I am not able in this brief essay to discuss the administrative threat to substantive rights, let me simply note that administrative power comes with profound costs for the freedoms of speech and religion—as when the FCC and FEC engage in prior licensing of political speakers or speech and the IRS restricts the political speech of churches.
- Last but not least, administrative power undermines equal voting rights. The people are told they have equal rights in voting for their lawmakers, but much lawmaking has been shifted out of the legislature.

Such has been the fate of civil liberties in America.

What is to be done? Part of the solution is candor—to talk about the problem in terms that avoid fictional, legitimizing labels. For example, rather than speak about "administrative law," we should talk about "administrative power"—to make clear that what we are discussing is a type of power, not a type of law. Similarly, the term "administrative law judges" should be placed in scare quotes.

Another part of the solution is to recognize administrative power as a threat to civil liberties. For too long, those who are skeptical of this sort of power have condemned it merely as a threat to business, free enterprise, and the economy. Such things are important, but administrative power is more basically an assault on the constitutional freedoms of all Americans. On this foundation, it will be possible to oppose the threat in a broad-based civil liberties movement.

Last but not least, the movement against administrative power needs to include litigation. Indeed, we need to litigate against administrative power in a manner that has not been done before. I have therefore started a new civil rights organization, the New Civil Liberties Alliance, to pick up where other civil rights organizations have left off—in particular to protect civil liberties from the sort of systemic threats that come from administrative power. The NCLA is the only civil rights organization largely devoted to checking the administrative state.

In the ongoing struggle, there is a role for everyone, not merely lawyers. If Americans are to defeat the administrative state's threat to civil liberties, each of us has to stand up for our constitutional freedoms. As I tell my students, do not expect anyone to stand up for your rights unless you are willing to stand up for theirs.

The Travel Bans

*Josh Blackman**

Introduction

Historically, landmark cases that present foundational constitutional questions trickle up to the Supreme Court over the course of several years. For example, *NFIB v. Sebelius* was decided more than three years after the Affordable Care Act was signed into law.[1] *Obergefell v. Hodges* built upon two decades of LGBT litigation.[2] And, during that deliberative process, advocates on both sides could develop arguments and implement a carefully crafted litigation strategy. Other landmark cases race to the Supreme Court following major crises. *Bush v. Gore* rushed through the judiciary in the wake of the disputed 2000 presidential election.[3] Likewise, the *Steel Seizure Case* concluded two months after President Truman nationalized the steel mills.[4] These latter cases arose out of true exigencies: the judiciary was forced to mobilize in response to an emergency that the other branches were unable to resolve.

Trump v. Hawaii fits into neither category: the legal issues were not difficult and the circumstances were not exigent.[5] Without question, the president has the statutory and constitutional authority to deny entry to aliens from certain countries based on national-security concerns. Yet the judiciary still moved at warp speed to

* Associate professor, South Texas College of Law Houston; adjunct scholar, Cato Institute. This essay builds on, and incorporates, prior writings about the travel bans that were published on the Lawfare Blog, *National Review Online,* and other outlets.

[1] 567 U.S. 519 (2012). See Josh Blackman, Unprecedented: The Constitutional Challenge to Obamacare (2013).

[2] 135 S. Ct. 2584 (2015).

[3] 531 U.S. 98 (2000).

[4] Youngstown Sheet & Tube Co. v. Sawyer, 343 U.S. 579 (1952).

[5] See Trump v. Hawaii, 138 S. Ct. 2392 (2018).

halt President Donald Trump's signature policy. Why? The "travel bans"—which denied entry to aliens from predominantly Muslim nations—traced their roots to overtly anti-Muslim statements made by then-candidate Trump. Furthermore, the government could only offer the faintest patina of a rational basis to defend the policies. Confronted with these facts, the lower courts uniformly enjoined the travel bans. Ultimately, only the Supreme Court upheld the final version in its entirety. This essay recounts the travel bans' 18-month litigation blitz.

Part I discusses the first iteration of the travel ban, which President Trump signed one week after his inauguration. There were no exigent circumstances that justified the entry ban, and its rollout was a colossal disaster. Within hours, courts intervened to block its enforcement. Within days, the judiciary entered the first raft of nationwide injunctions. Following defeats in the court of appeals, the acting solicitor general declined to petition for certiorari. Instead, Travel Ban 1.0, as it became known, was withdrawn. Part II dissects Travel Ban 2.0. After it was signed in March 2017, the self-professed "legal resistance" replayed its playbook: nationwide injunctions halting the policy were promptly affirmed by the courts of appeals. Except this time, the Supreme Court allowed most of the policy to go into effect. The message to the lower courts was apparent: treat this case like a normal case. Part III introduces Travel Ban 3.0, which was announced in September 2017. This policy—designed to be permanent—was promptly challenged in district courts. Once again, nationwide injunctions were affirmed by the courts of appeals. Yet, in December 2017, the Supreme Court permitted the *entire* policy to go into effect. This decision was a conclusive indication that the lower courts had gone astray. As a result, there should have been no surprises when, in June 2018, the Supreme Court upheld the third iteration in its entirety.

Now that this saga has drawn to an anti-climactic close, Part IV places the travel ban in perspective. First, this essay considers how the Court applies rational basis review to the proclamation: the judiciary must focus on *legality*, even if it conflicts with *reality*. Second, this essay contrasts the arguments raised by the "legal resistance" against the Trump administration with the presumption of regularity afforded by the Supreme Court. Finally, this section identifies how the law often applies differently to the president, through the "presidential avoidance canon."

The three iterations of the travel ban, like the president who signed them, were in all regards "unpresidented."[6]

I. Travel Ban 1.0

On Friday, January 27, 2017, one week after taking the oath of office, President Trump signed Executive Order No. 13769.[7] The order directed the executive branch to review information shared by foreign countries about their nationals who seek entry into the United States. During that 90-day period, the order suspended entry of aliens from seven countries: Iran, Iraq, Libya, Somalia, Sudan, Syria, and Yemen. To maintain the element of surprise, the White House did not provide any advance notice to the Departments of Justice, State, and Homeland Security. As a result, chaos erupted. Aliens from those seven nations, who were in transit while the order was signed, were detained upon landing at airports. Many of those aliens were Lawful Permanent Residents—that is, green-card holders—and had a statutory right to enter the United States. Over the next 24 hours, federal judges granted writs of habeas corpus, and ordered the release of those detained.[8] These emergency actions, which I dubbed "The Airport Cases," were the first round of litigation filed against the Trump administration.[9]

Soon the litigation would transition from releasing those in custody at airports, however, to halting the policy altogether. The Washington attorney general filed suit against Travel Ban 1.0. He asserted that Executive Order No. 13769 was unconstitutional, and sought a nationwide injunction.[10] After an expedited proceeding, on February 3, 2018, Judge James L. Robart barred enforcement

---

[6] See Donald J. Trump (@realDonaldTrump), Twitter (Dec. 17, 2016, 4:30 AM), archived at https://bit.ly/2KAA9tZ.

[7] 82 Fed. Reg. 8977 (2017).

[8] See e.g., Darweesh v. Trump, No. 17 CIV. 480 (AMD), 2017 WL 388504, at *1 (E.D.N.Y. Jan. 28, 2017); see also Josh Blackman, Nationwide Injunction (Stay, Really) Issued in Darweesh v. Trump, Josh Blackman's Blog, Jan. 28, 2017, https://bit.ly/2MhKUpZ.

[9] See Josh Blackman, The Procedural Aspects of "The Airport Cases," Josh Blackman's Blog, Jan. 29, 2017, http://bit.ly/2Kmqbfz.

[10] See Josh Blackman, Washington Seeks Nationwide Injunction of Immigration Order, Relying on Argument It Opposed U.S. v. Texas, Josh Blackman's Blog, Feb. 1, 2017, http://bit.ly/2M3XRDp.

of the travel ban.[11] The order had only the most threadbare analysis.[12] There was one paragraph describing the procedural background, and another two paragraphs reciting the standards for granting a temporary restraining order. (As a former district court clerk, I recognize copy-and-pasted boilerplate when I see it.) The actual legal analysis stretched across two conclusory paragraphs. The court did not cite any provision of the Constitution, or any statute that was violated. There was no real analysis here.

Even in times of conflict, courts have a duty to explain their reasoning through written opinions. This decision fell far, far short of that standard. Further, unlike the *Airport Cases*, which were decided in the wee hours after the executive order was issued, the Seattle court had several days to think about these issues. Such a momentous decision warrants some analysis. Yet, on this conclusory basis, the court issued a nationwide injunction against the executive order.

The government appealed. The U.S. Court of Appeals for the Ninth Circuit held oral arguments and, on February 10, 2017, declined to stay the nationwide injunction. I described the decision as a "contrived comedy of errors."[13] First, the court grossly erred by treating a temporary restraining order—that contained no reasoning—as a preliminary injunction. Second, the panel offered zero analysis of the underlying statutory scheme in the Immigration and Nationality Act (INA), which is exceedingly complex and intricate. While it is true that this approach would not resolve all claims—especially of those traveling on nonimmigrant visas—as Justice Robert Jackson reminded us six decades ago, the conjunction or disjunction between Congress and the presidency informs the exactness of judicial review.[14] This timeless lesson was lost on the panel, which, third, applied the strictest of scrutiny to assess whether the executive order was justified based on

---

[11] Washington v. Trump, No. C17-0141-JLR, 2017 WL 462040, at *2 (W.D. Wash. Feb. 3, 2017).

[12] See Josh Blackman, Instant Analysis Nationwide Injunction in Washington v. Trump, Josh Blackman's Blog, Feb. 4, 2017, http://bit.ly/2vDzbYq.

[13] Washington v. Trump, 847 F.3d 1151, 1156 (9th Cir. 2017) (per curiam); Josh Blackman, The 9th Circuit's Contrived Comedy of Errors in Washington v. Trump, 95 Tex. L. Rev. See Also 221 (2017), https://bit.ly/2Mc52tt.

[14] Youngstown Sheet & Tube Co., 343 U.S. at 635–39 (Jackson, J., concurring).

a real risk rather than alternative facts.[15] Fourth, the panel refused to narrow an overbroad injunction. Once again, a study of the underlying statutory scheme could have afforded a plausible method of saving part of the order, while excising the unconstitutional portions.

The government asked the Ninth Circuit to rehear the case en banc. That petition was denied over five dissenting opinions.[16] Instead of petitioning for certiorari, the Trump administration announced that the president would simply issue a new version.

II. Travel Ban 2.0

On March 6, 2017, President Trump signed Executive Order No. 13780, known as Travel Ban 2.0.[17] Like the earlier iteration, this new executive order called for a 90-day worldwide review to assess the risks of aliens entering the United States. During this period, nationals from Iran, Libya, Somalia, Sudan, Syria, and Yemen would be barred from the country. (Iraq was removed from the prior list.) The order noted that these six nations were selected because each was "a state sponsor of terrorism, has been significantly compromised by terrorist organizations, or contains active conflict zones."[18] This revised version cleaned up many of the deficiencies of its predecessor. For example, green-card holders were expressly exempted from the order. Travel Ban 2.0 was challenged in multiple fora. On March 15, 2017, the district court in Hawaii entered a nationwide injunction that blocked the entry ban; the following day, the district court in Maryland did the same.[19]

On May 25, 2017, the U.S. Court of Appeals for the Fourth Circuit, sitting en banc, found that Travel Ban 2.0 was unconstitutional.[20] Its analysis traced back to the campaign trail, when then-candidate Trump called for a "total and complete shutdown of Muslims entering the United States until our country's representatives can figure

[15] See Josh Blackman, Second-Guessing on National Security, Josh Blackman's Blog, Feb. 6, 2017, http://bit.ly/2vAJxbq.

[16] Washington v. Trump, 858 F.3d 1168 (9th Cir. 2017) (en banc).

[17] 82 Fed. Reg. 13209 (Mar. 6, 2017).

[18] *Id.*

[19] Hawai'i v. Trump, 241 F. Supp. 3d 1119 (D. Haw. 2017); Int'l Refugee Assistance Project v. Trump, 241 F. Supp. 3d 539 (D. Md. 2017).

[20] Int'l Refugee Assistance Project [IRAP] v. Trump, 857 F.3d 554 (4th Cir. 2017) (en banc).

out what is going on."[21] Then-candidate Trump also said "'Islam hates us' and asserted that the United States was 'having problems with Muslims coming into the country.'"[22] In her dissenting opinion, Justice Sonia Sotomayor would remark that "[a]s Trump's presidential campaign progressed, he began to describe his policy proposal in slightly different terms."[23] Specifically, "he characterized the policy proposal as a suspension of immigration from countries 'where there's a proven history of terrorism.'"[24] Closer to his election, "Trump reiterated that his proposed 'Muslim ban' had 'morphed into a[n] extreme vetting from certain areas of the world.'"[25]

On the basis of statements made by the president and his associates, before and after the inauguration, the Fourth Circuit ruled that Travel Ban 2.0 violated the Establishment Clause.[26] Specifically, Chief Judge Roger Gregory's majority opinion found that the executive order "drips with religious intolerance."[27] There were three concurring opinions, and three dissenting opinions.[28]

On June 12, 2017, a Ninth Circuit panel ruled that the travel ban violated the INA.[29] That court did not reach the constitutional question.

---

[21] Trump v. Hawaii, 138 S. Ct. 2392, 2417 (2018). The president did not remove that statement from his website until May 2017.

[22] Id.

[23] Id. at 2436 (Sotomayor, J., dissenting).

[24] Id.

[25] Id.

[26] See Josh Blackman, Analysis of IRAP v. Trump Part I: The Fourth Circuit's Reliance on Pre- and Post-Inauguration Statements, Lawfare, May 27, 2017, http://bit.ly/2KsKg3X; Josh Blackman, The Legality of the 3/6/17 Executive Order, Part II: The Due Process Clause Analysis, Lawfare, Mar. 12, 2017, http://bit.ly/2Mk9iUC; Josh Blackman, The Legality of the 3/6/17 Executive Order, Part III: The Establishment Clause, Lawfare, Mar. 15, 2017, http://bit.ly/2LXBxfP; Josh Blackman, Why Courts Shouldn't Try to Read Trump's Mind, Politico Mag., Mar. 16, 2017, https://politi.co/2M2XU2p.

[27] IRAP, 857 F.3d at 572.

[28] Josh Blackman, Analysis of IRAP v. Trump Part III: The Concurring Opinions of Judges Thacker, Keenan, and Wynn, Lawfare, May 30, 2017, http://bit.ly/2OLhfUn; Josh Blackman, Analysis of IRAP v. Trump Part IV: Judge Niemeyer's Dissent, Lawfare, June 2, 2017, http://bit.ly/2ncVUGQ; Josh Blackman, Analysis of IRAP v. Trump Part V: Judge Shedd and Judge Agee's Dissents, and the Government's Petitions for Certiorari and Applications for Stay, Lawfare, June 2, 2017, http://bit.ly/2Mp8gXy.

[29] Hawaii v. Trump, 859 F.3d 741, 755 (9th Cir. 2017) (per curiam). See Josh Blackman, The Legality of the 3/6/17 Executive Order, Part I: The Statutory and Separation of Powers Analyses, Lawfare, Mar. 11, 2017, http://bit.ly/2vz7SOO.

The acting solicitor general asked the Supreme Court to stay both rulings.[30] At the time, I urged the Supreme Court to provide closure on the legality of the travel ban.[31] A less-than-satisfactory result would leave far too many issues open.[32] The Court met me halfway.

On June 26, 2017—five months after Travel Ban 1.0 was signed—the Supreme Court finally intervened.[33] The per curiam opinion stayed the injunctions from the Fourth and Ninth Circuits, in part: the government could enforce the entry suspensions with respect to foreign nationals who lacked a "credible claim of a bona fide relationship with a person or entity in the United States."[34] Simply put, the justices split the baby. Some aliens with American relations would be admitted, but most aliens could be denied entry. Justices Clarence Thomas, Samuel Alito, and Neil Gorsuch would have allowed the policy to go into effect in its entirety.[35]

Once that stay was issued, the 90-day global review process began. During that time, the lower courts struggled to figure out what "bona fide" meant; but those disputes were to be short-lived.[36] The fact that a stay was granted, at least in part, was a positive omen for the government. Based on my research, "since Chief Justice John Roberts joined the Supreme Court in 2005, when the court grants a stay of a lower court decision and grants the petition for a writ of certiorari, in 22 out of 24 cases, the ultimate disposition is a reversal, at least in part."[37] More specifically, the Court always reversed when

[30] Josh Blackman, Analysis of IRAP v. Trump Part V, *Supra* note 28.

[31] Josh Blackman, America Needs Closure on the Travel Ban, N.Y. Times, June 11, 2017, https://nyti.ms/2O9YVTR.

[32] Josh Blackman, Six Possible Options for the Supreme Court's Review of the Travel Ban, Lawfare, June 24, 2017, http://bit.ly/2KtsRYI.

[33] Josh Blackman, The Scope of the Supreme Court's Decision in IRAP v. Trump, Lawfare, June 27, 2017, http://bit.ly/2Ml91kh.

[34] Trump v. Int'l Refugee Assistance Project, 137 S. Ct. 2080, 2088 (2017) (per curiam).

[35] *Id.* at 2089 (Thomas, J. concurring in part and dissenting in part).

[36] See Josh Blackman, A Nonchalant Conclusion to Trump v. IRAP, Lawfare, Oct. 13, 2017, http://bit.ly/2vGkZh1 ("This is the way *Trump v. IRAP* ends: not with a bang, but with a whimper. At least for now.").

[37] Josh Blackman, Understanding the Supreme Court's Equitable Ruling in Trump v. IRAP, SCOTUSblog, July 12, 2017, http://bit.ly/2OJgM59.

Justice Anthony Kennedy acquiesced in the grant of a stay, and certiorari is subsequently granted.

III. Travel Ban 3.0

After the 90-day global review period concluded on September 24, 2017, Travel Ban 2.0 expired on its own terms. That same day, President Trump issued Proclamation No. 9645, known as Travel Ban 3.0.[38] This final policy "placed entry restrictions on the nationals of eight foreign states whose systems for managing and sharing information about their nationals the President deemed inadequate."[39] Iran, Libya, Somalia, Syria, and Yemen remained on the list. Sudan was removed, but Chad, North Korea, and Venezuela were added. The proclamation explained that such restrictions were "most likely to encourage cooperation" while "protect[ing] the United States until such time as improvements occur."[40]

Once again, the proclamation was challenged in the Districts of Maryland and Hawaii. On October 17, 2017, both courts enjoined the entry bans.[41] The Fourth Circuit affirmed the nationwide injunction in its entirety, again finding that the entry ban violated the Establishment Clause.[42] The Ninth Circuit also affirmed the district court's injunction, again concluding that the entry ban violated the INA.[43]

On December 4, 2017, the Supreme Court put both preliminary lower-court rulings on hold.[44] The justices instructed the courts of appeals to "render their decision[s] with appropriate dispatch."[45] As a result, the entry ban could go into effect, in its entirety, while the lower courts considered the appeal on the merits. By that point, the writing was on the wall for the challengers. On December 22, 2017, the Ninth Circuit invalidated Travel Ban 3.0 on the same statutory

[38] 82 Fed. Reg. 45161 (Sept. 24, 2017).

[39] Trump, 138 S. Ct. at 2404.

[40] 82 Fed. Reg. 45161, 45164.

[41] Int'l Refugee Assistance Project v. Trump, 265 F. Supp. 3d 570 (D. Md. 2017); State v. Trump, 265 F. Supp. 3d 1140 (D. Haw. 2017).

[42] Int'l Refugee Assistance Project v. Trump, 883 F.3d 233 (4th Cir. 2018).

[43] Hawaii v. Trump, 878 F.3d 662 (9th Cir. 2017).

[44] See Trump v. IRAP, 138 S. Ct. 542 (2017) (Mem); Trump v. Hawaii, 138 S. Ct. 542 (2017) (Mem).

[45] *Id.*

grounds it set aside Travel Ban 2.0.[46] The government appealed that decision, and the Supreme Court granted certiorari on January 19, 2018. On February 15, 2018, the dilatory Fourth Circuit issued its decision, which invalidated Travel Ban 3.0 for substantially the same constitutional reasons it invalidated Travel Ban 2.0.[47]

Oral arguments were heard on the last scheduled day of the term: April 25, 2018. Ultimately, the Court sharply split 5-4 and upheld Travel Ban 3.0 in its entirety. Chief Justice Roberts wrote the majority opinion for the Court. He found that the proclamation did not violate the INA, nor did it run afoul of the Establishment Clause. Justice Kennedy concurred to explain why the president can exercise "discretion free from judicial scrutiny."[48] Justice Thomas also wrote a concurring opinion to criticize the usage of nationwide injunctions by district courts.

Justice Stephen Breyer, joined by Justice Elena Kagan, dissented on fairly narrow grounds: they contended that the failure of the government to faithfully implement the waiver program suggests that the program is in fact a Muslim ban. Justice Sotomayor, joined by Justice Ruth Bader Ginsburg, wrote a separate dissent. A "reasonable observer," they wrote, "would conclude that the Proclamation was motivated by anti-Muslim animus."[49] Neither dissent engaged the statutory analysis advanced by the majority.

A. Chief Justice Roberts's Statutory Analysis

The Court's statutory analysis begins with 8 U.S.C. § 1182(f), which was enacted in 1952. This provision enables the president to "suspend the entry of all aliens or any class of aliens," "for such period as he shall deem necessary," whenever he "finds" that their entry "would be detrimental to the interests of the United States." The challengers asserted that "§ 1182(f) confers only a residual power to temporarily halt the entry of a discrete group of aliens engaged in harmful conduct."[50] In other words, it cannot be used to deny entry to a class of aliens absent a showing of individualized harm.

---

[46] Hawaii v. Trump, 878 F.3d. 662 (9th Cir. 2017).

[47] IRAP v. Trump, 883 F.3d 233 (4th Cir. 2018) (en banc).

[48] Trump, 138 S. Ct. at 2424 (Kennedy, J., concurring).

[49] *Id.* at 2433 (Sotomayor, J., dissenting).

[50] *Id.* at 2408 (majority op.).

The Supreme Court swiftly dispatched this argument: "§ 1182(f) grants the President broad discretion to suspend the entry of aliens into the United States" based on "his findings . . . following a world-wide, multi-agency review . . . that entry of the covered aliens would be detrimental to the national interest."[51] Chief Justice Roberts added that "§ 1182(f) exudes deference to the President in every clause." He can decide "whether and when to suspend entry . . . whose entry to suspend . . . for how long . . . and on what conditions."[52] Therefore, the Proclamation fell "well within this comprehensive delegation" of authority from Congress.[53] The president was not required to make any *individualized* findings of harm for each excluded alien.

Furthermore, the Court rejected the challengers' argument that the president's finding must be made "with sufficient detail to enable judicial review."[54] Chief Justice Roberts found that "premise . . . questionable."[55] In other words, the Court strongly doubted that the findings need to meet *any* level of specificity that would allow judicial scrutiny. Such a "searching inquiry into the persuasiveness of the President's justifications," the Court explained, "is inconsistent with . . . the deference traditionally accorded the President in this sphere" of foreign affairs.[56] Yet, "even assuming that some form of review is appropriate, Roberts observed, "[t]he 12–page Proclamation— which thoroughly describes the process, agency evaluations, and recommendations underlying the President's chosen restrictions—is more detailed than any prior order a President has issued under § 1182(f)."[57] To call into question the sufficiency of President Trump's order would immediately call into question the sufficiency of similar orders issued by past presidents. Stated differently, because no one objected to orders issued by past president, the Court should hesitate before objecting to the order issued by the current president.

The challengers raised a second statutory argument, relating to 8 U.S.C. § 1152(a)(1)(A). It provides that "no person shall . . .

---

[51] *Id.*

[52] *Id.*

[53] *Id.*

[54] *Id.* at 2409.

[55] *Id.*

[56] *Id.* (citing Holder v. Humanitarian Law Project, 561 U.S. 1, 35 (2010)).

[57] *Id.* at 2409.

be discriminated against in the issuance of an immigrant visa because of the person's race, sex, nationality, place of birth, or place of residence." The challengers asserted that this nondiscrimination provision, enacted as part of the landmark 1965 INA, placed a limitation on the president's power to exclude aliens under § 1182(f). That is, the president could not deny entry on the basis of "race" or "nationality."

Early on in the litigation, I pointed out an obvious response to this argument: § 1182(f) concerns "entry" while § 1152(a)(1)(A) concerns the "issuance of an immigrant visa."[58] The provisions are not at all in tension. Unless an alien is admissible in the first place, it is irrelevant whether he has a visa. For example, an alien can arrive at an airport with a valid visa, but be denied entry if a federal official determines he is inadmissible. Moreover, Presidents Carter and Reagan had denied entry to Iranian and Cuban nationals, respectively.[59] No one claimed that these actions violated the INA. Furthermore, it would be unthinkable for Congress to deny the president the power to exclude aliens from belligerent nations, even absent a formal declaration of war. Sections 1182(f) and 1152(a)(1)(A) are best read to operate on different aspects of immigration law, rather than to conflict with each other.

The Supreme Court's analysis closely tracked my statutory arguments. First, Chief Justice Roberts observed that § 1152(a)(1)(A) does not affect "the *entire* immigration process" because it references "the act of visa issuance alone."[60] The challengers' construction, he wrote, "ignores the basic distinction between admissibility determinations and visa issuance that runs throughout the INA."[61] Specifically, the "concepts of entry and admission—but not issuance of a visa—are used interchangeably in the INA."[62] The chief justice explained

---

[58] See Josh Blackman, The Statutory Legality of Trump's Executive Order on Immigration, Josh Blackman's Blog, Feb. 5, 2017, http://bit.ly/2OdAhS7; Josh Blackman, The Statutory Legality of Trump's Executive Order on Immigration: Part II, Josh Blackman's Blog, Feb. 5, 2017, http://bit.ly/2AGLLf0; Josh Blackman, The Statutory Legality of Trump's Executive Order on Immigration: Part III, Josh Blackman's Blog, Feb. 7, 2017, http://bit.ly/2LR7ZQG; Josh Blackman, The Statutory Legality of Trump's Executive Order on Immigration: Part IV, Josh Blackman's Blog, Feb. 11, 2017, http://bit.ly/2OdBbOv.

[59] Exec. Order No. 12172, 3 C.F.R. 461 (1979), as amended by Exec. Order No. 12206, 3 C.F.R. 249 (1980); Proclamation No. 5517, 3 C.F.R. 102 (1986).

[60] Trump, 138 S. Ct. at 2414.

[61] *Id.*

[62] *Id.* at 2414 n.4.

that "a visa does not entitle an alien to enter the United States 'if, upon arrival,' an immigration officer determines that the applicant is 'inadmissible under this chapter, or any other provision of law'— including § 1182(f)."[63] The Court dismissed any construction under which the president could not "suspend entry from particular foreign states in response to an epidemic confined to a single region, or a verified terrorist threat involving nationals of a specific foreign nation, or even if the United States were on the brink of war."[64] Simply stated, "Sections 1182(f) and 1152(a)(1)(A) . . . operate in different spheres."[65]

The challengers' briefing before the Ninth Circuit and the Supreme Court focused almost entirely on the statutory argument. Yet, Chief Justice Roberts observed, "neither dissent even attempts any serious argument to the contrary."[66] Justice Sotomayor explained that she did not address the "complex statutory claims" because the constitutional question "prove[d] far simpler than the statutory one."[67]

B. Chief Justice Roberts's Constitutional Analysis

1. No "spiritual and dignitary" injury for Article III standing

After dismissing the statutory claims, the Court addressed whether "the Proclamation was issued for the unconstitutional purpose of excluding Muslims."[68] As a threshold matter, the Court declined to find Article III standing based on a purported "spiritual and dignitary" injury—that is, the Proclamation "establishes a disfavored faith."[69] Rather, the plaintiffs could only rely on a "more concrete injury" based on family reunification.[70]

---

[63] *Id.* at 2414.

[64] *Id.* at 2415.

[65] *Id.*

[66] *Id.* at 2415.

[67] *Id.* at 2434 (Sotomayor, J., dissenting).

[68] *Id.* at 2415 (majority op.).

[69] *Id.* at 2416.

[70] *Id.* I had correctly predicted that the Supreme Court would reject any injury based on mere "stigmatization." Josh Blackman, Analysis of IRAP v. Trump Part II: The Fourth Circuit's Misuse of Mandel, Din, Lemon, and Town of Greece, Lawfare, May 28, 2017, https://bit.ly/2nfVGib.

2. Domestic Establishment Clause cases do not apply

The Court's framing of the constitutional question was dispositive: "Relying on Establishment Clause precedents concerning laws and policies applied *domestically,* plaintiffs allege that the primary purpose of the Proclamation was religious animus and that the President's stated concerns about vetting protocols and national security were but pretexts for discriminating against Muslims."[71] The key word is "domestic." The Fourth Circuit had simply assumed that the Court's Establishment Clause precedents, which all concerned *domestic* policies, applied to the President's foreign policy decisions. There is good reason to exempt foreign policy decisions from the Court's domestic Establishment Clause cases, such as the so-called *Lemon* test, or the analysis established in *McCreary County v. ACLU.*[72]

Chief Justice Roberts found that this case "differs in numerous respects from the *conventional* Establishment Clause claim."[73] He observed that "[u]nlike the typical suit involving religious displays or school prayer," that is, mundane domestic matters, the challengers "seek to invalidate a national security directive regulating the entry of aliens abroad." As a result, this case "raises a number of delicate issues regarding the scope of the constitutional right and the manner of proof." Critically, in the domestic context, the Court in the past had no trouble looking to "extrinsic statements" to peek behind a facially neutral action, in order to ascertain whether the government had an impermissible, nonsecular purpose. With respect to the proclamation, however, the Court hesitated before "prob[ing] the sincerity of the stated justifications for the policy by reference to extrinsic statements—many of which were made before the President took the oath of office."[74]

In dissent, Justice Sotomayor faulted the majority for its "apparent willingness to throw the Establishment Clause out the window and forgo any meaningful constitutional review at the mere mention of

[71] Trump, 138 S. Ct. at 2417 (emphasis added).

[72] Lemon v. Kurtzman, 403 U.S. 602 (1971); McCreary County v. ACLU, 545 U.S. 844 (2005). See Josh Blackman, The Domestic Establishment Clause, 23 Roger Williams L. Rev. 435 (2018) (arguing that the Supreme Court's "domestic" Establishment Clause cases should not apply to the resolution of the travel ban's constitutionality).

[73] Trump, 138 S. Ct. at 2418 (emphasis added).

[74] *Id.*

a national-security concern."[75] The Court responded that applying "the *de novo* 'reasonable observer'" standard, as articulated in *Mc-Creary County v. ACLU*, was not appropriate for cases that involve "immigration policies, diplomatic sanctions, and military actions."[76] Chief Justice Roberts added that "a circumscribed inquiry applies to any constitutional claim concerning the entry of foreign nationals." There is no authority to support a "free-ranging inquiry . . . in the national security and foreign affairs context."[77]

Instead, Chief Justice Roberts proposed a POTUS-specific-framework: How should the Court consider "not only the statements of a particular President, but also the authority of the Presidency itself" when "reviewing a Presidential directive, neutral on its face, addressing a matter within the core of executive responsibility"?[78] This test is quite possibly the most important element of the entire decision. On the eve of oral arguments, *Washington Post* reporter Robert Barnes aptly summarized *Trump v. Hawaii* in a pithy headline: "In travel ban case, Supreme Court considers 'the president' vs. 'this president.'"[79] The majority opinion chose the former. Instead of focusing on the norm-busting behavior of the 45th president, the Court resolved this case with an eye toward all 45 presidents. "[W]e must consider not only the statements of a particular President," Chief Justice Roberts explained, "but also the authority of *the Presidency itself*."[80] Specifically, the Court concluded that "[t]he entry suspension is an act that is well within executive authority and could have been taken by any other President—the only question is evaluating the actions of this particular President in promulgating an otherwise valid Proclamation."[81]

The Court explained that "[t]he upshot of our cases in this context is clear: 'Any rule of constitutional law that would inhibit the flexibility' of the President 'to respond to changing world conditions should be

---

[75] *Id.* at 2441 n.6 (Sotomayor, J., dissenting).

[76] *Id.* at 2420 n.5 (majority op.).

[77] *Id.*

[78] *Id.* at 2418.

[79] Robert Barnes, In Travel Ban Case, Supreme Court Considers 'the President' vs. 'This President,' Wash. Post, Apr. 22, 2018, https://wapo.st/2vBlHfO.

[80] Trump, 138 S. Ct. at 2418 (emphasis added).

[81] *Id.* at 2423.

adopted only with the greatest caution,' and [the Court's] inquiry into matters of entry and national security is highly constrained."[82] Whatever precedents were set here, would constrain presidential power "in diverse contexts, including those presently unimagined, and will have the effect of [weakening] the Presidency [within] its constitutional bounds and undermining respect for the separation of powers."[83]

This principle, in large part, informed my personal approach to all three travel bans: "The judiciary should not abandon its traditional role simply because the president has abandoned his."[84]

3. The proclamation is "largely immune from judicial control"

Ultimately, the Court reviewed the Proclamation in an extremely deferential manner because it implicated "the admission and exclusion of foreign nationals," which "is a 'fundamental sovereign attribute exercised by the Government's political departments *largely immune from judicial control.*'"[85] *Kleindienst v. Mandel,* and not the Court's Establishment Clause cases, provides the appropriate "circumscribed judicial inquiry when the denial of a visa allegedly burdens the constitutional rights of a U.S. citizen."[86] Specifically, the Court's review was limited "to whether the Executive gave a 'facially legitimate and bona fide' reason for its action."[87] In my writings, I contended that the adjective "facially" modified *both* "legitimate" and "bona fide."[88] That is, the Court does not peek behind the

---

[82] *Id.* at 2419–20 (quoting Matthews v. Diaz, 426 U.S. 67, 81-81 (1976)).

[83] Cf. N.L.R.B. v. Noel Canning, 134 S. Ct. 2550, 2617–18 (2014) (Scalia, J., concurring) ("Sad, but true: The Court's embrace of the adverse-possession theory of executive power (a characterization the majority resists but does not refute) will be cited in diverse contexts, including those presently unimagined, and will have the effect of aggrandizing the Presidency beyond its constitutional bounds and undermining respect for the separation of powers.").

[84] Blackman, Why Courts Shouldn't Try to Read Trump's Mind, *Supra* note 26.

[85] Trump, 138 S. Ct. at 2418 (quoting Fiallo v. Bell, 430 U.S. 787, 792 (1977)) (emphasis added).

[86] *Id.* at 2419 (citing Kleindienst v. Mandel, 408 U.S. 753 (1972)).

[87] *Id.*

[88] See Blackman, Analysis of IRAP v. Trump Part II: *Supra* note 70 ("The operative phrase in *Mandel* is 'facially legitimate and bona fide reason.' Both 'legitimate' and 'bona fide' are best read as being modified by 'facially.' It is not 'legitimate' on the face, but 'bona fide' as a whole. The lack of good faith must be represented on the face of the action, not beyond its face.").

curtains to ascertain if the policy was not bona fide. Once again, the Court's analysis was consistent with my own.

Chief Justice Roberts explained that "'when the Executive exercises this [delegated] power negatively on the basis of a facially legitimate and bona fide reason, the courts will neither look behind the exercise of that discretion, nor test it by balancing its justification' against the asserted constitutional interests of U.S. citizens."[89] Critically, "'[j]udicial inquiry into the national-security realm raises concerns for the separation of powers'" by intruding on the president's constitutional responsibilities in the area of foreign affairs.[90] Finally, the Court added, Justice Kennedy's concurring opinion in *Kerry v. Din* reaffirmed the surface-deep-scrutiny required by the *Mandel* test.[91] The inquiry, and resolution, is straightforward: "A conventional application of *Mandel,* asking only whether the policy is facially legitimate and bona fide, would put an end to our review"—*regardless of* the statements that inform the policy's purpose.[92]

4. The proclamation survives rational basis scrutiny

Yet, the Court still probed just a bit below the surface. Why? Because the solicitor general "suggested that it may be appropriate here for the inquiry to extend beyond the facial neutrality of the order."[93] As a result, the Court "assume[d]" that it could "look behind the face of the Proclamation to the extent of applying rational basis review."[94] This alternative argument is important: absent the solicitor general's concession, the Court's precedents suggest applying a standard of review even *less* stringent than rational basis review. In his concurring opinion, Justice Kennedy aptly described this standard: "discretion *free* from judicial scrutiny."[95] Even applying some form of rational-basis review—is the "entry policy . . . plausibly related to the Government's stated objective to protect the country and improve

---

[89] Trump, 138 S. Ct. at 2419 (citations omitted).

[90] *Id.* (quoting Ziglar v. Abbasi, 137 S. Ct. 1843, 1861 (2017)).

[91] *Id.* (citing Kerry v. Din, 135 S. Ct. 2128, 2141 (2015) (Kennedy, J., concurring)).

[92] *Id.* at 2420.

[93] *Id.*

[94] *Id.*

[95] *Id.* at 2424 (Kennedy, J., concurring) (emphasis added).

vetting processes"[96]—results in a government victory. The extrinsic evidence can be "considered," but the policy must be upheld "so long as it *can reasonably be understood* to result from a justification independent of unconstitutional grounds."[97]

Critically, the justification need not be the actual justification. Rather, it must be a *reasonable* justification to support the policy. Justice Sotomayor is correct that "the Government remains wholly unable to articulate any *credible* national-security interest that would go unaddressed by the current statutory scheme absent the Proclamation."[98] The critical word, however is "credible." And, under current law, it is not for the judiciary to decide what interests are *credible*, or *wise*, or *justified*. Under rational basis review, the Court declined to "substitute [its] own assessment for the Executive's predictive judgments on such matters, all of which 'are delicate, complex, and involve large elements of prophecy.'"[99]

Based on the record, the majority opinion found, "there is persuasive evidence that the entry suspension has a legitimate grounding in national security concerns, quite apart from any religious hostility." Chief Justice Roberts did not deny the existence of any religious hostility, but the Court was still required to "accept that independent justification."[100] As a result, the extrinsic statements played no meaningful role in the majority's analysis. They were merely mentioned, and discarded. At bottom, "the Government has set forth a sufficient national security justification to survive rational basis review."[101]

C. Justice Kennedy's Concurring Opinion

The October 2017 term was unique: in 19 decisions that split 5-4, Justice Kennedy never joined the liberal quartet to form a majority. In 2 of those 19 cases, Chief Justice Roberts voted with the Court's

---

[96] *Id.* at 2420 (majority op.) (citing Railroad Retirement Bd. v. Fritz, 449 U.S. 166, 179 (1980)).

[97] *Id.* (emphasis added).

[98] *Id.* at 2444 (Sotomayor, J., dissenting)

[99] *Id.* at 2421 (majority op.) (quoting Chicago & Southern Air Lines, Inc. v. Waterman S.S. Corp., 333 U.S. 103, 111 (1948)).

[100] *Id.*

[101] *Id.* at 2423.

liberal bloc.[102] Even Justice Gorsuch crossed lines once.[103] But not Justice Kennedy, the Court's perennial swing vote. By way of comparison, in the October 2016 term, Justice Kennedy voted with the liberal bloc in 57 percent of the 5-4 decisions.[104] And in the October 2015 term, he joined the liberals in 75 percent of the 5-4 decisions. However, in his final term on the bench, that number dropped to *zero*. Justice Kennedy's concurring opinion in *Trump v. Hawaii* turned out to be his final writing as a member of the High Court. It warrants a careful study for what he said, and did not say.

First, he joined the Court's opinion in full, including its application of minimum-rational basis review. Critically, this concurrence was not one of Justice Kennedy's typical *conservatish* writings, where he concurred only in judgment, or watered down the majority opinion.[105] Second, he explained that "in some instances, governmental action may be subject to judicial review to determine whether or not it is 'inexplicable by anything but animus,'" such as "animosity to a religion."[106] But such "judicial review" is not appropriate for the entry ban. Third, Justice Kennedy cast doubt on whether future "judicial proceedings may properly continue in this case, in light of the substantial deference that is and must be accorded to the Executive in the conduct of foreign affairs."[107] Here, the soon-to-be-retired justice sent a subtle message to the inferior courts: their judgments remain inferior, and they should not supplant the Supreme Court's conclusive determination about the proclamation's legality. Specifically, Justice Kennedy sought to preemptively slam shut the door on "discovery and other preliminary matters" that may "intrude on the foreign affairs power of the Executive."[108]

[102] See Artis v. District of Columbia, 138 S. Ct. 594 (2008); Carpenter v. United States, 138 S. Ct. 2206 (2018).

[103] See Sessions v. Dimaya, 138 S. Ct. 1204 (2018).

[104] Kedar Bhatia, Final October Term 2017 Stat Pack and Key Takeaways, SCOTUSblog, June 29, 2018, http://bit.ly/2LWa4et.

[105] See e.g., Burwell v. Hobby Lobby Stores, Inc., 134 S. Ct. 2751, 2785 (Kennedy, J., concurring) ("It seems to me appropriate, in joining the Court's opinion, to add these few remarks").

[106] Trump, 138 S. Ct. at 2423–24 (Kennedy, J., concurring) (quoting Romer v. Evans, 517 U.S. 620, 632 (1996)).

[107] *Id.* at 2424.

[108] *Id.*

Fourth, Justice Kennedy made a "further observation." He explained that "[t]here are numerous instances in which the statements and actions of Government officials are not subject to judicial scrutiny or intervention."[109] Justice Kennedy does not explain why the proclamation is immune from "judicial scrutiny." Though, because he joined the majority opinion in full, the answer is straightforward: the government's denial of entry to noncitizens here is not subject to judicial intervention.

Justice Kennedy's fifth point is at once profound, yet perplexing: the fact that certain actions are "not subject to judicial scrutiny . . . does not mean those officials are free to disregard the Constitution and the rights it proclaims and protects."[110] For a generation, Justice Kennedy was content to serve as the moral compass of our polity: he cast the deciding vote on cases involving affirmative action, abortion, the death penalty, same-sex marriage, and countless other topics. For the travel ban, however, he is content to let the elected branches monitor their own actions.

Justice Kennedy closed his tenure on the Supreme Court with an ephemeral elegy for egalitarianism: "An anxious world must know that our Government remains committed always to the liberties the Constitution seeks to preserve and protect, so that freedom extends outward, and lasts."[111] Your guess is as good as mine as to the meaning of this sentence. Perhaps it's a fitting bookend to his "sweet mystery of life" passage from *Planned Parenthood v. Casey*. In any event, this "mic drop" was an elusive conclusion for the career of an elusive justice.

D. Justice Thomas's Concurring Opinion

Justice Thomas, as usual, would have gone further than did the majority. Instead of applying minimum rational basis review, Justice Thomas's concurring opinion contended that "Section 1182(f) does not set forth *any* judicially enforceable limits that constrain the President."[112] Full stop. Recall that Justices Thomas, Alito, and

---

[109] *Id.*

[110] *Id.*

[111] *Id.*

[112] *Id.* at 2424 (Thomas, J., concurring) (emphasis added).

Gorsuch would have upheld Travel Ban 2.0 in its entirety. Here, however, only Justice Thomas wrote separately.

Second, Justice Thomas reached a constitutional question the majority did not: he found "the President has *inherent* authority to exclude aliens from the country" under Article II.[113] The president's power to exclude aliens is supported by a unique amalgamation of inherent authority over foreign affairs, as well as explicit delegations of statutory authority. Note that this power is *inherent*, not *exclusive*.[114] That is, Congress can still impose meaningful limitations on this authority. And it should. The legislature, and not the judiciary, has the responsibility to enforce such constraints on immigration laws.

Third, while the majority was content to distinguish this case from other *domestic* Establishment Clause cases, Justice Thomas would simply eliminate the "reasonable observer" standard from the Court's jurisprudence altogether. Moreover, he would exclude from the ambit of the First Amendment any "alleged religious discrimination [that is] directed at aliens abroad."[115] Finally, though Justice Thomas found that the proclamation was not subject to any judicial review, he added that "the plaintiffs' proffered evidence of anti-Muslim discrimination is unpersuasive."[116]

Those four points would have been adequate to resolve the case. But Justice Thomas wrote further—at some length—to criticize the district courts' imposition of "universal" or "nationwide" injunctions. Justice Thomas added that "[d]istrict courts, including the one here, have begun imposing universal injunctions without considering their authority to grant such sweeping relief."[117] Such overly broad relief inflicts three distinct costs on the federal judiciary: "preventing legal questions from percolating through the federal courts, encouraging forum shopping, and making every case a national emergency for the courts and for the Executive Branch."[118]

---

[113] *Id.* (citing Knauff v. Shaughnessy, 338 U.S. 537, 542–43 (1950)) (emphasis added).

[114] Zivotofsky ex rel. Zivotofsky v. Kerry, 135 S. Ct. 2076, 2094 (2015) ("The weight of historical evidence indicates Congress has accepted that the power to recognize foreign states and governments and their territorial bounds is *exclusive to the Presidency*.") (emphasis added).

[115] Trump, 138 S. Ct. at 2424 (Thomas, J., concurring).

[116] *Id.*

[117] *Id.* at 2425.

[118] *Id.*

Hawaii v. Trump was not the appropriate case for the Court to decide the propriety of nationwide injunctions, because the Court ultimately found the policy lawful. But in a future case, Justice Thomas predicted, "this Court is dutybound to adjudicate" the propriety of nationwide injunctions.[119]

E. Justice Breyer's Dissenting Opinion

Justice Breyer dissented, joined by Justice Kagan. As a threshold matter, they did not conclude—as did Justices Sotomayor and Ginsburg—that the proclamation was "significantly affected by religious animus against Muslims."[120] Nor did they conclude, as did the majority, that the proclamation's purpose was to protect national security. Instead, Justices Breyer and Kagan took a far more circumspect route that would have left the nationwide injunction in place, at least temporarily.

Chief Justice Roberts's majority opinion highlighted the fact that "the Proclamation creates a waiver program open to all covered foreign nationals seeking entry as immigrants or nonimmigrants."[121] Even those aliens who are otherwise subject to the entry ban can still petition the government for a discretionary exemption. This "additional feature," the Court explained, bolstered the government's "claim of a legitimate national security interest."[122] The dissenting duo respectfully disagreed with this claim.

Instead, as Justice Breyer is wont to do, he crafted a carefully calibrated balancing test. If the waiver program was faithfully executed on a case-by-case basis, the government could rebut the presumption that the proclamation is a veiled Muslim ban. However, if the waiver program was not faithfully executed—that is, exemptions were arbitrarily denied—the government could not rebut the presumption that the proclamation was a veiled Muslim ban. In other words, "since the case-by-case exemptions and waivers apply without regard to the individual's religion, application of that system would help make clear that the Proclamation does not deny visas to numerous Muslim individuals (from those countries) who do not

---

[119] *Id.* at 2429.
[120] *Id.* at 2429 (Breyer, J., dissenting).
[121] *Id.* at 2422 (majority op.).
[122] *Id.*

pose a security threat." Alternatively, Justice Breyer explained, "denying visas to Muslims who meet the Proclamation's own security terms would support the view that the Government excludes them for reasons based upon their religion."[123]

Ultimately, based on his study of how the waivers have been issued, Justice Breyer found that "the Government is not applying the Proclamation as written."[124] In other words, no guidance existed that would explain how the exemptions should be issued. Additionally, too few waivers had been granted. As a result, the dissenters surmised, this process merely served as window dressing for a Muslim ban. Such selective enforcement supported the inference that the proclamation was in fact designed to implement anti-Muslim animus. Therefore, Justices Breyer and Kagan would "send this case back to the District Court for further proceedings" to determine whether the travel ban in fact "rest[s] upon a 'Muslim ban.'"[125] (Justice Sotomayor, in dissent, took this charge a step further: she concluded that "there is reason to suspect that the Proclamation's waiver program is nothing more than a sham."[126])

Chief Justice Roberts responded that Justice Breyer's analysis is premised on "selective statistics, anecdotal evidence, and a declaration from unrelated litigation" that is not "appropriate under rational basis review."[127] That's precisely the point: the mild dissenters duo did not conclude that minimum rationality was the correct standard. Justice Breyer hinted at that conclusion in the penultimate sentence of his dissent: "If this Court must decide the question without this further litigation, I would . . . find the evidence of antireligious bias, including statements on a website taken down only after the President issued the two executive orders preceding the Proclamation, along with the other statements . . . [would provide] a sufficient basis to set the Proclamation aside."[128] Justice Breyer was able to punt on this difficult question, however, because a future study of the waiver process could resolve the case more simply.

---

[123] Trump, 138 S. Ct. at 2430 (Breyer, J., dissenting).

[124] Id. at 2431.

[125] Id. at 2433.

[126] Id. at 2445 (Sotomayor, J., dissenting).

[127] Id. at 2423 n.7 (majority op.).

[128] Id. at 2433 (Breyer, J., dissenting).

F. Justice Sotomayor's Dissenting Opinion

Justices Breyer and Kagan wrote a cautious dissent that tried to avoid the implication that President Trump instituted a "Muslim ban." Justice Sotomayor, joined by Justice Ginsburg, made the charge explicitly. They faulted the Court for upholding "a policy first advertised openly and unequivocally as a 'total and complete shutdown of Muslims entering the United States' because the policy now masquerades behind a facade of national-security concerns." Furthermore, the dissent assailed the Court for "ignoring the facts, misconstruing our legal precedent, and turning a blind eye to the pain and suffering the Proclamation inflicts upon countless families and individuals, many of whom are United States citizens." Justice Sotomayor ultimately described that outcome as a "troubling result [that] runs contrary to the Constitution and our precedent."[129]

She offered an even blunter criticism for the Department of Justice: "Given President Trump's failure to correct the reasonable perception of his apparent hostility toward the Islamic faith, it is unsurprising that the President's lawyers have, at every step in the lower courts, *failed in their attempts to launder* the Proclamation of its discriminatory taint."[130] However, she added, "this new window dressing cannot conceal an unassailable fact: the words of the President and his advisers create the strong perception that the Proclamation is contaminated by impermissible discriminatory animus against Islam and its followers."[131]

Critically, unlike the majority, Justice Sotomayor's dissent applied the Court's domestic Establishment Clause precedents to find that the proclamation ran afoul of the constitutional guarantee of religious neutrality. "[A] reasonable observer would readily conclude that the Proclamation was motivated by hostility and animus toward the Muslim faith," and not "the Government's asserted national-security justifications."[132]

---

[129] *Id.* at 2433 (Sotomayor, J., dissenting).

[130] *Id.* at 2439.

[131] *Id.* at 2440.

[132] *Id.* at 2435, 2438. Cf. Josh Blackman, Hawaii v. Trump: What Would an "Objective Observer" Think of President Trump's Travel Ban?, Lawfare, May 16, 2017, http://bit.ly/2LYSCVN ("a handful of ambiguous post-inauguration statements, including Trump's declaration that 'we all know what that means' on signing the executive order, will be insufficient to demonstrate to an 'objective observer' an improper motive.").

Justices generally dissent "respectfully."[133] But this dissent was unadorned—and it didn't simply focus on the presidency in the abstract. It focused on *this* president. Indeed, Professor Will Baude pointed out that "Justice Sotomayor's dissent contains repeated references to 'President Trump,'" and "mentions the 'Trump administration.'" He added, "I doubt that either is an accident."[134] Indeed, during her announcement of the opinion, Justice Sotomayor referred to "President *Donald* Trump." Seated in the gallery, I was shocked she used the president's given name. Every time she uttered the word "Trump," her voice was filled with disdain. That sentiment pervaded the entire dissent.

IV. Placing the Travel Bans in Perspective

During the 18-month litigation blitz, numerous courts repeatedly invalidated the three iterations of the travel ban. Only the Supreme Court upheld it—and by a 5-4 vote. This final section places the travel bans in perspective.

A. Legality, Reality, and Rationality

In *Trump v. Hawaii*, the dissenting justices were troubled by the majority's unwillingness to consider what any "reasonable observer" would consider: namely, the President's blatantly anti-Islamic rhetoric that undergirded the travel ban. This precise question arose in December 2017, when the Fourth Circuit heard oral arguments in *Trump v. IRAP*. Judge James A. Wynn Jr. asked the Justice Department lawyer about the relevance of the president's inflammatory tweets to the Establishment Clause analysis.[135] "What do we do with that," he asked referring to the tweets. "Do we just ignore reality and look at the *legality* to determine how to handle this case?" Though the framing of his question was somewhat unclear, the premise was pellucid: What should a judge do if the law cuts one way, but reality cuts the other?[136]

---

[133] See Josh Blackman, Disrespectful Dissents on the Roberts Court, Josh Blackman's Blog, Mar. 25, 2015, http://bit.ly/2vFKcbs.

[134] Will Baude, Free Thoughts on Trump v. Hawaii, The Volokh Conspiracy, June 26, 2018, http://bit.ly/2OLIAGb.

[135] Oral Arg. Transcript at 24:20, Int'l Refugee Assistance Project v. Trump, 883 F.3d 233 (4th Cir. 2018) (No. 17-2231), http://bit.ly/2Ku5vlL.

[136] Josh Blackman, For Judges, 'Legality' Is Their Only 'Reality', Lawfare, Dec. 11, 2017, http://bit.ly/2vfA7Tu (emphasis added).

All courts, including the Supreme Court, exist only because of "legalities," and are limited by legalities. Article III jurisdiction is defined by legalities. The INA is constituted by a complicated scheme of legalities. The separation of powers embeds a host of legalities that restrict judicial power. The inherent powers of the president compose a legality that allows him to execute certain actions that no one else in the republic can execute. The difference between an op-ed and a published judicial opinion is a matter of "mere" legalities.

As for reality: the very nature of courts of limited jurisdiction requires courts to ignore reality unless the law makes it legally salient. If a fact is not present in the record, appellate courts cannot consider it. If parties are not properly injured and thus do not have standing, courts can take no action. If a case presents a political question, courts must look the other way. If Congress has deprived the court of jurisdiction, the case must be dismissed. Under the state-secret privilege, and related doctrines—like the executive-deliberative privilege—courts simply cannot inquire into the true reasons behind some actions.

In my writings, I accurately predicted that the Supreme Court would consider the proclamation under the rational basis review, based on the standard articulated in *Williamson v. Lee Optical*.[137] Under that level of scrutiny—which judges have no problem applying in other contexts—courts are required to imagine reasons why the government could have a rational basis, whether or not that reason has a basis in reality. Traditionally, courts have not held the government to an exacting means-ends scrutiny to justify actions taken to protect national security. Under this tier of scrutiny, laws are reviewed with a presumption of legality. The government's defense of the law doesn't need to be perfect, or even coherent. Indeed, under certain strands of rational-basis review, so long as the government provides a basis that could be the reason—even if it was not the real reason—courts will uphold it. As I tell my students, the word "rational" does not mean "logical" or "sensible," but rather "conceivable."[138]

---

[137] 348 U.S. 483, 488 (1955) ("The day is gone when this Court uses the Due Process Clause of the Fourteenth Amendment to strike down state laws, regulatory of business and industrial conditions, because they may be unwise, improvident, or out of harmony with a particular school of thought.").

[138] Josh Blackman, The Travel Ban and the Rational Basis Test, Lawfare, Oct. 23, 2017, http://bit.ly/2vGus8l.

If the Supreme Court wishes to revisit the uber-deferential rational basis test, it should do so in the context of a mundane domestic case; not a foreign-policy case in which the president acts with express statutory authority—as well as inherent constitutional authority—in order to exclude entry to non-U.S. persons.[139]

B. Resistance and Regularity

Perhaps my most lasting contribution to the legal discourse over the travel ban, and the Trump Administration as a whole, concerns the concept of "resistance." To be clear, I didn't invent that term! Before the inauguration, the self-proclaimed "legal resistance" emerged to develop legal strategies to frustrate the Trump administration.[140] This movement's first and most successful victories were the nationwide injunctions against the travel bans.[141] These actions were completely rational—and unsurprising from the party that (unexpectedly) lost the election.

What has garnered the most opposition to my work in this context is the concept of the "judicial resistance."[142] I didn't invent the concept of the "judicial resistance" either. It is derived from an essay titled "The Revolt of the Judges: What Happens When the Judiciary Doesn't Trust the President's Oath." Benjamin Wittes and Quinta Jurecic explained that the judiciary simply did not trust President Trump's oath of office. They asked whether courts would "actually treat Trump as a real president or, conversely, as some kind of accident—a person who somehow ended up in the office but is not quite the President of the United States in the sense that we would previously have recognized."[143] Such judicial resistance is not partisan. Nor do I think the judges are acting in bad faith. The judges are writing legal opinions. There are citations and precedents and modalities of arguments. It is law. My objection, however, is the manner in

---

[139] See Josh Blackman, The Burden of Judging, 9 N.Y.U J. L. & Liberty 1105 (2014).

[140] See Josh Blackman, The Legal Resistance, 9 Faulkner L. Rev. 45 (2017).

[141] See Josh Blackman, The Legal Resistance to President Trump, Nat'l Rev., Oct. 11, 2017, http://bit.ly/2OGwYnA.

[142] Josh Blackman, On the Judicial Resistance, Lawfare, Feb. 12, 2018, http://bit.ly/2vkyP9t.

[143] Benjamin Wittes & Quinta Jurecic, The Revolt of the Judges: What Happens When the Judiciary Doesn't Trust the President's Oath, Lawfare, Mar. 16, 2017, http://bit.ly/2nfsTKO.

which the courts have treated the president's role in the separation of powers.

Instead of resisting, the Supreme Court applied the "presumption of regularity" to the president's actions.[144] That is, the courts refused to modify their "screens of deference" in response to a norm-busting president.[145] Justice Kennedy's concurring opinion spoke directly to this issue. In his defense of the deferential standard of review applied to the proclamation, Justice Kennedy pointed to "[t]he oath that all officials take to adhere to the Constitution." Actions taken pursuant to this oath, he added, are beyond "those spheres in which the Judiciary can correct or even comment upon what those officials say or do." By virtue of taking the oath of office, a certain sphere of actions—including the "sphere of foreign affairs"—cannot be "correct[ed]" by the judiciary.[146]

Justice Kennedy had first-hand knowledge of this oath: he sat steps away from President Trump during the inauguration. And—unlike members of the inferior courts—Justice Kennedy was not troubled by President Trump's execution of his powers. Indeed, one day after *Hawaii v. Trump* was decided, Justice Kennedy announced his retirement. That decision allowed President Trump to appoint his replacement, and shift the balance of the Court for a generation. Because President Trump has "discretion free from judicial scrutiny" in these broad areas, it is "all the more imperative for him . . . to adhere to the Constitution and to its meaning and its promise."[147] But such adherence would not be compelled by the courts.

Going forward, *Trump v. Hawaii*—coupled with the imminent arrival of a new justice—should further lower the temperature of the judiciary toward President Trump. A ruling against the president, however, would have sent the opposite signal to an emboldened lower-court judiciary. Still, the lower courts will no doubt take notice of the fact that the Supreme Court considered extrinsic evidence—including preinauguration campaign-trail statements. Although that evidence did not tip the balance in this case, under the deferential

[144] See Josh Blackman, IRAP v. Trump: Applying the "Presumption of Regularity" in "Uncharted Territories," Lawfare, May 9, 2017, http://bit.ly/2vnwqLi.

[145] Josh Blackman, "Neutral Principles" and the "Presumption of Regularity" in the Era of Trump, Lawfare, Sept. 7, 2017, https://bit.ly/2gPrOcD.

[146] Trump, 138 S. Ct. at 2424 (Kennedy, J., concurring).

[147] *Id.*

standard of review the Court applied, such evidence may yield a different result in cases involving domestic affairs—such as the ongoing Deferred Action for Childhood Arrivals (DACA) litigation—with more stringent scrutiny.

C. The Presidential Avoidance Canon

In her dissenting opinion, Justice Sotomayor faulted the majority—and by extension, Justice Kennedy—for a double standard. She noted that in *Masterpiece Cakeshop*, decided earlier in the term, the Court found a violation of religious freedom based on "less pervasive official expressions of hostility" to faith.[148] Sotomayor added that in both *Trump v. Hawaii* and *Masterpiece Cakeshop*, "the question is whether a *government actor* exhibited tolerance and neutrality in reaching a decision that affects individuals' fundamental religious freedom."[149] But who is that "government actor?"

During oral arguments, Justice Kennedy asked the solicitor general about the relevance of "hateful statements" made by a "local mayor . . . as a candidate."[150] Justice Kennedy chose to focus on a "local mayor," quite deliberately. His concurring opinion illustrated that a "*local* mayor" is very different from the president of the United States. Likewise, the president of the United States is in a very different position from that of a mere member of the Colorado Civil Rights Commission, who disparaged the beliefs of Jack Phillips, the owner of the Masterpiece Cakeshop.

Both the majority and concurring opinions in *Hawaii* reflect a principle I've referred to as the "presidential avoidance canon": because of his unique role in the separation of powers, the law applies differently to the president than it does to anyone else.[151] Without

---

[148] *Id.* at 2439 (Sotomayor, J., dissenting) (citing Masterpiece Cakeshop, Ltd. v. Colo. Civil Rights Comm'n, 138 S. Ct. 1719, 1732 (2018) ("The official expressions of hostility to religion in some of the commissioners' comments—comments that were not disavowed at the Commission or by the State at any point in the proceedings that led to the affirmance of the order—were inconsistent with what the Free Exercise Clause requires").

[149] *Id.* at 2447 (emphasis added).

[150] Transcript of Oral Arg. at 28, Trump v. Hawaii, 138 S. Ct. 2392 (2018) (No. 17-965).

[151] See Josh Blackman, Preview of New Article: "Presidential Speech," Josh Blackman's Blog, Apr. 15, 2018, https://bit.ly/2MIEmrl.

question, the president is not "above the law."[152] The far more important question is: What "law" applies to the president?[153] In *Hawaii v. Trump,* the Court recognized that domestic Establishment Clause precedents cannot restrict the president's statutory and constitutional power to exclude.

Conclusion

This essay is somewhat bittersweet. In my prior contributions to the *Cato Supreme Court Review,* I wailed the law professor's evergreen lamentation: the majority opinion failed to adopt my legal analysis![154] Yet, *Trump v. Hawaii* largely tracked the legal arguments I developed throughout 2017 and 2018 on at least seven discrete issues.

First, standing was premised on a "concrete injury" based on family reunification, not a "spiritual and dignitary injury."[155] Second, there was no conflict between Section 1182(f) of the INA, which allows the president to suspend *entry* to certain aliens, and Section 1152(a)(1)(a), which concerns the issuance of *visas.* These provisions "operate in different spheres."[156] Third, the former provision does not impose temporal or other limitations on the president's authority; rather, it "exudes deference to the President in every clause."[157] Fourth, the travel ban does not run afoul of the nondelegation doctrine.[158] Fifth, the Court declined to apply its "Establishment Clause precedents concerning laws and policies applied domestically."[159] Sixth, *contra* Justice Sotomayor's dissent, the Court afforded President Trump the "presumption of regularity." Finally, the Court concluded

[152] See, e.g., Nixon v. Fitzgerald 457 U.S. 731, 758 n.41 (1982).

[153] See Josh Blackman, What Obstruction Law Applies to the President?, Lawfare, June 6, 2018, http://bit.ly/2vgadis.

[154] See Josh Blackman, U.S. v. Texas (Scalia, J., concurring), 2015–16 Cato Sup. Ct. Rev. 79 (2016); Alan Gura, Ilya Shapiro & Josh Blackman, The Tell-Tale Privileges or Immunities Clause, 2010–11 Cato Sup. Ct. Rev. 163 (2010).

[155] Trump, 138 S. Ct. at 2416.

[156] *Id.* at 2414.

[157] *Id.* at 2408.

[158] Josh Blackman, The Travel Ban, Article II, and the Nondelegation Doctrine, Lawfare, Feb. 22, 2018, https://bit.ly/2OMa5iG.

[159] Trump, 138 S. Ct. at 2417.

that the comparison between the travel ban and *Korematsu v U.S.* was inapposite.[160]

Why then, is the essay bittersweet? Because in *Trump v. Hawaii*, the law enabled a capricious president to arbitrarily separate families with only the faintest patina of a rational basis. These egregious orders were borne, at least in part, on religious animus. The entry bans would have no discernible impact on homeland security, and would instead weaken American interests at home and abroad. Yet, the president could implement them based on broad delegations of statutory authority, as well as his own inherent powers. Furthermore, under longstanding doctrine, the judiciary was required to show the president great deference in the area of foreign affairs and national security. Simply put, the travel ban was awful, but lawful.

During the 18 months between the issuance of Travel Ban 1.0 and the Supreme Court's decision upholding Travel Ban 3.0, I found myself in what has become a familiar position: defending an unpopular action I detest, because of my far greater concerns for maintaining the separation of powers. Indeed, I took the inverse position concerning President Obama's deferred action policies, DACA and Deferred Action for Parents of Americans and Lawful Permanent Residents (DAPA): good policy, but bad law.[161] This task is unforgiving, thankless, and largely misunderstood.

To that end, I deliberately did not file any amicus briefs in this case. Instead, I contented myself with advocating for the standard of review expressed in Justice Kennedy's final concurring opinion: "the very fact that an official may have broad discretion, *discretion free from judicial scrutiny*, makes it all the more imperative for him or her to adhere to the Constitution and to its meaning and its promise."[162] Mr. Bumble expressed the sentiment in *Oliver Twist* far more simply: in this case, "the law is an ass."

---

[160] Josh Blackman, The Simple Answer to Judge Paez's Question about Korematsu, Lawfare, May 19, 2017, http://bit.ly/2MkTile.

[161] Cf. Ilya Shapiro, Good Policy, Bad Law: Obama Correctly Rejected Again on Immigration Reform, Cato at Liberty, Nov. 10, 2015, http://bit.ly/2OFMMqR. Indeed, the editor of this volume and I often share the frustration of having our policy preferences and legal analyses go in opposite directions, particularly on immigration-related issues. See, e.g., Ilya Shapiro, Executive DACA Had to End, but Congress Must Now Legislate It, Cato at Liberty, Sept. 5, 2017, https://bit.ly/2OTS16u.

[162] Trump, 138 S. Ct. at 2424 (Kennedy, J., concurring).

The Ghost Ship of Gerrymandering Law

*Walter Olson**

Commentators spent much of the 2017–18 term in a state of high excitement over the Court's agreement to revisit the longstanding question of whether the Constitution provides a remedy for partisan gerrymandering. The Wisconsin and Maryland cases the Court was hearing featured tortured maps, colorful statehouse gossip, a tech angle (could a new test accurately measure the badness of gerrymanders?) and high constitutional theory (should the Court ground a remedy in Equal Protection or turn instead to the First Amendment?). Everyone understood that these cases might serve as a legacy for Justice Anthony Kennedy, nearing the end of his long and distinguished career, given that his position as swing vote might determine the outcome. Kennedy had played the same role a decade and a half earlier in 2004's *Vieth v. Jubelirer*,[1] in which his concurrence, by leaving the door open to possible future relief, had prepared the path for this day.

What floated into harbor instead was something of a ghost ship—sails handsomely rigged, the captain's table set with polished silver and china, but evacuated by its crew. Citing standing in the Wisconsin case and timing in the Maryland, the Court avoided the merits entirely and sent the disputes back to the lower courts. In particular, it said the Wisconsin complainants in *Gill v. Whitford*[2] would need to establish that gerrymandering affected districts in which they themselves lived, and it said the Maryland complainants in *Benisek v. Lamone*[3] were not entitled to a preliminary injunction

* Senior fellow, Cato Institute; co-chair, Maryland Redistricting Reform Commission. The commission, an advisory body appointed by Maryland Gov. Larry Hogan, was not involved in the litigation discussed here.

[1] 541 U.S. 267 (2004).

[2] 138 S. Ct. 1916 (2018).

[3] 138 S. Ct. 1942 (2018).

although additional facts and legal developments might entitle them to relief as the case proceeded. Both cases remained alive as to nearly all of their factual and legal contentions.

Strikingly, both decisions were unanimous as to result, with *Benisek* affirmed *per curiam* and *Gill*—written by Chief Justice John Roberts, not by Kennedy—decked with reasonably cordial concurrences from justices on each respective ideological wing. All was harmony and cooperation.

Why did the Court back off the merits? What allowed it to assemble at least surface unanimity? Does the outcome reflect Kennedy's personal take, or the thinking of the justices more generally? And what if anything does the decision augur about the state of the gerrymandering issue at the Court with Kennedy retired?

What *Vieth* Teed Up

Cicadas in the mid-Atlantic region tend to come back every 13 or 17 years, and gerrymandering visitations at the high court have been on a not dissimilar cycle. The 2017–18 crop arrived 14 years after *Vieth v. Jubilerer*, which in turn emerged from its burrow 18 years after the decision in *Davis v. Bandemer*.[4] (For completeness one would need to add 2006's *LULAC vs. Perry*,[5] a mixed race-and-politics case that, for most purposes, did little more than confirm the *Vieth* divisions.)

Vieth left the law in a condition of suspenseful equipoise that might not have been expected to last 14 months, let alone years. Arising from a challenge to Pennsylvania congressional districts, it had called forth a spirited plurality manifesto from Justice Antonin Scalia, drawing a hard line: Even if political gerrymandering did violate the Constitution, there was no practicable way for the courts to ensure political fairness consistent with preserving a proper and limited judicial role—which meant that the whole project should be given up as not justiciable.[6]

The Court's four liberals—John Paul Stevens, David Souter, Ruth Bader Ginsburg, and Stephen Breyer—vigorously defended the courts' presence in the area on equal protection grounds and argued that the Pennsylvania gerrymander was bad enough to deserve

[4] 478 U.S. 109 (1986).
[5] 548 U.S. 399 (2006).
[6] Vieth, 541 U.S. at 281.

correction.[7] At the same time, they proposed sharper definitions and tests to improve on the confusing standards prescribed back in *Davis v. Bandemer*, which had led to virtually no striking down of gerrymanders despite much futile litigation.[8]

Kennedy, in a separate concurrence later to be studied and parsed as if it were a religious text, took a middle position. The first two paragraphs give an overview:

> A decision ordering the correction of all election district lines drawn for partisan reasons would commit federal and state courts to unprecedented intervention in the American political process. The Court is correct to refrain from directing this substantial intrusion into the Nation's political life. While agreeing with the plurality that the complaint the appellants filed in the District Court must be dismissed, and while understanding that great caution is necessary when approaching this subject, I would not foreclose all possibility of judicial relief if some limited and precise rationale were found to correct an established violation of the Constitution in some redistricting cases.
>
> When presented with a claim of injury from partisan gerrymandering, courts confront two obstacles. First is the lack of comprehensive and neutral principles for drawing electoral boundaries. No substantive definition of fairness in districting seems to command general assent. Second is the absence of rules to limit and confine judicial intervention. With uncertain limits, intervening courts—even when proceeding with best intentions—would risk assuming political, not legal, responsibility for a process that often produces ill will and distrust.[9]

Kennedy agreed with the conservatives that "comprehensive and neutral principles" along with "rules to limit and confine judicial intervention" were not yet available to prevent disputes from multiplying beyond reason and generating "disparate and inconsistent" results from one challenge to the next.[10] For now, therefore, the Pennsylvania challenge would have to be thrown out, even as the

---

[7] See, e.g., *id.* at 319 (Stevens, J., dissenting).

[8] See, e.g., *id.* at 344 (Souter, J., dissenting).

[9] *Id.* at 306–7 (Kennedy, J., concurring).

[10] *Id.* at 308.

door was left open for better approaches. He showed scant interest in his liberal colleagues' suggestions for new tests that might work. He even held out as a definite possibility that the Scalia bloc might in time woo him over: The "weighty arguments for holding cases like these to be nonjusticiable . . . may prevail in the long run."[11] But the long run had not yet arrived.

With Kennedy installed as the fulcrum on a Court otherwise divided 4-4, there were two possibilities for those who might seek a different result: Wait for the Court's composition to change, or persuade Kennedy that "clear, manageable, and politically neutral standards" had been discovered.

Through most of the 14 years that followed, waiting for the Court's composition to change was a path that, at least as to gerrymandering, led nowhere. Stevens and Souter were replaced by Elena Kagan and Sonia Sotomayor on the one side, and Sandra Day O'Connor and William Rehnquist by Samuel Alito and John Roberts on the other, but few expected those changes to disturb the 4-4 split. The same was true of the eventual replacement of Scalia by Justice Neil Gorsuch.

Which left Kennedy as the liberal target. How could he be brought around?

In 2014, University of Chicago law professor Nicholas Stephanopoulos and political scientist Eric McGhee published an article in the *University of Chicago Law Review* proposing a measure of partisan distortion they called the "efficiency gap."[12] It depended in turn on a concept termed "wasted votes," defined in a distinctive way to include both votes cast for losing candidates *and* votes cast for winning candidates that are surplus to the number of votes needed to win. In this construct, if a Democratic candidate wins a district by a margin of 60 votes to 40, the Republican side has racked up 40 wasted votes—all those cast for the loser—while the Democratic side has racked up 19 wasted votes, namely the 60 actually cast for the winner less the 41 votes needed to win. Totaling the Democrats' wasted votes for all districts statewide, doing the same for the Republicans, subtracting the lesser number from the greater, and dividing the difference by the total number of votes cast, yields a ratio that can be said to measure the efficiency with which a gerrymandered map

---

[11] *Id.* at 309.

[12] Nicholas O. Stephanopoulos & Eric M. McGhee, Partisan Gerrymandering and the Efficiency Gap, 82 U. Chi. L. Rev. 831 (2015).

permits the winning party to convert votes to seats, other things being equal—an "efficiency gap."

If this sounds confusing, it is: This is not how casual observers or experts alike are used to talking about elections. But the practical use of the measure, it was argued, is that it can detect and rate in severity deliberate partisan gerrymanders—those in which the objective is "packing" opposing partisans into as few districts as possible while dispersing or "cracking" other concentrations of opponents among a larger number of districts where the gerrymandering party is likely to prevail. Because both packing and cracking tend to inflict wasted votes on the disfavored party, it was argued, successful gerrymanders will score high on the efficiency gap measure.

Stephanopoulos and McGhee went on to make another contention that was of some legal significance. Once a state's efficiency gap was higher than about 0.07, or 7 percent, they said, it reached a point where a dominant party might win time after time even if it could not muster actual majority support among voters. This was especially relevant to state legislators, who (in a triumph of self-interest) draw maps for themselves. And it opened up the prospect at least in theory that a party with modest minority standing among voters, say 47-53, might nonetheless keep itself in office indefinitely.

The Origins of *Gill v. Whitford*

In 2011, following the 2010 Census, Wisconsin's Republican legislature adopted districting maps for the state assembly after consultation with experts who assured them that the map was likely to yield the Republican Party a majority of assembly districts. In the following year's elections, to quote one account, "Wisconsin Republicans won 48.6 percent of the two-party vote but took 61 percent of the Assembly's 99 seats."[13]

In 2015, Wisconsin residents sympathetic to the Democratic Party sued in federal court to challenge the 2011 map as a partisan gerrymander, with Prof. Stephanopoulos, coauthor of the efficiency gap test, as their lead lawyer. His test, and whether it fulfilled *Vieth's* quest for a reliable and objective test for partisan gerrymandering, was at the heart of the case. In November 2016, a three-judge district

---

[13] Michael Wines, Judges Find Wisconsin Redistricting Unfairly Favored Republicans, N.Y. Times, Nov. 21, 2016, https://www.nytimes.com/2016/11/21/us/wisconsin-redistricting-found-to-unfairly-favor-republicans.html.

court accepted the plaintiffs' contentions and declared the redistricting unlawful under the Constitution, over a dissent from Judge William Griesbach.[14] The plan, said the majority, imposed serious partisan burdens on Wisconsin Democrats, could not be justified in terms of nonpartisan redistricting principles, and tended to entrench Republicans in a self-perpetuating manner.

Under the distinctive procedure that applies to redistricting challenges, challenges of this sort start with three-judge panels and proceed directly on appeal to the U.S. Supreme Court, bypassing the federal circuit courts of appeals. In virtually a foregone conclusion given the prominence of the case and its result, the Court duly took up the case.

Gerrymandering, which stretches back to the rise of representational systems, had long been a target of good-government forces, but by 2017 it had emerged as something else: a heated subject in the Red-Blue political wars. Over the past couple of census cycles, Republicans had employed a superior playbook to out-organize and outmaneuver Democrats, using under-the-radar campaigns to install majorities in state legislatures and then apply specialized talent to the process of drawing maps. By 2017, there were more Republican gerrymanders than Democratic ones around the country, affecting both the state legislatures and congressional representation in such populous states as Texas, Pennsylvania, Ohio, Michigan, and North Carolina. Although Democrats had also gerrymandered some states such as Illinois and Maryland, there was no doubt that the Republicans had greater impact, which accounted for at least some of the Republican edge of 40–50 seats in the U.S. House of Representatives. More passionate Democrats even claimed that the entire margin arose from gerrymandering.

By 2017, to some on the left, partisan gerrymandering had come to stand not merely as an enduring political evil of many places and times, but as part of an interlocking set of abuses and advantages— so-called voter suppression, the presidential Electoral College, the small-state advantage in the U.S. Senate, and more, by which Republicans had "rigged" national politics so as to hold power whether or not they could command the loyalty of a voter majority.[15]

---

[14] Whitford v. Gill, 218 F. Supp. 3d 837 (2016).

[15] See, e.g., Michelle Goldberg, Tyranny of the Minority, N.Y. Times, Sept. 25, 2017, https://www.nytimes.com/2017/09/25/opinion/trump-electoral-college-minority.html.

Many on the right, of course, saw this critique as overblown at best. They pointed out that among Republicans' other electoral conquests at this point were a host of offices not elected by district and thus not subject to gerrymandering, including a lopsided majority of state governorships (33 to 16, with 1 independent), and even a 27-22 majority among state attorney generalships, an office where Democrats had traditionally done well. The U.S. Senate, of course, was also a body free of gerrymandering, and although it did favor small states, Democrats enjoyed many small-state strongholds of their own in places like New England and Hawaii.

Even so, the we-was-robbed tone of much popular commentary put the Supreme Court on notice: It was now being drawn into an exceptionally partisan battle.

Adding the Maryland Case

Just as Republicans in Wisconsin had enacted a thoroughgoing gerrymander based on the 2010 Census, so Democrats in Maryland led by Gov. Martin O'Malley had drawn one of the most bizarre congressional maps in the country. Maryland's third district was compared by a federal judge to a "broken-winged pterodactyl."[16] One of the successful objectives had been to secure the defeat of longtime GOP Rep. Roscoe Bartlett by dissecting his western Maryland redoubt into two serpentine components, each of which could be attached to a Democratic-majority district anchored in the Montgomery County suburbs of Washington, D.C.

In 2013, Republican voters challenged the map. A three-judge panel's 2016 decision let the suit go forward, over one dissent.[17] Unlike Wisconsin's statewide suit, the challenge by this point had been pared down to just one district, the sixth, the one from which Bartlett had been ousted. In 2017, the panel declined the plaintiffs' request for a preliminary injunction, instead staying the case pending the expected high court ruling in *Gill v. Whitford*. Plaintiffs asked

[16] Carrie Wells, Gerrymandering Opponents Highlight Convoluted Districts, Baltimore Sun, July 17, 2017, http://www.baltimoresun.com/news/maryland/politics/blog/bs-md-gerrymander-meander-20170716-story.html.

[17] Benisek v. Lamone, 266 F. Supp. 3d 799 (2017). The case's circuitous path had earlier taken it to the Supreme Court on the issue of whether plaintiffs were entitled to a three-judge panel to hear their claim: see Shapiro v. McManus, 136 S. Ct. 450 (2015) (unanimous Court holds that three-judge panel is required).

the Court to review the case and, to some surprise, the Court agreed to do so: *Benisek v. Lamone* would become a companion case with its own separate oral argument in March (*Gill* had been argued in October).

What did the Maryland case bring that was not already present in the Wisconsin case? Notably, while Wisconsin's suit followed the main line of Court precedent by invoking equal protection theory, the Maryland plaintiffs had argued a theory of First Amendment retaliation: The state had identified them as a political minority based on their past electoral decisions and had taken adverse action against them by subjecting them to a hostile map. And that was significant because Kennedy's concurring opinion in *Vieth* had declared that the First Amendment "may be the more relevant constitutional provision in future cases that allege unconstitutional partisan gerrymandering":

> After all, these allegations involve the First Amendment interest of not burdening or penalizing citizens because of their participation in the electoral process, their voting history, their association with a political party, or their expression of political views. Under general First Amendment principles those burdens in other contexts are unconstitutional absent a compelling government interest. Representative democracy in any populous unit of government is unimaginable without the ability of citizens to band together in promoting among the electorate candidates who espouse their political views. As these precedents show, First Amendment concerns arise where a State enacts a law that has the purpose and effect of subjecting a group of voters or their party to disfavored treatment by reason of their views. In the context of partisan gerrymandering, that means that First Amendment concerns arise where an apportionment has the effect of burdening a group of voters' representational rights.[18]

In fact, the First Amendment road-not-taken had prompted a sharp exchange in the *Vieth* opinions. Scalia for the plurality had sniped that upholding a First Amendment challenge "would render unlawful all consideration of political affiliation in districting."[19] Kennedy retorted that it was not so broad as that: A court would have to find

[18] 541 U.S. at 314 (Kennedy, J., concurring).
[19] 541 U.S. at 294.

that the mapmakers had not just taken into account citizens' political affiliation, but laid a burden on them because of it.[20]

By accepting the Maryland case, at any rate, the Court in 2018 squarely faced Kennedy's suggestion to ground gerrymandering suits on a new constitutional rationale. And there was another advantage: The Court would be reviewing one gerrymander inflicted by Republicans and one by Democrats. Whichever way it decided, it could hope for greater cross-partisan legitimacy by showing that it would apply its rules to the sins of both parties alike.

As it did so, the Court was sure to draw lessons from its own modern history in two important areas in which it has sought to supervise electoral fairness: the one-person-one-vote cases, and the effort to correct disparate electoral treatment (including districting) based on race.

Equal Population and Racial Gerrymandering

The one-person-one-vote redistricting cases, *Baker v. Carr*[21] and *Reynolds v. Sims*,[22] are among the best known of the Warren Court era. Many of the 50 states did not regularly reapportion their legislative or congressional maps to reflect Census updates on population shifts, and some states organized the upper houses of their legislature by a criterion other than population—for example, providing each county with two senators. As with the U.S. Senate, that practice resulted in extreme variances in numbers of constituents per lawmaker, typically to the disadvantage of populous cities.

The results of the Court's decisions in *Baker v. Carr* and *Reynolds v. Sims* recall the anatomy of the bumblebee—theoretically dubious but in practice a great success. The theoretical skepticism arises because it is hard to picture either the Constitution's original language, or the Fourteenth Amendment of 1868 with its equal protection guarantee, as having been publicly understood at the time to bar the apportionment of state upper houses based on geography. Many state legislatures that ratified the post-Civil War Fourteenth Amendment had an upper house modeled on the U.S. Senate—yes, notoriously, the Framers had based the upper house of the federal

---

[20] *Id*. at 315 (Kennedy, J., concurring).

[21] 369 U.S. 186 (1962).

[22] 377 U.S. 533 (1964).

government's own legislative branch on geography rather than population. Appealing though state-level reform might be, the justices agonized over whether it could fairly be read into the Constitution under such circumstances.

Although criticized by some legal theoreticians,[23] the one-person-one-vote decisions quickly scored as a practical success. They were embraced and taken to heart by the public, the legal profession, and even to a remarkable extent the rural political elites whose power they had displaced. Proposals to overturn the decisions spluttered and went nowhere. Nor, notwithstanding Justice Felix Frankfurter's warnings about the "political thicket" the Court was entering,[24] were the decisions widely thought to have improperly dragged the courts into politics in ways that undermined their legitimacy. Even staunch conservatives who detested the Warren Court often spared the reapportionment cases their odium. After some turmoil in state legislatures, litigation subsided quickly, and by 1973 Justice William Brennan could write of the "truly extraordinary record of compliance with the constitutional mandate" of the cases.[25]

What accounts for that development? Above all, the one-person-one-vote formula triumphed because it was objective, predictable, easily understood, readily applied, and neutral: Count the people and divide by the number of districts. There were admittedly a few further wrinkles—the Court was more forgiving about state legislative districts than about congressional, for example, allowing a plus-or-minus population variance of five percent.[26] But even that exception functioned in practice as a bright-line rule.

And with that rule, everyone knew what they had to do, whether they be mapmakers, potential objectors, or judges hearing a challenge: They all could count and divide. Whether a Republican or Democrat judge heard the case you would get the same answer. Although the subject was politics of a sensitive kind, the standard's mechanical quality helped insulate the courts from ill will and political attack.

---

[23] See, e.g., Robert H. Bork, Neutral Principles and Some First Amendment Problems, 47 Indiana L. Rev. 1 (1971).

[24] Colegrove v. Green, 328 U.S. 549, 556 (1946).

[25] White v. Regester, 412 U.S. 755, 779 (1973) (Brennan, J., dissenting).

[26] Brown v. Thomson, 462 U.S. 835, 842 (1983).

Race and Partisanship

A second area in which the modern Court had sought to correct the electoral process was that of disparate treatment in electoral practices (including gerrymandering) based on race. Here its experience had been somewhat different: While the constitutional basis for stepping in was much clearer, it had not been so easy to apply clear and consistent standards.

Because race was at the very center of the post-Civil War amendments, there was no real doubt about whether the Constitution authorized the Court to remedy invidious local actions that burdened racial minorities in voting and campaigning for public office. All justices agreed that it did. But that still left plenty of room for disagreement. Were unintended burdens to be subject to remedies, or only those inflicted on purpose? What exactly counted as invidious, in cases where members of a racial minority might not agree on, say, the grouping of communities to be desired in a district map? Should gerrymanders to the disadvantage of white voters be handled in the same way as those disadvantaging black? What should happen in mixed motive cases, in which race-conscious lines were drawn in part (perhaps predominant part) for old-fashioned partisan motives?

As the courts struggled with these issues, they did not always come up with predictable and consistent answers. True, Congress's enactment of the Voting Rights Act meant that many issues could be resolved on the basis of statute without probing the constitutional text. Still, there was wobble in the ongoing jurisprudence, and cases kept arriving in which the Court was asked for clarification.

It was an open secret that maps favorable to black representation were often also favorable to Republican representation: Because blacks tended to vote Democratic as a bloc, constructing districts where they could elect their own often left remaining districts with a Republican tilt. In fact, more than one map devised with the approval, or at the instigation, of courts concerned to enhance minority representation was later cited in press accounts as an example of extreme partisan gerrymandering—though of course some of the maps might have been drawn from a mix of compliance motives and partisanship.

Parenthetically, it was a unifying and significant feature of the *Gill* and *Benisek* cases that neither presented race as a major complicating factor. The Court had good reason—as did many of the private interest groups and amici—not to want public discussions of racial and of partisan gerrymandering to get too entangled.

The Court's Experience with Gerrymandering

In part through its review of racial gerrymandering claims, the Court had grown quite familiar with the details of redistricting, and with the lack of any consensus as to when a normal or acceptable level of political motivation, assuming there is such a thing, shades into an extreme or objectionable level.

Consider, for example, the common practice of consulting incumbents about what they would like their new district to look like. That practice is baldly political, and accordingly damned by many good-government advocates (who correctly see it as tending to entrench incumbents). Unsurprisingly, it is popular among incumbents themselves. And it need not necessarily amount to *partisan* gerrymandering, since incumbents of both parties may be accorded the privilege.

Then there's redistricting that inflicts an awkward or difficult district on a particular incumbent who, let's say, is considered less than collegial. This sets off even more tripwires on good government grounds, especially if the target is unpopular not so much with colleagues as with legislative bosses. Yet some legislators privately or publicly defend this practice as a prerogative that helps rein in fractious mavericks and enforce cooperativeness.

Does it make sense to attach farm counties to the district of an incumbent who has shown neither interest nor expertise in farm issues? It's hard to separate that judgment from politics. What about the widespread practice of basing new maps on old, so as not to needlessly shunt large populations around between districts? That's fraught with political implications for incumbents' chances of reelection.

Bandemer: Not a Good Start

In the Court's first major encounter with political gerrymandering, *Davis v. Bandemer*,[27] it took up the issues that have puzzled it ever since: Are claims of partisan gerrymandering justiciable, and if so what standards should be used to adjudicate them?

Bandemer arose from a challenge to an Indiana statehouse map. There was no lack of partisan effect: Hoosier Republicans had

[27] 478 U.S. 109 (1986).

tinkered with districting in ways that seemed to have little rationale except to dunk the Dems, who in the subsequent election proceeded to win only 43 of 100 assembly seats though receiving 52 percent of the vote. Interestingly, considering the later evolution of the issue, the Republican National Committee entered the case as amicus alongside the American Civil Liberties Union and Common Cause to urge the overturning of what its own state party had done.

On one level, *Bandemer* was a win for the liberals, with the Court breaking 6-3 in favor of the proposition that partisan gerrymandering claims are indeed justiciable (earlier cases had left some doubt on that). In dissent, Justice Sandra Day O'Connor argued that the courts should know to stay out of an area that always and everywhere was going to be imbued with politics. There was "no clear stopping point," she warned.[28] Indeed, O'Connor—who unlike most of her colleagues had served for years in a state legislature—came close to defending baldly political motives in redistricting, hinting that they might serve to advance a "strong and stable two-party system."[29] Chief Justice Warren Burger and future Chief Justice William Rehnquist joined her.

But the six-justice majority could not agree on a standard for how to rule on such claims, and neither of its attempts provided clear guidance. Four justices, led by Justice Byron White, took the view that some politics in the process was okay, but that courts should step in to keep it from becoming "excessive," so as to prevent an "electoral system [from being] arranged in a manner that will consistently degrade a voter's or a group of voters' influence on the political process as a whole."[30] Such consistent degradation, they said, had not been shown here, so the maps would be upheld. Two others—Justice Lewis Powell, joined by John Paul Stevens—favored a totality-of-the-circumstances test and believed the Indiana gerrymander flunked it.

How to Address *Bandemer*'s Failure?

The headline take-aways from *Vieth v. Jubelirer*, as noted above, were its vigorous Scalia plurality opinion and somewhat coy Kennedy concurrence. But *Vieth* is most usefully read in conjunction

---

[28] *Id.* at 147 (O'Connor, J., concurring in the judgement).

[29] *Id.* at 144.

[30] 478 U.S. at 132.

with *Bandemer* as part of a single interrupted conversation, like a doubleheader played by the same two baseball teams with an intervening gap of 18 years.

By the time the Court reconvened, the dimpled babies of 1986 had grown into the college freshmen of 2004, and almost everyone agreed that the limp "consistently degrade" plurality language from *Bandemer* had flopped. Lots of partisan gerrymandering was going on, but virtually no successful challenges to it were getting through the federal courts. But how exactly had it failed, and what should replace it? Once again, the Court was split with no overall majority, but the arguments had been sharpened, with Justice Scalia taking up the lance on behalf of what were now four conservatives (Burger having departed the Court, and Scalia and Clarence Thomas having joined).

Scalia began by noting that the Framers knew of the problem of political gerrymandering and had given Congress express power to fix the issue at least as to U.S. House seats: Article I, Section 4 of the Constitution confers on the legislative branch a power to prescribe regulations for the holding of House elections, and Congress has at times used this power to regulate districting.

Meanwhile, he wrote, attempts to apply the *Bandemer* standard in practice had been "one long record of puzzlement and consternation" in the lower courts: "Eighteen years of judicial effort with virtually nothing to show for it."[31] In fact "several districting plans . . . were upheld despite allegations of extreme partisan discrimination, bizarrely shaped districts, and disproportionate results." And this lack of results was due to the flawed standard: "The lower courts were set wandering in the wilderness for 18 years not because the *Bandemer* majority thought it a good idea, but because five justices could not agree upon a single standard, and because the standard the plurality proposed turned out not to work."[32]

Then Scalia went a step further: not only had the effort failed, but any future efforts were destined to fail too. No standard was forthcoming that would parallel the "easily administrable standard of population equality" from the one-person-one-vote cases.[33] Even if political gerrymandering *did* violate the Equal Protection

[31] Vieth, 541 U.S. at 281.

[32] *Id.* at 303.

[33] *Id.* at 290.

Clause—and he came close to conceding that in some circumstances it did—the Court should quit trying to provide a remedy, there being no good reason to risk "the delay and uncertainty that brings to the political process and the partisan enmity it brings upon the courts."[34]

The liberal justices split among three dissents. Stevens was most unyielding on the need for a broad, even if that meant disruptive, remedy: "The concept of equal justice under law requires the State to govern impartially."[35] Unlike most of the other justices, he also saw the Court's jurisprudence on race-based gerrymandering as providing a judicially manageable standard even when applied to the more multifarious arena of political belief, which, as O'Connor had pointed out, ordinarily lacks the external visible dimension associated with race and comes in any number of varieties (parties have internal factions, for example), each potentially entitled to an equal protection guardian. Justice Souter, joined by Ginsburg, proposed breaking the inquiry into stages, at least some of which—such as checking for compactness and respecting the boundaries of political subdivisions—relied on traditional criteria of redistricting that lent themselves well to quantification and objective review. (Maps can be scored for compactness according to mathematical formulas, for instance, or for congruence based on how many or few county splits they impose.) Not enough, retorted Scalia: Subjectivity and uncertainty would still creep back in at various points, especially since the test's bottom line was the prevention of a vaguely described "extremity of unfairness."[36]

Justice Stephen Breyer took a different tack, conceding that "pure politics often helps to secure constitutionally important democratic objectives," but noting that political influences could become destructive.[37] He proposed that judges should "test for" situations in which a political minority had managed to entrench itself indefinitely as a majority through the gerrymander device.[38] Whatever the theoretical attractions of focusing the investigation this way, the question was whether such an inquiry would depend on too many uncertain

---

[34] *Id.* at 301.

[35] *Id.* at 317 (Stevens, J., dissenting).

[36] 541 U.S. at 295.

[37] *Id.* at 355 (Breyer, J., dissenting).

[38] *Id.* at 356.

evidentiary findings to yield a manageable standard. Was a single election result somehow typical of how things would go next time? How much depended on such vagaries as the running of a strong or weak candidate? As Scalia wrote, referring to one of the other proposed standards, "requiring judges to decide whether a districting system will produce a statewide majority for a majority party casts them forth upon a sea of imponderables, and asks them to make determinations that not even election experts can agree upon."[39]

A Court-ful of Misgivings

Reading both cases leaves it clear that Kennedy in his much-studied concurrence wasn't the only justice troubled about the floodgates problem and ensuring that courts' decisions were consistent and understandable. The *Bandemer* plurality was troubled as well: Not only had it erected various barriers to diagnosing an equal protection violation, but it warned against "[i]nviting attack on minor departures from some supposed norm" and cautioned courts to confine themselves to "serious" abuses.[40] Souter and Ginsburg were content to focus on cases with an "extremity of unfairness," and the Breyer indefinite entrenchment standard would probably have given courts even less to do. Even Stevens had signed onto Powell's *Bandemer* partial concurrence, which called for imposing a "heavy burden of proof" on plaintiffs since federal courts were "ill-equipped" to review districting decisions.[41]

The floodgates issue, incidentally, extended beyond the nation's 435 congressional districts and roughly 7,300 state legislative districts. Federal courts might also be required to review district lines for county and city councils and more specialized government bodies.

On other issues, too, liberal and not just conservative justices had expressed doubts about broad judicial supervision—doubts that found echoes in the *Gill* and *Benisek* cases. For example, the dispute over whether challenges should be brought statewide or to particular districts began early on, with many of the liberals' opinions, including that of Souter and Ginsburg, nodding toward the idea that

[39] 541 U.S. at 290.

[40] 478 U.S. at 133.

[41] *Id.* at 185 (Powell, J., concurring in part and dissenting in part).

individual-district challenges might be superior both in ease of assessment and in reflecting the nature of equal protection as an individual right.[42] In its remand of the Wisconsin case, of course, the Court as a whole did eventually side with the idea that courts should entertain complaints that people file about their own districts, rather than those filed by persons who feel aggrieved at how their party is faring in districts not their own.[43]

Finally, members of both liberal and conservative blocs had expressed misgivings about basing unfairness findings on snapshots representing performance in a single election, since political tides ebb and flow, individual candidates in any one round may be strong or weak, and so forth. A version of this issue came up both in *Gill*, as we will see below, and in *Benisek*. In the latter, the state of Maryland's defense pointed out that even if Democrats schemed to make the sixth district unwinnable for Republicans, the GOP had come close to winning the seat in 2014 anyway, a wave year for local Republicans.

Expert Attacks

With Kennedy known to be the likely target of persuasion, the litigants' arguments and expert submissions focused on some of the concerns flagged in his *Vieth* concurrence. Was the efficiency-gap standard suitably neutral, objective, resistant to manipulation, and related to the constitutional text? Kennedy was such a stickler on the neutrality point that his concurrence had even raised doubts about whether judges could properly enforce the measures of good redistricting practice in widest use around the states—those of compactness and of congruence with county and city boundaries.[44] The problem, as he saw it, is that those standards are not free from partisan impact: In present-day America, Democrats tend to congregate in cities, which means maps drawn to achieve neutral standards such as compactness and congruence tend to generate a slight Republican advantage, maybe two percentage points.

Opponents assailed the efficiency-gap theory as pretending to a neutrality that it would in no way embody in practice. For example,

---

[42] Vieth, 541 U.S. at 353 (Souter, J., dissenting).

[43] Gill, 138 S. Ct. at 1930.

[44] Vieth, 541 U.S. at 308 (Kennedy, J., concurring).

if even a sublimely impartial map drawn by the hand of the Recording Angel would saddle Democrats with more wasted votes owing to city concentration, then proclaiming a 7-percent gap as trigger starts Republicans out closer to the penalty line, meaning that Democrats can commit considerably more mischief before getting caught at it. In fact some of the maps that scored worst on the efficiency gap in plaintiffs' own submissions were drawn up by putative neutrals such as bipartisan commissions or courts themselves.

Nor was the efficiency gap free from problems of snapshots and their timing. (Indeed, its advocates recognized and sought to analyze that.) Also disturbing, if a test were elevated to the status of evidence with vital legal consequences, actors might find ways of manipulating wasted-vote scores. For example, parties often decide not to run a sacrificial-lamb candidate in a district that is safe for the other side, thus accepting a zero vote when they could have obtained (say) a 25-percent share. But that decision influences efficiency gap scores, giving each party an artificial reason to contest futile races—or alternatively request that scores be based on the vote totals missing nominees "should" have gotten had they run, a dangerous speculation.

Foreshadowing

There were early clues that *Gill* was not going to be an easy sell to Kennedy. Within hours of taking the case, the Court issued a stay of the order below, with Kennedy siding with the conservative wing over dissents from the four liberals. Decisions on stays often provide a peek into justices' preliminary thinking.[45]

By February, more clues suggested that the Supreme Court was leaning against a big decision. Rather than fast-track consideration of its second case, *Benisek*, the Court instead set an oral argument date of March 28. Any decision announcing the applicability of a new constitutional standard would throw one or both states into confusion: Absentee military primary ballots are printed as early as the spring, and the Maryland legislature, for one, adjourns for the year in early April. Of course the Court might have tried to introduce

---

[45] See Josh Blackman, On the Roberts Court, A Grant of a Stay, Followed by a Cert Grant, Almost Always Yields a Reversal, JoshBlackman.com, July 10, 2017, http://joshblackman.com/blog/2017/07/10/on-the-roberts-court-a-grant-of-a-stay-followed-by-a-cert-grant-almost-always-yields-a-reversal.

a new standard in a staged or prospective way, but its lack of a sense of urgency was hard to miss.

At each of the two oral arguments, the first comment from the bench foreshadowed the disposition of the case. In *Gill*, Justice Kennedy jumped in almost at once to cast doubt on whether standing should be statewide as opposed to by-district,[46] while in *Benisek*, Justice Ginsburg started off by questioning whether a preliminary injunction was needed when adequate relief was to be had later.[47]

Concerns about manageability and floodgates were also much in evidence. In *Benisek*, for example, at least four justices of varying stripes (Alito, Roberts, Kagan, and Breyer) all brought up the prospect that a First Amendment standard would require the application of strict scrutiny to even the faint whiff of politics in an otherwise reasonable plan, thereby encouraging more challenges. There were also other concerns: At the *Gill* oral argument, Gorsuch, Breyer, Kagan, and Chief Justice Roberts all expressed floodgates concerns. Roberts also warned that if courts presumed to enforce an opaque mathematical test relying on "sociological gobbledygook," ordinary citizens would start to assume that judges were ruling for one party because they wanted that party to win. "And that is going to cause very serious harm to the status and integrity of the decisions of this Court in the eyes of the country."[48]

The ultimate anticlimax thus came as little surprise. The Wisconsin complainants would have to go back and configure their case so as to demonstrate standing in their own home districts; the Maryland complainants would have to go back and develop the record further. Concurring on behalf of the four liberals, Justice Elena Kagan was of the opinion that once the complainants lined up plaintiffs who lived in the right districts, they could proceed to introduce statewide evidence and seek statewide remedies, which would leave them with more or less the full scope of what liberal litigation groups had wanted.[49] Only Justices Thomas and Gorsuch, although they concurred in the judgment, would have ended the Wisconsin complainants' case outright rather than permit a standing do-over.[50]

[46] Transcript of Oral Arg. at 4, Gill v. Whitford, 138 S. Ct. 1916 (2018) (No. 16-1161).

[47] Transcript of Oral Arg. at 4, Benisek v. Lamone, 138 S. Ct. 1942 (2018) (No. 17-333).

[48] Gill, Transcript, *supra* note 46, at 40.

[49] Gill, 138 S. Ct. at 1934 (Kagan, J., concurring).

[50] *Id.* at 1941 (Thomas, J., concurring).

Conclusion

Some commentators claimed to see in the 2017–18 term the Year of the Sidestep, given the other big cases that ended anticlimactically, notably *Masterpiece Cakeshop*, in which the Court dodged the expected Culture War clash by going off on a less contentious tangent to send the case back for more processing.

But such comparisons are not needed here. In the end, the Court saw little temptation to jump either way and thus face high risks to its institutional legitimacy. The framing of the issue in the liberal press as one of systematic national election-stealing by Republicans meant that a 5-4 decision to uphold the maps and rule out future relief would expose the Court to another bitter, sustained attack on its institutional role like the brouhaha that followed *Citizens United*. To the conservatives, at least, a jump into an open-ended new standard would risk a loss of political legitimacy just as surely, even if the slow way.

Following Justice Anthony Kennedy's decision to retire, it would not be surprising if liberal forces seek to avoid a showdown at the high court on this issue for a while, as they bide their time waiting for a more favorably disposed Court.

But whatever happens at the Court, there are good reasons for states to act on their own to curb the evils of partisan gerrymandering without looking to One First Street. Measures to prescribe strong standards of compactness and congruence; take line-drawing out of the hands of self-interested incumbents; provide for transparency, open data access, and public map submission; and ensure strong judicial review in state courts made sense on June 17, 2018, and they continued to make sense on June 19. Moreover, they do not require waiting on a Court that may stay perched on its fence for many years to come.

The Court has kicked the issue down the road. The rest of us shouldn't. Partisan gerrymandering remains a distinctive political evil, a force for entrenching undeserving incumbency, and a worthy target for efforts at reform.

Katz Nipped and Katz Cradled: Carpenter and the Evolving Fourth Amendment

Trevor Burrus* and James Knight**

Introduction

In October of 1983, Motorola sold the first commercial version of its portable, mobile telephone for the equivalent of $10,000 in today's dollars.[1] In the three-and-a-half decades since that first sale, cell phones have become so ubiquitous as to be "almost a 'feature of human anatomy.'"[2] While Motorola's original 1983 product was truly just a phone, modern smartphones are "in fact minicomputers that also happen to have the capacity to be used as a telephone."[3] Because of the vast array of functions available on smartphones, individuals "compulsively carry cell phones with them all the time"[4] such that "nearly three-quarters of smart phone users report being within five feet of their phones most of the time."[5] This means that if you know where a person's phone is, you likely know where they are as well. And, because of the way cell phone networks have been structured, carriers *do* know approximately where a customer's phone is whenever it connects to the network, which is to say most of the time.

---

* Research fellow, Cato Institute Robert A. Levy Center for Constitutional Studies.

** Legal intern, Cato Institute.

[1] Tas Anjarwalla, Inventor of the Cell Phone: We Knew Someday Everybody Would Have One, CNN, Jul. 9, 2010, http://www.cnn.com/2010/TECH/mobile/07/09/cooper.cell.phone.inventor/index.html.

[2] Carpenter v. United States, 138 S. Ct. 2206, 2218 (2018) (quoting Riley v. California, 134 S. Ct. 2473, 2484 (2014)).

[3] Riley, 134 S. Ct. at 2489.

[4] Carpenter, 138 S. Ct. at 2218.

[5] Riley, 134 S. Ct. at 2490 (citing Harris Interactive, 2013 Mobile Consumer Habits Study (June 2013)).

When the phone connects to the network, its approximate location is automatically stored by the carrier in a "time-stamped record known as cell-site location information (CSLI)."[6] CSLI allows anyone accessing it to virtually "travel back in time to retrace a person's whereabouts, subject only to the retention policies of the wireless carriers, which currently maintain records for up to five years."[7] This "provides an intimate window into a person's life, revealing not only his particular movements, but through them his 'familial, political, professional, religious, and sexual associations.'"[8] Despite the sensitive nature of CSLI, the government could, until recently, acquire, access, and inspect these records without first obtaining a warrant, because CSLI was believed to fall into a gap in Fourth Amendment protection known as the "third-party doctrine."

In *Carpenter v. United States*, the Supreme Court was asked to decide whether the warrantless seizure and search of 127 days of a customer's CSLI was permitted by the Fourth Amendment. The case promised to be one of the biggest Fourth Amendment decisions in recent history, and it did not disappoint. Whereas much of the Court's usual Fourth Amendment docket consists of narrow, fact-bound issues that only moderately tinker with the existing doctrine, *Carpenter* held the possibility of radically overhauling that jurisprudence.

In the end, the majority opinion mostly tinkered with the law, but in an important and privacy-protecting way. And while the result in *Carpenter* is a significant victory for civil liberties, the case will eventually be bigger than its holding. Due to the conceptual shortcomings of the majority opinion, coupled with individual dissents from Justices Clarence Thomas and Neil Gorsuch calling for Fourth Amendment jurisprudence to be rethought from the ground up, *Carpenter* will likely be seen by future generations as the beginning of significant changes to the law of the Fourth Amendment.

Justice Gorsuch's dissent in particular reads like the opening salvo in what will likely be a career-long attempt to re-work the Court's Fourth Amendment jurisprudence. Only in his second term on the Court, Gorsuch seems to have chosen the Fourth Amendment as one

---

[6] Carpenter, 138 S. Ct. at 2211.

[7] *Id.* at 2218.

[8] *Id.* at 2217.

of his battlegrounds. His timing could not be better, as technological changes in both data storage and surveillance have led many scholars to question the continued viability of the framework created a half-century ago by the famous case of *Katz v. United States.*[9]

In *Katz*, the Court rejected the textual, property-based approach to the Fourth Amendment that had been followed until that point and substituted an inquiry into whether the challenged government action violated an individual's "reasonable expectation of privacy."[10] In the 1970s, in *United States v. Miller* and *Smith v. Maryland,* the Court, using this new Fourth Amendment test, concluded that "a person has no legitimate expectation of privacy in information he voluntarily turns over to third parties" and that such information is therefore not entitled to Fourth Amendment protection.[11] Because CSLI is held by carriers, not customers, it appeared to fall under this doctrine. The confluence of cellular network architecture and judicial reinterpretation of the Fourth Amendment had thus appeared to create a situation where the government could legally engage in warrantless, retrospective location-tracking of U.S. citizens.

The Court in *Carpenter* sought to rectify this unintended consequence of its Fourth Amendment jurisprudence, explicitly taking up Justice Louis Brandeis's call for the Court "to ensure that the 'progress of science' does not erode Fourth Amendment protections."[12] Unwilling to disturb *Katz* or its offspring *Miller* and *Smith,* the Court instead crafted a narrow exception to the third-party doctrine designed for the "unique nature of cell phone location information" and requiring the government to obtain a warrant in most cases before compelling carriers to turn over a customer's CSLI.[13]

In this article, we will first explore the factual and legal background of the *Carpenter* case, including a brief overview of the development of the Fourth Amendment leading up to the decision. Next, we turn

---

[9] 389 U.S. 347 (1967).

[10] *Id.* at 361 (1967) (Harlan, J., concurring). The reasonable-expectation-of-privacy standard set out in Justice Harlan's concurrence was adopted by a majority of the Court the following year in *Terry v. Ohio,* 392 U.S. 1, 9 (1968).

[11] Smith v. Maryland, 442 U.S. 735, 743–44 (1979); United States v. Miller, 425 U.S. 435, 443 (1976).

[12] Carpenter, 138 S. Ct. at 2223 (quoting Olmstead v. United States, 277 U.S. 438, 473–74 (1928) (Brandeis, J., dissenting)).

[13] *Id.* at 2220.

to the Court's decision itself. Chief Justice John Roberts's majority opinion is of course important for establishing the ultimate holding in the case, and the dissents of Justices Anthony Kennedy, Thomas, and Samuel Alito provide valuable critiques of the majority opinion. But we focus more on Justice Gorsuch's dissent, which calls for a rethinking of Fourth Amendment law. We will try to help with that rethinking by placing the Fourth Amendment into philosophical and legal context. By using positive law to help delineate when the Fourth Amendment has been triggered, future jurists can help create a more textually grounded and philosophically justified jurisprudence. Ultimately, we believe that is the appropriate result both as a matter of originalism and as a matter of privacy protection.

I. Fourth Amendment Background

The Fourth Amendment places limitations on the government's search-and-seizure powers. In relevant part, the amendment reads: "The right of the people to be secure in their persons, houses, papers, and effects, against unreasonable searches and seizures, shall not be violated."[14] The Supreme Court's jurisprudence on the amendment through the late-19th and early-20th centuries remained close to the literal meaning of the text, with the Court focusing on the amendment's property-centric language in cases such as *Ex parte Jackson* (1878), *Weeks v. United States* (1914), and *Agnello v. United States* (1925).[15] In *Ex parte Jackson*, for example, the Court held that the Fourth Amendment's protections of a person's "papers" and "effects" were not limited to those papers and effects which are kept in the safety of one's own home. Letters and packages in the mail were just as protected, and the Fourth Amendment protects against "unreasonable searches and seizures" of a person's papers and effects "wherever they may be."[16]

The property-centric view of the Fourth Amendment continued in *Olmstead v. United States* (1927), when the Court held that the warrantless wiretapping of defendants' phone lines, was not a "search" or "seizure" of "persons, houses, papers, [or] effects," rejecting a

[14] U.S. Const. amend. IV.

[15] Ex parte Jackson, 96 U.S. 727 (1878); Weeks v. United States, 232 U.S. 383 (1914); Agnello v. United States, 269 U.S. 20 (1925).

[16] Ex parte Jackson, 96. U.S. at 732–33.

proposed analogy to *Ex parte Jackson's* protection of letters in the mail.[17] In the following decades the Court drew a hard line on a physical property-based interpretation of the amendment, finding that microphones placed against the wall of an adjoining room did not trigger Fourth Amendment protections,[18] but a "spike mike" that physically pierced the property did.[19]

In 1967, *Katz* overturned *Olmstead*, but instead of simply adapting the Fourth Amendment's protection of "persons, houses, papers, and effects" to reflect new forms of intrusions on those things, the Court rejected the property-based approach entirely, holding that "the Fourth Amendment protects people, not places."[20] While the *Katz* majority did not develop a test laying out precisely what this change meant, Justice John Marshall Harlan's concurring opinion formulated what is now referred to as the *Katz* "reasonable expectation of privacy" test.[21] This test, adopted by a majority of the Court the following year in *Terry v. Ohio*,[22] essentially replaced the Fourth Amendment inquiry of whether a search or seizure of a person, house, paper, or effect has occurred with an inquiry into whether the government had invaded a person's "actual (subjective) expectation of privacy . . . that society is prepared to recognize as 'reasonable.'"[23]

Despite the rise of the "reasonable expectation of privacy" doctrine in Fourth Amendment jurisprudence, modern cases have demonstrated that the traditional, property-based protections still apply. In *Soldal v. Cook County*, for example, the Court unanimously found that local sheriffs' aid of a landlord in conducting a self-help eviction through physical removal of a tenant's mobile home constituted a Fourth Amendment seizure despite there being no privacy violation.[24] The Court was "unconvinced that any of [its] prior cases supports the view that the Fourth Amendment protects against unreasonable seizures of property only where privacy or liberty is also

---

[17] Olmstead v. United States, 277 U.S. 438, 464 (1928).

[18] Goldman v. United States, 316 U.S. 129, 135 (1942).

[19] Silverman v. United States, 365 U.S. 505, 511 (1961).

[20] Katz, 389 U.S. at 351.

[21] *Id.* at 361 (Harlan, J., concurring).

[22] Terry, 392 U.S. at 9.

[23] Katz, 389 U.S. at 361 (Harlan, J., concurring).

[24] Soldal v. Cook Cty., Ill., 506 U.S. 56 (1992).

implicated," noting examples of existing Fourth Amendment jurisprudence, such as the "plain view" rule, that provided similar protection in the absence of privacy interests.[25]

The Court reaffirmed the principle behind this holding in 2012 in *United States v. Jones*, where the warrantless placement of a GPS tracker on defendant's vehicle with the aim of tracking his movements was found to be a Fourth Amendment violation on the grounds that the tracker was a "physical intrusion" that undoubtedly "would have been considered a 'search' within the meaning of the Fourth Amendment when it was adopted."[26] Writing for the majority, Justice Antonin Scalia reaffirmed the holding of *Soldal*, noting that "the *Katz* reasonable-expectation-of-privacy test had been *added to*, not *substituted for*, the common-law trespassory test."[27] Scalia clarifies that *Katz* "did not repudiate [the] understanding" held for "most of our history" that the Fourth Amendment embodies "a particular concern for government trespass upon areas . . . it enumerates."[28]

Jones was the most significant case dealing with mass data surveillance before *Carpenter*. Some thought that *Jones* presaged the possible end of the third-party doctrine, and others thought it more significant for its use of traditional trespass concepts applied to modern surveillance. With CSLI, however, there is nothing "attached" that could count as a trespass. Just having your phone turned on and on your person is all that is needed to track your location.

II. *Carpenter v. United States*

Cell phones function by sending signals to and from "cell sites," sets of radio antennas mounted on "tower[s] . . . light posts, flag poles, church steeples, or the sides of buildings."[29] Cell phones connect to these cell sites whenever they send or receive texts, phone calls, and data.[30] CSLI is protected under the Stored Communications Act (SCA), which allows the government to use a court order to compel carriers to turn over such records whenever it could offer "'specific

[25] *Id.* at 65–66.

[26] United States v. Jones, 565 U.S. 400, 404–05 (2012).

[27] *Id.* at 409.

[28] *Id.* at 406–07.

[29] Carpenter, 138 S. Ct. at 2211.

[30] *Id.* at 2211–12.

and articulable facts showing that there are reasonable grounds to believe' that the records sought 'are relevant and material to an ongoing criminal investigation.'"[31] Notably, this standard is lower than the probable-cause standard required for warrants.

In 2011, federal prosecutors and law enforcement officers were attempting to catch the perpetrators of a series of robberies in the Detroit area. From a previous suspect arrested in the case, officers had received a list of suspects, their phone numbers, and the arrested suspect's call records from the time of the robberies. Using this information, "the prosecutors applied for court orders under the Stored Communications Act to obtain cell phone records for petitioner Timothy Carpenter and several other suspects." Federal magistrate judges granted the prosecutors' requests, signing two orders compelling MetroPCS and Sprint, two wireless carriers with whom Carpenter had accounts, to disclose CSLI for the "origination and . . . termination [of] incoming and outgoing calls" to Carpenter's cell phone "during the four-month period when the string of robberies occurred."[32]

These requests resulted in "the Government obtain[ing] 12,898 location points cataloging Carpenter's movements—an average of 101 data points per day."[33] Using these location points, the prosecution was able to place Carpenter's phone near four of the robberies. After presenting that information at trial, Carpenter was convicted of almost all counts charged and received a prison sentence of more than 100 years.

Following his conviction, Carpenter appealed to the Sixth Circuit. The court affirmed his conviction on third-party doctrine grounds, finding that "Carpenter lacked a reasonable expectation of privacy in the location information collected."[34] Because the location data is voluntarily shared with the wireless carrier by the user, the court ruled that the "the resulting [CSLI] business records are not entitled to Fourth Amendment protection."[35] Carpenter then filed a petition for certiorari, which the Supreme Court granted.

[31] *Id.* at 2212 (quoting 18 U.S.C. § 2703(d)).

[32] *Id.*

[33] *Id.*

[34] *Id.* at 2213.

[35] *Id.*

A. Katz *Cradled: Chief Justice Roberts's Majority Opinion*

Chief Justice Roberts wrote the majority opinion, joined by Justices Ruth Bader Ginsburg, Stephen Breyer, Sonia Sotomayor, and Elena Kagan. Roberts framed the issue of government requests for CSLI within the *Katz* framework, which determines whether a "search" has occurred—and thus whether Fourth Amendment protections are triggered—by asking whether the government has infringed upon a person's "reasonable expectation of privacy." Roberts explicitly rejected a contention by Justice Kennedy that, even under *Katz*, "property-based concepts" provide the rubric for resolving "which expectations of privacy are entitled to protection."[36] The Court has "repeatedly emphasized," argued Roberts, "that privacy interests do not rise or fall with property rights."[37] Instead, Roberts took a more holistic approach, arguing that "the analysis is informed by historical understandings 'of what was deemed an unreasonable search and seizure when [the Fourth Amendment] was adopted,'" and that prior case law gives us "basic guideposts of Fourth Amendment privacy concerns."[38] Among these guideposts are "securing the privacies of life against arbitrary power, and placing obstacles in the way of a too permeating police surveillance."[39]

Roberts wrote, "As technology has enhanced the Government's capacity to encroach upon areas normally guarded from inquisitive eyes, this Court has sought to 'assure[ ] preservation of that degree of privacy against government that existed when the Fourth Amendment was adopted.'"[40] Combined with the guideposts he identifies above, language such as this strongly implies that a chief rationale behind the *Carpenter* decision is, as Orin Kerr has argued, "equilibrium-adjustment."[41] Kerr argues that "[w]hen technology dramatically expands the government's power under an old legal rule . . . the Court changes the legal rule to restore the prior level

---

[36] *Id.* at 2213–14, 2214 n.1.

[37] *Id.* at 2214 n.1.

[38] *Id.* at 2213–14 (quoting Carroll v. United States, 267 U.S. 132, 149 (1925)).

[39] *Id.* at 2214 (cleaned up).

[40] *Id.* (quoting Kyllo v. United States, 533 U.S. 27, 34 (2001)).

[41] See, e.g., Orin Kerr, When Does a Carpenter Search Start—and When Does It Stop?, Lawfare, Jul. 6, 2018, https://www.lawfareblog.com/when-does-carpenter-search-start-and-when-does-it-stop.

of government power."[42] Roberts, ever the incrementalist, appears to have taken that approach in *Riley v. California*, where he wrote for a unanimous Court that a warrant is required before searching the digital contents of a cell phone incident to an arrest.[43] In *Carpenter*, Roberts also saw something "qualitatively different" distorting the existing legal protections.[44] The existing rules of the Court's Fourth Amendment doctrine would dictate less protection than Roberts thinks the amendment requires, but instead of reassessing the Court's entire Fourth Amendment jurisprudence to judge whether this deviation is justified, Roberts carved out a special "cell phone exception."

This exception comes about because Roberts saw government acquisition of CSLI as sitting "at the intersection of two lines of cases, both of which inform our understanding of the privacy interests at stake."[45] The first line of cases he referred to, exemplified by *Jones*, "addresses a person's expectation of privacy in his physical location and movements," while the second is the third-party doctrine of *Smith* and *Miller* where, Roberts wrote, "the Court has drawn a line between what a person keeps to himself and what he shares with others."[46] While the first line of cases would appear to grant Fourth Amendment protection to CSLI as highly sensitive location data, the second rules out such protection on the grounds that CSLI is held by a third party.

It is notable that Roberts focused not on *Jones's* majority opinion, which resolved the case on property grounds, but rather on the concurrences of Justices Alito and Sotomayor, who both used broader *Katz* privacy analysis to determine that "longer term GPS monitoring in investigations of most offenses impinges on expectations of privacy."[47] Both lines of cases that Roberts analyzes are thus attempts to apply the *Katz* test, and yet the two applications appear to contradict one another in the case of CSLI. Roberts, however, did

---

[42] *Id.*

[43] 134 S. Ct. 2473, 2489–93 (2014).

[44] Carpenter, 138 S. Ct. at 2216.

[45] *Id.* at 2214–15.

[46] *Id.* at 2215–16.

[47] Jones, 565 U.S. at 430 (Alito, J., concurring in judgment); see also *id.* at 415 (Sotomayor, J., concurring).

not seem to take this internal contradiction as a mark against *Katz*. Instead, he simply treated CSLI, which is both location data and third-party information, as a special category, emphasizing that it is a "new phenomenon," is "qualitatively different from telephone numbers and bank records," and has a "unique nature."[48] This "unique nature" thus allowed Roberts to take the novel approach of applying both lines of precedent to CSLI, balancing the concerns against one another.

On the location side, Roberts discussed how the time and expense that tailing someone for extended periods used to require has resulted in a societal expectation against extensive secret monitoring of a person's movements, an expectation which warrantless acquisition of CSLI contravenes. The private nature of a person's movements, the sensitive information it may reveal, and the extensive set of retrospective data that CSLI offers all weigh in favor of strong privacy interests for Roberts. "Accordingly, when the Government accessed CSLI from the wireless carriers, it invaded Carpenter's reasonable expectation of privacy in the whole of his physical movements."[49]

Against this conclusion Roberts weighed the third-party doctrine concerns of *Smith* and *Miller*. Here again he emphasized that CSLI is a "distinct category of information" from the categories already covered by the doctrine and deemphasized the determinacy of the act of sharing within the third-party doctrine.[50] Instead, Roberts argued that *Smith* and *Miller* "considered 'the nature of the particular documents sought' to determine whether 'there is a legitimate expectation of privacy concerning their contents.'"[51] A "detailed chronicle of a person's physical presence compiled every day, every moment, over several years . . . implicates privacy concerns far beyond those considered in *Smith* and *Miller*."[52] Accordingly, while the expectation of privacy was not present in *Smith* and *Miller*, it was present as strongly in *Carpenter* as it was in *Jones*.

Combined with an increased expectation of privacy is a decreased presence of third-party sharing. CSLI "is not truly 'shared' as one

---

[48] Carpenter, 138 S. Ct. at 2216–17.

[49] *Id.* at 2219.

[50] *Id.*

[51] *Id.* (quoting Miller, 425 U.S. at 442).

[52] *Id.* at 2220.

normally understands the term," since the "sharing" occurs automatically "without any affirmative act on the part of the user beyond powering up."[53] Roberts's solution to the intersection between *Jones's* locational privacy interest and *Smith* and *Miller's* third-party doctrine was to weigh them against one another. With the increased privacy interest and the decreased degree of third-party sharing, Roberts came to the "narrow" holding that cell phone location data is a special case worthy of special protection, and thus the government must obtain a warrant for CSLI in most cases.

B. Justice Kennedy's Dissent

Justice Kennedy dissented from the majority, writing an opinion joined by Justices Thomas and Alito. Kennedy's primary criticism of the court's ruling was that it misconstrued precedent in such a way as to put "needed, reasonable, accepted, lawful, and congressionally authorized criminal investigations at serious risk in serious cases" through undue restrictions on law enforcement.[54] Specifically, Kennedy was critical of the line the Court attempted to draw between CSLI and other types of business records that traditionally fell under the third-party doctrine, calling the distinction "unprincipled and unworkable."[55] He argued that cell-site records are far less accurate than GPS, revealing only "the general location of the cell phone user," that the contracts users sign with carriers authorizes the carriers to keep CSLI records, and that law enforcement access to these records "can serve as an important investigative function."[56] Kennedy also criticized the methodology Roberts employed, arguing that the third-party doctrine does not involve balancing privacy interests with third-party disclosure.

While Kennedy did not advocate abandoning *Katz*, he did take a far more property-centric view of the *Katz* test than Roberts, writing that "property-based concepts . . . have long grounded the analytic framework that pertains in these cases."[57] For Kennedy, "the only question necessary to decide was whether the Government searched

[53] *Id.*
[54] *Id.* at 2223 (Kennedy, J., dissenting).
[55] *Id.* at 2224.
[56] *Id.* at 2225.
[57] *Id.* at 2224.

anything of Carpenter's when it used compulsory process to obtain cell-site records from Carpenter's cell phone service providers."[58] And, according to Kennedy, the third-party doctrine dictates that "the answer is no."[59]

Kennedy believed that *Katz* was a useful way to move beyond "arcane distinctions developed in property and tort law" but that "'property concepts' are, nonetheless, fundamental 'in determining the presence or absence of the privacy interests protected by that Amendment.'"[60] This is true, he argued, both because "individuals often have greater expectations of privacy in things and places that belong to them, not to others," and because "the Fourth Amendment's protections must remain tethered to the text," and therefore to "persons, houses, papers, and effects."[61] The closest Carpenter came to meeting this property-based standard was when he argued that 47 U.S.C. § 222 gave him a Fourth Amendment interest in the cell-site records, but Kennedy found this unconvincing, citing the statute's limited confidentiality protections and the customer's lack of "practical control over the records."[62]

C. Katz *Nipped, Part I: Justice Thomas's Dissent*

Although Justice Thomas joined Justice Kennedy's dissent, agreeing that Supreme Court precedent would dictate the result Kennedy advocated, he separately argued that the entire *Katz* doctrine should be overruled and the Court should return to a more originalist, textualist, and property-based interpretation of the Fourth Amendment. "This case should not turn on 'whether' a search occurred. It should turn, instead, on *whose* property was searched."[63]

Thomas believed that under this inquiry, Carpenter could not assert a Fourth Amendment right to the CSLI, arguing that the cell-site records belonged solely to the carriers in question. Carpenter "did not create the records, he does not maintain them, he cannot control them, and he cannot destroy them. Neither the terms of his

---

[58] *Id.* at 2226.

[59] *Id.*

[60] *Id.* at 2227 (quoting Rakas v. Illinois, 439 U.S. 128, 143, 143–44 n.12 (1978)).

[61] *Id.*

[62] *Id.* at 2229.

[63] *Id.* at 2235 (Thomas, J., dissenting).

contracts nor any provisions of law make the records his."[64] Accordingly, none of Carpenter's property was searched, and he can make no Fourth Amendment claim.

Though Thomas thought that the case at hand was straightforward, he used it as an opportunity to argue that "the *Katz* test has no basis in the text or history of the Fourth Amendment," and that it therefore "invites courts to make judgments about policy, not law," "distort[s] Fourth Amendment jurisprudence," and should be abandoned.[65] Thomas conducted a lengthy review of 20th-century Fourth Amendment doctrine and underscored the lack of legal grounding for *Katz* and the reasonable-expectation-of-privacy standard: "Justice Harlan did not cite anything for this 'expectation of privacy' test, and the parties did not discuss it in their briefs."[66] Indeed, "[t]he test appears to have been presented for the first time at oral argument by one of the defendant's lawyers" who drew an analogy to the "reasonable person" test in tort law.[67] The resultant test defines "'search' to mean 'any violation of a reasonable expectation of privacy,'" which, Thomas argued, is "not a normal definition of the word 'search'" and "misconstrues virtually every one" of the words of the relevant part of the Fourth Amendment.[68]

For Thomas, a central flaw of the *Katz* test is its focus on "the concept of 'privacy,'" as "[t]he word 'privacy' does not appear in the Fourth Amendment (or anywhere else in the Constitution for that matter)."[69] Instead, Thomas wrote, the right protected by the Fourth Amendment is "'[t]he right of the people to be secure,'" limited to "'persons' and three specific types of property."[70] The Fourth Amendment is thus closely connected with property, not privacy. Thomas described how the Fourth Amendment's protection of security in property was a reaction to the Crown's use of writs of assistance against the American colonists in the years leading up to the

[64] *Id.*

[65] *Id.* at 2236–38 (quoting Minnesota v. Carter, 525 U.S. 83, 97 (1998) (Scalia, J., concurring)).

[66] *Id.* at 2237.

[67] *Id.* (citing Peter Winn, *Katz* and the Origins of the "Reasonable Expectation of Privacy" Test, 40 McGeorge L. Rev. 1, 9–10 (2009); Harvey A. Schneider, *Katz v. United States*: The Untold Story, 40 McGeorge L. Rev. 13, 18 (2009)).

[68] *Id.* at 2238.

[69] *Id.* at 2239.

[70] *Id.* (quoting U.S. Const. amend. IV).

revolution, undermining *Katz's* assertion that "the Fourth Amendment protects people, not places."[71]

Thomas argued that *Katz's* emphasis on "expectations of privacy" has now led the Court to further distort the text of the Fourth Amendment—while the text's use of the word "their" makes clear that "at the very least, [ ] individuals do not have Fourth Amendment rights in *someone else's* property," "under the *Katz* test, individuals can have a reasonable expectation of privacy in another person's property."[72] Thomas found Carpenter's arguments that the cell-site records are his "papers" unpersuasive as "[n]othing in the text [of § 222] pre-empts state property law or gives customers a property interest in the companies' business records."[73] If Section 222 or another statute *did* explicitly give Carpenter such a property interest in his CSLI, it seems that Thomas would be willing to find Fourth Amendment protection, though he appeared to have reservations concerning Congress's authority in this area.[74]

Finally, Thomas found *Katz* unclear and potentially circular because, even as the Court is supposed to enforce society's privacy expectations, those expectations are in turn shaped by the Court's rulings. Thomas argued that the Court is really asking the normative question of "whether a particular practice *should* be considered a search under the Fourth Amendment," rather than the descriptive question that the *Katz* test purports to require.[75]

D. Justice Alito's Dissent

Justice Alito focused his dissent (which was joined by Justice Thomas) on the negative effects he saw the majority decision having on subpoena law, arguing that "the Court ignores the basic distinction between an actual search . . . and an order merely requiring a party to look through its own records and produce specified documents."[76] Actual searches, Alito argued, require probable cause, while a subpoena doesn't. Not only can Carpenter not assert that the

---

[71] *Id.* at 2239–41.

[72] *Id.* at 2242.

[73] *Id.* at 2243.

[74] *Id.* at 2242.

[75] *Id.* at 2246.

[76] *Id.* at 2247 (Alito, J., dissenting).

SCA court order here requires probable cause, Alito wrote, he cannot object at all, because it is "object[ing] to the search of a third party's property." The Court, he warned, "will be making repairs—or picking up the pieces—for a long time to come."[77]

Alito argued that the SCA court order was "the functional equivalent" of a subpoena, and that there "is no evidence that these writs were regarded as 'searches' at the time of the founding."[78] To illustrate this point, Alito traced the development of subpoenas from the Court of Chancery and argued that "the Fourth Amendment, as originally understood, did not apply to the compulsory production of documents at all."[79] Instead, it was targeted at "physical intrusion" and the "taking of property by agents of the state."[80] Absent these violations, people in the Founding Era would not have thought that the Fourth Amendment applied.

The majority opinion, Alito argued, places at risk long-settled precedents concerning subpoenas and the vital law enforcement purposes they serve. The government met the requirements for a subpoena and conducted neither a search nor a seizure, particularly not of any property belonging to Carpenter. Alito viewed the Court's decision as confusingly and improperly granting Carpenter *"greater* Fourth Amendment protection than the party actually being subpoenaed," namely the carrier.[81] Rejecting Carpenter's Section 222 argument that he had a property interest in the CSLI, Alito concluded that "there is no plausible ground for maintaining that the information at issue here represents Carpenter's 'papers' or 'effects.'"[82]

E. Katz *Nipped Part II: Justice Gorsuch's Dissent*

As discussed previously, *Katz* and its progeny did not completely excise property law from the Fourth Amendment. Property law featured prominently in *Jones,* as well as in *Florida v. Jardines,* when the Court held that bringing a drug sniffing dog on a porch was a search because *Katz* did "not subtract anything from the Amendment's

[77] *Id.*
[78] *Id.*
[79] *Id.* at 2250.
[80] *Id.*
[81] *Id.* at 2255.
[82] *Id.* at 2259.

protections when the Government does engage in a physical intrusion of a constitutionally protected area."[83]

And in *Byrd v. United States*, also decided last term, the Court wrestled with whether and how positive property rights affect the reasonable expectation of privacy for the driver of a rental car who is not listed as an authorized driver on the rental agreement.[84] Examining some of the issues in *Byrd*, as well as some of the questions Gorsuch asked, can help us better contextualize Gorsuch's *Carpenter* opinion.

Byrd was pulled over driving a rental car for which his fiancé had signed the agreement and then given him permission to drive. Because of this, the troopers reasoned that they did not need his consent to search the trunk, and they subsequently discovered drugs. At oral argument, Justice Gorsuch pursued a line of questioning that predicted his *Carpenter* dissent. There were two theories advanced by Byrd's counsel: "One, a property law theory, essentially, as I understand it, that possession is good title against everybody except for people with superior title. And – and I understand that. That's an ancient common law rule. I can go back and find that in treatises all the way back to Joseph Story."[85] The other theory was the reasonable-expectation-of-privacy test, which seemed inadequate to Gorsuch for the same reasons he would later express in his *Carpenter* dissent. In fact, since *Carpenter* was argued in late November 2017 and *Byrd* was argued in January 2018, Gorsuch may have already been researching and writing his *Carpenter* dissent.

Justice Kennedy wrote for a unanimous Court in *Byrd*, holding that the unauthorized driver does enjoy a reasonable expectation of privacy. Kennedy's opinion examined "property concepts" in order to inform "'the presence or absence of the privacy interests protected by that Amendment.'"[86] However, the problem with the property law theory raised by Byrd—arguing that "common-law property interest in the rental car as a second bailee that would have provided him with a cognizable Fourth Amendment interest in the vehicle"—was he did not "raise this argument before the District Court or Court of Appeals, and those courts did not have occasion to address whether

---

[83] Florida v. Jardines, 569 U.S. 1, 5 (2013) (cleaned up).

[84] Byrd v. United States, 138 S. Ct. 1518 (2018).

[85] Transcript of Oral Arg. at 24, Byrd v. United States, 138 S. Ct. 1518 (2018) (No. 16-1371).

[86] Byrd, 138 S. Ct. at 1526 (quoting Rakas, 439 U.S. at 144).

Byrd was a second bailee or what consequences might follow from that determination."[87] The Court was left to apply the reasonable-expectation-of-privacy test, yet still borrowed heavily from positive property law to aid "the Court in assessing the precise question."[88] Gorsuch would lament Byrd's belated attempt to raise arguments based on positive property law in his *Carpenter* dissent.

Gorsuch begins his *Carpenter* dissent with many of the same criticisms posed by the other dissenters, finding the line Roberts attempted to draw between CSLI and other types of third-party business records unsatisfying. Unlike the other dissenters, however, Gorsuch believes that the line should have been pushed the other way, such that many of the types of information now covered by the third-party doctrine should be protected by the Fourth Amendment. Regardless of the eventual solution, however, he thinks the current distinctions are untenable and that the Court was left with three options: (1) "ignore the problem, maintain *Smith* and *Miller*, and live with the consequences"; (2) "set *Smith* and *Miller* aside and try again using the *Katz* 'reasonable expectation of privacy' jurisprudence that produced them"; or (3) "look for answers elsewhere."[89]

Weighing the first option, Gorsuch concluded that *Smith* and *Miller* seem to be unprincipled and would lead to untenable results. "Can the government demand a copy of all your e-mails from Google or Microsoft without implicating your Fourth Amendment rights?" Gorsuch asked. "*Smith* and *Miller* say yes it can—at least without running afoul of *Katz*. But that results strikes most lawyers and judges today—me included—as pretty unlikely."[90] Both subjectively and objectively, Gorsuch found it hard to believe that a person should *never* expect privacy in the "information they entrust to third parties, especially information subject to confidentiality agreements."[91] He concluded his analysis of *Smith* and *Miller* by characterizing the third-party doctrine as "[a] doubtful application of *Katz* that lets the government search almost whatever it wants whenever it wants."[92]

---

[87] *Id.* at 1526–27.

[88] *Id.* at 1527.

[89] Carpenter, 138 S. Ct. at 2262 (Gorsuch, J., dissenting).

[90] *Id.*

[91] *Id.* at 2263.

[92] *Id.* at 2264.

The second option Gorsuch offered is scrapping *Smith* and *Miller* and returning to *Katz's* straight "reasonable expectation of privacy" approach. This too is unappealing, however, because he found many of the same problems with *Katz's* interpretation of the text of the Fourth Amendment as Justice Thomas. "[T]he framers chose not to protect privacy in some ethereal way dependent on judicial intuitions. They chose instead to protect privacy in particular places and things—'persons, houses, papers, and effects'—and against particular threats—'unreasonable' governmental 'searches and seizures.'"[93] "Even on its own terms," Gorsuch argued, "*Katz* has never been sufficiently justified" since it is not clear where one should look for "reasonable expectations of privacy" nor "why judges rather than legislators should" be doing the looking.[94] "As a result" of these issues, "*Katz* has yielded an often unpredictable—and sometimes unbelievable—jurisprudence."[95] As examples of this tendency, Gorsuch criticized the two "guideposts" named by the Roberts in the majority opinion, asking, "[a]t what point does access to electronic data amount to 'arbitrary' authority? When does police surveillance become 'too permeating'? And what sort of 'obstacles should judges 'place' in law enforcement's path when it does? We simply do not know."[96]

In the face of these unappealing, unworkable, and unprincipled options, Gorsuch wrote that there was another way to go. This other way is the traditional, pre-*Katz* Fourth Amendment approach, but with updates to deal with the problems posed by modern technology. "[T]he traditional approach asked if a house, paper or effect was *yours* under law. No more was needed to trigger the Fourth Amendment."[97] This approach has several advantages, not least that it removes from a judge the ability to decide Fourth Amendment cases based on "personal sensibilities about the 'reasonableness of your expectations or privacy," or to supplant the legislature's judgments on matters of policy.[98] "Under this more

---

[93] *Id.*
[94] *Id.* at 2265.
[95] *Id.* at 2266.
[96] *Id.*
[97] *Id.* at 2267–68.
[98] *Id.*

traditional approach, Fourth Amendment protections for your papers and effects do not automatically disappear just because you share them with third parties."[99]

This line of reasoning raises the questions of "what kind of legal interest is sufficient to make something *yours*? And what source of law determines that? Current positive law? The common law at 1791, extended by analogy to modern times? Both?"[100] Gorsuch acknowledged that more work needs to be done before this theory could be fully implemented, but he offered five thoughts.

First, he proposed using a legal concept known as a bailment to partially address the third-party doctrine issue. "A bailment is the 'delivery of personal property by one person (the *bailor*) to another (the *bailee*) who holds the property for a certain purpose'" and "normally owes a legal duty to keep the item safe." Adopting this property-law principle into Fourth Amendment jurisprudence could help to preserve Fourth Amendment interests even after information is transferred to a third-party. His starting point for applying bailments to Fourth Amendment law was *Ex parte Jackson*, where the Court wrote that "[t]he constitutional guaranty of the right of the people to be secure in their papers against unreasonable searches and seizures extends to *their papers*, thus closed against inspection, *wherever they may be*." Similarly, "[j]ust because you entrust your data—in some case, your modern-day papers and effects—to a third party may not mean you lose any Fourth Amendment interest in its contents."[101]

While on the U.S. Court of Appeals for the Tenth Circuit, Gorsuch applied similar reasoning to email and found that, under *Jones*, the government had improperly performed a warrantless search when it opened an email obtained from defendant's email provider on the grounds that opening the message constituted a trespass into the defendant's "effects."[102] Applying similar reasoning to other types of

---

[99] *Id.* at 2268.

[100] *Id.*

[101] *Id.* at 2269.

[102] United States v. Ackerman, 831 F.3d 1292, 1308 (10th Cir. 2016) ("Of course, the framers were concerned with the protection of physical rather than virtual correspondence. But a more obvious analogy from principle to new technology is hard to imagine and, indeed, many courts have already applied the common law's ancient trespass to chattels doctrine to electronic, not just written, communications.").

digital analogues of "papers" and "effects" seems like the first step towards a modernized, originalist Fourth Amendment doctrine.

Second, and somewhat contrary to his fellow dissenters' skepticism of Carpenter's Section 222 argument, Gorsuch "doubt[ed] that complete ownership or exclusive control of property is always a necessary condition to the assertion of a Fourth Amendment right."[103] This principle is already reflected in Fourth Amendment law because tenants and resident family members without legal title still "have standing to complain about searches of the houses in which they live."[104] One of the largest hurdles to Carpenter's case was that the CSLI was not a record over which he retained full ownership. The carrier had, at the very least, part ownership of the CSLI it had created and maintained. For Gorsuch's property-centric approach to work in *Carpenter*, allowing people to claim Fourth Amendment protection on property in which they have an incomplete ownership interest is essential.

Seemingly as an aside, Gorsuch also noted that the Court's language in *Riley* concerning how the "use of technology is functionally compelled by the demands of modern day life," could be used to argue that "stor[ing] data with third parties may amount to a sort of involuntary bailment."[105] In this way, even though the carrier is the originator of the data, it could be treated as a bailee under law, providing another path around partial ownership.

Third, Gorsuch was open to the notion of positive law "provid[ing] detailed guidance on evolving technologies without resort to judicial intuition. State (or sometimes federal) law often creates rights in both tangible and intangible things."[106] As he did in *Byrd*, Gorsuch explored the idea of state-created, positive-law digital property rights during oral arguments when he asked Carpenter's lawyer whether, if "a thief broke into T-Mobile, stole this information and sought to make economic value of it," would Carpenter "have a conversion claim . . . under state law?"[107] Carpenter's lawyer seemed to have

---

[103] Carpenter, 138 S. Ct. at 2269 (Gorsuch, J., dissenting).

[104] *Id.*

[105] *Id.* at 2270.

[106] *Id.* at 2269–70.

[107] Transcript of Oral Arg. at 38, Carpenter v. United States, 138 S. Ct. 2206 (2018) (No. 16-402).

been caught off-guard by the question. Gorsuch later brought up the topic with the government's counsel, asking whether the existence of a viable conversion claim would make accessing CLSI "a search of . . . paper or effect under the property-based approach approved and reminded us in *Jones*?"[108] The government lawyer fought the hypothetical and refused to answer the question on the grounds that no such positive-law property right existed, but the exchange demonstrates that this approach to Fourth Amendment law had been on Gorsuch's mind throughout the case and was also on his mind in *Byrd*. If legislatures start acting to create these positive-law property rights, Gorsuch believes that "that may supply a sounder basis for judicial decisionmaking than judicial guesswork about societal expectations."[109]

Gorsuch's fourth point is, in truth, a caveat to his third. He wanted to make clear that the positive-law train goes only one way: "while positive law may help establish a person's Fourth Amendment interest there may be some circumstances where positive law cannot be used to defeat it." *Ex parte Jackson*, for instance, "suggests the existence of a constitutional floor below which Fourth Amendment rights may not descend. Legislatures cannot pass laws declaring your house or papers to be your property except to the extent the police wish to search them without cause."[110]

Fifth, Gorsuch made a brief remark concerning subpoenas, noting that "this constitutional floor may, in some instances, bar efforts to circumvent the Fourth Amendment's protection through the use of subpoenas."[111] He largely left this up to further historical research on the original meaning of the amendment, but noted that the Fifth Amendment may be the source of stronger protection against subpoenas, not the Fourth. At the same time, he was wary of returning to *Boyd v. United States*, a case which, on similar reasoning, restricted the use of nearly all subpoenas and eventually proved unworkable. [112]

Finally, Gorsuch understood that constructing a non-*Katz* version of the Fourth Amendment based in property rights and positive

---

[108] *Id.*at 52.

[109] Carpenter, 138 S. Ct. at 2270.

[110] *Id*. at 2271.

[111] *Id*.

[112] Boyd v. United States, 116 U.S. 616 (1886).

law was difficult and underexplored. This is particularly true when there is a lack of complete ownership, as in the case with transfers of rental cars and the third-party doctrine. Unlike Justices Thomas and Kennedy, Gorsuch thought it was "entirely possible a person's cell-site data could qualify as *his* papers or effects under existing law."[113] *Carpenter* argued in his merits brief that a "property-based analysis under the Fourth Amendment provides an independent ground for holding that the government conducts a search."[114] Those arguments, however, were not developed before the district court and the court of appeals. For Gorsuch, "Mr. Carpenter's discussion of his positive law rights in cell-site data was cursory." "He offered no analysis, for example, of what rights state law might provide him with" in addition to federal law.[115]

Despite the limited briefing, Gorsuch pointed out that, while the telephone carrier possesses the customer's information in some sense, the Wireless Communication and Public Safety Act of 1999 (WCPSA) describes that information as "customer proprietary network information"[116] (CPNI) and "generally forbids a carrier to 'use, disclose, or permit access to individually identifiable' CPNI without the customer's consent, except as needed to provide the customer's telecommunications services."[117] Moreover, "Congress even afforded customers a private cause of action for damages against carriers who violate the Act's terms."[118]

Given those federal protections, "those interests might even rise to the level of a property right," but the "problem is that we don't know anything more" due to Carpenter's unwillingness to develop the argument further.[119] Thus, to Gorsuch, the *Carpenter* case "offers a cautionary example" to those in the future who fail to adequately explore the relationship between the Fourth Amendment and positive law in their briefs to the Court.

---

[113] Carpenter, 138 S. Ct. at 2272 (Gorsuch, J., dissenting).

[114] Brief for Petitioner at 32, Carpenter v. United States, 138 S. Ct. 2206 (2018) (No. 16-402).

[115] Carpenter, 138 S. Ct. at 2272 (Gorsuch, J., dissenting).

[116] 47 U.S.C. § 222 (2012).

[117] Carpenter, 138 S. Ct. at 2272 (quoting 47 U.S.C. § 222(c)(1)).

[118] *Id.* (citing 47 U.S.C. § 207).

[119] *Id.*

III. The Evolving Fourth Amendment[120]

Justice Gorsuch's dissent offered many stirring and interesting critiques of Fourth Amendment doctrine post-*Katz*. If the Fourth Amendment were to be based on positive property law and other positive law, what would that look like? Moreover, are there any philosophical and jurisprudential reasons to re-think Fourth Amendment jurisprudence as grounded in positive law?

We believe there are. In this section we will examine the philosophical justifications for grounding the Fourth Amendment in positive law—namely, that a Fourth Amendment rooted in positive law is a source of legitimacy for state actors' presumptive violations of property rights. Positive law delineates where non-state actors are allowed to go and what non-state actors are allowed to do. Positive law determines, or can determine, whether non-state actors are allowed to fly a drone over another's yard, secretly record someone's conversations in a phone booth, collect someone's DNA, or attach a GPS monitor to someone's car. It also determines when someone has been falsely imprisoned, harassed, stalked, or had his privacy otherwise invaded. If a state actor violates one of those rules, something must differentiate his actions from that of a common thief or kidnapper. In our view, the Fourth Amendment's reasonableness and warrant requirements are the source of that legitimacy, and the requirements kick-in as soon as a state actor has done what a non-state actor is prohibited from doing—namely, violating positive law.

Next, we will explore how positive property law has been used in the context of the Takings Clause, allowing it to evolve but keeping it rooted in the text and original meaning. It may seem strange to ground a constitutional provision in rules and definitions created by state and federal law, but it's been done before. Finally, we will briefly explore how positive law can help clarify the application of the Fourth Amendment in two emerging areas: drones and DNA collection.

A. *The Fourth Amendment and the Legitimacy of State Action*

Governments have special privileges and powers that ordinary people do not. Those powers are exemptions to general rules of conduct

---

[120] This section was heavily influenced by William Baude & James Y. Stern, The Positive Law Model of the Fourth Amendment, 129 Harv. L. Rev. 1821 (2016). It seems that Justice Gorsuch also found the article illuminating, as he cites it twice in his dissent. This prescient scholarship made our task much easier.

that are applicable to everyone in nearly every circumstance: don't steal, assault, murder, kidnap, trespass, extort, or break into and search someone's property. On initial reflection, it's not clear why government officials are allowed to break generally applicable moral rules, especially after it becomes clear that "the mass of mankind has not been born with saddles on their backs, nor a favored few booted and spurred, ready to ride them legitimately, by the grace of God."[121] Enlightenment thinkers such as Locke, Montesquieu, and Hobbes spent much of their lives articulating justifications and limitations for the moral exemptions granted to governments. Thomas Jefferson was greatly influenced by those thinkers, particularly Locke, when he wrote:

> We hold these truths to be self-evident, that all men are created equal, that they are endowed by their Creator with certain unalienable Rights, that among these are Life, Liberty and the pursuit of Happiness. *That to secure these rights,* Governments are instituted among Men, deriving their just powers from the consent of the governed.[122]

Our Constitution is based on those founding tenets and on the understanding that a government that is sufficiently powerful to accomplish useful public functions is also one powerful enough to trample on the rights of the people. That was James Madison's "great difficulty": "You must first enable the government to control the governed; and in the next place oblige it to control itself."[123] In order to ensure that government officials don't abuse the moral exemptions granted to them, the Constitution imposes numerous restrictions on when, where, and how those officials can use their powers.

Within the Bill of Rights, the Fourth Amendment is somewhat unique in that it describes how the government is to carry out certain rights-endangering activities. This differentiates it from many of the other provisions of the Bill of Rights that are described as outright prohibitions rather than descriptions of how state actors are to behave. Thus, when the First Amendment says "Congress shall make no law . . . abridging the freedom of speech, or of the press," it doesn't describe the strictures to be obeyed in making such a law. Similarly, "the right

---

[121] Letter from Thomas Jefferson to Roger Weightman, Mayor of Wash. D.C. (June 24, 1826), http://www.loc.gov/exhibits/jefferson/214.html.

[122] Declaration of Independence para. 2 (U.S. 1776) (emphasis added).

[123] The Federalist No. 51 (Madison).

to keep and bear arms shall not be infringed,"[124] and "[e]xcessive bail shall not be required, nor excessive fines imposed, nor cruel and unusual punishments inflicted,"[125] to name a few more. In this way, the Fourth Amendment is like the Takings Clause—both implicitly acknowledge that, if done properly, searching and taking property are legitimate functions of government in a way that suppressing speech is not. And, as will be discussed more *infra*, the Fourth Amendment and the Takings Clause are also similar in their reliance on positive law.

The Fourth Amendment, like the Takings Clause, presupposes property through its use of the term "their"—that is, "the right of the people to be secure in *their* persons, houses, papers, and effects, against unreasonable searches and seizures, shall not be violated."[126] Understanding that state officials would be given exemptions to violate individual's property rights, the Fourth Amendment attempts to limit and define how those exemptions are granted. As Professors Lillian BeVier and John Harrison write:

> Under the sub-constitutional law that protects private property, people are not free to enter another's home, or physically seize another's person, without permission. As a result, it is much easier for people to keep secrets from one another than it otherwise would be. But governments routinely authorize their agents to search for evidence of wrongdoing in ways that would be unlawful for a private person. Search warrants are a classic example; they empower officers to use physical force, if necessary, to enter private property without the owner's permission. Warrants, and other sources of special authority to search, thus present a threat to rights-holders that the private law does not deal with because it does not apply to the government as it does to others. The Fourth Amendment adds an additional layer of rules that the ordinary legislative process may not alter—rules designed specifically for the special search and seizure powers of officials. It does permit searches that a private person could never undertake, but requires that they be reasonable. It does allow the special exception to private rights created by warrants but regulates their issuance and content.[127]

[124] U.S. Const. amend. II.

[125] U.S. Const. amend. VIII.

[126] U.S. Const. amend. IV (emphasis added).

[127] Lillian BeVier & John Harrison, The State Action Principle and Its Critics, 96 Va. L. Rev. 1767, 1790 (2010).

If we understand the Fourth Amendment as delineating limits on the exemptions granted to government, it becomes important to clarify what, precisely, government actors are being exempted from—namely, what can normal people (that is, non-state actors) do and what are they prohibited from doing? Government actors can certainly do what normal people do—in ordinary circumstances, joining the government doesn't reduce your rights as a private citizen—but they must act in accordance with the strictures of the Fourth Amendment when doing what is prohibited to normal people, such as forcibly entering a house, searching it, and/or seizing another person's property or body.

Viewed this way, the Fourth Amendment restrictions on searches and seizures by government officials are not merely there to protect the people from abuses, although they do that too. More fundamentally, the restrictions of the Fourth Amendment are a source of *legitimacy* for state action. A bill must pass both houses of Congress and be signed by the president to become a law[128]—thus becoming a presumptive justification for the legitimate use of force by state agents. But, just as the president doesn't wield kingly authority to pronounce the laws,[129] a properly conducted search or seizure must conform to the Fourth Amendment to be legitimate.

Such requirements of legitimate state action are what separate, at least in theory, state officials from common criminals, or, perhaps, mere "stationary bandits."[130] A burglar and a searching-and-seizing police officer are quite similar at first glance, but it is not the uniform that authorizes the police officer to commit ostensibly immoral actions. The officer must carry out his search according to law to be legitimate, and he is subsequently liable if he transgresses those requirements.

At least, that's how it used to be, before the growth of qualified immunity and the advent of the exclusionary rule.[131] As Professor Richard Re notes, "Early in American history—many decades before

128 INS v. Chadha, 462 U.S. 919, 952–59 (1983).

129 The myriad problems with the administrative state notwithstanding. See generally, Philip Hamburger, Is Administrative Law Unlawful? (2014) (spoiler: yes it is).

130 Mancur Olson, Dictatorship, Democracy, and Development, 87 Am. Pol. Sci. Rev. 567 (1993).

131 Richard M. Re, The Due Process Exclusionary Rule, 127 Harv. L. Rev. 1885, 1918–20 (2014).

the modern category of constitutional criminal procedure was invented—unreasonable searches and seizures were generally viewed as a species of tort in the same legal category as trespasses perpetrated by private parties."[132] For most of American history "[u]nconstitutional searches were adjudicated according to a three-step process: (i) the aggrieved party brought a trespass action; (ii) the federal officer claimed immunity, usually based on a warrant; and (iii) to overcome the asserted immunity defense, the aggrieved party alleged violation of the Fourth Amendment."[133]

Note what happened in this process, particularly in the context of classical liberal theories of legitimate government action: (1) A citizen claims that a government agent was a mere trespasser, as any normal person would be if they searched private property without consent; (2) the government agent claims that, no, he should be given the benefit of the special governmental exemption from standard moral rules, or in other words, he deserves the special *immunity* conferred upon state actors who commit presumptively immoral property violations; and (3) the citizen responds by arguing that such exemptions are *only* granted by acting in conformity with the Fourth Amendment, which the state actor did not. In a sense, by not acting in conformity with the Fourth Amendment, the state actor has converted himself into a private actor, stripping himself of the cloak of immunity derived from acting in conformity with law.

This is, in essence, what famed and influential English jurist Sir Matthew Hale meant when he attacked the legitimacy of general warrants in 1736. By being illegitimate, such warrants gave state official no exemption from general property rules: "searches made by pretense of such general warrants give no more power to the officer or party than what they may do by law without them."[134]

Under this understanding, it's no wonder that alleged Fourth Amendment violations were adjudicated as private-law tort claims because the argument was, in essence, that the state actor became a private actor by performing an unreasonable search or seizure. In so doing, the state actor became someone who, according to law and custom, had gone where he wasn't allowed to go and done what

---

[132] *Id.* at 1918–19 (footnote omitted).

[133] *Id.* at 1920.

[134] Matthew Hale, 2 Historia Placitorum Coronae 150 (Rider 1800).

he wasn't allowed to do. As Professor Re writes, the original Fourth Amendment "ensured that 'unreasonable' federal officials would be treated just like private common law trespassers."[135]

B. The Use of Property Law in the Takings Clause

Positive law informs the acceptable behavior of normal people and, therefore, also informs when state actors have moved beyond that acceptable behavior. An examination of positive law can lead us to an alternative way of defining when a "search" occurred, free from the unpredictable *Katz* framework. When the rules of positive law are not obeyed, the Fourth Amendment kicks in and a "search" or "seizure" has occurred. This may seem like a radical departure from standard Fourth Amendment law, but in many ways it's not.

Using positive law to illuminate the meaning of constitutional provisions is not new, and in fact, is often necessary. The Takings Clause of the Fifth Amendment is the most obvious example. As Justice Gorsuch says in his *Carpenter* dissent, "In the context of the Takings Clause we often ask whether those state-created property rights are sufficient to make something someone's property for constitutional purposes. A similar inquiry may be appropriate for the Fourth Amendment."[136]

By prohibiting the taking of private property except for public use and with just compensation, the Takings Clause presupposes the existence of private property. The states, as the pre-existing sovereigns that came together to create the Constitution, define property law. "Because the Constitution protects rather than creates property interests," the Court has said, "the existence of a property interest is determined by reference to 'existing rules or understandings that stem from an independent source such as state law.'"[137]

Perhaps, in an alternate constitutional historical timeline, a creative justice would have severed the Takings Clause from its roots in independent sources of state property law. Opining that the Takings Clause "protects people, not places,"[138] our hypothetical justice

---

[135] Re, *supra* note 131, at 1920.

[136] Carpenter, 138 S. Ct. at 2270 (Gorsuch, J., dissenting).

[137] Phillips v. Wash. Legal Found., 524 U.S. 156, 164 (1998) (quoting Bd. of Regents of State Colleges v. Roth, 408 U.S. 564, 577 (1972)).

[138] Katz, 389 U.S. at 351.

creates a test that protects an individual's "reasonable expectation of property." That test would then be applied to situations such as occurred in *Murr v. Wisconsin*: two adjacent lots are purchased separately but are later effectively merged by subsequent state and local rules.[139] The reasonable expectation of property test would protect the reasonable expectation that the lots would remain separate.[140]

This, of course, did not happen, but if it did, many scholars and judges would be complaining that the Takings Clause had become unmoored from the Constitution. Instead, the Takings Clause has been consistently connected to evolving concepts of property law, and the Court has held that "a mere unilateral expectation or an abstract need is not a property interest entitled to protection."[141] As positive law delineates new species of property not known at the Founding, the Court has taken those changes into account. Thus, the Court has extended the Takings Clause to cover a materialman's lien established by Maine law,[142] real estate liens,[143] trade secrets,[144] and valid contracts.[145] Few if any justices have argued that the Takings Clause should only protect forms of property recognized at the Founding (at least these authors couldn't find one). In fact, expanding the Takings Clause to cover new forms of property is more often characterized as closely adhering to the original intent. In applying the Takings Clause to "the interest accruing on an interpleader fund deposited in the registry of the county court," the Court said that "this is the very kind of thing that the Taking Clause of the Fifth Amendment was meant to prevent."[146]

It's doubtful, of course, that something as specific as interest on a bank account was "the very kind of thing" that the Framers intended the Takings Clause to prevent. What the Court meant was that the Takings Clause was meant to prevent the more abstract

---

[139] Murr v. Wisconsin, 137 S. Ct. 1933 (2017).

[140] In applying the "reasonable investment-backed expectations" prong of the *Penn Central* test, the courts already arguably do something relatively similar. Penn Cent. Transp. Co. v. New York City, 438 U.S. 104, 127–29 (1978).

[141] Webb's Fabulous Pharms. v. Beckwith, 449 U.S. 155, 161 (1980).

[142] Armstrong v. United States, 364 U.S. 40, 44, 46 (1960).

[143] Louisville Joint Stock Land Bank v. Radford, 295 U.S. 555, 596–602 (1935).

[144] Ruckelshaus v. Monsanto Co., 467 U.S. 986 (1984).

[145] Lynch v. United States, 292 U.S. 571, 579 (1934).

[146] Webb's Fabulous Pharms., 449 U.S. at 155, 164.

concern of turning "private property into public property without compensation."[147] That abstract concern is not dissimilar from the abstract concerns animating the Fourth Amendment. State actors are granted a privilege that normal people don't have—namely, the ability to forcibly take someone's property for a public use— and therefore certain strictures must be obeyed if that taking is not mere theft for personal gain. Like the Fourth Amendment, the requirements of the Takings Clause are about legitimacy; by obeying certain constraints, a presumptive violation of general moral rules can become a legitimate state action.

C. How Positive Law Can Be Used in the Fourth Amendment

You've received a new drone for Christmas. It flies nimbly through the air and constantly films high-resolution video. You take it outside to try it out and direct it to hover over your neighbor's yard. He's always had this strange building on his lot, and you know the ceiling is glass. Even at 300 feet in the air, the drone's zoom is good enough to get a glimpse.

Or, perhaps you've always wondered about the ethnicity of your co-worker. Sure, she says she's English with a little bit of Polish, but you're pretty sure that she has some South Asian in her. If she is South Asian, she can come to your monthly South Asian meet-up, which you think she'll enjoy. Plus, it might be a nice surprise for her to find out something about her genetic history. One day you grab from the trash a coffee cup she used and swab it for DNA, which you send to 23andMe.

Most people would question the legality of the actions in both these situations—and they would be right to do so. On the question of drones, common law defined trespass by aircraft fairly narrowly: an aircraft flown "above the land of another is a trespass if, but only if, (a) it enters into the immediate reaches of the air space next to the land, and (b) it interferes substantially with the other's use and enjoyment of his land."[148] That rule seems somewhat antiquated in a world of drones, and states throughout the country have been passing laws regulating their use. According to the National Conference of State Legislatures, "41 states have enacted laws addressing

---

[147] *Id.* at 164.

[148] Restatement (Second) of Torts § 159(2) (Am. Law. Inst. 1965).

[drones] and an additional three states have adopted resolutions."[149] Some laws, such as North Dakota's, prohibit "any private person to conduct surveillance on any other private person" via a drone.[150]

States have also begun regulating "DNA theft."[151] In Alaska, for example, "a person may not collect a DNA sample from a person, perform a DNA analysis on a sample, retain a DNA sample or the results of a DNA analysis, or disclose the results of a DNA analysis unless the person has first obtained the informed and written consent of the person."[152] Alaska also creates a property right in your "DNA sample and the results of a DNA analysis performed on the sample."[153]

While states are experimenting with various positive laws that can help manage the emerging problems associated with drones and DNA testing, the Supreme Court is stuck in the past. In 1985, the Supreme Court, relying on *Katz's* reasonable expectation of privacy test, ruled that the Fourth Amendment "simply does not require the police traveling in the public airways . . . to obtain a warrant in order to observe what is visible to the naked eye."[154] And in 2013, in *Maryland v. King*, the Court ruled that "taking and analyzing a cheek swab of the arrestee's DNA is . . . a legitimate police booking procedure that is reasonable under the Fourth Amendment."[155]

With both aerial surveillance and DNA, we see how a positive-law theory of the Fourth Amendment can illuminate whether and how these emerging technologies should be restricted under the Fourth Amendment. A state's drone laws define what private people can do with their unmanned aircraft and should also define when state-actors have searched private property. And while the Court in *King* ruled that a cheek swab of an arrestee was search, albeit a reasonable one, future cases will have to deal with the surreptitious

---

[149] Current Unmanned Aircraft State Law Landscape, Nat. Conf. of State Legislatures, Feb. 1, 2018, http://www.ncsl.org/research/transportation/current-unmanned-aircraft-state-law-landscape.aspx.

[150] N.D. Cent. Code § 29.29.4-05(2) (2015).

[151] See generally, Elizabeth E. Joh, DNA Theft: Recognizing the Crime of Nonconsensual Genetic Collection and Testing, 91 B.U. L. Rev. 665 (2011).

[152] Alaska Stat. § 18.13.010(a)(1) (2004).

[153] *Id.* at (a)(2).

[154] California v. Ciraolo, 476 U.S. 207, 215 (1985).

[155] Maryland v. King, 569 U.S. 435, 465–66 (2013).

collection of DNA, as occurred when the "Golden State Killer" was captured by comparing a clandestinely obtained sample from a suspect with an online genetic database.[156]

Finally, it is important to highlight the sense of unlawfulness that most people would experience if they either surveilled a neighbor with a drone or furtively collected a colleague's DNA. In some sense, such actions *feel* wrong, and rightfully so. Yet police across the country are currently free to conduct aerial surveillance and collect DNA without asking for an exemption to general moral rules—that is, a warrant or a determination that a search is reasonable. Ultimately, bringing the Fourth Amendment into better alignment with the rules that govern private actors could help police earn more legitimacy and respect. There's nothing quite so upsetting as a state-sanctioned lawbreaker.

Conclusion

Carpenter v. United States was a blockbuster case, but perhaps not for the reasons many expected. Cell-site location information is now protected by the Fourth Amendment, albeit in a still unclear manner. That's a victory for privacy.

But it's still a small victory. The unworkable and antiquated third-party doctrine remains, and it is unclear whether the holes punched in it by *Carpenter* will expand. The third-party doctrine, as well as the *Katz* reasonable-expectation-of-privacy test, still stand on shaky doctrinal and theoretical grounds, and it's likely shakier now due to *Carpenter*.

Yet for those who have long been frustrated by the Fourth Amendment's bizarre reasonable-expectation-of-privacy test, *Carpenter* represents the beginning of what will likely be growing shift away from *Katz* and its progeny. Justice Thomas expressed extreme skepticism towards *Katz*—just as in *Jones*, both Justice Sotomayor and Justice Alito indicated doubts that the Fourth Amendment condoned the uses of certain types of mass surveillance.

Ultimately, it is Justice Gorsuch's opinion that will prove to be the most important aspect of *Carpenter*. Not only did Gorsuch raise

---

[156] Matt Ford, How the Supreme Court Could Rewrite the Rules for DNA Searches, New Republic, Apr. 30, 2018, https://newrepublic.com/article/148170/supreme -court-rewrite-rules-dna-searches.

trenchant criticisms of *Katz*, but he took the time to offer an alternative: A Fourth Amendment jurisprudence based in property law and positive law rather than one based in the bizarre and atextual use of the reasonable expectation of privacy. And while that view is still undertheorized, Gorsuch has signaled that he's willing to listen.

And that's how Fourth Amendment law slowly begins to change. Savvy future litigants will no longer ignore positive-law arguments when bringing their cases to the Court. When warranted, Justice Gorsuch is likely to write separate opinions expounding upon positive-law theory and, in so doing, slowly develop a coherent alternative to current Fourth Amendment jurisprudence rooted in classical liberal philosophy and better committed to the text. Whether any justices will go along with him remains to be seen, but it will be exciting to watch.

Class v. United States: Bargained Justice and a System of Efficiencies

*Lucian E. Dervan**

Introduction

In 2018, the United States Supreme Court ruled in *Class v. United States* that a defendant does not inherently waive his or her right to appeal constitutional claims simply by entering an unconditional plea of guilty. Rather, the Court determined such waivers must be express.[1] While the issue decided in *Class* was relatively straightforward, the case stands more importantly as another pillar in the growing body of modern plea-bargaining jurisprudence. In particular, *Class* is of note because the facts of the case and the discussions surrounding the appeal raise fundamental questions regarding the operation of the plea-bargaining machine, the psychology of defendant decisionmaking, and the voluntariness of plea bargaining given our growing understanding of the phenomenon of factually innocent defendants falsely pleading guilty.

This article begins with an examination of *Class*, including the incentives that led the defendant to plead guilty despite his belief that the statute of conviction infringed his constitutional rights. The article then examines the shadowy rise of plea bargaining during the 19th and 20th centuries and the recent focus on plea bargaining by the Supreme Court since its 2010 decision in *Padilla v. Kentucky*.[2]

---

* Associate professor of law and director of criminal justice studies at Belmont University College of Law in Nashville, Tennessee. He currently serves as chair of the American Bar Association Criminal Justice Section. You can follow him on twitter @LucianDervan. The views expressed herein are solely his own.

[1] See Class v. United States, 138 S. Ct. 798, 800 (2018). Factual description and case background is also taken from Petition for Writ of Certiorari at 5, Class v. United States, 138 S. Ct. 798 (2018) (No. 16-424) and Brief for the United States at 3, Class v. United States, 138 S. Ct. 798 (2018) (No. 16-424).

[2] 559 U.S. 356.

This analysis of recent plea-bargaining case law will illustrate that fundamental issues are beginning to rise to the surface regarding defendant decisionmaking and voluntariness in the plea context, including the reliability of admissions of guilt in return for plea bargains and the phenomenon of false pleas. The article, therefore, next examines recent psychological research on these topics, including research demonstrating that factually innocent individuals will falsely confess in return for the benefits of a bargain and research finding that pretrial detention is a driver of false pleas. Finally, the piece considers the ramifications of growing evidence that plea bargaining has a voluntariness and reliability problem. Along with considering ways to address these concerns, the article proposes that these revelations will inevitably lead us to face a broader question. What does it mean if we have adopted a criminal justice system that embraces efficiency at the expense of accuracy?

The *Class* Saga

In 2013, Rodney Class was indicted by a federal grand jury in Washington, D.C., for violating 40 U.S.C. § 5104(e)(1), which makes it illegal to "carry . . . on the Grounds or in any of the Capitol Buildings a firearm." The charge stemmed from events that began in May of that year when Class parked his jeep in an employee parking lot on the grounds of Capitol Hill. After exiting his vehicle, Class proceeded to various congressional office buildings. While Class was inside, a U.S. Capitol police officer observed that Class's vehicle did not have a parking permit. Upon closer inspection, the officer saw a large blade and a gun holster.

Several hours later, Class returned to his vehicle and encountered the police. Although he refused to consent to a search of the jeep, he did admit that there were weapons inside. Police informed Class that it was illegal to possess weapons on the grounds of the Capitol. According to Class, he had been unaware that he had parked in such an area or that weapons were prohibited there. Moreover, there were no signs indicating that the parking lot was within the grounds of the Capitol or that weapons were prohibited in that location. Class was arrested, and police obtained a search warrant for the vehicle. During their search, officers discovered weapons and ammunition, including a 9mm Ruger pistol, .44 caliber Taurus pistol, and .44 caliber Henry rifle, all of which lawfully belonged to Class.

During a later interrogation by the Federal Bureau of Investigation, Class admitted that he traveled with weapons to assist him in "enforcing" federal criminal laws against federal judges as a "constitutional bounty hunter."

After Class's indictment, he waived his right to counsel and represented himself during subsequent proceedings. He filed several pro se motions in an attempt to have the case against him dismissed. Those motions raised, among other things, issues related to the Second Amendment and fair notice. The district court examined the claims in light of the Supreme Court decision in *District of Columbia v. Heller*[3] and concluded that the applicable statute was valid. Class's case was then set for trial.

When the date of Class's trial arrived, he failed to appear after having provided the court with a letter stating that he would no longer participate in the case. As would be expected, the court issued a bench warrant, and Class was later arrested. Facing the possibility of additional charges for failing to appear under 18 U.S.C. § 3146(a)(1), which carries a possible sentence of up to five years in prison, Class took the road so frequently traveled by defendants today and pleaded guilty in return for the benefits of a plea bargain. In return for giving up his constitutional right to a jury trial, the government agreed that it would not charge Class with his failure to appear. Further, the government agreed that it would recommend a sentence at the low end of the applicable federal sentencing range of 0 to 6 months imprisonment along with a fine of $500 to $5,000 for the weapons charge.

Class was certainly not alone in pleading guilty in federal court that year. In 2014, the year in which he pleaded guilty, 97.1 percent of convictions in the federal system were obtained through guilty pleas.[4] Further, it is likely that around 75 percent of those pleading guilty did so in return for a promise of leniency or in response to a threat

[3] 554 U.S. 570 (2008).

[4] See U.S. Sentencing Commission, 2014 Sourcebook of Federal Sentencing Statistics, Figure C, https://www.ussc.gov/sites/default/files/pdf/research-and-publications/annual-reports-and-sourcebooks/2014/FigureC.pdf. In the last reported year from the Federal Sentencing Commission, 2017, 97.2 percent of criminal convictions in the federal system resulted from a plea of guilty. See U.S. Sentencing Commission, 2017 Sourcebook of Federal Sentencing Statistics, Figure C, https://www.ussc.gov/sites/default/files/pdf/research-and-publications/annual-reports-and-sourcebooks/2017/FigureC.pdf.

of further punishment.[5] For Class, the offer of leniency in return for waiving his right to a jury trial was significant. The statutory maximum term of imprisonment for the weapons charge was five years in prison.[6] For failure to appear, it was an additional five years in prison, which, according to the statute, "shall be consecutive to the sentence of imprisonment for any other offense."[7] It is hard to imagine that anyone—whether guilty or innocent, whether believing the statute to be valid or not—would reject an offer to go home immediately when the alternative was to risk up to 10 years in prison. As promised, Class received a remarkably light sentence when compared with the statutory maximum. He was sentenced to time served, which was 24 days, and 12 months of supervised release.[8]

The issue that eventually brought this case to the Supreme Court involved questions about what rights were waived as a result of Class accepting the government's proposed plea agreement. According to Justice Stephen Breyer's majority opinion, Class's written plea agreement contained the following express waivers:

> (1) [A]ll defenses based upon the statute of limitations; (2) several specified trial rights; (3) the right to appeal a sentence at or below the judicially determined, maximum sentencing guideline range; (4) most collateral attacks on the conviction and sentence; and (5) various rights to request or receive information concerning the investigation and prosecution of his criminal case.[9]

At the same time, the plea agreement contained express areas in which Class could challenge issues on appeal, including claims based upon "(1) newly discovered evidence; (2) ineffective assistance of counsel; and (3) certain statutes providing for sentence

---

[5] According to the assistant solicitor general who argued for the government in *Class*, approximately 25 percent of pleas in the federal system are so-called "open pleas" that do not involve any conditions or promises from the government in exchange for the defendant's agreement to plead guilty. Accordingly, the remaining 75 percent of plea agreements are in fact plea bargains featuring some promise of favorable treatment by the government. See Transcript of Oral Arg. at 61–62, Class v. United States, 138 S. Ct. 798 (2018) (No. 16-424).

[6] See 40 U.S.C. § 5109(a) (2018).

[7] 18 U.S.C.A. § 3146(b)(2) (West 2018).

[8] See Class, 138 S. Ct. at 802.

[9] *Id.* at 802.

reductions."[10] Despite Class's having raised the issue of the constitutionality of the weapons statute during earlier proceedings, the plea agreement said nothing about whether his right to appeal based on this argument was waived.

During the court's Rule 11 plea hearing, a proceeding during which defendants enter their plea of guilty and are advised, among other things, of the various rights they are waiving as a result, there was also no specific mention of whether Class had waived this right. At one point, the court discussed the issue of appeal, but the discussion did not specifically address the Second Amendment challenges the defendant had previously brought or constitutional challenges more generally.

> THE COURT: All right. Now, by pleading guilty, you would be generally giving up your rights to appeal. Do you understand that?
>
> THE DEFENDANT: Yes.
>
> THE COURT: Now, there are exceptions to that. You can appeal a conviction after a guilty plea if you believe that your guilty plea was somehow unlawful or involuntary or if there is some other fundamental defect in these guilty-plea proceedings. You may also have a right to appeal your sentence if you think the sentence is illegal. Do you understand those things?
>
> THE DEFENDANT: Yeah. Pretty much.[11]

Although the government would later argue that most appellate rights were waived once the plea was entered and accepted by the district court, Class appears not to have understood or agreed with that assessment as he appealed his conviction to the U.S. Court of Appeals for the D.C. Circuit just a few days later.

The appeal centered on the issues raised by Class unsuccessfully in the lower court, namely, whether the statute of indictment violated the Second Amendment and whether the lack of notice afforded that weapons were prohibited in the lot in which he parked violated the Due Process Clause. Rather than address the substantive challenges to the statute, however, the appeals court determined that those issues could not be raised because Class had waived his right to appeal on those

---

[10] *Id.*

[11] Joint Appendix at 63, Class v. United States, 138 S. Ct. 798 (2018) (No. 16-424).

grounds by pleading guilty. "It is well-established law," the appellate court wrote, "that '[u]nconditional guilty pleas that are knowing and intelligent . . . waive the pleading defendant['s] claims of error on appeal, even constitutional claims."[12] Despite the fact that the plea agreement in the case contained no express waiver of the right to appeal on constitutional grounds, the appellate court nonetheless concluded that Class should have invoked Rule 11's provisions for conditional pleas if he wished to preserve the opportunity to challenge the constitutionality of the statute of conviction after pleading guilty.[13] In essence, the court determined that an inherent result of Class's decision to plead guilty was the waiver of his ability to raise on appeal his constitutional challenges to the prosecution. Class appealed that holding to the Supreme Court.

In a 6-3 decision handed down on February 21, 2018, the Supreme Court concluded that a guilty plea by itself does not bar a federal criminal defendant from challenging the constitutionality of the statute of conviction on direct appeal, and therefore "Class did not relinquish his right to appeal the District Court's constitutional determinations simply by pleading guilty."[14]

Justice Stephen Breyer wrote for the majority that the issue in *Class* had been previously raised in the 1968 case of *Haynes v. United States*, in which the Court concluded that a defendant's "plea of guilty . . . did not waive his previous [constitutional] claim."[15] The rationale for the holding, as explained by the Court particularly by reference to *Blackledge v. Perry*[16] and *Menna v. New York*,[17] was that a guilty plea reflected a "confession of all the facts," but it did not preclude a challenge based on the notion that the "facts alleged and admitted do not constitute a crime."[18] Applying these principles to *Class*, the Court

[12] Class v. United States, No. 15-3015, 2016 WL 10950032, at *22 (D.C. Cir. July 5, 2016) (citing United States v. Delgado–Garcia, 374 F.3d 1337, 1341 (D.C. Cir. 2004)) (brackets and ellipsis in original).

[13] See Fed. R. Crim. P. 11(a)(2).

[14] Class, 138 S. Ct. at 803. The majority opinion was written by Justice Breyer and joined by Chief Justice John Roberts and Justices Ruth Bader Ginsburg, Sonia Sotomayor, Elena Kagan, and Neil Gorsuch. Justice Samuel Alito wrote a dissenting opinion that was joined by Justices Anthony Kennedy and Clarence Thomas.

[15] Haynes v. United States, 390 U.S. 85, 87 n.2 (1968).

[16] 417 U.S. 21 (1974).

[17] 423 U.S. 61 (1975).

[18] Class, 138 S. Ct. at 804 (citing Commonwealth v. Hinds, 101 Mass. 209, 210 (1869)).

wrote, "In sum, the claims at issue here do not fall within any of the categories of claims that Class' plea agreement forbids him to raise on direct appeal. They challenge the Government's power to criminalize Class' (admitted) conduct."[19] In so ruling, the Court rejected the contentions that (1) Class had inherently waived his constitutional claims simply by pleading guilty; (2) Federal Rule of Criminal Procedure 11(a)(2) required him to affirmatively preserve his right to appeal through a conditional plea; and (3) Class expressly waived his right to appeal during the plea colloquy in the district court.

In a dissenting opinion, Justice Samuel Alito began by concluding, with relative brevity, that waivers are permissible and, with one exception, Rule 11 makes "clear that . . . a defendant who enters an unconditional plea waives all nonjurisdictional claims."[20] Justice Alito then spent most of the remainder of the dissent focusing on that exception in Rule 11, which is contained in the Advisory Committee Notes. The exception noted by Justice Alito, labeled the "*Menna-Blackledge* doctrine," referring to the two cases discussed in the majority opinion and noted above, holds that "a defendant has the right under the Due Process Clause of the Fourteenth Amendment to contest certain issues on appeal even if the defendant entered an unconditional guilty plea."[21] Justice Alito makes clear from his dissent that he believes *Menna* and *Blackledge* represent inconsistent and unjustified departures from prior precedent that established that "[w]hen a defendant pleaded guilty to a crime, he relinquished his right to litigate all nonjurisdictional challenges to his conviction (except for the claim that his plea was not voluntary and intelligent)."[22] Justice Alito concludes, therefore, that Rule 11 should govern this case, which would lead to a conclusion that Class had, in fact, waived his rights to appeal.

Class in Context

The decision in *Class* is certainly a narrow one and, in many respects, it is not surprising given the language in *Blackledge* and *Menna*. The Court was simply asked to determine whether Rule 11 creates a default waiver of constitutional claims in unconditional

[19] *Id*. at 805.
[20] Class, 138 S. Ct. at 808 (Alito, J., dissenting).
[21] *Id*. at 809 (Alito, J., dissenting).
[22] *Id*.

pleas or whether, if the government seeks such a waiver, the prosecution must expressly include pertinent waiver language in the plea agreement. To dismiss *Class* because of its limited focus, however, is to miss the important larger picture that begins to emerge when it is placed alongside other recent Supreme Court decisions from the last decade involving the increasingly problematic question of bargained justice. Plea bargaining arose informally in the shadows of the criminal justice system and was largely ignored for most of its journey to dominance. But the Court has begun paying more attention to the many concerns presented by this expeditious yet extraconstitutional mechanism for resolving criminal cases. And this new focus means that the Court should soon confront one of the most haunting questions in American criminal justice today: How do we respond to plea bargaining's innocence issue and the growing concerns this phenomenon creates regarding the voluntariness and reliability of modern plea-bargaining practice?

To understand the necessity of the Supreme Court's work regarding plea bargaining over the last decade and the significance of where the Court might be moving next, one must step back and gain a historical view of where this journey began. Though many assume that plea bargaining has old common-law roots, the reality is that bargained justice is an American invention with a relatively short history.[23] One need only look to English common law to see how far the law in this area has moved over the last centuries. In the 1783 English case of *Rex v. Warickshall*, for example, the accused was taken into custody for receiving stolen goods.[24] Eventually, Warickshall confessed after obtaining a "promise of favor."[25] Consistent with earlier precedent, the English court struck down the confession, stating, "[A] confession forced from the mind by the flattery of hope, or by the torture of fear, comes in so questionable a shape . . . that no credit ought to be given to it."[26] Language similar to this appeared in American case law as well. For example, in the 1897 case

[23] See Lucian E. Dervan, Bargained Justice: Plea Bargaining's Innocence Problem and the Brady Safety-Valve, 2012 Utah L. Rev. 51 (2012); see also George Fisher, Plea Bargaining's Triumph: A History of Plea Bargaining in America (2003); Albert W. Alschuler, Plea Bargaining and Its History, 79 Colum. L. Rev. 1 (1979).

[24] Re. v. Warickshall, 168 Eng. Rep. 234 (1783).

[25] *Id.* at 234.

[26] *Id.* at 235.

of *Bram v. United States*, the Supreme Court said, "[The] true test of admissibility is that the confession is made freely, voluntarily and without compulsion or inducement *of any sort*."[27]

Despite such strong language prohibiting offers of leniency or threats of punishment to induce guilty pleas, appellate courts in America began seeing plea bargains around the time of the American Civil War. Given existing precedent, it is no surprise that these deals were disfavored, as evidenced by examination of some of the language used by the courts at this time. One court wrote, "when there is reason to believe that the plea has been entered through inadvertence . . . and mainly from the hope that the punishment, to which the accused would otherwise be exposed, may thereby be mitigated, the Court should be indulgent in permitting the plea to be withdrawn."[28] Another court said, "[plea bargaining is] hardly, if at all, distinguishable in principle from a direct sale of justice."[29]

Nevertheless, such deals continued to grow in the shadows of the American criminal justice system for at least two reasons. First, some judges, prosecutors, and defense counsel realized that plea bargaining offered a vehicle to hide their own corruption. Thus, in the early 20th century, bribes were sometimes used to secure "bargains" containing reduced sentences. This was particularly prevalent in Chicago, where "fixers," located in front of the courthouse, arranged deals for defendants.[30] Second, as overcriminalization became more prominent in the United States after the turn of the century, court systems in the early 1900s became overburdened and unable to process the increasing number of cases appearing on the dockets. This issue was particularly pronounced during the prohibition era as the number of offenses and offenders swelled.[31] In response, prosecutors began offering defendants incentives to plead guilty to help clear dockets and reduce caseloads.

While the practice of plea bargaining grew more common in the trenches during the first half of the 1900s, the Supreme Court

---

[27] Bram v. United States, 168 U.S. 532, 548 (1897) (emphasis added). It is worth noting that both *Warickshall* and *Bram* involved police confessions. However, until the mid-20th century, a plea of guilty was treated using the same law. See Alschuler, *supra* note 23.

[28] People v. McCrory, 41 Cal. 458, 462 (1871).

[29] Wight v. Rindskopf, 43 Wis. 344, 354 (1877).

[30] See Alschuler, *supra* note 23, at 24–25.

[31] See Fisher, *supra* note 23, at 210–12.

remained relatively inactive in this area of law. In the few cases involving bargained-for guilty pleas that came before it prior to 1970, the Supreme Court typically went no further than to indicate that guilty pleas must be voluntary and note that it generally did not favor deals creating significant incentives for defendants to waive their right to trial. The Court, however, failed to rule definitively on the question of the constitutionality of bargained justice more broadly.[32] Without a direct ruling from the Court echoing the skeptical sentiments from *Warickshall* and *Bram*, the use of incentives to induce defendants to plead guilty became more widely accepted and began to emerge from the shadows. In 1968, for example, the American Bar Association wrote about the supposed benefits of plea bargaining in an overwhelmed criminal justice system.

> [A] high proportion of pleas of guilty and *nolo contendere* does benefit the system. Such pleas tend to limit the trial process to deciding real disputes and, consequently, to reduce the need for funds and personnel. If the number of judges, courtrooms, court personnel and counsel for prosecution and defense were to be increased substantially, the funds necessary for such increases might be diverted from elsewhere in the criminal justice process. Moreover, the limited use of the trial process for those cases in which the defendant has grounds for contesting the matter of guilt aids in preserving the meaningfulness of the presumption of innocence.[33]

These words from the ABA in 1968 revealed the challenge the Supreme Court would face three years later when asked to definitively determine the legitimacy of plea bargaining in the seminal case of *Brady v. United States*.[34] Were the cautionary words from *Warickshall*, *Brams*, and the post-Civil War cases still relevant in a criminal justice system that had come to rely on plea bargaining to function? Not surprisingly, the answer was no.

The defendant in the 1970 *Brady* case pleaded guilty to kidnapping after being charged under a statute that permitted the death penalty

---

[32] See, e.g., Machibroda v. United States, 368 U.S. 487 (1962); Walker v. Johnston, 312 U.S. 276 (1941).

[33] A.B.A. Project on Standards for Crim. Just., Standards Relating to Pleas of Guilty 2 (1968).

[34] 397 U.S. 742 (1970).

only if recommended by a jury. By pleading guilty, Brady ensured that he would not be executed. After pleading guilty, however, the defendant changed his mind and argued that the plea should be withdrawn because the incentives to acquiesce were so large that his "confession" was involuntary. The defendant's argument relied on the requirement that pleas be voluntary, something discussed in those few early 20th-century Supreme Court cases that explicitly addressed pleas of guilty, and which is still present in plea-bargaining jurisprudence and expressly provided for in Rule 11 today.[35] Given that Brady faced losing his life if he exercised his right to trial, as opposed to a term of imprisonment if he pleaded guilty, many assumed that the Supreme Court would allow the plea to be withdrawn and rule that such incentives to plead guilty were impermissible. The Court, however, determined that Brady's plea was voluntary and went on to explain that offers of leniency and threats of punishment are permissible, as long as they do not overbear the will of the defendant.

While the *Brady* decision was a shift away from the language of *Warickshall*, *Brams*, and the post-Civil War cases, it should not have been surprising given the Court's limited options by that time. By 1970, almost 90 percent of cases in the United States were being resolved through pleas of guilty.[36] As the ABA had pointed out, plea bargaining offered a solution to the growing problem of overburdened dockets, and a decision by the Court prohibiting the practice would certainly have thrown the system into disarray. The necessity of relying on plea bargaining became even more pronounced around this time because the Supreme Court's due-process revolution of the 1960s had substantially increased the complexity, length, and cost of trials. One study, for example, demonstrated that the length of criminal trials almost doubled from the beginning to the end of that decade.[37] The Court also likely recognized that plea bargaining would persist regardless of whether it received the Court's blessing. In the 1978 case of *Bordenkircher v. Hayes*, the Court

[35] Fed. R. Crim. P. 11(b)(2) ("Before accepting a plea of guilty or nolo contendere, the court must address the defendant personally in open court and determine that the plea is voluntary and did not result from force, threats, or promises (other than promises in a plea agreement).").

[36] See Dervan, *supra* note 23, at 81.

[37] See Alschuler, *supra* note 23, at 38.

wrote, "a rigid constitutional rule that would prohibit a prosecutor from acting forthrightly in his dealings with the defense could only invite unhealthy subterfuge that would drive the practice of plea bargaining back into the shadows from which it has so recently emerged."[38]

Important both to an understanding of the Court's decision in *Brady* and to an analysis of where the Court might be moving today is a realization that the *Brady* decision contained both a significant assumption and a vital caveat. In the concluding paragraphs of the decision, the justices discussed their vision for how the now officially recognized plea-bargaining system might operate. In this regard, the Court envisioned a system in which plea bargains would assist jurisdictions in saving resources for "cases in which there is a substantial issue of the defendant's guilt or in which there is substantial doubt that the State can sustain its burden of proof."[39] Further, the Court specifically emphasized the requirement that bargains be voluntary, which meant that the incentives should not be so large as to "overbear[] the will" of a defendant.[40] Finally, near the end of the opinion the Court addressed an issue that inevitably looms over the whole institution of plea bargaining and that will be addressed in some detail in the remainder of this essay, namely, the risk that plea bargaining poses to innocent defendants. Regarding this concern, the Court stated that it did not believe innocents would be convicted with any greater frequency as a result of plea bargaining. But this was not a statement based on any data or psychological research. Rather, it was merely the Court's assumption about human behavior and decisionmaking. Apparently recognizing that this surmise could be mistaken or that the incentives used in plea bargaining might grow so large as to begin to capture a significant number of innocents, the Court offered this final thought: "we would have serious doubts about this case if the encouragement of guilty pleas by offers of leniency substantially increased the likelihood that defendants, advised by competent counsel, would falsely condemn themselves."[41]

[38] 434 U.S. 357, 365 (1978).

[39] *Brady*, 397 U.S. at 752.

[40] *Id.* at 750.

[41] *Id.* at 758.

Thus, albeit with a caveat, the modern plea-bargaining system was born in 1970 as the Court brought official recognition to an institution that had previously operated in the shadows of the criminal justice system. There were several important plea-bargaining cases decided by the Supreme Court in the years following *Brady*, each of which focused on the same general principles laid down in the original decision. Plea bargaining was permissible, but there must be caution to ensure pleas remain voluntary. And to be voluntary, incentives should not be so large as to result in "overbearing the will" of defendants.

The Modern Era of Plea Bargaining

Though it is difficult to pinpoint the most appropriate moment in time at which to begin an analysis of what might be termed the modern era of plea-bargaining jurisprudence, I believe the best place to start is the 2010 case of *Padilla v. Kentucky*.[42] Padilla had been a lawful permanent resident of the United States for 40 years when he was arrested for drug distribution in 2001. After conferring with counsel, Padilla decided to plead guilty pursuant to an agreement that resulted in the dropping of one charge. In reaching his decision to plead guilty, Padilla relied on his attorney's advice that "he did not have to worry about immigration status since he had been in the country so long."[43] Contrary to his counsel's statement, however, Padilla's conviction all but created a requirement that he be deported. On appeal, Padilla argued that his counsel's failings amounted to ineffective assistance of counsel under the Sixth Amendment, and the Supreme Court agreed. The Court found that the Sixth Amendment did require that a criminal defense attorney advise a client when the client's decision to plead guilty might result in deportation. While the *Padilla* decision was limited to matters involving immigration consequences, on another level the case represented the beginning of a realization by the Court that plea bargaining and its mechanics were more complex and significant than reflected in *Brady* and in *Brady's* early progeny. Plea bargaining thus deserved more rigorous attention.

This more exacting scrutiny of plea bargaining came in a pronounced manner just two years later in *Lafler v. Cooper*[44] and *Missouri*

[42] 559 U.S. 356 (2010).

[43] *Id.* at 359 (internal quotation marks omitted).

[44] 566 U.S. 156 (2012).

v. Frye.[45] The *Lafler* and *Frye* cases were similar to *Padilla* in that they involved Sixth Amendment ineffective assistance of counsel claims. The cases were unique, however, because the defendants rejected advantageous plea offers due to the alleged ineffective assistance of their attorneys. In ruling on the issue, the Supreme Court concluded that plea bargaining is a "critical stage" of a criminal prosecution and, therefore, the Sixth Amendment right to effective assistance of counsel applies. *Lafler* and *Frye* are particularly significant holdings in a sequence of modern plea cases that has worked to expand the protections afforded defendants during the plea-bargaining process. But the two cases are perhaps most significant for the Court's remarks about the role of plea bargaining.

Lafler and *Frye* addressed the fundamental question of how significant plea bargaining has become in our modern criminal justice system. Justice Anthony Kennedy in *Lafler* wrote, "criminal justice today is for the most part a system of pleas, not a system of trials."[46] In *Frye*, Justice Kennedy elaborated on this concept:

> Because ours "is for the most part a system of pleas, not a system of trials," it is insufficient simply to point to the guarantee of a fair trial as a backstop that inoculates any errors in the pretrial process. "To a large extent . . . horse trading [between prosecutor and defense counsel] determines who goes to jail and for how long. That is what plea bargaining is. It is not some adjunct to the criminal justice system; it *is* the criminal justice system."[47]

Far from the tenor of *Brady*, which focused on plea bargaining mostly as a tool for increasing the resources available for trials, *Lafler* and *Frye* shifted focus toward the bargains themselves. This recognition that we live in a world of pleas is vital in explaining the Court's persistent focus on plea bargaining over the last decade, contemplating the Court's recent plea-bargaining precedents, and speculating where the Court might go next.

While *Lafler* and *Frye* answered a fundamental initial question about modern plea practice, I believe that the *Class* decision, as well

[45] 566 U.S. 134 (2012).

[46] Lafler, 566 U.S. at 170.

[47] Missouri, 566 U.S. at 143–44 (internal citations omitted; ellipsis and brackets in original).

as *Lee v. United States,*[48] which was delivered just a few months earlier, serves to guide us in identifying additional fundamental issues the Supreme Court must address as it continues to shape modern plea-bargaining law. As noted above, the first of these issues is to consider defendant decisionmaking more closely, including reexamining the reliability of admissions of guilt in the plea context along with the phenomenon of false pleas. In the decades that have passed since *Brady,* a case in which the Court expressed concern about the possibility of an innocence problem, the justices have failed to return in a meaningful way to the early assumptions about the accuracy of plea bargaining in capturing guilty, not innocent, defendants. If one examines the Court's two most recent plea-bargaining cases, however, it appears that at least some of the justices might be amenable to taking up this issue in the near future.

In June 2017, just a few months before *Class* was argued, the Court delivered an opinion in *Lee.* This case examined whether a defendant who had agreed to plead guilty in reliance on his attorney's mistaken assurances that he would not be deported should be afforded relief. Writing for the majority, Chief Justice John Roberts wrote:

> But for his attorney's incompetence, Lee would have known that accepting the plea agreement would *certainly* lead to deportation. Going to trial? *Almost* certainly. If deportation were the "determinative issue" for an individual in plea discussions, as it was for Lee; if that individual had strong connections to this country and no other, as did Lee; and if the consequences of taking a chance at trial were not markedly harsher than pleading, as in this case, that "almost" could make all the difference.[49]

Applying this logic, the Court reversed the lower court, which had denied the petitioner's request to vacate his conviction and withdraw his guilty plea. Chief Justice Roberts's framing of the discussion as one about "determinative issues" is important because it reflects a realization that defendants plead guilty for a variety of reasons, some of which might have little to do with the underlying facts of the case. While *Lee* is only a small foray into the fundamental issue of defendant decisionmaking, one must wonder whether Chief Justice Roberts

---

[48] 137 S. Ct. 1958 (2017).

[49] *Id.* at 1968–69.

considered how far this idea might extend beyond the specific facts of the *Lee* case. Would an innocent defendant with a "determinative issue" separate from factual guilt, such as an offer of immediate release from pretrial detention, be willing to falsely plead?

Interestingly, while Chief Justice Roberts's discussion in *Lee* appeared to open the door to a fresh review of defendant decisionmaking, Justice Clarence Thomas offered a dissent in *Lee* that harkened to the assumptions found in early plea-bargaining cases. Justice Thomas argued in his dissent that the Sixth Amendment does not require "'counsel to provide accurate advice concerning the potential removal consequences of a guilty plea,'" a position he has held since dissenting in *Padilla*.[50] During his discussion, Justice Thomas raised the issue of the reliability of guilty pleas by referring to two cases. First, he quoted from the 1985 case of *Hill v. Lockhart* for the premise that "guilty pleas are themselves generally reliable. Guilty pleas 'rarely' give rise to the 'concern that unfair procedures may have resulted in the conviction of an innocent defendant.'"[51] He then went on to quote the 1975 case of *Menna v. New York* for the proposition that "'a counseled plea of guilty is an admission of factual guilt so reliable that, where voluntary and intelligent, it quite validly removes the issue of factual guilt from the case.'"[52]

Justice Sonia Sotomayor also touched on the issue of defendant decisionmaking in her questioning of the government in the *Class* case just over three months after the *Lee* decision. Taking an approach in sharp contrast to Justice Thomas in *Lee*, Justice Sotomayor expressed concern regarding the coercive power of plea bargaining during an exchange with the government regarding appeal waivers. She said, "Mr. Feigin, all you are saying is how much power you have and how much power to coerce you have."[53] Justice Sotomayor later went on to describe one such tool of the prosecution in creating strong incentives. In discussing the ability of prosecutors to deny defendants acceptance of responsibility credit under the Federal Sentencing Guidelines, she said, "And I know of many prosecutors' offices

---

[50] *Id.* at 1969 (Thomas, J., dissenting) (quoting Padilla v. Kentucky, 559 U.S. 356, 388 (2010) (Scalia, J., dissenting, joined by Thomas, J.)).

[51] *Id.* at 1973 (Thomas, J., dissenting) (quoting Hill v. Lockhart, 474 U.S. 52, 58 (1985)).

[52] *Id.* (quoting Menna v. New York, 423 U.S. 61, 62 n.2 (1975)).

[53] Transcript of Oral Arg. at 33, Class v. United States, 138 S. Ct. 798 (2018) (No. 16-424).

who routinely tell Judges if a defendant seeks to preserve an appeal right, they have not accepted responsibility."[54] If having "determinative issues" is one factor potentially leading to unreliable admissions of guilt and false pleas, "coercion" and the creation of incentives that might "overbear the will" of defendants is certainly another. What the varying perspectives from Justices Roberts, Thomas, and Sotomayor might mean is unclear, but the broader issue at least appears to be in the wind.

Whether the justices will further explore issues surrounding the reliability of plea bargaining in the future is unclear, but if they are interested, an amicus brief in *Class* makes clear that those in the trenches of the criminal justices system are ready for that discussion. Although *Class* was styled by many as mostly concerning the Second Amendment or basic pleading practice under Rule 11, at least one group thought the case represented an opportunity to begin examining the issue of defendant decisionmaking more closely.

In its amicus brief in *Class*, the Innocence Project directly raised not only the issue of defendant decisionmaking, but the related issue of plea bargaining's innocence problem—that is, the very real possibility that coercive plea bargaining results in the convictions of nontrivial numbers of innocent people. The timing and content of the brief are fascinating. Though submitted one month before the decision in *Lee*, the Innocence Project brief seemed to speak to the concept of "determinative issues" proposed by Chief Justice Roberts in that case. Further, the brief soundly refuted the surmise regarding the reliability of guilty pleas expressed in *Brady*, *Menna*, and *Hill*, as well as Justice Thomas's subsequent dissent in *Lee*. The Innocence Project explained:

> The criminal justice system's reliance on pleas places pressure on all defendants to plead guilty. . . . Neither innocent nor guilty defendants want to receive the most severe punishments available under the law or endure the stress and uncertainty of trial, and their decisions to plead guilty or not are informed by these pressures. Put differently, life and liberty are often the prevailing considerations, rather than guilt or innocence.[55]

[54] *Id.* at 39.

[55] Brief of the Innocence Project as Amicus Curiae in Support of Petitioner at 6, Class v. United States, 138 S. Ct. 798 (2018) (No. 16-424).

The Innocence Project brief then went on to discuss our growing understanding of the psychology of defendant decisionmaking, including the findings of my 2013 study on innocence with Dr. Vanessa Edkins.

> The available evidence confirms the disparity between sentences handed down after trial and those entered in connection with guilty pleas. . . .
>
> Defense attorneys make their clients aware of these sentencing differentials in presenting the potential costs of exercising their right to trial, and "defendants would be a good deal less willing to plead guilty in the absence of a sentence-related inducement." Such inducements appeal to guilty and innocent defendants alike, as demonstrated by a recent empirical study that attempted to replicate the choice put to an innocent defendant who is offered a lenient plea bargain or a hearing on more severe charges.[56]

While the Supreme Court in *Class* did not specifically address the innocence issues raised in the Innocence Project brief, the empirical research it discussed, along with other studies from recent years, are exactly what the Court must consider if and when it takes up this fundamental issue. It seems worthwhile, therefore, to take a moment to consider how much we have learned about defendant decisionmaking since those early years and the—we can now assert with some confidence, deeply flawed—assumptions about the reliability of plea bargaining that appeared in the *Brady* decision nearly 50 years ago.

The Psychology of Plea Bargaining

Our understanding of the psychology of plea bargaining has advanced enormously in recent years. For example, in the pathbreaking study discussed above by the Innocence Project, Dr. Edkins and I asked students to participate in a research project that would compare group work to individual work through a series of test questions.[57] Unbeknownst to the students, the study was not really about group work, but was designed to employ a deception paradigm that would

[56] *Id.* at 8–9 (internal citations omitted).

[57] See Lucian E. Dervan & Vanessa A. Edkins, The Innocent Defendant's Dilemma: An Innovative Empirical Study of Plea Bargaining's Innocence Problem, 103 J. of Crim. L. & Criminology 1 (2013).

explore the issue of false guilty pleas. To examine this phenomenon, all of the students who participated in the test were accused of cheating on the individual work portion. Through the use of a confederate in the room, the study was structured so that only about half of the students actually engaged in cheating. The other half completed the test without any misconduct occurring. Regardless of factual guilt or innocence, and without yet knowing which of the participants had actually cheated, all of the participants were offered a bargain in return for confessing to the alleged offense. If the student admitted to cheating, they would lose their compensation for participating in the study. This was viewed as akin to probation or time served.

The participant was also informed that if they refused the deal, the matter would be referred to an "Academic Review Board." This board was described to the participants in a manner that made it sound very similar to a criminal jury trial, including the right to present evidence and testify. If convicted before the board, the participants were told that they would lose their compensation, their faculty adviser would be notified, and they would be required to attend an ethics course. This ethics course was viewed as a loss of time, akin to a period of incarceration. While this scenario did not perfectly recreate the actual criminal justice system, the anxieties experienced by participants were similar to, though presumably not as intense as, those experienced by people facing criminal charges. Further, this research advanced our understanding of defendant decisionmaking in ways that earlier studies utilizing only hypothetical scenarios could not.

In response to our cheating paradigm, 89 percent of the guilty participants took the plea offer. With regard to the innocent students, 56 percent of the participants were willing to falsely confess to an offense they had not committed in return for the benefits of the bargain. For the majority of innocent students who knew definitively that they had not violated the rules, it appears that accepting the deal simply made more sense. As the Innocence Project wrote in its brief, "Innocent defendants, like guilty defendants, plead guilty in exchange for lighter sentences because the benefits of doing so outweigh the costs of facing trial."[58] It is interesting to further consider

---

[58] Brief of the Innocence Project as Amicus Curiae in Support of Petitioner at 9, Class v. United States, 138 S. Ct. 798 (2018) (No. 16-424).

the application of these findings in the actual criminal justice system, where laws are often unclear and where factual guilt or innocence is sometimes less than certain even in the mind of the defendant.

To assist in validating our study data, we compared the results of our experiment to data regarding false pleas in mass exoneration cases.[59] In the Rampart mass-exoneration case in California, for example, authorities determined that dozens of officers had engaged in misconduct, including "hundreds of instances in which evidence or contraband was planted on suspects, false statements were coerced or fabricated, and police officers offered perjured testimony in court."[60] These findings led to approximately 156 felony convictions being dismissed or overturned, though it is clear from the evidence that not all of the exonerated defendants were actually innocent of the charged conduct. In examining this mass exoneration, Professor Russell Covey determined that the plea rate among those who were not actually innocent, though they were exonerated in the aftermath of the scandal, was 89 percent, exactly the same number as observed in our study. In that same research, Professor Covey concluded that actually innocent exonerees in the Rampart matter had pleaded guilty at a rate of 77 percent, much higher than that observed in our cheating paradigm. It is not surprising that fewer individuals falsely plead guilty when facing the possibility of an ethics class, however, as opposed to actual incarceration in jail or prison. But this only lends further support to concerns that when faced with the kinds of incentives typically involved, some significant percentage of innocent defendants in the criminal justice system will plead guilty.

Dr. Edkins's and my 2013 deception study has been repeatedly replicated and validated in various forms as other psychology labs around the world continue exploring this and related issues to develop a broader understanding of plea bargaining. In fact, Dr. Edkins and I, along with members of a large international research team, have spent the last two years running an updated and expanded version of this cheating-paradigm study in the United States, Japan, and South Korea. In the new version of the study, we have amended certain aspects of the paradigm to gain deeper insights into defendant

[59] See Russell Covey, Police Misconduct as a Cause of Wrongful Convictions, 90 Wash. U. L. Rev. 1133 (2013).

[60] Id. at 1138.

decisionmaking, including creating a role for defense counsel, requiring cooperation against codefendants, and further testing the impact of varying differential sizes. The term "differential" here describes the difference between the sentence or punishment a defendant receives in return for pleading guilty and the sentence or punishment a defendant risks if they proceed to trial.

Many have theorized that the larger the differential, the greater the likelihood a defendant—including an innocent one—will plead guilty. Creating research paradigms that examine the impact of differentials, therefore, is a critical step in better understanding defendant decisionmaking in the plea context. Our ongoing comparative research in Japan, South Korea, and the United States will help decide whether plea bargaining will be allowed in South Korea, where the practice is currently prohibited. In Japan, which only recently adopted plea bargaining, the study will be of significance in identifying risks associated with bargained justice and in creating a strategy for the implementation of new rules of criminal procedure to address these concerns. Early data from each country indicate that the plea rates by factually guilty and factually innocent participants are consistent with our earlier findings. Further, our results to date appear to demonstrate that the same innocence issues identified in our original 2013 study are present in different countries, cultures, and legal systems. The innocence issue, we are coming to find, is a global one.

Since the release of our cheating paradigm study results in 2013, the interest in plea-bargaining research within the psychology community has grown substantially. As new studies are released every year, we learn more and more about the psychology of defendant decisionmaking within the system of plea bargaining that now dominates the U.S. criminal justice system. Earlier this year, Dr. Edkins and I released a new plea-bargaining study that examined the issues of innocence, pretrial detention, and collateral consequences by utilizing several different hypothetical scenarios.[61] The study asked participants to review three hypotheticals involving a student charged with a drug offense, a nurse charged with assault,

---

[61] See Vanessa A. Edkins & Lucian E. Dervan, Freedom Now or a Future Later: Pitting the Lasting Implications of Collateral Consequences against Pretrial Detention in Decisions to Plead Guilty, 24 Psychol., Pub. Pol'y, & L. 204 (2018).

and an unemployed individual living with two children in public housing and charged with breaking and entering. For each, roughly half of the participants were asked to decide whether to accept a plea deal without being told the collateral consequences of conviction. The other half were informed of the specific collateral consequences that would apply after conviction, such as loss of the right to vote, ineligibility for students loans, loss of professional licenses, and ineligibility for public housing and food stamps. The research also tested whether the guilt or innocence of the defendants impacted the outcome, along with the effect of pretrial detention on plea decisionmaking.

The results of this new study confirm in several ways Justice Sotomayor's concern about the power of plea bargaining and speak directly to Chief Justice Roberts's notion of potentially "determinative issues," which are issues other than the underlying facts of the case that might lead a defendant, including an innocent one, to plead guilty. First, the study found participants assigned to both the factually guilty and factually innocent conditions electing to plead guilty, thus once again confirming the innocence phenomenon. Second, direct knowledge of relevant collateral consequences did not alter defendant decisionmaking, despite the sometimes life-long impact of these measures. Though disturbing, this finding is consistent with psychological research on temporal discounting, which posits that later consequences have less impact on decisionmaking than immediate ones. Here, more immediate considerations, such as reduced sentences or release from pretrial detention, drove the participants' choices. Third, the study found that pretrial detention significantly influenced plea decisions. Of particular importance here, the rate of innocent individuals who pleaded guilty tripled in the pretrial scenarios. The data in this recent study suggest, therefore, that sentencing differentials and pretrial detention are two examples of "determinative issues" in the plea context that might lead a defendant's will to be overborn, regardless of factual guilt.

As noted in a recent article examining research in the area of defendant decisionmaking in the plea-bargaining context, "it is beyond dispute that factually innocent defendants have pled guilty."[62]

---

[62] Allison D. Redlich, Vanessa A. Edkins, Stephanos Bibas & Stephanie Madon, The Psychology of Defendant Plea Decision Making, 72 Am. Psychologist 339, 348 (2017).

Beyond the numerous studies discussed above that confirm the un-reliability of plea bargaining and the fact that innocents are will-ing to falsely confess, there is empirical evidence from actual cases. Consider, for example, a 2015 report from the National Registry of Exonerations on the issue of "Innocents Who Plead Guilty."[63] Of the first 1,700 exonerees in the database, 15 percent had pleaded guilty to an offense they had not committed. The rates in certain areas are staggering.

For example, drug crimes comprised 40 percent of all guilty-plea exonerations, with 66 percent of exonerations involving a false plea of guilty. In Harris County (Houston), Texas, the report noted that there had been 71 drug exonerations since 2014, and the defendant in every case had pleaded guilty. Consistent with the new defen-dant decisionmaking and collateral-consequences study described above, the National Registry of Exonerations reported that "most of these defendants accepted plea bargains to possession of illegal 'drugs' because they faced months in jail before trial, and years more if convicted."[64] These defendants decided that their "determinative issue" was the finality of release from pretrial detention, despite the fact that they had not engaged in the alleged conduct. As noted in a 2017 report, the large number of exonerations from Harris County is due to the work of the district attorney's office's Conviction Integrity Unit and a practice of testing drug samples even after the entry of a guilty plea.[65] One can only wonder what the rate of false pleas might look like nationally if all jurisdictions employed these practices in drug cases.

The impact of incentives on false pleas was also present else-where in the National Registry of Exonerations data set, including in murder cases. The 2015 report found that the larger the sentencing differential—something achieved through, for example, allowing a defendant to plead guilty to a reduced charge—"the higher the proportion of exonerated homicide defendants who plead guilty."[66]

[63] Innocents Who Plead Guilty, Nat'l Registry of Exonerations (Nov. 24, 2015), http://www.law.umich.edu/special/exoneration/Documents/NRE.Guilty.Plea.Article1.pdf.

[64] *Id*. at 2.

[65] See Exonerations in 2016 Report, Nat'l Registry of Exonerations (Mar. 7, 2017) at 8, http://www.law.umich.edu/special/exoneration/Documents/Drug_Cases_2016.pdf.

[66] See Innocents Who Plead Guilty, *supra* note 63.

As an illustration, 49 percent of those exonerated for manslaughter had pleaded guilty.[67] In considering this data from the National Registry's database, it is important to note that actual rates of false pleas are likely much higher than reflected in the data set because of the many hurdles defendants who have pleaded guilty face in demonstrating their actual innocence. Regarding self-reported rates of false pleas, studies have found numbers ranging from 18 percent for juvenile offenders to 37 percent for offenders with mental illness.[68]

These various studies and anecdotes demonstrate that the assumptions in *Brady, Hill, Menna,* and countless other early plea-bargaining cases about the reliability of this institution were wrong. The idea that people only plead guilty because they are in fact guilty, and for no other reason, ignores the many other "determinative issues" that might be driving these decisions. During his plea hearing, Class engaged in the standard colloquy with the Court.

> THE COURT: Are you pleading guilty because you are guilty and for no other reason?
>
> THE DEFENDANT: All right. Yeah.
>
> THE COURT: Is that a yes?
>
> THE DEFENDANT: Yeah.
>
> THE COURT: All right.[69]

Although every defendant is made to stand and utter these words, we know there is much more at work than a mere desire to confess guilt and that there are, in fact, "other reason[s]" for a defendant deciding to take this path. Even the government admitted as much in its summary of the argument in *Class.* "A defendant who voluntarily pleads guilty," the government wrote, "has made a strategic choice in which he accepts an adverse legal judgment in return for sentencing considerations and other potential benefits."[70]

---

[67] *Id.* at 1, table 1.

[68] See Redlich et al., *supra* note 62, at 348.

[69] Joint Appendix at 79, Class v. United States, 138 S. Ct. 798 (2018) (No. 16-424).

[70] Brief for the United States at 9, Class v. United States, 138 S. Ct. 798 (2018) (No. 16-424).

Where Do We Go from Here?

We know today, based on the research described above along with a steadily increasing number of real-world examples, that the incentives to plead guilty can be overpowering—indeed, so overpowering that even innocent defendants will sometimes take this path. When the Court addresses the fundamental question of defendant decisionmaking, it will have to wrestle with this reality and decide how best to proceed with the development of its plea-bargaining jurisprudence. Recall that in *Brady,* the Court said, "[W]e would have serious doubts about this case if the encouragement of guilty pleas by offers of leniency substantially increased the likelihood that defendants, advised by competent counsel, would falsely condemn themselves."[71] Yet, that is exactly where we find ourselves almost 50 years later, waiting on the Court both to recognize and to address that fact in light of all that we now know.

Does this portend that the Court might one day reverse course and decide that its 1970 approval of what has since become a veritable plea-bargaining machine was a mistake? I think not. Even if some of the justices desired this path, the Supreme Court of today stands in an even worse position than the Court of 1970 to stop plea bargaining's triumph. Plea bargaining has become a fully accepted part of our criminal justice system and, because of that acceptance, our system has grown even more reliant on bargained justice for its continued functioning. But completely prohibiting plea bargaining is likely an unnecessary step, and indeed a step too far, if our focus is plea bargaining's innocence problem. That concern is best addressed, I believe, through more focused efforts to fill in the various gaps that were created over the many years during which plea bargaining evolved and expanded in the shadows without much consideration of its operation or ramifications. Given that all but three to five percent of convictions each year in America come from guilty pleas, the Court must provide defendants greater rights before, during, and after the plea-bargaining process. Examples might include meaningful grand jury reform; better access to information, including exculpatory information, before pleading guilty; and reasonable limitations on the size of sentencing differentials sometimes used to punish those who exercise their constitutional right to trial.

---

[71] Brady v. United States, 397 U.S. 742, 758 (1970).

Fortunately, this is the type of work the Court has been focused on in the plea-bargaining context for a number of years as it has worked to provide defendants greater rights. We must now encourage the continuation of this journey so that the Court might expand on its previous work and reach these and other new and important topics.

Finally, before concluding, one must also observe that embracing the realities of plea bargaining's innocence issue raises another fundamental question the Court must address in this long journey to create modern plea-bargaining law. If, even knowing the alarming power of plea bargaining to ensnare the innocent, we continue forward, are we not conceding that beyond being merely a system of pleas, today's criminal justice system is, for the most part, actually a system of efficiencies? As a recent article regarding plea bargaining observed, "Though there are several reasons underlying the rise in plea bargains, the primary reason—efficiency—remains true today and is the most-often-cited reason for maintaining the practice."[72] What does it means to concede that the criminal justice system today is more about efficiency and less about justice than our Founders might ever have envisioned? What does it mean that in a system that values individual liberty, we have marginalized the right to a jury trial because of our inability to operate an overcriminalized system without bargained justice? While I do not know how those questions will be answered, I do think they are the concerns to which a deep examination of plea bargaining must eventually lead us—and the Court.

---

[72] Redlich et al., *supra* note 62, at 340–341. The role of efficiency in the criminal justice system more generally is discussed at length in Darryl K. Brown, The Perverse Effects of Efficiency in Criminal Process, 100 Va. L. Rev. 183 (2014).

Masterpiece Cakeshop: A Romer for Religious Objectors?

*Thomas C. Berg**

Masterpiece Cakeshop, Ltd. v. Colorado Civil Rights Commission[1] seemed set to rank among the major rulings of the Supreme Court's 2017 term. Reviewing the case of the baker who declined on religious grounds to "design and create a custom cake to celebrate [a] same-sex wedding,"[2] the Court seemed primed to address multiple issues affecting other wedding vendors (florists, photographers, wedding planners) and religious objectors (colleges, adoption agencies, etc.) facing penalties for sexual-orientation discrimination arising from their traditional beliefs. When does a commercial product or service—for example, creating a cake—embody a message such that the Free Speech Clause protects a business against being compelled to provide it? Is there a compelling governmental interest in prohibiting refusals of service based on sexual orientation and, if so, does that interest remain sufficiently compelling when a small proprietor refuses to provide personal services for a wedding and many other providers are readily available?

But the unveiling of *Masterpiece* proved to be less dramatic, as the decision put off those questions. Instead the Court, by a 7-2 vote, overturned the state commission's ruling against the baker on the ground that the commission, in adjudicating the case, had displayed "hostility" and bias against his religious belief in limiting marriage

---

* James L. Oberstar Professor of Law and Public Policy, University of St. Thomas School of Law (Minnesota). Portions of this article draw from the amicus brief that Professor Douglas Laycock and I drafted in *Masterpiece Cakeshop*. Brief of Christian Legal Society et al. as Amici Curiae Supporting Petitioners, Masterpiece Cakeshop, Ltd. v. Colo. Civil Rights Comm'n, 138 S. Ct. 1719 (2018) (No. 16-111) [hereinafter "Masterpiece Amicus Brief"].

[1] 138 S. Ct. 1719 (2018).

[2] Craig v. Masterpiece Cakeshop Inc., 370 P.3d 272, 276 (Colo. App. 2015).

to one man and one woman.[3] The commission thus violated the Free Exercise Clause requirement that "laws be applied in a manner that is neutral toward religion."[4] In concluding that the state had acted with hostility, the Court found a violation of what it had previously called "the minimum standard" of free exercise rights.[5] It therefore reached no conclusion whether, in a proceeding untainted by official hostility, the objectors' speech or religious rights, or the government's nondiscrimination interests should prevail.

The ruling left LGBT-rights activists disappointed and, in some cases, angry that the Court had labeled criticism of the baker's belief as hostility. But many also expressed relief that the holding appeared so narrow.[6] Activists on the baker's side had inverse reactions: tempered cheering for a narrowly grounded win.[7] And everyone moved on. Until three weeks later—when Justice Anthony Kennedy, author of the *Masterpiece Cakeshop* majority opinion, announced his retirement, giving Republicans a chance to solidify a conservative majority on the Court. The scope of religious liberty for traditionalists objecting to facilitating same-sex relationships is among the issues that splits the Court ideologically, with Kennedy the swing vote.[8] So the question arises whether *Masterpiece Cakeshop*'s holding based on case-specific strains of hostility will serve as prelude to broader protection for religious dissenters whose beliefs clash with sexual-orientation nondiscrimination laws.

[3] Masterpiece, 138 S. Ct. at 1729–32.

[4] *Id.* at 1732.

[5] Church of Lukumi Babalu Aye v. City of Hialeah, 508 U.S. 520, 543 (1993) (holding that ordinances targeting Santeria animal-sacrifice rituals "f[e]ll well below the minimum standard necessary to protect First Amendment rights").

[6] For examples of both reactions, see *infra* notes 50, 82–84 and accompanying text.

[7] See, e.g., Rod Dreher, Religious Liberty Wins Small, The American Conservative, June 4, 2018, https://bit.ly/2M3XAk1 (describing result as "a big deal . . . but not as big a deal as I would have liked"); Editorial, Broad Enough to Matter, National Review, June 4, 2018, https://bit.ly/2Hkofmg (although "the Court should have issued a broader ruling," "Phillips's victory is broad enough to earn our applause").

[8] Kennedy's vote was decisive in 5-4 rulings in *Zubik v. Burwell*, 136 S. Ct. 1557 (2016) (requiring federal government to consider further accommodations of religious nonprofits that objected to insuring contraception); Burwell v. Hobby Lobby Stores, Inc., 134 S. Ct. 2751 (2014) (ruling for closely held businesses that objected to Obama administration's contraception-insurance mandate); Christian Legal Society v. Martinez, 561 U.S. 661 (2010) (ruling against Christian student group denied recognition by state law school).

Such a progression in a civil right, from narrow holdings condemning government hostility in a particular instance to broader recognition of a key liberty, has appeared at least once before—with gay rights themselves. The Court's first ruling for gay rights, *Romer v. Evans* in 1996, held that a Colorado constitutional amendment, adopted by voters, was so broad, withdrawing such a wide range of gay-rights legal claims, that it showed a "bare desire to harm"—"animus" toward—the state's gay and lesbian persons.[9] The opinion, written (like *Masterpiece Cakeshop*) by Justice Kennedy, avoided deciding whether government discrimination against gays and lesbians was a suspect classification triggering heightened equal protection scrutiny. And the Court continued to avoid that question as it issued further gay-rights rulings, written by Kennedy, striking down state anti-sodomy laws in *Lawrence v. Texas*[10] and Section 3 of the federal Defense of Marriage Act (DOMA) in *United States v. Windsor*.[11] *Windsor* continued the pattern of deciding such cases narrowly by holding that DOMA reflected animus toward gays and lesbians. Only when the Court finally invalidated state denials of same-sex civil marriage in 2015[12]—Kennedy again—did it change its focus from government's anti-gay animus to same-sex couples' fundamental right to marry.

This article examines *Masterpiece Cakeshop* and the unresolved religious-liberty questions through the lens of the similarities with *Romer* and, potentially, with the later rulings that expanded and solidified gay rights. Part I describes the resemblances between the two cases, suggesting how *Masterpiece* can be seen as a "*Romer* decision" in the context of religious objectors to gay-rights laws. In particular, both opinions find animus or hostility as a "minimalist" holding that avoids committing to broad implications for future cases. But that modesty comes with a cost: To find animus, the Court must denounce the decisionmakers in the immediate case as especially unjustified, even malicious, and that conclusion can cause equal or greater anger compared with broader holdings, such as declaring a suspect classification or fundamental right. In the final parallel with

---

[9] Romer v. Evans, 517 U.S. 620, 634, 644 (1996).

[10] 539 U.S. 558 (2003).

[11] 570 U.S. 744 (2013).

[12] Obergefell v. Hodges, 135 S. Ct. 2584 (2015).

Romer, I sketch how the finding of unequal, hostile treatment in *Masterpiece* can develop into broader protection of religious traditionalists' right to decline to facilitate same-sex marriages.

I then turn to general parallels between gay-rights and religious-freedom claims—parallels that call for sympathizing with and protecting both sides. Those parallels depend less on the improper motives or attitudes (animus/hostility) of the regulators, and more on the seriousness of the interests and predicaments of those harmed by government action (same-sex couples denied marriage rights, religious objectors penalized for following their beliefs). Developing sympathy for their respective predicaments, I argue, is more likely to calm our society's serious problem of negative polarization—while condemning others for animus is more likely to aggravate such polarization. That in turn, I suggest, makes an argument for relying on heightened-scrutiny rationales in these cases, rather than findings of animus or hostility.

I. The Parallels in *Romer* and *Masterpiece*

A. Animus/Hostility, Inferred from the Government Action

Both *Romer* and *Masterpiece Cakeshop* found that the government action rested on animus or hostility, inferred from, at least in part, the action's terms and operation. *Romer* invalidated, by a 6-3 vote, Colorado's Amendment 2, by which referendum voters had added a provision to the state constitution to overturn gay-rights ordinances that had passed in Aspen, Boulder, Denver, and other localities. The amendment provided that no state or local government or agency could "adopt or enforce" any law or other policy "whereby homosexual . . . orientation, conduct, practices, or relationships" could be the basis for anyone "to have or claim any minority status, quota preferences, protected status or claim of discrimination."[13] The Court inferred animus from the "sheer breadth" of Amendment 2: Its ban on all gay-rights laws, state or local, in Colorado was "so discontinuous with the reasons offered for it that the amendment seems inexplicable by anything but animus toward the class it affects."[14]

The state had offered two justifications for the provision: respecting freedom of association, "in particular the liberties of landlords

---

[13] Romer, 517 U.S. at 624 (quoting Colo. Const. art. II, § 30(b)).
[14] *Id.* at 632.

or employers who have personal or religious objections to homosexuality," and "conserving resources to fight discrimination against other groups."[15] But the Court said that "[t]he breadth of the amendment is so far removed from these particular justifications that we find it impossible to credit them"; it was "a status-based enactment divorced from any factual context from which we could discern a relationship to legitimate state interests."[16] The broad disadvantage imposed raised an "inevitable inference" that the amendment rested on "a bare desire to harm a politically unpopular group," which even under the lowest level of judicial scrutiny, "cannot constitute a *legitimate* governmental interest."[17] Amendment 2 flunked that lowest level, rational-basis scrutiny.[18]

In *Masterpiece Cakeshop*, the Court invalidated the state order against Jack Phillips, the baker who refused to design the same-sex wedding cake, without ruling on whether his cake involved protected speech or whether requiring him to provide it served a compelling government interest against discrimination. Instead, the Court said that whatever the proper result on those "difficult to resolve" issues,[19] the commission in adjudicating the case had displayed hostility toward Phillips's religious belief in traditional marriage. It had therefore violated "the First Amendment's guarantee that our laws be applied in a manner that is neutral toward religion."[20]

The finding of hostility rested on two kinds of evidence. The first involved hostile on-record statements by two of the seven commissioners. Most aggressively, one commissioner compared Phillips's actions to slavery and the Holocaust—asserting that religion and

---

[15] *Id.* at 635.

[16] *Id.* Although the Court provided no further analysis, presumably religious objections could receive protection through exemptions to nondiscrimination laws, instead of through total bans on enacting such laws.

[17] *Id.* at 634 (cleaned up).

[18] The *Romer* opinion suggested, in an unsystematic way, other possible rationales. Amendment 2 attacked statutory protections not merely for same-sex conduct, but for orientation itself; it restricted gays and lesbians' political rights by requiring a constitutional amendment to pass any gay-rights legislation, *id.* at 627–29; and it arguably withdrew such a wide range of protections that it was "a denial of equal protection of the laws in the most literal sense," *id.* at 634. But those rationales (valid or not) were inapplicable in *Windsor*, which relied only on animus.

[19] Masterpiece, 138 S. Ct. at 1732.

[20] *Id.*

religious freedom had been used to justify both evils—and added that "it is one of the most despicable pieces of rhetoric that people can use[:] to use their religion to hurt others."[21] The Supreme Court held such statements "inappropriate" for an adjudicatory body charged with "fair and neutral enforcement of Colorado's anti-discrimination law."[22]

The other evidence of anti-religious hostility in *Masterpiece* involved not statements but official action: the commission's disparate treatment of a separate set of cases, in which three bakers had refused a conservative Christian's request that they bake cakes with religious symbols and quotations hostile to same-sex relationships.[23] The Christian customer brought claims of religious discrimination, but the commission rejected them, protecting the bakers' refusals. As the Supreme Court found, the state's treatment "of Phillips' religious objection did not accord with its treatment of these other objections."[24] For example, the commission said that any message from the same-sex wedding cakes "would be attributed to the customer, not to [Phillips], but it did not address that point" with respect to the protected bakers. The commission also had treated the protected bakers' willingness to make other cakes with Christian themes for Christian customers as exonerating, but had treated "Phillips' willingness to sell [other cakes] to gay and lesbian customers as irrelevant."[25]

Masterpiece Cakeshop held that this inconsistent treatment of Phillips and the protected bakers showed hostility towards Phillips's religious faith: The state had been neither "neutral [nor] tolerant," as free-exercise

---

[21] *Id.* at 1729 (citing transcript of commission's hearing from July 25, 2014, see Transcript of Oral Arg. at 11–12).

[22] *Id.* By contrast, *Romer* cited no such "smoking-gun" statements, perhaps because none could be remotely probative of the intent of a million-plus referendum voters. But in later striking down DOMA Section 3, the *Windsor* Court did cite animus it said was reflected in the House committee report on the statute. 570 U.S. at 770; see also Dale Carpenter, *Windsor* Products: Equal Protection from Animus, 2013 Sup. Ct. Rev. 183, 264–75 (cataloging statements in DOMA's legislative history showing "malice" or indifference toward gay-lesbian persons and relationships).

[23] Masterpiece Cakeshop, 138 S. Ct. at 1732; *id.* at 1730 (citing Jack v. Gateaux, Ltd., Charge No. P20140071X; Jack v. Le Bakery Sensual, Inc., Charge No. P20140070X; Jack v. Azucar Bakery, Charge No. P20140069X).

[24] *Id.* at 1730.

[25] *Id.* There were several other inconsistencies, as the amicus brief that Professor Laycock and I filed detailed. See Masterpiece Amicus Brief, *supra* n.*, at 18–21.

principles require, but had acted on "a negative normative 'evaluation of the particular justification' for his objection."[26]

B. *The Minimalist Rationale for Animus/Hostility Holdings*

In both *Romer* and *Masterpiece Cakeshop*, attributing animus was not necessarily the most convincing basis for the decision. Still, the Court decided to write the two opinions that way, and probably for similar reasons. What Cass Sunstein said of the *Romer* case could also be said of *Masterpiece*: The holding of animus or hostility was "more minimalist" than the alternative grounds for decision.[27] The Court wanted to step gingerly in its early confrontation with a topic to avoid a holding that announced broad implications.

1. *Romer*

As to *Romer*, it was unusual for the Court to infer animus under rational-basis scrutiny. It was not unheard of, as *Romer*'s cite to *Dept. of Agriculture v. Moreno* shows.[28] But it was very much the exception: Countless decisions had held that unless the classification triggered heightened scrutiny, a state "does not violate the Equal Protection Clause merely because the classifications made by its laws are imperfect."[29] Even if the classification is "both underinclusive and overinclusive, . . . 'perfection is by no means required.'"[30]

The Court had allowed government bodies—regardless of an individual's circumstances—to exclude all persons over age 60 (or sometimes even 50) from specific government jobs,[31] exclude all persons undergoing

---

[26] *Id.* at 1731 (quoting Church of the Lukumi Babalu Aye v. City of Hialeah, 508 U.S. 520, 537 (1993)).

[27] Cass R. Sunstein, Foreword: Leaving Things Undecided, 110 Harv. L. Rev. 4, 53–54 (1996).

[28] See Romer, 517 U.S. at 634 (quoting Dept. of Agriculture v. Moreno, 413 U.S. 528, 534 (1973), as stating "[i]f the constitutional conception of 'equal protection of the laws' means anything, it must at the very least mean that a bare . . . desire to harm a politically unpopular group cannot constitute a legitimate governmental interest").

[29] Dandridge v. Williams, 397 U.S. 471, 485 (1970).

[30] Vance v. Bradley, 440 U.S. 93, 108 (1979) (quotation omitted).

[31] *Id.* at 111 (excluding persons over 60 from foreign-service jobs) ("In an equal protection case [under rational basis scrutiny], those challenging the legislative judgment must convince the court that the legislative facts on which the classification is apparently based could not reasonably be conceived to be true."); Massachusetts Bd. of Retirement v. Murgia, 427 U.S. 307, 314–17 (1976) (per curiam) (exclusion of persons over 50 from police jobs).

methadone treatment from any government job,[32] and exclude persons from retirement benefits (despite their longstanding reliance on those benefits) because they no longer currently worked in an industry.[33] The Court did not find that there was hostility or prejudice toward, for example, older Americans in the workplace.[34] The Court recently reiterated that it "hardly ever strikes down a policy as illegitimate under rational basis scrutiny."[35] Under classic low-level, near-"rubber stamp" rationality review, the fact that some Colorado businesses or individuals had objections to same-sex conduct or relationships might have supported even a severely overbroad provision like Amendment 2.[36]

A prime objection to the courts' reluctance to infer animus is that laws discriminating against gays and lesbians are "invidious": They "circumscribe a class of persons characterized by some unpopular trait or affiliation" and thus "create or reflect [a] special likelihood of bias on the part of the ruling majority."[37] But that feature typically contributes to treating the classification involved as suspect or semi-suspect, triggering heightened scrutiny rather than rationality review. Neither *Romer* nor its successors, *Lawrence* and *Windsor*, declared sexual-orientation classifications suspect. By the time of *Windsor*, lower courts had fully articulated the grounds for adopting heightened scrutiny,[38] yet the Court held back from that step even as it kept ruling for gay-rights claimants. *Windsor* held, again, that DOMA reflected a "bare desire to harm" gays and lesbians.[39] The "animus" approach was idiosyncratic to Justice Kennedy, the key vote; other justices might have been happy to declare sexual-orientation classifications suspect. But that raises the question of what motivated Kennedy to prefer "animus" holdings.

[32] N.Y. Transit Authority v. Beazer, 440 U.S. 568 (1979).

[33] R.R. Retirement Bd. v. Fritz, 449 U.S. 166 (1980).

[34] This despite later congressional action based on just such a finding via the Age Discrimination in Employment Act, 29 U.S.C. §§ 621–34.

[35] Trump v. Hawaii, 138 S. Ct. 2392, 2420 (2018).

[36] See Carpenter, *supra* note 22, at 247 ("In *Romer*, an attempt to conserve state resources for combatting other forms of discrimination could have saved Amendment 2 [under low-level rational-basis scrutiny].").

[37] Beazer, 440 U.S. at 593 n.40.

[38] See, e.g., Windsor v. United States, 699 F.3d 169, 185 (2d Cir. 2012), aff'd on other grounds, 570 U.S. 744; Varnum v. Brien, 763 N.W.2d 862, 885–96 (Iowa 2009); Kerrigan v. Comm'r of Public Health, 289 Conn. 135, 174–214, 957 A.2d 407, 431–54 (2008); In re Marriage Cases, 43 Cal. 4th 757, 840–44, 183 P.3d 384, 441–44 (2008).

[39] 570 U.S. at 769–70.

Setting aside inquiries into Justice Kennedy's psyche, the best explanation of the approach from *Romer* through *Windsor* is minimalism: The Court proceeded cautiously, seeking to send incremental signals. Making sexual orientation a suspect classification would have suggested that multiple other discriminatory provisions might fall: "don't ask, don't tell" for gay and lesbian military personnel, and ultimately the denial of civil marriage to same-sex couples.[40] In 1996, when *Romer* was decided, there were significant pragmatic concerns about the responses to such rulings. Likewise, in 2003, in striking down sodomy prohibitions on personal privacy grounds, the Court noted that it was not addressing "whether the government must give formal recognition to any relationship that homosexual persons seek to enter."[41]

In Sunstein's assessment, the Court proceeded slowly beginning in 1996 partly because the justices were unsure "exactly what the Constitution require[d]" concerning sexual orientation, as to which societal understandings were steadily changing, "and partly because of strategic considerations having to do with the timing of judicial interventions into politics."[42] In Dale Carpenter's view, animus holdings were a "minimalist alternative" to "more adventurous theories of constitutional substance" such as declaring sexual orientation a suspect classification or same-sex partnerships a fundamental right.[43] Even in 2013, when the trend for gay rights was clear, the biggest issue of all remained undecided: same-sex marriage in the states. By continuing to apply a form of rationality review in *Windsor*, the Court could still signal an incremental approach, preserving the possibility of saying that states' traditional powers allowed them to limit marriage to opposite-sex couples even if Congress's unusual intervention into the subject in DOMA was invalid.[44]

[40] See Carpenter, *supra* note 22, at 231 ("[Holding] that classifications based on sexual orientation always warrant heightened scrutiny . . . would immediately have called into question all marriage laws and the ban on military service by openly gay people codified under 'Don't Ask, Don't Tell.'").

[41] Lawrence, 539 U.S. at 578.

[42] Sunstein, *supra* note 27, at 64.

[43] Carpenter, *supra* note 22, at 230.

[44] For example, Carpenter, writing immediately after *Windsor* in 2013, argued, "The Court's decision does not necessarily condemn all laws limiting marriage to opposite-sex couples. . . . The animus holding . . . is so closely tied to federalism concerns that it is not obvious the Court would come to the same conclusion about a *state* law defining marriage as one man and one woman." Carpenter, *supra* note 22, at 284.

2. *Masterpiece Cakeshop*

Masterpiece Cakeshop shows the same pattern in the free-exercise context: a ruling based on official "hostility"—that is, animus—in the particular case. The majority opinion again, by Kennedy, punted on the key underlying issues, saying only that however they should be resolved, "Phillips was entitled to the neutral and respectful consideration of his claims in all the circumstances of the case."[45]

The opinion indeed suggested that all the circumstances of the case mattered. It said that some of the commissioners' statements could be read as non-hostile to religious beliefs—but not when combined with the more egregious statements calling Phillips's acts "despicable" and analogizing them to slavery and the Holocaust.[46] The opinion said that the disparate treatment of Phillips compared with the protected bakers was "[a]nother indication of hostility,"[47] leaving open whether a change in any of the facts might change the conclusion. The majority even avoided saying that the disparate treatment could have no justification.[48] It pointed out that the state's actual reasoning in the two sets of cases either was inconsistent—for example, attributing the message to the customer one time, but implying it would be attributed to the baker the other—or rested on a judgment about the "offensiveness" of the requested message.[49] Commentators on both left and right took *Masterpiece* as narrow.[50] Precisely because the majority left open whether there was a way to

---

[45] 138 S. Ct. at 1729.

[46] One commissioner said twice that Phillips would have to set aside his religious beliefs if he wanted to "'do business in this state'"; the Court said this could be read as denigrating Phillips's interest in following his faith, or as merely asserting that the state's interest in nondiscrimination was overriding in commercial contexts. *Id.* (quoting commission Transcript of Oral Arg. at 23, 30).

[47] *Id.* at 1730.

[48] *Id.* at 1728 ("[t]here were, to be sure, responses to the[] argument[]" that the treatment of the two sets was inconsistent).

[49] *Id.* at 1731.

[50] Amanda Marcotte, Supreme Court Dodges the Big Issue in *Masterpiece Cakeshop* Ruling: Is There a loophole for Bigots?, Salon, June 4, 2018, https://bit.ly/2JlyWa6 ("it's fair to say the high court punted"); Jeff Jacoby, The Real Significance of the Masterpiece Cakeshop Decision, Boston Globe, June 4, 2018, https://bit.ly/2MLQWLX ("[the] majority opinion sidestepped the hard questions posed by this litigation") (citing commentators on both sides).

justify treating the bakers differently, the concurrences by Justices Elena Kagan and Neil Gorsuch rushed in to debate the issue.[51]

As in *Romer*, one could question *Masterpiece*'s conclusion of hostility. For one thing, the reliance on contemporaneous statements by the commissioners sits uneasily with the jurisprudence of the majority's conservative members, who tend to focus on text rather than intent.[52] (The Court's opinion answered this objection by noting that the case involved adjudicators,[53] whose displays of bias are typically matters of especially serious concern.) One could also question whether the statements were so plainly hostile as to be impermissible. Even the commissioner who compared Phillips's acts to slavery and the Holocaust arguably meant only that religious motivation cannot justify impositions on others' rights.[54]

Yet the inference of improper hostility was justified. There is no other explanation for the statement labeling Phillips's position a "despicable . . . use [of] religion." As the Court said, that label "disparage[d] his religion" not just by calling it despicable, but by "characterizing it as merely rhetorical—something insubstantial and even insincere."[55] As for comparisons to the Holocaust, we call the tendency to resort to them "Godwin's Law";[56] the eponymous creator of that term aimed it at "poorly reasoned [and] hyperbolic invocations of Nazis or the Holocaust" that "usually [operate] as a kind of rhetorical hammer to express rage or contempt for one's opponent."[57]

---

[51] Cf. 138 S. Ct. at 1733–34 (Kagan, J., concurring); with *id.* at 1734–40 (Gorsuch, J., concurring); see *infra* Part I.C.

[52] For example, in *Lukumi*, which involved a city's nonneutral ordinances prohibiting animal sacrifices by the Santeria sect, only two justices had considered contemporaneous statements of city councilmen to show the council's anti-Santeria hostility. 508 U.S. at 542 (Kennedy and Stevens, JJ.). And Justice Antonin Scalia wrote separately to criticize reliance on those statements. *Id.* at 558-59 (Scalia, J., concurring in the judgment).

[53] Masterpiece Cakeshop, 138 S. Ct. at 1730.

[54] Overwhelming as those two evils were, one could make analogies to them for limited points without equating them in every way.

[55] 138 S. Ct. at 1729.

[56] "As an online discussion grows longer, the probability of a comparison involving Hitler approaches 1." Godwin's Law, Wikipedia, https://bit.ly/1k8wXqb (last visited Aug. 20, 2018).

[57] Mike Godwin, Sure, Call Trump a Nazi. Just Make Sure You Know What You're Talking About, Wash. Post, Dec. 14, 2015, https://bit.ly/2LWSKG9; see Mike Godwin, I Seem to Be a Verb: 18 Years of Godwin's Law, Jewcy, Apr. 30, 2008 (claiming that his aim was to challenge people who "glibly compared someone else to Hitler or to Nazis to think a bit harder about the Holocaust").

Comparing Phillips's act with overwhelming evils was hyperbolic—sufficiently so to support an inference of hostility. Above all, the hyperbole, even if tolerable in other contexts, was "inappropriate for [adjudicators] charged with the solemn responsibility of fair and neutral enforcement of Colorado's antidiscrimination law."[58]

The Court in *Masterpiece Cakeshop*, as in *Romer*, likely focused on case-specific animus in order to proceed cautiously and avoid broader questions in its early ruling on a subject—here, on the clash between religious freedom, expressive speech, and nondiscrimination in relatively public settings like commercial businesses. The Court avoided directing substantive resolutions for the disputes and simply admonished that they be decided "with tolerance" and respect for both sides.[59] In ruling for Phillips, the Court avoided suggesting that a wide range of refusals of service would be protected—as in *Romer*, ruling for gays and lesbians, it had avoided suggesting that a wide range of laws discriminating against same-sex conduct or relationships might fall. The Court perhaps hoped that after its admonition for tolerance and respect, objectors like Phillips might win in a limited set of circumstances, or at least that decisionmakers would consider their predicament seriously—as Court in *Romer* perhaps hoped in 1996 that an admonition to social conservatives might have prompted greater consideration for the lives and interests of same-sex couples.

In *Romer*, it appeared the Court felt constrained to adopt a narrow holding because it did not wish to adopt a new rule that sexual-orientation classifications were suspect. In *Masterpiece Cakeshop*, the Court was constrained by its free-exercise precedents. It had held in *Employment Division v. Smith* that a law or regulation did not violate the Free Exercise Clause if it was "neutral [toward religion and] generally applicable";[60] it applied that same general standard in its other leading decision, *Church of the Lukumi Babalu Aye v. City of Hialeah*.[61] The Court was also somewhat constrained—albeit with substantial wiggle room—in addressing Phillips's expressive speech claim. In *Rumsfeld v. Forum for Academic and Institutional Rights, Inc.*, for

---

[58] Masterpiece Cakeshop, 138 S. Ct. at 1729.

[59] *Id.* at 1732.

[60] 494 U.S. 872, 879–80 (1990).

[61] 508 U.S. at 533–34.

example, the Court had rejected a law school's argument that allowing military recruiters implied approval of "Don't Ask, Don't Tell."[62]

Still, despite such constraints, *Masterpiece Cakeshop* creates (as *Romer* created) seeds for later decisions to expand the rights they recognized. Louis Michael Seidman correctly predicted that *Romer's* "lack of technical discussion of precedent and doctrine" created a pervasive "ambiguity" that would make the opinion "generative" of broader holdings.[63] One might say the same of *Masterpiece Cakeshop's* holding that the state violated neutrality given all the facts of the case. That holding too could have broad implications, as the next section discusses.

C. The Next Parallel? Expanding Protection of Religious Objectors

Romer proved be the first of several gay-rights rulings, culminating in the declaration of same-sex marriage rights in *Obergefell*. We do not know whether *Masterpiece Cakeshop* will start a similar series recognizing religious-conscience rights to decline to facilitate same-sex marriages or relationships. Will bakers, florists, or photographers prevail in cases where the initial decisionmaker does not display hostility or bias against their beliefs and claims? How will courts handle the many cases involving objections to nondiscrimination laws by religious nonprofit organizations—for example, when adoption agencies decline to place children in same-sex families, colleges decline to provide same-sex married housing or accept transgender students' chosen identity, or religious entities require employees to limit sexual intimacy to male-female marriage?

Strict scrutiny will govern these cases if they involve federal regulation—triggering the Religious Freedom Restoration Act (RFRA)[64]—or arise in a state that has its own religious-liberty statute or broad constitutional guarantee (which Colorado does not). But in other situations, the First Amendment precedents, including *Masterpiece*, will determine the courts' analysis.

As already noted, the *Masterpiece Cakeshop* majority sent some signals that the decision should be construed narrowly. For example,

---

[62] 547 U.S. 47 (2006) (Students "can appreciate the difference between speech a school sponsors and speech that the school permits because [it is] legally required to do so.").

[63] Louis Michael Seidman, *Romer's* Radicalism: The Unexpected Revival of Warren Court Activism, 1996 Sup. Ct. Rev. 67, 69–70.

[64] 42 U.S.C. § 2000bb et seq.

insofar as the Court's finding of hostility rested on "smoking gun" statements by commissioners, future decisionmakers can easily evade it. They will now be more careful to conceal their hostile attitudes toward traditionalist religious beliefs. But those attitudes can still drive decisions silently, and the attitudes are widespread.

But there are potentially broad religious-freedom implications in the other ground for finding hostility in *Masterpiece Cakeshop*: the inconsistent treatment of Phillips versus the bakers who were permitted to refuse the "anti-gay" cake.[65] To say that inconsistent, more favorable treatment of analogous secular claims shows unconstitutional hostility toward religion is potentially a powerful principle. Left-leaning states and cities will be unwilling to force socially liberal vendors to produce goods with conservative religious messages in violation of their consciences. Those states cannot then turn around and require religiously conservative vendors to produce goods in violation of their consciences. Religious objectors facing litigation can send testers to smoke out such uneven enforcement of anti-discrimination law.

Of course, states will try to manipulate rules to rationalize unequal treatment of objectors with whom they agree and disagree. In *Masterpiece*, four justices accepted such a rationalization. Justice Kagan's concurrence argued (and Justice Ruth Bader Ginsburg's dissent agreed) that the state could treat the cases differently because the protected bakers refused "to make a cake (one denigrating gay people and same-sex marriage) that they would not have made for any customer," while Phillips refused to sell same-sex couples "a wedding cake that [he] would have made for an opposite-sex couple."[66]

As Justice Gorsuch explained in his concurring opinion, this reaches a preordained result by manipulating categories: saying that the "anti-gay" cake had a distinctive message, but treating the cake for the same-sex wedding as merely generic.[67] If the category is cakes with a message, as the protected bakers' cases show, then one must consider the message of a custom cake designed for a same-sex wedding. Often such a cake will have some indication, even if symbolic

---

[65] See Douglas Laycock & Thomas C. Berg, *Masterpiece Cakeshop*—Not as Narrow as May First Appear, SCOTUSblog, June 5, 2018, https://bit.ly/2xQBhbK.

[66] 138 S. Ct. at 1733 (Kagan, J., concurring, joined by Breyer, J.); accord *id.* at 1750–51 (Ginsburg, J., dissenting, joined by Sotomayor, J.).

[67] *Id.* at 1735–40 (Gorsuch, J., concurring).

or implicit, indicating approval of the marriage—two brides, the couple's names, a rainbow—and that is a cake that Phillips would not sell to anybody. Justice Ginsburg's dissent—as well as Justice Kagan's concurrence—made much of the fact that the same-sex couple, Charlie Craig and David Mullins, "were turned away before any specific cake design could be discussed."[68] But if Phillips's conversation with them had continued a little longer, symbolism in the design almost certainly would have arisen. Phillips testified that his regular process involved learning about the customers' "desires, their personalities, their personal preferences and . . . their wedding ceremony and celebration" so as to "design the perfect creation for the specific couple."[69] It is hard to imagine how such a design would not affirm the goodness of their marriage, which is a message that Phillips says he cannot affirm.

If Phillips had lost because of the brevity of the conversation, the meaning of the ruling would have been extremely narrow. Under that rationale, he would prevail if he had begun discussing the "perfect creation for the specific couple" and then withdrawn.

Even without explicit symbols, the cake still sends an affirming message. As the Colorado appeals court tellingly put it, Craig and Mullins asked Phillips to "design and create a cake to celebrate their same-sex wedding."[70] The cake says, explicitly or implicitly, "this marriage is to be celebrated," and, in context, that celebration is of a same-sex marriage.[71] Context is critical: As Justice Samuel Alito observed at oral argument, a cake saying "November 9, the best day in history" means something different when provided for a birthday party instead of a Kristallnacht anniversary celebration.[72] It is irrelevant that "[t]he cake requested was not a special 'cake celebrating

---

[68] *Id.* at 1751 n.9 (Ginsburg, J., dissenting) (distinguishing "between a cake with a particular design and one whose form was never even discussed"); *id.* at 1733 n.* (Kagan, J., concurring) ("Phillips did not so much as discuss the cake's design before he refused to make it").

[69] Joint Appendix ["J.A."] at 161.

[70] Craig, 370 P.2d at 276.

[71] See Sherif Girgis, Filling in the Blank Left in the *Masterpiece* Ruling: Why Gorsuch and Thomas Are Right, The Public Discourse, June 14, 2018, https://bit.ly/2M5ebUC.

[72] Transcript of Oral Arg. at 68, Masterpiece Cakeshop, Ltd. v. Colo. Civil Rights Comm'n, 138 S. Ct. 1719 (2018) (No. 16-111). The hypothetical does not violate Godwin's Law (*supra* notes 56–57)—it compares Nazism for only a limited purpose, and not for rhetorical or emotional impact.

same-sex marriage.'"[73] Phillips's convictions about the general issue of marriage are strong enough that he objects to celebrating any particular same-sex marriage, no matter the couple's virtues. Right or wrong, he is entitled to that belief.

Three justices in *Masterpiece Cakeshop*, including Gorsuch, said the two sets of bakers' refusals should have been treated the same.[74] Justice Kennedy was not among those three, but his seat on the Court will now likely go to Brett Kavanaugh, who has shown sympathy to religious liberty claims by (among others) social conservatives.[75] So too has Chief Justice John Roberts,[76] even though he kept his cards close to the vest in *Masterpiece Cakeshop* by joining only Kennedy's majority opinion. The prospects seem good for a solid 5-4 majority that will give significant weight in religious-objector cases to the fact that other objectors were permitted to refuse to sell products whose message they opposed.

D. The Problem with Animus/Hostility Holdings in a Polarized Society

Although a holding of animus or hostility can have broader implications, it usually remains a strategy for ruling narrowly in the immediate case. But that strategy creates its own problems. To rule narrowly, the court must portray the decisionmakers in that case as exceptionally unjustified, insensitive, or even malicious. If their action were not exceptionally bad, the ruling invalidating it would have broad rather than narrow implications. Thus, although an "animus" holding may avoid suggesting broad further consequences, it is aggressive in another way: denouncing the decisionmakers for their hostility.

---

[73] 138 S. Ct. at 1733 n.* (Kagan, J., concurring).

[74] Masterpiece, 138 S. Ct. at 1734–40 (Gorsuch, J., concurring, joined by Alito, J.); *id.* at 1740 (Thomas, J., concurring in part and in the judgment) (joining Gorsuch's analysis).

[75] See Priests for Life v. U.S. Dept. of Health & Human Servs., 808 F.3d 1, 14–26 (D.C. Cir. 2015) (Kavanaugh, J., dissenting from denial of rehearing en banc) (arguing that nonprofit objectors to Obama administration's contraception mandate should prevail under RFRA).

[76] See Obergefell, 135 S. Ct. at 2625 (Roberts, C.J., dissenting) ("Many good and decent people oppose same-sex marriage as a tenet of faith, and their freedom to exercise religion is—unlike [same-sex marriage rights]—actually spelled out in the Constitution.").

Those who are denounced take umbrage, as they did in response to *Romer, Windsor,* and *Masterpiece.* Justice Scalia's dissent in *Romer* said the Court had "verbally disparage[d] as bigotry adherence to traditional attitudes" and thereby ruled in a way that was "nothing short of insulting."[77] After *Windsor* similarly found animus behind DOMA, conservative commentator Hadley Arkes complained that the Court had denigrated arguments for the centrality of male-female marriage as "so much cover for malice and blind hatred"—that denigration, Arkes claimed, was itself "hate speech" against traditionalists.[78] Other commentators, like Rick Garnett, worried about the consequences for rights to dissent from same-sex marriage. A holding of animus, he warned, suggested that traditionalists "are best regarded as backward and bigoted, unworthy of respect. Such a view is not likely to generate compromise or accommodation and so it poses a serious challenge to religious freedom."[79]

Even Michael Perry, who supported *Windsor* based on same-sex couples' fundamental freedom to marry, criticized the Court's finding of animus as "tendentious in the extreme, and demeaning to all those who for a host of non-bigoted reasons uphold the traditional understanding of marriage as an essentially heterosexual institution."[80] In short, to accuse traditionalists of demeaning LGBT people can itself be demeaning. "Perhaps animus doctrine is animus based."[81]

Now *Masterpiece* has accused pro-gay-rights officials of showing "hostility" and intolerance toward religious conservatives, and progressives have likewise taken umbrage. The shoe is on the other foot, and progressives dislike how it feels. One law professor excoriated the Court for "an utterly absurd finding of 'taint' and supposed religious animus."[82] Another commentator wrote that the majority

---

[77] Romer, 517 U.S. at 652 (Scalia, J., dissenting).

[78] Hadley Arkes, Worse Than It Sounds, and It Cannot Be Cabined, Bench Memos, Nat'l Rev. Online, June 26, 2013, https://bit.ly/2nnhA3j.

[79] Richard W. Garnett, Worth Worrying About?: Same-Sex Marriage & Religious Freedom, Commonweal, Aug. 5, 2013, https://bit.ly/2Mt3x7e.

[80] Michael J. Perry, Right Result, Wrong Reason: Same-Sex Marriage & The Supreme Court, Commonweal, Aug. 5, 2013, https://bit.ly/2vv10D5.

[81] Carpenter, *supra* note 22, at 185 (considering but rejecting the argument).

[82] Neil H. Buchanan, Kennedy's Sadly and Unnecessarily Tainted Legacy, Verdict: Justia, July 3, 2018, https://bit.ly/2voFY8Z ("Somehow, [the Court] found anti-religious bigotry in a person's revulsion at the thought of using religion to justify bigotry. That is an impressive feat of thinking backward (and backward thinking).").

acted as if "conservative Christians are special snowflakes who have to be given a safe space"—"as if the central matter [in the case] . . . was an urgent need to police the tone of civil rights commissioners."[83] In yet another view, Justice Kennedy had "assiduously . . . labored to find government 'hostility' to Phillips' religion" based on "tepid evidence" of "a 'slip-up' by a public official."[84]

We can see the difficulty with animus holdings through the prism of the nation's current ideological and cultural polarization. Kennedy seemingly intended the *Masterpiece Cakeshop* majority opinion to address the angry divide over traditional religion and LGBT rights; he admonished progressives to treat traditionalist believers with respect, the same way he had previously admonished conservatives to treat same-sex couples. Thus the opinion's summation that "these disputes must be resolved with tolerance, without undue disrespect to sincere religious beliefs, and without subjecting gay persons to indignities when they seek goods and services in an open market."[85]

Calming conflict is an understandable aim, for American politics and society are deeply polarized. Even before the inflammatory election and presidency of Donald Trump, polls reported that "[m]embers of the two parties are more likely today [than any time in 50 years] to describe each other . . . as selfish, as threats to the nation, even as unsuitable marriage material."[86] Polarization has become so much more poisonous because it is increasingly "negative." "Americans increasingly are voting against the opposing party more than they are voting for their own party."[87] In that environment, "politicians need only incite fear and anger toward the opposing party to win and maintain power."[88] The conflict between LGBT people and religious traditionalists is a prime locus of

[83] Ian Millhiser, Supreme Court Holds that Religious Conservatives Are Special Snowflakes Who Need a Safe Space, ThinkProgress, June 4, 2018, https://bit.ly/2M2Kdxx.

[84] Sarah Posner, The 'Masterpiece Cakeshop' Decision Is Not as Harmless as You Think, The Nation, June 4, 2018, https://bit.ly/2Jaw0AX.

[85] 138 S. Ct. at 1732.

[86] Emily Badger and Niraj Chokshi, How We Became Bitter Political Enemies, N.Y. Times, June 15, 2017, https://nyti.ms/2OPPvOf (describing polls up to and through 2016).

[87] Alan Abramowitz and Steven Webster, 'Negative Partisanship' Explains Everything, Politico, Sept./Oct. 2017, https://politi.co/2MeAlny.

[88] Id.

fear-based polarization; the two groups remain today, as a 1990s book called them, "perfect enemies."[89]

To mitigate such conflict, our constitutional tradition relies heavily on civil liberties, including the rights both to form families and to exercise religion. As Madison wrote in his *Memorial and Remonstrance against Religious Assessments*, "equal and compleat liberty" in matters of conscience is the best solution for "religious discord": "if [such liberty] does not wholly eradicate [such conflict, it] sufficiently destroys its malignant influence on the health and prosperity of the State."[90] Civil rights and liberties ideally reduce the stakes in sociocultural conflict; they reduce each side's existential fear that a hostile majority will successfully attack their core commitments. If same-sex couples can marry and religious opponents of same-sex marriage can live according to their beliefs, their deep disagreement will generate less in "malignant" bitterness and alienation.

But is condemning improper hostility an effective means of countering negative polarization? Admittedly, in some cases hostility is so clear and so damaging that condemnation is necessary. Arguably *Romer* and *Masterpiece* were such cases, the former because the disability imposed on gays and lesbians was especially wide-ranging, the latter because hostile expression by adjudicators is especially improper.

And yet, as already noted, relying on condemning animus or hostility creates its own problems. Labeling the contenders in a legitimate socio-cultural-political dispute as "bigots" may inflame rather than calm the situation; it may simply add further charges and countercharges, in a vicious cycle. Dahlia Lithwick described the irony of *Masterpiece*: "[A] case that was ultimately decided in large part on the basis of how we speak to one another about religion and discrimination further polarized and distorted the national discourse about religion and discrimination."[91]

Moreover, conclusions of animus can come too easily. Even Dale Carpenter, who defends the anti-animus principle at length,

---

[89] Chris Bull and John Gallagher, Perfect Enemies: The Religious Right, the Gay Movement, and the Politics of the 1990s (1996).

[90] James Madison, Memorial and Remonstrance against Religious Assessments (June 20, 1785), ¶ 11, https://bit.ly/1MHiLmr.

[91] Dahlia Lithwick, Anthony Kennedy's Suffering Olympics, Slate, June 6, 2018, https://slate.me/2McVQF0.

acknowledges the "substantial concerns" that it "is prone to judicial abuse [and] is difficult to apply even when not abused"—that it risks becoming "an attempt to hush debate about deeply contested moral and legal controversies" such as, for example, over the nature of marriage.[92] He answers that the principle "should be used sparingly, and only in extraordinary cases," such as against the broad attacks on same-sex relationships in *Romer* and *Windsor*, or when there is an "utter failure of alternative explanations" to justify the law.[93] But if animus/hostility is the only doctrinal ground for constitutional attack, there will be pressure for the courts to expand the category. They will have incentives to stretch and reach conclusions of hostility in order to provide relief on the only available theory. Progressives may appreciate that danger after the Court's controversial attributions of hostility in *Masterpiece Cakeshop*.

The limits of animus holdings became plain when the Court finally struck down state exclusions of same-sex marriage in *Obergefell*. That decision relied overwhelmingly on the fundamental right to marry, holding that "the reasons marriage is fundamental under the Constitution apply with equal force to same-sex couples."[94] Only one section of the opinion suggested a finding of animus or hostility: The Court said that "[i]t demeans gays and lesbians for the State to lock them out of a central institution of the Nation's society."[95] But that passage is brief compared with the fundamental-right discussion, and it focuses only on the demeaning effect, drawing no conclusion about hostile purpose.

Obergefell, I'd suggest, reflected the Court's sense that to call states' opposite-sex-only marriage laws the product of "animus" would have hurt the cause of getting acceptance for the decision. If the Court needed to calm a polarized public's response, an animus conclusion would have been disastrous and insulting—especially if it had rested on "the utter failure of alternative explanations"[96] to make out even a rational basis for the same-sex exclusion. Instead, the Court went out of its way to say that "[m]any who deem same-sex marriage to be wrong reach that conclusion based on decent and

[92] Carpenter, *supra* note 22, at 233, 185.

[93] *Id.* at 232, 246.

[94] Obergefell, 135 S. Ct. at 2599.

[95] *Id.* at 2602.

[96] Carpenter, *supra* note 22, at 246.

honorable religious or philosophical premises, and neither they nor their beliefs are disparaged here."[97] In other words, an animus holding would itself have been disparaging.

Having discussed the parallels between *Romer* and *Masterpiece Cakeshop*, especially in the advantages and disadvantages of their focus on animus/hostility, I now discuss a set of parallels between gay rights and religious freedom generally.

II. Parallels between Gay Rights and Religious Freedom

It is right to give strong constitutional protection to both the commitments of same-sex couples and the religious exercise of objectors to same-sex marriage. The classic American response to deep conflicts like that between gay rights and free exercise is to protect the liberty of both sides. The very arguments that underlie protection of same-sex marriage also support strong protection for religious liberty.[98] Religious traditionalists and same-sex couples each argue that the government should not act against a fundamental feature of their identity: faithfulness to the demands of the divine (as understood by the believer) for the former, and love and commitment to a life partner for the latter.

Moreover, both groups argue that their identity cannot be separated from their conduct so as to give government *carte blanche* to regulate their conduct. Courts have rejected a distinction between sexual orientation and marital conduct, finding that both the orientation and the conduct that follows from it are central to a person's identity.[99] Status and conduct are equally intertwined for the religious believer: "[B]elievers cannot fail to act on God's will, and it is no more reasonable for the state to demand that they do so than for the state to demand celibacy of all gays and lesbians. Both religious believers and same-sex couples feel compelled to act on those things constitutive of their identity."[100]

---

[97] Obergefell, 135 S. Ct. at 2602.

[98] The arguments following appear at greater length in, e.g., Masterpiece Amicus Brief, *supra* n.*, at 8–12; Douglas Laycock and Thomas C. Berg, Protecting Religious Liberty and Same-Sex Marriage, 99 Va. L. Rev. Online 1, 3–5 (2013), https://bit .ly/2vKimen; Thomas C. Berg, What Same-Sex Marriage and Religious Liberty Claims Have in Common, 5 Nw. J. L. & Soc. Pol'y 206, 212–26 (2010).

[99] See, e.g., Marriage Cases, 43 Cal. 4th at 841–42, 183 P.3d at 442–43; Kerrigan, 289 Conn. at 185–86, 957 A.2d at 438; Varnum, 763 N.W.2d at 885, 893.

[100] Laycock and Berg, *supra* note 98, at 4.

Both groups also claim the right to live their identities in public settings. Same-sex couples, once wrongly told to keep their relationships closeted, now have the right to participate in the institution of civil marriage. And because of public-accommodation laws, they rightly have full access to most goods and services in the marketplace, including wedding-related goods. But religious believers likewise have strong interests in being able to live according to their religious identity in their workplaces, where people "spend more of their waking hours than anywhere else except (possibly) their homes."[101] We can reconcile these two claims by recognizing religious exemptions for small businesses that conscientiously object to providing personalized goods and services directly to same-sex marriages (primarily through weddings) when other providers are readily available.

Masterpiece Cakeshop fits, at a general level, with this project of protecting both sides. The majority opinion sets the right tone, reaffirming the right of same-sex couples to dignity and equality and the right of objecting religious believers to tolerance and respect. The opinion presents each side's claims and perspectives in some detail. It emphasizes that "gay persons and gay couples cannot be treated as social outcasts or as inferior in dignity and worth" and that frequent refusals of service in the market would impose "a community-wide stigma."[102] As to Phillips's perspective, the opinion explains that because his cakes involved personal artistic design, "the customers' rights to goods and services became a demand for him to exercise the right of his own personal expression for their message, a message he could not express in a way consistent with his religious beliefs."[103] Although the opinion avoids deciding between these claims, the very act of presenting them can engender sympathy for the real human concerns on both sides. The opinion thus has a "performative" character by, in Joshua Matz's words, "seek[ing] to model a conception of civility that takes seriously the claims on both sides" given "our pluralistic society."[104]

---

[101] Eugene Volokh, Freedom of Speech and Workplace Harassment, 39 UCLA L. Rev. 1791, 1849 (1992).

[102] 138 S. Ct. at 1727.

[103] *Id.* at 1728.

[104] Joshua Matz, Fury and Despair over the Masterpiece Cakeshop Ruling Are Misplaced, The Guardian, June 6, 2018, https://bit.ly/2M5WhB1.

With that said, we should note that the above parallels between same-sex couples and religious objectors concern the strength of their interests and the depth of their predicament when faced with burdensome laws. The parallels lie in the fundamental feature of identity for both, the intertwining of that identity with conduct (marrying a partner, acting consistently with God's will), and the painfulness or impossibility of changing that identity or the conduct that necessarily flows from it. Both same-sex couples and religious believers also face hostility from others—the focus of the holdings in *Romer* and *Masterpiece*—but that is a distinct point from the strength of the interests that the couples and the believers have.[105]

There are advantages to focusing on how important these interests are to the persons affected by regulation—the same-sex couples, the religious objectors—and disadvantages to focusing on the hostility of the regulators. As already discussed in Part I.D., emphasizing the regulators' animus/hostility or the "utter failure" of the case for regulation runs the risk of perpetuating a cycle of accusations and counter-accusations. But the dynamic can be different if the court instead holds that even if the decisionmakers' motives are pure, and even if the regulation is rational, the case for applying the regulation is not strong enough to overcome the important interests of those whom the regulation harms. Focusing on the important interests of the regulated persons more closely resembles heightened scrutiny than "animus" analysis. Thus, the final part of this essay discusses heightened scrutiny as an alternative to "animus."

III. Beyond Animus/Hostility: Protecting Both Rights

Heightened scrutiny, based on either a suspect classification or a fundamental interest, avoids certain problems that an animus holding creates. The Court applying heightened scrutiny need not reach to condemn the asserted justifications for the regulation in question as irrational or an "utter failure"—it need only conclude they are

---

[105] Animus/hostility analysis can take some account of the seriousness of the effect on the disadvantaged person. In race-discrimination cases, "[t]he impact of the official action whether it 'bears more heavily on one race than another,' may provide an important starting point" in showing intent. Vill. of Arlington Heights v. Metro. Hous. Dev. Corp., 429 U.S. 252, 266 (1977) (quoting Washington v. Davis, 426 U.S. 229, 242 (1976)). But as a general matter, impact is only one among many factors contributing to finding animus or hostility, and the focus will be elsewhere.

not strong enough to meet the higher level of scrutiny. And heightened scrutiny rests on far more than a negative judgment about the regulators' prejudice or hostility. It also typically rests on factors that will more likely evoke positive sympathy for the affected persons. As such, heightened scrutiny may be better suited to counter our age of negative polarization.

A. Heightened Scrutiny of Sexual-Orientation Discrimination

Were the Court to declare that classifications based on sexual orientation trigger heightened (say, intermediate) scrutiny, that determination would rest on several factors. True, one criterion for calling the classifications suspect overlaps with an animus holding: that they "are so seldom relevant to the achievement of any legitimate state interest that [they] are deemed to reflect prejudice and antipathy."[106] But there are several other relevant criteria, including whether the class characteristic is "beyond the individual's control" and would be painful or impossible to change.[107] For example, before *Obergefell*, lower courts distilled and followed these factors in deciding whether excluding same-sex couples from civil marriage violated their equal-protection rights.[108]

State supreme courts, in addition to finding that gays and lesbians have been subject to "invidious discrimination" resting on "historical prejudice," have laid out the other reasons for intermediate scrutiny:

> The characteristic that defines the members of this group—
> attraction to persons of the same sex—bears no logical
> relationship to their ability to perform in society, either
> in familial relations or otherwise as productive citizens.
> Because sexual orientation is such an essential component
> of personhood, even if there is some possibility that a
> person's sexual preference can be altered, it would be wholly
> unacceptable for the state to require anyone to do so.[109]

[106] City of Cleburne v. Cleburne Living Center, 473 U.S. 432, 440 (1985).

[107] *Id.* at 441 (quotation omitted).

[108] See Varnum, 763 N.W.2d at 887–88 ("The Supreme Court has considered: (1) the history of invidious discrimination against the class burdened by the legislation; (2) whether the characteristics that distinguish the class indicate a typical class member's ability to contribute to society; (3) whether the distinguishing characteristic is "immutable" or beyond the class members' control; and (4) the political power of the subject class.").

[109] *Id.* at 895–96 (quoting Kerrigan, 957 A.2d at 432).

Much of the case for calling the classification suspect, then, rests on how essential the feature is to personhood, and how difficult or disorienting it would be for the person to try to change it or act inconsistently with it. These criteria support heightened scrutiny positively, by recognizing how gay and lesbian people are situated and the interests they have at stake, rather than negatively, by attributing animus or bigotry to the other side. The positive case is suited to generate understanding for the lives and claims of gay people, not merely anger at those who fail to show such understanding. That positive focus is less likely to perpetuate the polarizing cycle of condemnations and counter-condemnations.

The features justifying heightened scrutiny also overlap substantially with the commonalities or parallels between same-sex couples and religious conservatives. In addition to the existence of prejudice—against religious conservatives in some degree as well as against same-sex couples—there is the parallel of "an essential component of personhood,"[110] whether in committed intimate relationships or having a committed religious faith. There is also a parallel in the difficulty of changing such a core component of personhood—a difficulty that makes it "wholly unacceptable for the state to require" or pressure such change,[111] either significantly disfavoring same-sex relationships or significantly penalizing religious commitments, without very strong reasons.

B. Stronger Scrutiny for Free-Exercise Claims

To protect both sides, the Court could also solidify the protection of free exercise—resting it on something more than accusing decisionmakers of hostility or bias against religion. There are two ways forward.

1. Forbidding devaluing religion compared with secular analogues

First, the Court could adhere to the free-exercise test of "neutrality and general applicability" from *Employment Division v. Smith* and *Church of the Lukumi*,[112] but read it in a protective rather than nonprotective way. Some lower courts have confined unconstitutionality under the *Smith/Lukumi* test to cases in which the government

---

[110] *Id.* (quoting Kerrigan, 957 A.2d at 432).

[111] *Id.*

[112] See *supra* notes 60–61 and accompanying text.

targets or singles out religion (or a particular faith) or displays animus or hostility toward it.[113] But other courts have read the test more broadly. Under their approach, free exercise prevents the state not just from showing active "animus" toward religion, but also from "devaluing" it—that is, treating it as less important than analogous secular claims. These decisions hold that when the state recognizes even one or a few exceptions to a law for secular conduct, it must recognize an analogous religious exception. Without the exception, the law would burden religion in a way neither neutral nor generally applicable.

In the most prominent case invoking this principle, the U.S. Court of Appeals for the Third Circuit held that two Muslim police officers must be permitted to wear beards for religious reasons, despite a police department's no-beard policy, when other officers were permitted an exception for medical reasons.[114] The court held that the "department has made a value judgment that secular (i.e., medical) motivations for wearing a beard are important enough to overcome its general interest in uniformity but that religious motivations are not."[115] The policy had to survive strict scrutiny because it "devalued their religious reasons for wearing beards by judging them to be of lesser import than medical reasons."[116] Other courts have applied the same rationale in several other situations, including to protect Native Americans seeking to possess bird feathers when the law barring such possession already contained exemptions for taxidermists and others[117] and to protect Orthodox Jews building a synagogue when the zoning laws made an exception for "private clubs and lodges."[118] The cases applying this approach come from, at a minimum, four federal circuits, two federal district courts, and two state appellate courts.[119]

---

[113] See, e.g., Thomas v. Anchorage Equal Rights Comm'n, 165 F.3d 692, 701–02 (9th Cir. 1999), vacated on ripeness grounds, 220 F.2d 1134 (9th Cir. 2000) (en banc).

[114] Fraternal Order of Police v. City of Newark, 170 F.3d 359 (3d Cir. 1999) (Alito, J.).

[115] Id. at 366.

[116] Id. at 365.

[117] Horen v. Commonwealth, 479 S.E.2d 553 (Va. App. 1997).

[118] Midrash Sephardi v. Town of Surfside, 366 F.3d 1214, 1234–35 (11th Cir. 2004).

[119] See Douglas Laycock & Steven T. Collis, Generally Applicable Law and the Free Exercise of Religion, 95 Neb. L. Rev. 1, 19–23 (2016).

These decisions did not find full-fledged "hostility" toward religion, but simply a devaluation of its importance when compared with analogous secular interests that the government values. Those secular interests can be relatively few, or even just one, as in the medical exception for the no-beard policy.

The more protective approach best explains the Supreme Court's cases. True, the facts of *Lukumi* involved laws targeting and singling out a religion. The ordinances struck down there were manipulated to such a degree that they applied to "Santeria adherents but almost no others."[120] But that, the Court said, made the case unusual and extreme: The ordinances fell "well below the minimum standard necessary to protect First Amendment rights," and it was therefore unnecessary to "define with precision the standard used to evaluate whether a prohibition is of general application."[121] That is, targeting and animus were merely obvious instances of free-exercise violations; they did not exhaust the category. Moreover, the protective interpretation of *Smith* is the only one that can explain *Sherbert v. Verner*[122] and other decisions holding that religious minorities cannot be denied unemployment benefits when they refuse particular work for sincere religious reasons.[123] Those decisions protected religious reasons for refusing work, without any finding that the state had singled out religious reasons alone or was hostile to them. Rather, religious reasons had to be protected because state law already protected a few secular reasons for refusing work (but far from all secular reasons).[124]

This broader protection follows not just from precedent but from constitutional logic. Treating religious interests as less important than the analogous secular interests that are exempted is inconsistent with the status of religious exercise as a constitutional right. If free exercise protects only against "animus" directed uniquely at religion, it allows religion to be treated as badly as other interests the state regards as unimportant. But the Constitution's text deems

[120] 508 U.S. at 536.

[121] *Id.* at 543.

[122] 374 U.S. 398 (1963).

[123] See also Frazee v. Dept. of Employment Security, 489 U.S. 829 (1989); Hobbie v. Unemployment Appeals Comm., 480 U.S. 136 (1987); Thomas v. Review Bd., 450 U.S. 707 (1981).

[124] See Smith, 494 U.S. at 884 (explaining *Sherbert* on this basis).

religious exercise as an important interest, and free exercise should be treated as well as the state treats other interests that it values. When the government deems some private interests and activities sufficiently important to protect and others insufficiently important, religious exercise should be treated like the important interests, not the unimportant ones.

It would not be surprising if the Court, after experience with the *Smith* rule, decided explicitly to read the rule in a protective way rather than a wholly unprotective way. The Court has already announced an important limit on *Smith*'s reach: strong protection for religious organizations, even against generally applicable laws, when the organizations employ ministers and resolve "internal governance" issues.[125] Many thought that a constitutionally mandated exception for organizations' governance was inconsistent with *Smith*; the Court unanimously held otherwise.[126]

Masterpiece Cakeshop itself should come out the same way under either an "animus" or a "devaluing" standard. True, the Court found for Phillips on the basis of a single situation where analogous secular objections were protected (the other bakers' refusals of anti-gay cakes). But those cases made for evidence of animus toward his beliefs—not just devaluing of them—because those protected objections were squarely on the opposite side from Phillips on the divisive question of same-sex marriage. The commission targeted Phillips's belief for disfavor; it did not merely treat it as less than vitally important. But for other cases protecting religious minorities, it matters whether free-exercise protection is narrowly confined to targeting and hostility or extends further to prevent devaluing.

2. Overruling *Smith*

The more consequential step would be for the Court to overrule *Smith* and hold that laws substantially burdening religious exercise must satisfy heightened scrutiny even if they are neutral and generally applicable. This is not the place to review the voluminous claims (and responses to them) that *Smith* is in tension with the constitutional

---

[125] Hosanna-Tabor Evangelical Lutheran Church & School v. EEOC, 565 U.S. 171, 188 (2012).

[126] *Id.* at 190 (confining *Smith* to regulation "of only outward physical acts," versus as "internal church decision").

text,[127] the original understanding,[128] counter-majoritarian protection of unfamiliar or unpopular religious minorities,[129] or other criteria of constitutional interpretation.

As Professor Laycock and I argued in the amicus brief we filed in *Masterpiece Cakeshop*,[130] *Smith* can be reconsidered because it has not become embedded in the law; its rule about generally applicable laws has been interpreted only in *Lukumi* and now in *Masterpiece*, both of which would have come out the same way under either standard. *Smith* was not applied in *Hosanna-Tabor*, which stated a separate doctrine about internal church governance, nor was it applied in other major religious-exercise cases that were decided under federal religious-liberty legislation.[131]

Overturning *Smith* would shift the focus in free-exercise cases to the impact a law has on the important, constitutionally recognized interest in religious exercise. It would shift focus away from the question whether the relevant regulation was hostile—a focus that invites the cycle of charges and counter-charges of bigotry and intolerance. Turning focus away from a law's "general applicability" would also remove the element of "constitutional luck" in which a person's religious practice is protected only because the government happens to have protected someone else.[132]

---

[127] Cf. Stephanie H. Barclay & Mark L. Rienzi, Constitutional Anomalies or As-Applied Challenge? A Defense of Religious Exemptions, 59 B.C. L. Rev. 1595, 1608–31 (2018) (defending free-exercise exemption claims as "as applied" challenges), with Nicholas Quinn Rosenkrantz, The Subjects of the Constitution, 62 Stan. L. Rev. 1209, 1263–68 (2010) (arguing that the phrase "make no law prohibiting" excludes as-applied challenges).

[128] Cf. Michael W. McConnell, The Origins and Historical Understanding of Free Exercise of Religion, 103 Harv. L. Rev. 1409 (1990), with Philip A. Hamburger, A Constitutional Right of Religious Exemption: An historical perspective, 60 Geo. Wash. L. Rev. 915 (1992).

[129] See, e.g., Thomas C. Berg, Minority Religions and the Religion Clauses, 82 Wash. U.L.Q. 919, 964–72 (2004); Michael W. McConnell, Free Exercise Revisionism and the *Smith* Decision, 57 U. Chi. L. Rev. 1109, 1130–32 (1990).

[130] Masterpiece Amicus Brief, *supra* n.*, at 35.

[131] Holt v. Hobbs, 135 S. Ct 853 (2015) (Religious Land Use and Institutionalized Persons Act); Burwell v. Hobby Lobby, 134 S. Ct. 2751 (RFRA); Gonzales v. O Centro Espirita Beneficiente Uniao do Vegetal, 546 U.S. 418 (2006) (RFRA).

[132] Christopher C. Lund, A Matter of Constitutional Luck: The General Applicability Requirement in Constitutional Jurisprudence, 26 Harv. J. L. & Pub. Pol'y 627 (2003).

Heightened scrutiny would provide a means of protecting the essential interests of both same-sex couples and religious dissenters. As the next subsection briefly discusses, nondiscrimination rules in the commercial sphere usually serve important or even compelling interests and thus prevail even under heightened scrutiny. But in a few cases they do not. A rule of strict (or at least heightened) scrutiny takes account of the weight of the competing constitutional interests and thus would do justice more often than a rule like *Smith's*, which ignores those interests if the law in question is neutral and generally applicable.

When the Court decided *Smith*, it expressed confidence that the political branches would protect religious minorities.[133] But that confidence rested on the premise that American society "believes in the negative protection accorded to religious belief,"[134] a premise that is being undercut by today's intensifying polarization in which beliefs in and about religion lie at the heart of the divide. Polarized politicians and interest groups are increasingly unwilling to consider how to avoid imposing burdensome penalties on religious practice. Sometimes progressives have little regard for the effect of penalties on conservative believers; sometimes, as in the case of President Trump's travel ban,[135] conservatives have little regard for the effect of penalties on Muslims. Whether the majority in a jurisdiction minimizes the importance of religious practice to religious believers in general, or just to those in a particular faith, the result is that the majoritarian branches are insensitive to particular free-exercise claims. That's when the courts must play an important, although obviously not exclusive, role.

3. The scope of exemptions

Finally, it is worth emphasizing that broadened protection for religious objectors will by no means be absolute, especially in the commercial marketplace. While dodging all the ultimate issues, the

---

[133] Smith, 494 U.S. at 890 ("[A] society that believes in the negative protection accorded to religious belief can be expected to be solicitous of that value in its legislation as well. It is therefore not surprising that a number of States have made an exception to their drug laws for sacramental peyote use.").

[134] *Id.*

[135] Cf. Trump, 138 S. Ct. 2392 (upholding travel ban based on deference to executive's immigration power, despite president's clear statements of anti-Muslim animus).

Court in *Masterpiece Cakeshop* did say that "any decision in favor of the baker would have to be sufficiently constrained, lest all purveyors of goods and services who object to gay marriages for moral and religious reasons [be able to refuse], something that would impose a serious stigma on gay persons."[136] This is indeed right, for there are important interests in ensuring, first, that gay persons have access to goods and services and, second, that they not face repeated refusals.

As such, protections for religious objectors in commercial cases should be limited to those situations (primarily weddings) where the objector provides personal services directly to facilitate the marriage and other providers are readily available.[137] This principle covers the facts of *Masterpiece*, where the baker would provide cakes to same-sex couples for any other event besides a wedding,[138] and where close to 70 bakeries in the Denver metro area (including one a tenth of a mile from the Masterpiece Cakeshop store) listed themselves as serving same-sex weddings.[139] In cases involving religious nonprofits, protection should apply as long as clients, students, or employees have notice of the organization's religious character and its adherence to religious norms, as well as adequate alternatives.[140]

Such limited protection for religious objectors in the commercial sphere means that same-sex couples will very occasionally be referred elsewhere and feel insulted and demeaned. But some dignitary harms must be tolerated in order "to give adequate 'breathing space' to the freedoms protected by the First Amendment."[141]

---

[136] Masterpiece, 138 S. Ct. at 1728–29.

[137] My defense here of this scope of exemption is brief. For fuller defenses, see, e.g., Masterpiece Amicus Brief, *supra* n.*, at 29–34; Thomas C. Berg, Religious Exemptions and Third-Party Harms, 17 J. Fed. Soc'y 50, 53–56 (Oct. 2016), https://fedsoc.org/commentary/publications/religious-exemptions-and-third-party-harms); Thomas C. Berg, Religious Accommodation and the Welfare State, 38 Harv. J. L. & Gend. 103, 128–30, 137–39, 141–42 (2015).

[138] 138 S. Ct. at 1724.

[139] Brief of Law and Economics Scholars as Amici Curiae Supporting Petitioners, Masterpiece Cakeshop, Ltd. v. Colo. Civil Rights Comm'n, at 15–16, 138 S. Ct. 1719 (2018) (No. 16-111).

[140] For more detailed discussion, see Thomas C. Berg, Partly Acculturated Religion: A Case for Accommodating Religious Nonprofits, 91 Notre Dame L. Rev. 1341, 1369–73 (2016).

[141] Hustler Magazine, Inc. v. Falwell, 485 U.S. 46, 56 (1988).

Although *Masterpiece Cakeshop* correctly expresses concern for the dignity of same-sex couples, it should not be read to say that such referrals elsewhere are never protected. Without such an exemption, conscientious objectors like Jack Phillips must permanently surrender either their conscience or their livelihood. That permanent harm outweighs the real but short-term dignitary harm to same-sex couples. A narrow exception to gay-rights laws, in a religiously significant context of intense importance to conscientious objectors, holds the best hope of protecting both sides.

Conclusion

Courts were correct to protect same-sex couples in *Romer* and subsequent cases, and they are also right to protect religious objectors to same-sex marriage in defined circumstances. *Masterpiece Cakeshop* starts that project, which may expand just as gay-rights holdings expanded after *Romer*. It seems doubtful, however, that condemning the regulators' "animus" or "hostility" provides the best ground for protecting both sides, since it may simply increase negative polarization. We should give more weight to doctrines, like heightened scrutiny, that directly portray the important interests of the regulated parties—same-sex couples and religious believers—and directly encourage sympathy for their predicaments.

To Speak or Not to Speak, That Is Your Right: *Janus v. AFSCME*

*David F. Forte**

Some Supreme Court precedents go through extensive death spasms before being interred. *Lochner v. New York,*[1] *Plessy v. Ferguson,*[2] and *Austin v. Michigan Chamber of Commerce*[3] come to mind.[4] Others like *Chisholm v. Georgia*[5] and *Minersville School District v. Gobitis*[6] incurred a swift and summary execution. Still others, overtaken by subsequent cases, remain wraith-like presences among the Court's past acts: *Beauharnais v. Illinois*[7] and *Buck v. Bell*[8], for example, remain "on the books."

I. *Abood*

Abood v. Detroit Board of Education[9] falls into the first category. Over what turned out to be a prescient objection by Justice Lewis Powell—"Collective bargaining in the public sector is 'political' in any meaningful sense of the word"[10]—the majority in *Abood* held

---

* Professor of law, Cleveland State University.

[1] 198 U.S. 45 (1905), effectively overturned by West Coast Hotel v. Parrish, 300 U.S. 379 (1937).

[2] 163 U.S. 537 (1896), effectively, though not explicitly, overruled by Brown v. Board of Education, 347 US 483 (1954).

[3] 494 U.S. 652 (1990), overruled, Citizens United v. FEC, 558 U.S. 310 (2010).

[4] One might say that, with the Civil War, the death spasms of *Dred Scott v. Sandford*, 60 U.S. 393 (1857), were quite literal. The case was superseded by U.S. Const. amend. XIII (1866) and amend. XIV (1868).

[5] 2 U.S. 419 (1793), superseded, U.S. Const. amend. XI (1795).

[6] 310 U.S. 586 (1940), overruled, West Virginia State Bd. of Educ. v. Barnette, 319 U.S. 624 (1943).

[7] 343 U.S. 250 (1952).

[8] 274 U.S. 200 (1927).

[9] 431 U.S. 209 (1977).

[10] *Id.* at 257 (Powell, J., concurring).

that a union of public employees is no different from a union of private employees in its right to collect "agency fees" from nonunion members of the bargaining unit that the union represents. Acting as an "agent" of the nonunionized workers, the union could justifiably collect fees for the collective bargaining and dispute resolution services it provided to the nonunion employees.

Abood was originally seen as an advance in First Amendment freedoms. First Amendment casebooks seemed to categorize the case in that way.[11] The Court held that public employees could not have their union dues or nonunion agency fees used for political or ideological purposes. Thus, union assessments on workers fell into two categories: chargeable fees for services that the union provides, and nonchargeable fees subsidizing a union's political activities, such as some forms of lobbying or electioneering (to the extent constitutionally permitted).

Janus v. American Federation of State, County, and Municipal Employees[12] put an end to *Abood* and its distinction between a union's collective bargaining with a public employer and a union's political activity. Justice Powell's common-sense observation that everything that a union and a public employer agree upon is a political decision became the basis for the holding. Following recent Supreme Court First Amendment doctrine, the decision is based on the notion, as in *Citizens United v. FEC*,[13] that money talks and the Constitution protects that kind of talk. Along with *National Institute of Family and Life Advocates v. Becarra*, decided this term, *Janus* continues to cast protections around citizens who object to being compelled by state action to speak out against their beliefs. *Masterpiece Cakeshop v. Colorado Civil Rights Commission*, also decided this term, sidestepped the issue in favor of deciding the case on religious discrimination grounds, but *Janus* will certainly have salience when that issue returns to the courts. Money as speech, public-union contracts as political decisions, and the prohibition on compelled speech are the three legs on which *Janus* stands.

---

[11] See, e.g., Kathleen M. Sullivan & Noah Feldman, First Amendment Law 494–95 (6th ed. 2016).

[12] 138 S. Ct. 2448 (2018).

[13] 558 U.S. 310 (2010).

II. *Abood's* Confused Legacy

To the majority in *Janus, Abood's* legacy was wasteful and ambiguous. To the dissent, *Abood* was an "embedded" precedent upon which much law had been built. Following the *Abood* decision, the issues that bedeviled the courts included (1) whether public-sector unions had to ask permission from their members to spend a percentage of their dues on political activities, or whether it was up to the worker to find out the percentage so spent and ask for a refund or for it not to be withheld; and (2) how to determine the line between chargeable and nonchargeable expenses for calculating the agency fee for nonunion workers.

For example, in *Lehnert v. Ferris Faculty Association*,[14] the Court had to weave through a number of disputed charges on nonunion workers and decide on which side of the line the following charges fell: activities of the union's state and national affiliates, outside litigation, public relations expenditures, and expenses for carrying on an illegal strike. In *Ellis v. Brotherhood of Railway Employees*,[15] the Court confronted differentiating expenses related to conventions, social activities, litigation, organizing, publishing, and death benefits. In *Locke v. Karass*,[16] the Court approved a fee to nonunion members for the cost of litigation undertaken by the national union. In *Chicago Teachers Union, Local No. 1 v. Hudson*,[17] the Supreme Court disapproved the idea of rebates for improper assessments, because the funds taken from the nonunion workers had already been improperly utilized. In that case, the Court did require unions to provide sufficient notice to union and nonunion members for assessments that were earmarked for political purposes. But the Court failed to address the "opt out" problem, which still left the onus on the worker to initiate his claim not to have a portion of his fees taken. In response, the state of Washington required a union to gain prior permission from nonunion members before assessing any fees for political purposes, a law that the Supreme Court ultimately upheld.[18]

---

[14] 500 U.S. 507 (1991).

[15] 466 U.S. 435 (1984).

[16] 555 U.S. 207 (2009).

[17] 475 U.S. 292 (1986).

[18] Davenport v. Washington Educ. Ass'n, 551 U.S. 177 (2007).

The Supreme Court's taxonomical quest was just the tip of the iceberg. There were hundreds of lower court decisions attempting to parse out *Abood*'s imprecise formula, and the Court considered some when it finally questioned the basis of *Abood*. In particular, the Court recognized the nearly insurmountable obstacles facing a nonunion worker who sought a refund of his improperly charged agency fees.[19]

III. The Ticking Clock

By 2012, the Court began signaling that *Abood*'s characterization of agency fees as collective bargaining service payments was mistaken. In *Knox v. SIEU, Local 1000*,[20] Justice Samuel Alito declared for the Court, "Because a public-sector union takes many positions during collective bargaining that have powerful political and civic consequences, the compulsory fees constitute a form of compelled speech and association that imposes a 'significant impingement on First Amendment rights.'"[21] Two years later, in *Harris v. Quinn*,[22] the Court declared that persons who were not "full-fledged employees" of the state could not be assessed union imposed fees simply because they worked in a state-run program. In his opinion for the Court, Alito engaged in an extended critique of *Abood*, declaring that it paid insufficient attention to First Amendment concerns in the imposition of agency fees. He also expounded on the long list of cases attempting to deal with the chargeable/nonchargeable distinction and described the heavy burden on nonunion employees who sought to obtain their right not to contribute to causes they did not believe in.

But for the death of Justice Antonin Scalia, it is virtually certain that *Abood* would have fallen in 2016 in *Friedrichs v. California*

---

[19] See Jibson v. Michigan Ed. Assn.-NEA, 30 F.3d 723 (6th Cir. 1994); Price v. Int'l Union, United Auto, Aerospace & Agricultural Implement Workers of Am., 927 F.2d 88 (2d Cir. 1991); Andrews v. Educ. Assn. of Cheshire, 829 F.2d 335 (2d Cir. 1987); Am. Fed. of TV & Recording Artists, Portland Local, 327 N.L.R.B. 474 (1999); Calif. Knife & Saw Works, 320 N.L.R.B. 224 (1995), all of which were cited by the Supreme Court in its attack on *Abood* in *Harris v. Quinn*, 134 S.Ct. 2618, 2636–38 (2014).

[20] 567 U.S. 298 (2012).

[21] *Id.* at 310–11 (citing Ellis v. Brotherhood of Ry. Emp., 466 U.S. 435, 455 (1984)) (holding that a union could not unilaterally increase fees for political purposes without notice to the employee).

[22] 134 S. Ct. 2618 (2014).

Teachers Association.[23] In that case, public school teachers who had resigned their union membership protested paying *any* fees, citing their free-speech and associational rights under the First Amendment. Their complaint was dismissed at the district court level, a decision the U.S. Court of Appeals for the Ninth Circuit summarily affirmed.[24] At oral argument before the Supreme Court, most observers noted Scalia's hostile tone and expected a decision against *Abood.* With his passing, however, an evenly divided Court affirmed the Ninth Circuit per curiam. When Neil Gorsuch joined the Court in April 2017, Alito was at last able to drop the other shoe. With the predicted 5-4 vote in *Janus*, the Supreme Court overruled *Abood.*

IV. Employment Speech or Political Speech?

The central question separating the Court and the dissenters in *Janus* was whether compulsory agency fees constituted speech about the conditions of the workplace or instead was political speech dealing with public issues. Justice Elena Kagan's dissent centered on the *Pickering* test. She argued that because the speech in question was employment related, it did not matter if it also had political content. Thus, it was not a question of whether these fees were speech at all: The dissent did not contest the claim that personal financial expenditure can constitute political speech, and it accepted *Abood's* rule that nonunion employees could not be compelled to contribute to political causes. Instead, Kagan simply emphasized throughout that the speech was workplace related.

The *Pickering* test, as developed in *Pickering v. Board of Education*,[25] *Connick v. Myers*,[26] and *Garcetti v. Cebellos*,[27] holds that an employee's private speech about a matter of public concern is protected by the First Amendment unless the speech causes harm to the efficiency or harmonious operation of the workplace. However, if the employer has a reasonable belief that the speech will cause disruption, even

[23] 136 S. Ct. 1083 (2016).

[24] Friedrichs v. Cal. Teachers Ass'n, No. SACV 13-676-JLS (CWx), 2013 U.S. Dist. LEXIS 188995 (C.D. Cal. Dec. 5, 2013); aff'd 2014 U.S. App. LEXIS 24935 (9th Cir. Cal., Nov. 18, 2014).

[25] 391 U.S. 563 (1968).

[26] 461 U.S. 138 (1983).

[27] 547 U.S. 410 (2006).

if the speech concerns a matter of public concern, the employee has no First Amendment protection. Kagan's argument was straightforward. Because unions are legally bound to represent the interests of all members of the bargaining unit, the employer may wish to agree to agency fees for the sake of harmony in the workplace. Removing compulsory agency fees threatens the network of relations built up between employer and union to the detriment of a smoothly functioning governmental enterprise.

Kagan cited *Abood*'s view that permitting compulsory agency fees would alleviate the possibility of "inter-union conflict," for the *Abood* Court had feared that without compulsory union fees, workers might split into rival unions. But for the *Janus* majority, the idea that agency fees were necessary to avoid workplace disruption was chimerical. As Alito countered, no such disruption had ever occurred, either at the time of *Abood* or after.

Justice Alito used the example of the federal postal union. Under federal law, "a union chosen by majority vote is designated as the exclusive representative of all the employees."[28] Yet no agency fees are allowed under federal law. How then is harmony disrupted?, the majority asked. Twenty-eight states forbid agency fees. This is not a question of "inter-union conflict,"[29] as the dissent put it, for nobody disputes that a public employer can agree to a union's exclusive representation of the workers.

Kagan then tried another line. She offered examples of employee disruption that might happen under the majority's holding. "Suppose a government entity disciplines a group of (non-unionized) employees for agitating for a better health plan at inopportune times and places."[30] Would they claim that they were engaging in protected political speech? Or, "suppose a public employer penalizes a group of (non-unionized) teachers who protest merit pay in the school cafeteria." But the dissent undercut the force of the example by positing the disruptive circumstances of the protest itself. Alito easily disposed of the objections: A letter written by an employee to management asking for increased merit pay could hardly be seen to cause harm to the workplace, but a demonstration in the workplace could. He pointed

[28] Janus v. AFSCME 138 S. Ct. 2448, 2466 (2018).

[29] *Id.* at 2489.

[30] *Id.* at 2496 (Kagan, J., dissenting).

out that the facts of each case could show that the manner of protest would be disruptive, and hence the "political" nature of the protest would be outbalanced by the needs of the workplace.[31] Compulsory agency fees do not prevent workers from being impolite.

Kagan's main argument was that the speech in question did not reach even the first step of the *Pickering* analysis: namely, that agency fees were about supporting the union's position on working conditions, and not about matters of general public concern. "[E]veryone knows the difference between politicking and collective bargaining,"[32] she wrote, so there was nothing to balance. For the majority, however, collective bargaining with a public employer *is* politicking, and there is no way to lever them apart. It is a question of scale. When an individual asks for a raise, that is a matter of private concern. But when a public-sector union of thousands of employees asks for raises for its members, the effect on public policy can be enormous. And that only increases when, for example, teachers unions bargain over tenure, teacher assignments, descriptions of duties, and administrative arrangements.

Alito's contrast between an individual and thousands of workers asking for a raise would have left him with a problem had he ended his analysis there, for it made the political nature of the speech dependent on its quantitative impact. In fact, he quotes his own majority opinion in *Harris* to that effect: "[I]t is impossible to argue that the level of . . . state spending for employee benefits . . . is not a matter of great concern.'"[33] A quantitative test on whether a union's activity affects public policy would require the courts to decide on a case-by-case basis whether the First Amendment applied or not.

On the other hand, later, Justice Alito made the more qualitative argument that public worker employment arrangements are by nature political. Where Kagan declared tautologically, "[a]rguing about the terms of employment is still arguing about the terms of employment,"[34] Alito noted that unions negotiate and "express

[31] *Id.* at 2477 (majority op.).

[32] *Id.* at 2498 (Kagan, J., dissenting).

[33] *Id.* at 2475 (majority op.) (citing Harris, *supra* note 22).

[34] *Id.* at 2497 (Kagan, J., dissenting). Perhaps Kagan was retaliating for Chief Justice John Roberts' famous trope, "The way to stop discrimination on the basis of race is to stop discriminating on the basis of race." Parents Involved in Community Schools v. Seattle School Dist. No. 1, 551 U.S. 701, 748 (2007).

opinions" over far wider issues, such as minority rights, school assignments for children, affirmative action, evolution, healthcare, and educational policy. These are, of their nature, central concerns of the polity, not just the workplace. This kind of qualitative definition of political action would cover all public-union activities, without the need to measure the extent of the impact in any particular instance.

In this debate, Justice Alito clearly has the more accurate perception of what happens in public-union negotiations. "When a large number of employees speak through their union, the category of speech that is of public concern is greatly enlarged, and the category of speech that is of only private concern is substantially shrunk. By disputing this, the dissent denies the obvious." From their own experience, most Americans would likely agree.

V. *Stare Decisis*

It seems that whenever the Court moves in a different direction—no matter what the direction—the dissenters call out, *"stare decisis"*! And so, the *stare decisis* dance begins. The dissenters list the criteria for maintaining a precedent and argue that the majority has violated the criteria. The majority says that it has not really changed the law—it merely reinterpreted the issue (see, for example, the *Casey* plurality's handling of *Roe v. Wade*, and Scalia's response[35])—or that the criteria for maintaining the precedent no longer exist.

Justice Kagan vigorously defended the continuing validity of *Abood* on the ground of *stare decisis*. Even if a decision is wrong, she intoned, it does not justify jettisoning it if the norms of *stare decisis* call for its retention. Above all, she concluded, the reliance factor compels adhering to *Abood*: It has stood for 40 years. Not only courts, but legislatures and private and public actors had all channeled their conduct in light of its principles. The Court "wreaks havoc" on these "entrenched" arrangements.

Overruling *Abood*, Kagan continued, will disrupt many states' complex and interrelated labor law legislative schemes. Thousands of contracts with agency fee provisions will be changed (perhaps she could have rhetorically used the word "impaired") and will have to be renegotiated in a legislative atmosphere of real uncertainty.

---

[35] Compare Planned Parenthood v. Casey, 505 U.S. 833, 853, 861, 871 (plurality), with *id.* at 882–84 (Scalia, J., dissenting) (1992).

Moreover, *Janus* affects contracts in key state service sectors such as police, health, and safety. Were Kagan an originalist, or even a judicial traditionalist, she could have bolstered her arguments with the Framers' understanding of the independent role of the states in social legislation, or the fact that these state-bound contracts were essentially local and not national in character. One suspects that Chief Justice William Rehnquist might have taken that line of argument.

Alito's response was methodical, but dismissive. Where Kagan cited numerous ways the Court had previously championed the importance and necessity of *stare decisis*, Alito retorted with quotes attesting to its disposability. Precedents can be overcome if there are "strong reasons for doing so," he wrote. "The doctrine 'is at its weakest when we interpret the Constitution.'" And it has "least force of all to decisions that wrongly denied First Amendment rights."[36]

Alito then listed the factors that permitted an overruling and found them easily applicable to *Abood*: its reasoning was poor, the rule it created was unworkable, it was inconsistent with decisions in the allied field, and subsequent developments had made it irrelevant. Alito saved for last the factor that Kagan had most relied upon: reliance.

In the most detailed part of his analysis, Alito critiqued *Abood*'s reasoning, focusing on the manner in which *Abood* wrongly read two precedents that it had relied upon.[37] *Abood* used deferential scrutiny in a case replete with admitted free-speech interests, and consequently, it did not accurately evaluate the strength (or weakness) of the government's interests in allowing compulsory agency fees. The Court in *Abood* presumed but did not investigate whether agency fees did in fact contribute to labor peace. Nor did it recognize the differences in the effect that agency fees in the private sector had compared to the public sector. It thus failed to acknowledge how collective bargaining in the public sector had political ends. Lastly, it was blind to the administrative problems that would arise in distinguishing between chargeable and nonchargeable expenditures.

[36] Janus, 138 S. Ct. at 2476.

[37] The precedents were *R.R. Employees v. Hanson*, 351 U.S. 225 (1956), and *Machinists v. Street*, 367 U.S. 740 (1961).

Moreover, the rule announced in *Abood* was unworkable, Alito averred. He did not repeat the extensive history of line-drawing difficulties that he had made in *Harris v. Quinn*, satisfying himself with a brief summary. But he did emphasize the difficulties that non-union members would face in having their claims for their agency fees determined and adjudicated.

Subsequent developments had eroded the credibility of the *Abood* decision, he continued, stating again that exclusive representation was not tied to the institution of agency fees, and hence, labor peace was not threatened. *Abood* was dated. It was decided just when public-sector unions were beginning to expand and few saw how they would drive state expenditures.

Abood was also inconsistent with Court precedents dealing with political action by government employees. While the Court has protected government workers from being forced to support a particular political party, *Abood* permits the forced subsidy of political action (i.e., collective bargaining with governmental agencies) by the same governmental employees. Finally, Alito turned to reliance interests.

Here his position was far less potent, which, of course, is why he put the stronger arguments first. He dismissed the effect that overruling would have on extant union contracts containing agency fees. They were of short duration, and anyway, such contracts usually severed provisions dealing with agency fees. He tried a distracting rhetorical flourish: "[I]t would be unconscionable to permit free speech rights to be abridged in perpetuity in order to preserve contract provisions that will expire on their own in a few years' time."[38] Besides, he said problematically, unions were on notice since 2012 that the Court had doubts about *Abood*.

Kagan pounced. She proclaimed the Court's arguments on *stare decisis* "the worst part" of the opinion. The majority, ignoring 40 years of settled law, embedded *dicta* into two previous cases (*Knox* and *Harris*), ready to be used for the final *coup de grace*. "Relying on them is bootstrapping—and mocking *stare decisis*. Don't like a decision? Just throw some gratuitous criticisms into a couple of opinions and a few years later point to them as 'special justifications.'"[39]

[38] Janus, 138 S. Ct. at 2485.

[39] *Id.* at 2499 (Kagan, J., dissenting).

There is a predictable irony in the battle over *stare decisis*. Beginning in the late 1930s, the Supreme Court overturned decades of precedents protecting contractual and other economic liberties. In the 1960s and 1970s, the Court jettisoned precedents in many other areas, such as criminal procedure, apportionment, and social traditions. In those cases, many justices in the minority bemoaned the loss of respect for *stare decisis*. In recent years, however, where there is a reversal of some of those judicial decisions, or when the present Court strikes out in a new direction, the new minority grieves over the loss of "long-standing precedent," most of which were born in those previously activist decades. Nor is the idea of salting opinions with *dicta* for later use new. Justice William Brennan famously used the technique.[40] And so, the *stare decisis* dance continues.

VI. Compelled Speech

We now return to the core arguments of the Court: money as speech, public-union contracts as political decisions, and the prohibition on compelled speech. The dissent did not contest that money can be expression for First Amendment purposes, nor could it. Whatever restrictions have been permitted by campaign finance laws or judicial decisions since the time of *Buckley v. Valeo*,[41] the Supreme Court has made clear that money is not only a means of expression, it is an indispensible element of political expression:

> A restriction on the amount of money a person or group can spend on political communication during a campaign necessarily reduces the quantity of expression by restricting the number of issues discussed, the depth of their exploration, and the size of the audience reached. This is because virtually every means of communicating ideas in today's mass society requires the expenditure of money.[42]

[40] In *Eisenstadt v. Baird*, Brennan issued the following *dictum*, knowing that *Roe v. Wade* was soon to be decided: "If the right of privacy means anything, it is the right of the individual, married or single, to be free from unwarranted governmental intrusion into matters so fundamentally affecting a person as the decision whether to bear or beget a child." 405 U.S. 438, 453 (1972).

[41] 424 U.S. 1 (1976).

[42] *Id.* at 19.

The second element that the majority needed to show was that collective bargaining issues in the public sector were ineluctably political. To do so, the majority had to demonstrate that the development of public-sector unions had made their actions essentially political in contrast to private-sector unions. Without recent history to back it up, the majority may have had a more difficult time freeing itself from the grasp of *Abood*. And that is why the majority's reliance on recent history left an opening for the dissent to claim that the Court was making up new law in defiance of *stare decisis*.

There is no doubt that public-sector unionization has had a major effect on the direction of public policy, particularly in education. In 1972, when *Abood* was decided, public-sector unionization had only begun its growth following the passage of collective bargaining statutes by most states. Wisconsin had been the first in 1959. By 2017, unionization was 34.4 percent public-sector workers, five times greater than in the private sector, in which only 6.5 percent were members of unions. States with a high percentage of public-sector workers, such as California (53 percent), New York (70 percent), and Illinois (52 percent), had granted them significant benefits, including pensions, creating economic stress that has had major effects on their state budgets in other areas.[43]

In *Janus*, Justice Alito noted that the "ascendance of public-sector unions has been marked by a parallel increase in public spending." In constant 2017 dollars, state and local government spending had risen from $4,000 per capita in 1970 to $10,238 per capita in 2014. He brought up Illinois' embarrassing underfunded pension obligations, spoke of "multiple municipal bankruptcies," and concluded that today, collective-bargaining issues have a high degree of "political valence."[44]

One might ask whether this constitutional doctrine is dependent on political and economic conditions that might vary from time to time? If public-sector unions' influence on public spending drastically contracted, would the unions still be barred by the Constitution from obtaining agency fees, even though their "political valence" had become marginal? Is there an argument that even today, some

[43] See Daniel DiSalvo, The Trouble with Public Sector Unions, 5 Nat'l Aff. 3 (Fall 2010).

[44] Janus, 138 S. Ct. at 2483.

small public-sector unions do not have enough public-policy clout to be called political rather than economic actors? Are large teachers unions "in" but small parking enforcement unions "out" of constitutional limitations here? Alito did distinguish between an individual's complaint regarding pay, which would not rise to a matter of public interest under *Pickering,* and the same complaint by a union of many thousands. But where to draw the line? If *Abood* had problems in line-drawing, *Janus* may not be any better.

Elsewhere in his opinion, as noted above, Alito pointed to the other kinds of social and political issues that unions have become engaged with, issues that might stir the disagreement or even ire of many workers. They include issues such as climate change, the civil war, sexual orientation, and sexual identity. These are by nature political issues, where the size of the union matters not. If a union tries to argue that no agency fees are assessed for such position taking, the question reduces again to *Abood's* unenforceable chargeable/ nonchargeable distinction.

On either count, then, Justice Alito is justifiably confident that the new doctrine of union public speech will stand. Either the union affects policies by its economic demands or, on noneconomic issues, it is impossible to make an accurate division between appropriate chargeable fees and nonchargeable fees.

On the third prong, compelled speech, the Court's argument is strongly persuasive. But it depends on the dissent's reliance on *Pickering* not being applicable, for under *Pickering,* not only may employee speech be silenced or punished if it is disruptive to the workplace—no matter what its "public" content—an employee may legitimately be compelled to speak in putting forth the policy of the government entity. But once Alito disposes of the *Pickering* objection, the result cannot be gainsaid: state action that compels a person to speak against his beliefs is patently contrary to the notion of a republican government based on the consent of free individuals.

The facts of this case illustrate the majority's position clearly. Illinois law permitted agency fee deductions from a worker's pay without any form of consent. By doing so, the state violated the worker's First Amendment rights, Alito emphatically declares, "unless the employee affirmatively consents to pay. By agreeing to pay, nonmembers are waiving their First Amendment rights, and such a waiver cannot be presumed."[45]

In a tight argument, Alito calls on a run of precedents including, among others, *Wooley v. Maynard* ("freedom of speech 'includes both the right to speak and the right to refrain from speaking at all'").[46] He quotes the famous pronouncement of Justice Robert Jackson in *West Virginia v. Barnette*: "If there is any fixed star in our constitutional constellation, it is that no official, high or petty, can prescribe what shall be orthodox in politics, nationalism, religion, or other matters of opinion or force citizens to confess by word or act their faith therein."[47]

Recall how pernicious forced affirmation can be. In 1860, Abraham Lincoln, speaking to the people of New Haven, described those positions of the North that alone would satisfy the South of the North's good faith: "[W]hat will convince them? This, and this only; cease to call slavery wrong, and join them in calling it right. And this must be done thoroughly—done in acts as well as in words. Silence will not be tolerated—we must place ourselves avowedly with them."[48]

In the most eloquent portion of his opinion, Justice Alito expressed the centrality of freedom of speech to the "search for truth" and "to our democratic form of government." If state action compels people "to voice ideas with which they disagree, it undermines these very ends." He warms to a point that will have salience when the next *Masterpiece Cakeshop* dispute reaches the Court: "When speech is compelled, however, additional damage is done. In that situation, individuals are coerced into betraying their convictions."[49]

In the face of Alito's extensive arguments, Kagan's only objection to the compelled speech doctrine was the tepid observation that it had not been often used by the Supreme Court. It is certain that the compelled speech doctrine has a future.

---

[45] *Id.* at 2486.

[46] *Id.* at 2463 (citing Wooley v. Maynard, 430 U.S. 705, 714 (1977)).

[47] *Id.* (citing West Virginia Bd. of Educ. v. Barnette, 319 U.S. 624, 642 (1943)).

[48] Abraham Lincoln, Speech at New Haven, Mar. 6, 1860, http://www.historyplace.com/lincoln/haven.htm.

[49] Janus, 138 S. Ct. at 2464.

VII. Level of Scrutiny

Having established that collective bargaining in the public sector is a form of political speech and hence is covered by the First Amendment, one might expect that the Court would apply a strict scrutiny test to the government's attempt to limit that speech by the device of compulsory agency fees. But Justice Alito takes a different route. In the preview cases to *Janus* (*Knox* and *Harris*), Alito speculated on the appropriate test that should be used. In *Knox,* he noted that the Court had previously voided a federal compulsory contribution requirement for marketing mushrooms that had been levied on a mushroom farmer and that such schemes should be subject to "exacting First Amendment scrutiny."[50] This was different both from strict scrutiny and from the traditional *Central Hudson* intermediate scrutiny test for commercial speech.

The formal strict scrutiny test demands that, for a statute that infringes on a protected fundamental right to pass muster, the government must demonstrate that the end sought to be achieved is "compelling," and that the means are "narrowly tailored" to achieve that end (a recent and somewhat more relaxed means/ends standard than the previous "least burdensome alternatives" test). In contrast, as set by the Court in *Central Hudson Gas & Electric Corp. v. Public Service Commission* (the "*Central Hudson*" test), governmental restrictions on commercial speech are tested by a form of intermediate scrutiny:

> At the outset, we must determine whether the expression is protected by the First Amendment. For commercial speech to come within that provision it at least must concern lawful activity and not be misleading. Next, we ask whether the asserted governmental interest is substantial. If both inquiries yield positive answers, we must determine whether the regulation directly advances the governmental interest asserted, and whether it is not more extensive than is necessary to serve that interest.[51]

As restated in *Janus,* the new *Knox* formulation would be an amalgam of strict and intermediate scrutiny. The compelled agency fee must "serve a compelling state interest that cannot be achieved through means significantly less restrictive of associational freedoms."[52]

[50] 567 U.S. 298, 310 (citing United States v. United Foods, Inc., 533 U.S. 405 (2001)).

[51] 447 U.S. 557, 566 (1980).

[52] Janus, 138 S. Ct. at 2465.

By ginning up the (formerly) intermediate scrutiny test closer to strict scrutiny, Alito paralleled Justice Ruth Bader Ginsburg's enhancement of the intermediate test on issues of sex discrimination: "Parties who seek to defend gender-based government action must demonstrate an 'exceedingly persuasive justification' for that action,"[53] though Alito increased the ends component of the test he was using while Ginsburg strengthened the means component.

Previously in *Harris*, Alito had inserted a doubt whether even a strengthened intermediate scrutiny test was appropriate. After all, if agency fee "expression" is, in its nature, political speech, then only strict scrutiny would suffice. Yet, despite the unquestionable grounding of the decision on the premise that public union collective bargaining *is* political action, Alito did not take that final step in *Janus* and call for strict scrutiny. The Court finds "it unnecessary to decide the issue of strict scrutiny because the Illinois scheme cannot survive even under the more permissive standard applied in *Knox* and *Harris*."[54]

Perhaps, Alito (along with the other four justices in the majority) was considering that collective bargaining in the public sector is both commercial and political and that it does not fit into either category entirely. If so, we should likely expect that the "*Janus* test" will be yet another arcane intermediate scrutiny test that will take its place in First Amendment jurisprudence along with Time, Place, and Manner,[55] the *O'Brien* test,[56] and the *Central Hudson* test.

VIII. Due Process

As noted, Justice Alito found *Abood* wanting on every asserted ground. It was "poorly reasoned" and "inconsistent with other First Amendment cases," there have been new developments since *Abood*

---

[53] United States v. Virginia, 518 U.S. 515, 531 (1996).

[54] Janus, 138 S. Ct. at 2465.

[55] Restrictions on speech are constitutional if (1) they are content neutral (2) they are narrowly tailored to serve a governmental interest; and (3) they leave open ample alternative means of expression. See Cox v. New Hampshire, 312 U.S. 569 (1941).

[56] Where expression has both verbal and nonverbal elements, the regulation at issue must (1) be within the constitutional power of the government to enact, (2) further an important or substantial government interest, (3) ensure that interest is unrelated to the suppression of speech, and (4) prohibit no more speech than is essential to further that interest. United States v. O'Brien, 391 U.S. 367, 377 (1968).

was issued, and there were insufficient justifications for maintaining the holding on the grounds of *stare decisis*.

But throughout the opinion, Alito takes pains to emphasize the essential arbitrariness in distinguishing between chargeable and unchargeable fees, as well as the lack of effective notice to nonunion members as to what fees are being deducted and the justifications for their deductions. In sum, without saying it in so many words, Alito found that compulsory agency fees violate due process.

As long tradition, precedents, and academic discourse have revealed, "procedural" due process has two prongs: to be legally valid, (1) a governmental action must accord with the "Law of the Land,"[57] and 2) its enforcement must comport with fair judicial procedures.[58] The first prong has expanded into the "Principle of Legality". Laws that cannot be understood are void for vagueness. Laws that lack any rational connection between means and ends are "arbitrary" and invalid. Laws that lack any public purpose and are instituted merely to advance one group's interest over another's (taking from A and giving to B) are also void. And, of course, laws or governmental actions that do not come from a legitimate lawgiver lack authority (Law of the Land).[59]

---

[57] The Law of the Land is often, though not incontestably, associated with the Magna Carta. "No free man shall be seized or imprisoned, or stripped of his rights or possessions, or outlawed or exiled, or deprived of his standing in any way, nor will we proceed with force against him, or send others to do so, except by the lawful judgment of his equals or by the law of the land." Magna Carta, § 39 (1215).

[58] The scholarly consensus is that its source is the Statute of Edward III, which declared, "That no Man of what Estate or Condition that he be, shall be put out of Land or Tenement, nor taken, nor imprisoned, nor disinherited, nor put to Death, without being brought in Answer by due Process of the Law." Statute of 1354 (Edw. III). Another opinion holds that the principle of fair judicial process can be found, or is at least prefigured, in Section 39 of the Magna Carta or in Section 40: "To no one will we sell, to no one deny or delay right or justice."

[59] The provenance of the principle of legality reaches back to many sources including the Magna Carta, as well as the philosophy of St. Thomas Aquinas. "Now laws are said to be just, both from the end, when, to wit, they are ordained to the common good—and from their author, that is to say, when the law that is made does not exceed the power of the lawgiver—and from their form, when, to wit, burdens are laid on the subjects, according to an equality of proportion and with a view to the common good." Summa Theologiae, I-II, q. 96, art. 4.

A famous more modern jurisprudential expositor was Lon Fuller. See Lon L. Fuller, The Morality of Law (1964).

First, concerning the principle of legality prong of procedural due process, Alito notes the essential arbitrariness in the distinction between chargeable and nonchargeable fees. The very list that the union made illustrates the problem. "Nonmembers were told that they had to pay for lobbying, social and recreational activities, advertising, membership meetings and conventions, and litigation, as well as other unspecified services that may ultimately inure to the benefit of the members of the local bargaining unit."[60] Each term is difficult to parse as either workplace related or political.

The Court found that the "line between chargeable and non-chargeable union expenditures has proved to be impossible to draw with precision."[61] The Court had previously attempted to give that line some definition in *Lehnert v. Ferris Faculty Association*,[62] but decades of litigation over the issue of lobbying expenses, for example, not only showed that the standard was "unworkable" (and not just for *stare decisis* purposes), but trenched into due process vagueness territory. In fact, AFSCME agreed at oral argument that the "chargeable–non-chargeable line suffers from 'a vagueness problem.'"[63]

The second prong of procedural due process is the guarantee of fair adjudicative procedures. Its application has expanded greatly over the decades but the principle remains the same: lack of fair notice and of access to effective remedies is a violation of due process. In *Chicago Teachers Union v. Hudson*,[64] the Court directed unions to send an adequate notice as to the basis of the chargeable assessments so the nonunion members would have the ability to challenge the categorization. But the Court in *Janus* concluded that experience has taught that, not only have notices been inadequate, but nonunion members "face a daunting and expensive task if they wish to challenge union chargeability determinations."[65]

A much discussed example of the principle of legality is Justice Samuel Chase's opinion in *Calder v. Bull,* and it may be significant that the examples he gives of invalid laws were also prohibited by the positive law of the Constitution. 3 U.S. 386, 387–89 (1798).

[60] Janus, 138 S. Ct. at 2461 (cleaned up).

[61] *Id.* at 2481.

[62] 500 U.S. 507 (1991).

[63] Janus, 138 S. Ct. at 2481.

[64] 475 U.S. 292 (1986).

[65] Janus, 138 S. Ct. at 2481.

The Court reproduced in the body of its opinion the notice of chargeable and nonchargeable fees that the union had made in this case:[66]

Category	Total Expense	Chargeable Expense
Salary and Benefits	$14,718,708	$11,830,230
Office Printing, Supplies, and Advertising	$148,272	$127,959
Postage and Freight	$373,509	$268,107
Telephone	$214,820	$192,721
Convention Expense	$268,855	$268,855

The Court then asked rhetorically how a nonunion member could ever determine what constitutes these categorizations and whether they were properly attributed without his incurring enormous expense in hiring lawyers and experts. It then noted that chargeability issues rarely surfaced at the court of appeals level simply because the nonunion members did not have the wherewithal to determine if they had a case.

The union answered that a nonunion member could still obtain justice through arbitration, which the union pays for, and he would not even have to attend the arbitration. But Alito pointed out that the nonunion member still has to pay for "attorneys and experts to mount a serious challenge." He concludes that the union's "suggestion that an objector could obtain adequate review without even showing up at an arbitration" is simply "farfetched."[67] In sum, under the Court's analysis, the nonunion member lacks due process protections.

IX. Originalism

In what would seem to be an unnecessary aside, Alito took a diversion in his opinion to answer an originalist argument that the union had put forward in its brief. Out of its 59 pages, the brief spent but three in proposing that the originalist understanding would not

---

[66] *Id.* at 2482.

[67] *Id.*

have accorded workplace speech any First Amendment protection.[68] But those three pages were enough to raise Alito's ire.

That the proponents of maintaining the constitutionality of compulsory agency fees would resort to an originalist argument—however brief—is of crucial moment. It signals that even those who do not espouse originalism as a valid interpretive methodology believe themselves compelled to present it to the Court, many of whose members understand and utilize originalism. It is also of significance that Kagan did not deal with her side's originalist argument. One speculates that she held back because she thought the argument foolish, or futile, or, more likely, that she did not want to validate a method of interpretation that she opposes.

But Alito did think that the union's argument was foolish; he wanted to show its futility; and he did want to validate an appropriately rigorous method of originalism. It was as if he were saying to the respondents, "You want to make an originalist argument? Let me show you how it's really done." With raised eyebrows, Alito begins, "The most surprising of these new arguments is the Union respondent's originalist defense of *Abood*."[69]

First of all, he writes, if the union wants to make an originalist argument, then why does it emphasize *stare decisis* in its brief? *Stare decisis* is not supposed to trump originalism. Further, if the union is correct that the Framers never intended the First Amendment to protect employee speech, then even *Pickering*'s limited support for employee speech on matters of public concern would fall. Why, then, does the union embrace *Pickering* so strongly in its brief? In fact, Alito scolds, the union wants us to apply "[t]he Constitution's original meaning only when it suits them. . . . We will not engage in this halfway originalism."[70] He then punctures the union's argument. First, any restrictions placed by the First Congress on government employees limited their outside business dealings, not their speech. Early restrictions on men in the military from using disrespectful words against the president are easily justified as a

---

[68] See Brief of Respondent American Federation of State, County, and Municipal Employees, Council 31 ["AFSCME Brief"] at 17–20, Janus v. AFSCME, 138 S. Ct. 2448 (2018) (No. 16-1466).

[69] Janus, 138 S. Ct. at 2469.

[70] *Id.* at 2470.

matter of military discipline. Lastly, the union relies on *dictum* from a 20th-century case, *Connick v. Myers*, that "a public employee had no right to object to conditions placed upon the terms of employment,"[71] as if it bolstered its originalist argument. That case, Alito points out, is by definition separate from and an alternative to an originalist interpretation. Alito leaves the union's originalist argument in tatters, and Justice Kagan was wise not to touch it.

In fact, Alito argues, originalism points in the other direction. History shows that the Founders had no experience with unions or collective bargaining. But they knew about compelled speech. As a fundamental principle, the Framers rejected government coercion to compel support for particular beliefs. To that end, Alito points to Thomas Jefferson's attack on religious assessments in Virginia: "[T]o compel a man to furnish contributions for the propagation of opinions which he disbelieves and abhor[s] is sinful and tyrannical."[72] Unfortunately, Alito gives little more Founding-era evidence. It is a question, therefore, whether this one Jeffersonian swallow doth make for an originalist spring on compelled speech. Jefferson's position on religious assessments has been tied to contested notions of the original understanding of the Establishment Clause; it applied to one state only; and it may not have had evident parallels in the political realm.

More was needed it would seem, and Alito attempted to supply it in his opinion in *Knox v. SEIU*. There he put forward a series of closely related propositions, each supported by major Supreme Court precedents:

1. "The First Amendment creates an open marketplace in which differing ideas about political, economic, and social issues can compete freely for public acceptance without improper government interference."

2. "The government may not prohibit the dissemination of ideas that it disfavors, nor compel the endorsement of ideas that it approves."

[71] *Id.* (quoting Connick v. Myers, 461 U.S. 138, 143 (1983) and citing AFSCME Brief at 2, 17).

[72] *Id.* at 2464 (citing A Bill for Establish Religious Freedom, in 2 Papers of Thomas Jefferson 545 (J. Boyd ed., 1950)).

3. "The First Amendment protects 'the decision of both what to say and what not to say.' And the ability of like-minded individuals to associate for the purpose of expressing commonly held views may not be curtailed."[73]

Taking those propositions together with his defense in *Janus* of the citizen's right to search for truth based on his own freely informed conscience, we see that Alito treats the doctrine of compelled speech as the logical application of this moral axiom: Citizens in a representative republic possess rights of free inquiry in the search for truth, liberty to achieve association with fellow citizens, and protection and appropriate action from their government. This is, at bottom, a natural law proposition positivized in the First Amendment to the Constitution.[74] That, we can say, is the originalism of Justice Alito.

Justice Clarence Thomas has the reputation of being the most rigorous originalist on the Court. One might think that if he found Alito's analysis wanting, he would have appended a clarifying concurrence. But Thomas joined Alito's opinions in *Knox* and *Janus* without a separate concurrence. Nor did he himself make originalist argument for the protection of compelled speech in his opinion in *National Institute of Family and Life Advocates v. Becerra*, decided this term. We can conclude that Justice Thomas is in accord with Justice Alito's originalist and philosophical principles on the doctrine of compelled speech.

X. Weaponizing the Constitution

Justice Kagan's writing has sometimes been likened to Justice Scalia's. Her dissent in *Janus* is well structured, uses economy of language, and is bitingly ironic. There is another parallel to Scalia. Although she does not possess the same panache, she attacks the majority as Scalia would when he thought the Court was striking off in an unjustified direction. She just espouses a different direction. What does Kagan fear? What does she think is really going on here?

She, of course, believes that *Janus* will cripple public-sector unions. Unions will lose "a secure source of financial support," and without adequate funding they will be a less effective representative of

[73] Knox v SEIU, 567 U.S. 298, 309 (2012).

[74] See generally Hadley Arkes, Beyond the Constitution (1990).

workers. Nonunion workers do not lose out in an agency-fee regime, she claims. By law, the union must represent all workers. Without agency fees, free riders, being "economically rational actors," will maintain benefits without having to bear the costs.[75] Recent reports of union finances and membership losses since *Janus*, though others observe that without the crutch of agency fees, public-sector unions will become more aggressive and effective in recruiting members.[76]

Justice Alito pointed out that federal workers' unions, which by law cannot collect agency fees, are nonetheless very strong and enjoy exclusive representation. Kagan rejoined that the free rider problem in the federal workforce is, in fact, severe. Moreover, she noted that wages and benefits are not the subject of union-management negotiations in the federal sphere. Congress independently takes care of that. (Alito had found that avoidance of free rides was not a compelling interest sufficient to justify infringement of First Amendment rights.)

The decision, she pursues, "creates an unjustified hole in the law, applicable to union fees alone,"[77] for other forms of workplace speech continue to be governed by *Pickering*. This decision is, in sum, simply an anti-union diktat. Why did the Court overrule *Abood*? "[B]ecause it wanted to."[78] But Justice Kagan fears that there is something else afoot.

> There is no sugarcoating today's opinion. The majority overthrows a decision entrenched in this Nation's law—and in its economic life—for over 40 years. As a result, it prevents the American people, acting through their state and local officials, from making important choices about workplace governance. And it does so by weaponizing the First Amendment, in a way that unleashes judges, now and in the future, to intervene in economic and regulatory policy. [79]

And there you have her paradigm and her nightmare: The conservative court is readying a return to the years before 1938 when it used the Constitution to monitor and direct the economic policy

---

[75] Janus, 138 S. Ct. at 2491 (Kagan, J., dissenting).

[76] Compare, e.g., Kris Maher, Unions Take a Hit after Court Ruling, Wall Street J., Aug. 6, 2018, at A3, with David Griesing, The Janus Ruling Doesn't Have to Be a Death Knell for Public Unions, Chicago Tribune, Aug. 11, 2018, https://trib.in/Z+Pm8IP.

[77] Janus, 138 S. Ct. at 2491 (Kagan, J., dissenting).

[78] *Id.* at 2501.

[79] *Id.*

of the country. In the same way that the post-1938 Court—Justice Hugo Black most prominently—claimed that the Court had previously weaponized the Due Process Clause against economic reform and in favor of business, Kagan thinks this Court will use the First Amendment to the same end:

> [A]lmost all economic and regulatory policy affects or touches speech. So the majority's road runs long. And at every stop are black-robed rulers overriding citizens' choices. The First Amendment was meant for better things. It was meant not to undermine but to protect democratic governance—including over the role of public-sector unions.[80]

In fact, Alito dropped a footnote that might have raised Kagan's hackles even more. This, the most startling aspect to Alito's opinion, is his re-opening the door of *Lochner*-era substantive due process. In the section of the opinion in which he tries to develop an originalist defense for the compelled speech doctrine, he wrote, "Indeed, under common law, 'collective bargaining was unlawful,'[81] . . . and into the 20th century, every individual employee had the 'liberty of contract' to 'sell his labor upon such terms as he deem[ed] proper.'" At this point he cited *Adair v. United States*,[82] one of the most prominent cases upholding the substantive due process right of contract.

Although he tried to soothe—"We note this only to show the problems inherent in the Union respondent's argument; we are not in any way questioning the foundations of modern labor law."[83]— nonetheless, this may be one of the first times in the modern era that a justice writing a majority opinion has tied the substantive due process cases on liberty of contract to an originalist grounding.

But Kagan is heir, of course, to a line of cases in which the post-New Deal Court weaponized the Constitution to insert policies into the Constitution that would have been unrecognizable to the Framers and even to most justices who served prior to 1960. That Court was also removing issues of public concern from the democratic process altogether, as Justice Scalia time and again pointed out. In other

---

[80] *Id.* at 2502.

[81] *Id.* at 2471 (majority op.) (citing Teamsters v. Terry, 494 U.S. 558 (1990)).

[82] 208 U.S. 161 (1908).

[83] Janus, 138 S. Ct. at 2471, n. 7.

words, many originalists believe that the Court for decades has been weaponizing the Constitution in the culture wars, while heirs to the 1938 Supreme Court believe that the modern Court is using the Constitution as a weapon in an economic and class war.

XI. The Future

Despite Kagan's "the sky is falling" fears of an end to democratic decisionmaking, *Janus* marks an affirmation of the democratic ethos. It does so in three ways. First, it affirms the fundamental nature of the human person in political society: a rational, associative, truth-seeking individual with inalienable rights of conscience. Second, *Janus* is decided amidst a growing awareness that the decision-making process in this republican polity is distorted by independent groups—factions, in Madison's term—wielding power over governmental agencies to make policies over citizens without the citizens' consent. Third, *Janus* represents yet another chapter in the Roberts Court's championing of First Amendment protection over the right to espouse different kinds of expressions and the right to the sanctity of one's own opinions. If Brett Kavanaugh is confirmed for the Supreme Court, we can expect more movement in all of those ways.

But against this sanguine hope, there is a tempering apprehension. One side of the Court claims that the other is making economic policy. The other side says that the Court has been creating new cultural norms. Many senators today vote on nominees based on predictions about what side of the policy battles a nominee will align himself.[84] It may not be too far distant when this country sees "resistance," not only against particular federal office holders, against particular laws, or against particular election results, but against particular decisions of the Supreme Court. It is then that this country's commitment to the rule of law will be definitively tested.

---

[84] See generally Roger Pilon, Judicial Confirmations and the Rule of Law, Foreword, 2016–2017 Cato Sup. Ct. Rev. ix (2017).

NIFLA v. Becerra: A Seismic Decision Protecting Occupational Speech

by Robert McNamara* and Paul Sherman**

National Institute of Family and Life Advocates v. Becerra (*NIFLA*) had all the hallmarks of a classic culture-war showdown. On one side was a coalition of so-called crisis-pregnancy centers—organizations that provide certain prenatal services and counseling to pregnant women but do not perform or recommend abortions. On the other side were pro-choice groups that accused the pregnancy centers of misleading or outright deceiving pregnant women about the availability and possible risks of abortion or birth control.

So far, so familiar. But what sets *NIFLA* apart is not its well-trod battle lines between pro-life and pro-choice factions, but the unusual approach that the state of California took in mediating this dispute. California wanted pregnant women to know about the availability of state-financed abortions—and if crisis-pregnancy centers would not voluntarily give this information to their clients, California would force them to do so. What followed was a lawsuit that raised some of the most important unanswered questions in First Amendment law. What protection does the First Amendment afford to speech by "professionals"? How much power does the government have to compel truthful speech that it believes will benefit consumers? And what should courts do when economic or social regulation trenches upon an individual's free-speech rights?

The Supreme Court answered these questions, and its decision was a blockbuster. *NIFLA* is one of the most important First Amendment rulings in a generation, clarifying decades of muddled precedent and significantly expanding protection for speech in the commercial marketplace. Indeed, it is no exaggeration to say that *NIFLA* cements

* Senior Attorney, Institute for Justice.

** Senior Attorney, Institute for Justice.

the Roberts Court as the most libertarian in our nation's history on free-speech issues.

Below, we begin by summarizing the facts of *NIFLA* and the broader legal controversy surrounding crisis-pregnancy centers, which was by no means limited to California. We then explain the Ninth Circuit's ruling and compare that ruling to the approach other circuits had taken in cases with similar facts or raising similar issues of "professional speech." In the final two sections, we discuss the Supreme Court's ruling and its implications for future litigation over the abortion debate and beyond.

I. Facts of the Case and the Broader Controversy over Crisis-Pregnancy Centers

Although they have garnered increased attention in recent years, crisis-pregnancy centers are not a new phenomenon. The first appears to have been founded in California in 1968. Typically, these centers provide prenatal services, such as pregnancy testing, obstetric ultrasounds, and pregnancy counseling. And their numbers have grown rapidly; today, crisis-pregnancy centers outnumber abortion providers by nearly 1,000.[1]

For as long as they have existed, crisis-pregnancy centers have also drawn criticism from pro-choice groups for their tactics. Abortion-rights supporters say that these centers are rooted in deception, providing scientifically questionable information to their clientele and falsely holding themselves out as full-service medical clinics to draw in women who would otherwise seek abortions.

Only in 2015, however, did California, acting in response to these complaints, adopt the California Reproductive Freedom, Accountability, Comprehensive Care, and Transparency (FACT) Act.[2] The FACT Act imposed two notice requirements on facilities that provide pregnancy-related services—one for licensed facilities and one for unlicensed facilities. (Licensed facilities are those that the state licenses to provide primary or specialty care and that have the "primary purpose" of "providing family planning or pregnancy-related

[1] Family Research Council, A Passion to Serve: How Pregnancy Resource Centers Empower Women, Help Families, and Strengthen Communities (2d ed.), https://downloads.frc.org/EF/EF12A47.pdf (last visited Aug. 1, 2018).

[2] Cal. Health & Safety Code Ann. § 123470 et seq. (West 2018).

services."[3]) Additionally, the act covers only licensed facilities that engage in at least two enumerated activities, which include offering obstetric ultrasounds, offering pregnancy testing, collecting health information from clients, or advertising pregnancy-options counseling.[4]

The act contained several exemptions from this definition. Most notably, it did not apply to "clinic[s] that [are] enrolled as . . . Medi-Cal provider[s] and in the Family Planning Access, Care, and Treatment Program [Family PACT program]."[5] This exemption could never apply to crisis-pregnancy centers, however, because to participate in the Family PACT program a clinic must offer "the full scope" of family planning services, including sterilization and emergency contraception.[6]

Licensed clinics subject to the FACT Act had to provide a government-drafted notice to their clients. This "Licensed Notice" stated, "California has public programs that provide immediate free or low-cost access to comprehensive family planning services (including all FDA-approved methods of contraception), prenatal care, and abortion for eligible women. To determine whether you qualify, contact the county social services office at [insert the telephone number]."[7] Clinics had to print the notices in English and any other languages identified by state law.[8] In most counties throughout California this meant the notice must be printed in both English and Spanish, though some counties required translation into many additional languages. Los Angeles County, for example, required the notice in 13 different languages.[9]

The act also required disclosures by unlicensed facilities. These included any facility that the state did not license, that did not have a licensed medical provider on staff or under contract, and that had the "primary purpose" of "providing pregnancy-related services."[10]

---

[3] *Id.* at § 123471(a).

[4] *Id.*

[5] *Id.* at § 123471(c) (internal quotation marks omitted).

[6] Cal. Welf. & Inst. Code Ann. §§ 24005(c), 24007(a)(1), (2).

[7] Cal. Health & Safety Code Ann. § 123472(a)(1).

[8] *Id.* at § 123472(a).

[9] NIFLA v. Becerra, 138 S. Ct. 2361, 2369 (2018).

[10] Cal. Health & Safety Code Ann. § 123471(b).

As with licensed facilities, unlicensed facilities would be covered only if they engaged in certain conduct, such as offering ultrasounds or collecting client information. And as with licensed facilities, the act excluded unlicensed facilities enrolled in Medi-Cal and the Family PACT program.

The "Unlicensed Notice" required of unlicensed facilities stated that, "This facility is not licensed as a medical facility by the State of California and has no licensed medical provider who provides or directly supervises the provision of services."[11] The law required clinics to post the notice on site and on all advertising materials and that it be written in at least 48-point type.[12] When included in advertising material, the type had to be the same size or larger than all surrounding text.[13] And, like the Licensed Notice, the Unlicensed Notice had to be in both English and any other language required by state law.

California was not the only state to take issue with crisis-pregnancy centers, nor was *NIFLA* the first case to challenge state regulation of these centers. In 2011, for example, New York City adopted a law requiring facilities that had "the appearance of a licensed medical facility" to post mandatory disclosures for their clients. These disclosures had to inform clients (1) whether the center had a licensed medical provider on staff, (2) that the city's department of health encouraged pregnant women to consult with a licensed medical provider, and (3) whether the center provided referrals for abortion or emergency contraception. The U.S. Court of Appeals for the Second Circuit upheld the law in part and rejected it in part. The court held that the disclosures about whether the center was run by a licensed medical provider would survive even strict scrutiny under the First Amendment, but that the disclosure about abortion services (which "mandate[d] discussion of controversial political topics") and the requirement to convey the government's own message would fail under even intermediate scrutiny.[14]

---

11 *Id.* at § 123472(b)(1).

12 *Id.* at § 123472(b)(2).

13 *Id.* at § 123472(b)(3).

14 Evergreen Ass'n v. City of New York, 740 F.3d 233, 246–51 (2d Cir. 2014).

While it was not the first law to regulate crisis-pregnancy centers, the FACT Act was among the broadest. As compared to the New York law, it both required the centers to convey a more substantial government message and applied with a far broader sweep, as it did not hinge on whether a center *seemed* like a fully licensed medical facility. Litigation was inevitable.

II. The Litigation Below

Four days after the FACT Act was signed into law, NIFLA and two crisis-pregnancy centers in California (collectively "NIFLA") sued, alleging that the act violated the First Amendment's Free Speech and Free Exercise Clauses. NIFLA moved for preliminary injunction seeking to halt enforcement of the act during the litigation. The district court denied the injunction on both claims,[15] and NIFLA appealed to the Ninth Circuit, which affirmed the district court's ruling.[16]

The Ninth Circuit's analysis of NIFLA's religious-liberty claim was unremarkable and merits little discussion. Under the Supreme Court's 1990 ruling in *Employment Division v. Smith*, "the right of free exercise does not relieve an individual of the obligation to comply with a valid and neutral law of general applicability on the ground that the law proscribes (or prescribes) conduct that his religion prescribes (or proscribes)."[17] Such facially neutral laws will survive constitutional scrutiny so long as they satisfy the rational-basis test. The Ninth Circuit easily concluded that the FACT Act satisfied this deferential standard.[18]

Far more significant was the Ninth Circuit's ruling on NIFLA's free-speech claim, which held that the notice requirements for both licensed and unlicensed clinics survived First Amendment scrutiny.

---

[15] NIFLA v. Harris, No. 15cv2277, 2016 WL 3627327 (S.D. Cal. Feb. 9, 2016).

[16] NIFLA v. Harris, 839 F.3d 823 (9th Cir. 2016).

[17] 494 U.S. 872, 879 (1990) (cleaned up).

[18] NIFLA, 839 F.3d at 844–45. We note in passing that NIFLA also contended that the law was motivated specifically by hostility to the centers' religious beliefs, a contention that ultimately played little role in the resolution of this case but that does have elements in common with this term's decision in *Masterpiece Cakeshop v. Colo. Civil Rights Comm'n*, 138 S. Ct. 1719 (2018).

Before starting its analysis of the notice requirements' constitutionality, the Ninth Circuit first examined whether the requirements were "content-based" or "content-neutral." This is a crucial distinction in First Amendment law, because content-based speech restrictions—with few exceptions—are subject to strict scrutiny, the most searching form of judicial review. Content-neutral regulations, by contrast, are typically subject to a lower level of scrutiny.

Here, the Ninth Circuit split the difference, concluding that the act was indeed content-based but that the notice requirement for licensed pregnancy centers was not subject to strict scrutiny. To justify this result, the court invoked a rule that had become known as the "professional speech doctrine."[19]

Before describing the professional-speech doctrine, it helps to know a bit of background about the how the Supreme Court has treated other categories of lesser-protected speech. Although the general rule, again, is that content-based regulations of speech are subject to strict scrutiny, the Court has long recognized some categories of speech to which this does not apply. The most commonly cited are those categories of speech, "long familiar to the bar," that fall outside the scope of the First Amendment.[20] These categories include, among other things, true threats, child pornography, and defamation. Because these forms of speech have been treated as unprotected "from 1791 to the present," content-based regulation of such speech triggers no First Amendment scrutiny.[21]

In addition to these narrow categories of wholly unprotected speech, there is one other category of speech for which the Supreme Court has held that content-based restrictions do not trigger strict scrutiny: commercial advertising. Although the Court at first treated commercial speech as wholly unprotected, it reversed course in the 1970s.[22] Under the modern commercial-speech doctrine, government may regulate commercial speech based on its content, and these regulations are subject to only intermediate scrutiny. This standard

[19] NIFLA, 839 F.3d at 838–41.

[20] United States v. Stevens, 559 U.S. 460, 468 (2010).

[21] Id.

[22] Va. State Bd. of Pharmacy v. Va. Citizens Consumer Council, Inc., 425 U.S. 748 (1976).

is more easily satisfied than strict scrutiny, but it is not a rubber stamp; it imposes a meaningful burden on government to justify its restrictions.[23]

Absent from this list of second-class speech is what some courts have called "professional speech" (or what we prefer to call "occupational speech").[24] This is speech—often, though not exclusively, in the form of advice—between an expert speaker and a client. Examples abound: A lawyer advising a client is engaged in occupational speech, as is a tour guide describing points of interest, or a health coach recommending recipes. Or—to bring things back to *NIFLA*—a volunteer at a crisis-pregnancy center discussing prenatal health.

If the default rule in First Amendment law is that content-based restrictions on speech are subject to strict scrutiny, and if the Supreme Court has never held that occupational speech is an exception to this rule, then one would expect that burdens on occupational speech would get strict scrutiny. So how could the Ninth Circuit escape this conclusion? Enter: The Professional Speech Doctrine.

Although its formulation and scope vary from circuit to circuit, the professional-speech doctrine, at its base, is simply a rule that provides reduced protection for speech in a professional/client relationship. The Ninth Circuit first adopted this doctrine in *National Association for the Advancement of Psychoanalysis v. California Board of*

---

[23] See, e.g., Edenfield v. Fane, 507 U.S. 761, 770–71 (1993) (noting that the government's burden under intermediate scrutiny "is not satisfied by mere speculation or conjecture; rather, a governmental body seeking to sustain a restriction on commercial speech must demonstrate that the harms it recites are real and that its restriction will in fact alleviate them to a material degree"). Many commentators have questioned the validity of commercial speech's second-class status, and at least one Supreme Court justice has argued that the commercial-speech doctrine should be abandoned, and that content-based restrictions on commercial speech be subject to the same strict scrutiny as content-based restrictions on political speech. See, e.g., Alex Kozinski & Stuart Banner, Who's Afraid of Commercial Speech, 76 Va. L. Rev. 627 (1990); 44 Liquormart, Inc. v. Rhode Island, 517 U.S. 484, 522 (1996) (Thomas, J., concurring) ("I do not see a philosophical or historical basis for asserting that 'commercial' speech is of 'lower value' than 'noncommercial' speech.").

[24] We prefer the term "occupational speech" because it reflects more accurately the breadth of speech potentially affected by the professional speech doctrine. As we will discuss in more detail, *infra*, courts that have invoked "professional speech" have not limited the doctrine to speech occurring in what would commonly be understood as "professions." See, e.g., Moore-King v. Cty. of Chesterfield, 708 F.3d 560 (4th Cir. 2013) (applying the professional speech doctrine to regulation of fortune tellers).

Psychology, in which the court upheld California's licensure of psychologists against a First Amendment challenge.[25] More recently, the Ninth Circuit refined the doctrine in *Pickup v. Brown*, in which the court upheld a California law that prohibited licensed mental health professionals from engaging in any conduct—including speech, such as talk therapy—designed to change a minor's sexual orientation or gender expression.[26]

Under the Ninth Circuit's current statement of the professional-speech doctrine, speech uttered by "professionals" exists on a continuum of First Amendment protection. At one extreme is speech directed to the public at large, such as a public lecture, which receives full First Amendment protection. At the other extreme, is speech that is so integrally tied to professional conduct that it is the functional equivalent of conduct itself. In the Ninth Circuit's view, this speech is no different from performing brain surgery or dispensing medication and so receives no First Amendment protection.[27] In the middle is an ill-defined class of speech that occurs within a professional/client relationship, but that is more like speech than conduct. This speech receives some First Amendment protection—but not strict scrutiny. And it is into this category that the Ninth Circuit placed the notice requirement for licensed pregnancy centers.

The Ninth Circuit concluded that the Licensed Notice easily satisfied intermediate scrutiny. First, the court noted that California had "a substantial interest in the health of its citizens, including ensuring that its citizens have access to and adequate information about constitutionally-protected medical services like abortion."[28] The court also credited the California legislature's finding that "a substantial number of California citizens may not be aware of, or have access to, medical services relevant to pregnancy."[29]

Having found the state's interest substantial, the court next looked at the tailoring of the Licensed Notice. With seemingly little regard for the effect that compelled speech about the availability of state-funded abortion would have on NIFLA's ability to convey its pro-life

[25] 228 F.3d 1043 (9th Cir. 2000).
[26] 740 F.3d 1208 (9th Cir. 2014).
[27] *Id.* at 1227.
[28] NIFLA, 839 F.3d at 841.
[29] *Id.*

message, the court held that the Licensed Notice did not "contain any more speech than necessary." Instead, the notice merely informed readers of "the existence of publicly-funded family-planning services," without encouraging, suggesting, or implying that women should use those services.[30] Concluding that there was no reason to believe this notice would be ineffective, the court found the Licensed Notice was appropriately tailored to the state's interest.

In reaching this conclusion, the court dismissed the most obvious, narrower approach California might have taken: distributing information about family-planning services directly, rather than making NIFLA its unwilling mouthpiece. And this is where the shift from strict to intermediate scrutiny perhaps had its largest impact. For although strict scrutiny requires that government use the least-restrictive means of regulating speech, intermediate scrutiny imposes no such requirement.[31] Thus, the Licensed Notice survived.

The Ninth Circuit next turned to the notice requirement for unlicensed clinics. Unlike in its analysis of the requirement for licensed clinics, the court found it unnecessary to decide whether unlicensed clinics were engaged in professional speech. This is because the Ninth Circuit thought the notice required of unlicensed clinics survived even under strict scrutiny.[32]

For those who are familiar with the Supreme Court's strict-scrutiny jurisprudence, this conclusion is somewhat shocking. Although the cliché that strict scrutiny is "strict in theory but fatal in fact" is an overstatement,[33] strict scrutiny still places a heavy burden on the government. This is particularly true in the First Amendment context. Only twice in our nation's history has the Supreme Court upheld a speech restriction under strict scrutiny, and those cases involved concerns of national security and the integrity of the judiciary.[34]

Even so, the Ninth Circuit concluded that the Unlicensed Notice was narrowly tailored to serve a compelling government interest in ensuring that women are aware of whether a facility 'in which

[30] *Id.* at 842.

[31] *Id.*

[32] *Id.* at 843.

[33] See Adam Winkler, Fatal in Theory and Strict in Fact: An Empirical Analysis of Strict Scrutiny in the Federal Courts, 59 Vand. L. Rev. 793 (2006).

[34] See Holder v. Humanitarian Law Project, 561 U.S. 1 (2010); Williams-Yulee v. Florida Bar, 135 S. Ct. 1656 (2015).

they are receiving prenatal care is subject to the same level of state oversight as other facilities with which they may be familiar.[35] Absent from the court's analysis was any discussion of less-restrictive alternatives the state might have employed, such as maintaining a publicly available database of licensed and unlicensed clinics. The court seems to have concluded that, because the Second and Fourth Circuits had upheld similar notices in unlicensed clinics, it need not independently consider whether the state might achieve its goals equally well without compelling speech.

Having determined that NIFLA was unlikely to prevail on any of its First Amendment claims against either of the notice requirements, the Ninth Circuit denied NIFLA's motion for preliminary injunction.

III. How the Ninth Circuit's Ruling Fits in with Other Occupational-Speech Cases[36]

A. Origins of the Professional Speech Doctrine

The Ninth Circuit did not invent the professional-speech doctrine. The intellectual roots of the doctrine stretch back to a concurring opinion by Justice Robert Jackson in *Thomas v. Collins* in 1945. Agreeing with the Court's majority that the government could not require a speaker to get a license before giving a public speech endorsing membership in a labor union, Justice Jackson opined that "a rough distinction always exists" between the permissible regulation of a vocation and the impermissible regulation of speech.[37] For Justice Jackson, that distinction should be based on the presence or absence of an (unidentified) "other factor which the state may regulate so as to bring the whole within official control."[38]

No member of the Court took up the task of identifying what that factor might be until 1985. The case was *Lowe v. SEC*, in which the U.S. Securities and Exchange Commission brought an enforcement action against Christopher Lowe, a disgraced former investment adviser who had lost his registration and been prohibited from acting

---

[35] NIFLA, 839 F.3d at 843.

[36] Portions of this section are adapted from Paul Sherman, Occupational Speech and the First Amendment, 128 Harv. L. Rev. F. 183 (2015), https://harvardlawreview.org/2015/03/occupational-speech-and-the-first-amendment.

[37] 323 U.S. 516, 544–48 (1945) (Jackson, J., concurring).

[38] *Id.* at 547.

as an investment adviser following a conviction on various felony offenses.[39] Despite his conviction, Lowe continued to publish a newsletter that provided investing advice. The SEC believed this to violate the securities laws and filed a complaint against Lowe in federal court.

The SEC lost before the district court, but prevailed before the Second Circuit, after which the Supreme Court granted certiorari to consider "the important constitutional question whether an injunction against the publication and distribution of petitioners' newsletters is prohibited by the First Amendment."[40] But the Court never reached this constitutional question. Instead, in an opinion by Justice John Paul Stevens, a majority of the Court found on statutory grounds that the registration requirement did not apply to newsletter publishers.[41]

Justice Byron White, however, disagreed. Writing for himself, Chief Justice Warren Burger, and Justice William Rehnquist, White concluded that it was necessary to reach whether requiring newsletter publishers to register with the SEC violated the First Amendment.[42] In doing so, he laid out a test that would prove to have an outsized influence on the development of occupational-speech jurisprudence in lower federal courts.

The crux of Justice White's concurrence is a distinction between speech targeted at the public at large and speech targeted at specific individuals. As Justice White saw it, "[o]ne who takes the affairs of a client personally in hand and purports to exercise judgment on behalf of the client in the light of the client's individual needs and circumstances is properly viewed as engaging in the practice of a profession."[43] In this context, a professional's speech is incidental to the conduct of his profession, "[j]ust as offer and acceptance are communications incidental to the regulable transaction called a contract."[44] White therefore saw no First Amendment problem with "generally applicable licensing provisions limiting the class of persons who may practice [a] profession," even where the practice of that profession consists entirely of speaking.[45]

---

[39] 472 U.S. 181 (1985).

[40] *Id.* at 188–89 (majority opinion).

[41] *Id.* at 210–11.

[42] *Id.* at 212–13 (White, J., concurring in the result).

[43] *Id.* at 232 (footnotes omitted).

[44] *Id.*

[45] *Id.*

White expressly contrasted these "professionals" with speakers who do not have a "personal nexus" with their clients and who do not "purport to be exercising judgment on behalf of any particular individual with whose circumstances he is directly acquainted."[46] In that setting, White believed that "government regulation ceases to function as legitimate regulation of professional practice with only incidental impact on speech" and instead becomes "regulation of speaking or publishing as such," and, hence, subject to the First Amendment.[47]

White's concurrence is unusual in at least two respects. The first is that his extended discussion of why the government may permissibly regulate occupational speech in which there is a "personal nexus" between speaker and listener was unnecessary to the disposition of the case. There was no dispute that, with regard to the newsletters at issue, Christopher Lowe had no personal nexus with his readers. The second is that White drew his personal-nexus test almost entirely from his own imagination. White does not cite a single controlling opinion of the Supreme Court that supports the existence of a "personal nexus" exemption to the First Amendment, relying instead on Justice Jackson's concurring opinion in *Thomas v. Collins*.

Since Justice White's 1985 concurrence, neither the U.S. Supreme Court nor any individual justice has ever cited its personal-nexus test. But because it was the clearest statement that any justice had made on the intersection of occupational licensing and the First Amendment, it had a disproportionate influence on lower courts, which, until recently, have tended to accept uncritically Justice White's personal-nexus test as the law.[48]

Troublingly, this uncritical acceptance of Justice White's test had largely ignored his admonition that speech falls outside the First Amendment only when the speaker "takes the affairs of a client personally in hand and purports to exercise judgment on behalf of

[46] *Id.*

[47] *Id.*

[48] See, e.g., Locke v. Shore, 634 F.3d 1185, 1191 (11th Cir. 2011); Accountant's Soc'y of Va. v. Bowman, 860 F.2d 602, 604 (4th Cir. 1988); Tepeyac v. Montgomery Cnty., 779 F. Supp. 2d 456, 466–67 (D. Md. 2011); Accountants' Ass'n of La. v. State, 533 So. 2d 1251, 1254–55 (La. Ct. App. 1988); In re Rowe, 604 N.E.2d 728, 731 (N.Y. 1992); cf. Nat'l Ass'n for the Advancement of Psychoanalysis, 228 F.3d at 1053–55 (dismissing, based on Justice Jackson's concurrence in *Thomas v. Collins*, First Amendment challenge to California's licensing requirement for psychologists).

the client."[49] Justice White seems to have intended this limitation to protect consumers who enter into fiduciary relationships. Yet lower courts had generally found Justice White's test to be satisfied by the existence of any personal nexus between speaker and listener. As a result, rather than applying only to speakers in a fiduciary or quasi-fiduciary relationship with their listeners, lower courts have expanded Justice White's rule to include, among other things, the aesthetic recommendations of interior designers[50] and even the predictions of fortune tellers.[51]

This is not to say that the consequences of Justice White's concurrence have been wholly negative. Although Justice White was wrong, he was only half wrong: He was surely correct that the First Amendment fully protected Christopher Lowe's newsletters. And that conclusion—as opposed to his more expansive *dicta*—has had some positive consequences. Lower courts have relied on this portion of Justice White's *Lowe* concurrence to strike down registration requirements for people who publish information about commodities trading[52] and prohibitions on operating "for sale by owner" websites without being a licensed real estate broker.[53]

What emerged from these two lines of cases was a fairly consistent rule: The First Amendment prohibits requiring a speaker to secure a government-issued license to engage in speech published to the public at large, no matter how technical the speech's subject matter. But when speech consists of advice or recommendations made in the course of business, and is in any way tailored to the circumstances or needs of the listener, the First Amendment permits its regulation.[54]

B. The Growing Split in the Circuits

Ironically, this trend toward a broad professional-speech doctrine started to shift with *Pickup v. Brown*, the challenge to California's

---

[49] Lowe, 472 U.S. at 232 (White, J., concurring in the result).

[50] See Locke v. Shore, 682 F. Supp. 2d 1283, 1292 (N.D. Fla. 2010), aff'd, 634 F.3d 1185 (11th Cir. 2011), cert. denied, 565 U.S. 1111 (2012).

[51] See Moore-King v. Cty. of Chesterfield, 708 F.3d 560, 568 (4th Cir. 2013).

[52] See Taucher v. Born, 53 F. Supp. 2d 464, 482 (D.D.C. 1999).

[53] See ForSaleByOwner.com Corp. v. Zinnemann, 347 F. Supp. 2d 868, 876–79 (E.D. Cal. 2004).

[54] Exceptions to this general trend included a handful of cases striking down bans on fortune telling. See, e.g., Argello v. City of Lincoln, 143 F.3d 1152 (8th Cir. 1998).

ban on conversion therapy, which the Ninth Circuit had looked to in deciding *NIFLA*. More precisely, the trend started to shift with an opinion by Judge Diarmuid O'Scannlain, dissenting from denial of rehearing en banc in *Pickup*.[55]

The panel in *Pickup*, applying the professional-speech doctrine, had concluded that talk therapy was simply a form of professional conduct, entitled to no First Amendment protection. But, in Judge O'Scannlain's view, that conclusion could not be squared with modern First Amendment precedent.[56] Most notably, that conclusion was irreconcilable with the Supreme Court's 2010 decision in *Holder v. Humanitarian Law Project*.

Humanitarian Law Project involved an as-applied challenge to a federal statute that "prohibited the provision of 'material support or resources' to certain foreign organizations that engage in terrorist activity."[57] The law defined "material support or resources" to include both "training," defined as "instruction or teaching designed to impart a specific skill, as opposed to general knowledge," and "expert advice or assistance," defined as "advice or assistance derived from scientific, technical or other specialized knowledge."[58]

The plaintiffs in *Humanitarian Law Project* included two U.S. citizens and six domestic organizations that wished, among other things, to train members of the Kurdistan Workers' Party (PKK) "on how to use humanitarian and international law to peacefully resolve disputes" and to "teach[] PKK members how to petition various representative bodies such as the United Nations for relief."[59] The plaintiffs challenged the prohibition against their doing so on First Amendment grounds.

The government defended the law by arguing that the material-support prohibition was aimed at conduct, not speech, and thus only incidentally burdened the plaintiffs' expression. But the Supreme Court emphatically rejected the government's argument, holding that the material-support prohibition was a content-based regulation of speech subject to strict scrutiny. In doing so, the Court explained that when "the conduct triggering coverage under [a] statute consists

---

[55] 740 F.3d at 1215 (O'Scannlain, J., dissenting from denial of rehearing en banc).

[56] *Id.* at 1216.

[57] Humanitarian Law Project, 561 U.S. at 7.

[58] *Id.* at 12–13.

[59] *Id.* at 10, 14–15.

of communicating a message," applying the statute to that conduct is properly viewed as a content-based regulation of speech.[60] Applying that rule to the case before it, the Court easily concluded that the law was content-based:

> Plaintiffs want to speak to the PKK and the LTTE, and whether they may do so under § 2339B depends on what they say. If plaintiffs' speech to those groups imparts a "specific skill" or communicates advice derived from "specialized knowledge"—for example, training on the use of international law or advice on petitioning the United Nations—then it is barred. On the other hand, plaintiffs' speech is not barred if it imparts only general or unspecialized knowledge.[61]

Applying these principles in turn to California's ban on conversion therapy, Judge O'Scannlain thought it obvious that the ban targeted speech. As he pointed out, the plaintiffs in *Humanitarian Law Project*, who included lawyers and judges, "certainly purported to be offering professional services."[62] Yet the Supreme Court had rejected the government's attempt to relabel this speech as conduct. The same rule, O'Scannlain argued, should apply to talk therapy.

Judge O'Scannlain's dissent did not carry the day in *Pickup*, but it formed a significant basis for the Third Circuit's later decision in *King v. Governor of New Jersey*.[63] *King* involved a virtually identical ban on sexual orientation change efforts aimed at minors.[64] But unlike the Ninth Circuit, the Third Circuit acknowledged that *Humanitarian Law Project* was not distinguishable.[65] The court criticized "the enterprise of labeling certain verbal or written communications 'speech' and others 'conduct' [as] unprincipled and susceptible to manipulation."[66] Yet the court went on to conclude that occupational speech—while protected by the First Amendment—should receive the same reduced protection as commercial speech.[67] Thus, applying

---

[60] *Id.* at 28.

[61] *Id.* at 27 (internal citations omitted).

[62] Pickup, 740 F.3d at 1217 (O'Scannlain, J., dissenting from denial of rehearing en banc).

[63] 767 F.3d 216 (3d Cir. 2014).

[64] *Id.* at 220.

[65] See *id.* at 225 (applying *Humanitarian Law Project*).

[66] *Id.* at 228.

[67] *Id.* at 232–33.

the intermediate scrutiny set forth in *Central Hudson Gas & Electric Co. v. Public Service Commission*,[68] the court held that New Jersey's ban on sexual-orientation change efforts was constitutional.[69]

Judge O'Scannlain's dissent would later influence the en banc Eleventh Circuit's ruling in *Wollschlaeger v. Governor of Florida*,[70] which concerned a prohibition on doctors asking their patients about gun ownership when doing so was "not relevant" to their medical care.[71] Responding to the government's reliance on *Pickup v. Brown*, the Eleventh Circuit cited Judge O'Scannlain as having raised "serious doubts about whether *Pickup* was correctly decided."[72] Rejecting this approach, the court followed the lead of the Third Circuit and reviewed the challenged restrictions with intermediate scrutiny, which they could not survive.

Thus, from Judge O'Scannlain's dissent in *Pickup* grew a substantial circuit split. The Supreme Court, having waited 33 years to clarify the First Amendment status of occupational speech, could wait no longer.

C. The Professional Speech Doctrine at the Supreme Court

Despite this considerable doctrinal development in the lower courts, the Supreme Court (as discussed above) was writing on an essentially clean slate in addressing the question, which is reflected in the breadth of approaches suggested by the amicus briefs filed in *NIFLA* itself. Some briefs, like that filed by the United States, argued that the government should be permitted to "regulate speech by members of regulated professions related to their services" subject only to heightened (rather than strict) scrutiny.[73] Others, like Public Citizen, urged the Court to approach the broader professional-speech question with caution but to recognize a limited exception that would afford less-than-strict scrutiny to "disclosure requirements

---

[68] 447 U.S. 557 (1980).

[69] King, 767 F.3d at 233–40.

[70] 848 F.3d 1293 (11th Cir. 2017) (en banc).

[71] *Id.* at 1302.

[72] *Id.* at 1309. In doing so, the court also subtly criticized its own, earlier precedent in *Locke v. Shore*, which had reached largely the same conclusion as *Pickup*.

[73] Brief for the United States as Amicus Curiae Supporting Neither Party at 15–16, NIFLA v. Becerra, 138 S. Ct. 2361 (2018) (No. 16-1140).

that relate to the nature of the services to be provided and are material to the client's decision whether to enter into a [professional] relationship."[74] On the more speech-protective side, the Cato Institute urged the Court to strictly cabin any professional-speech exception along the lines suggested by Justice White—permitting the regulation only of "expert knowledge" that is tailored to "a particular client's circumstances."[75] And the Institute for Justice—our firm—argued that the "professional speech doctrine" was, at its core, a deeply dangerous "doctrinal innovation" that should be rejected root and branch.[76]

In short, the breadth of available approaches—not just different outcomes, but fundamentally different rules of law—was strikingly wide, as one would expect after 30 years of silence from the Court. And that meant that the Supreme Court's actual decision could be expected to have consequences that swept far beyond the specific context of crisis-pregnancy centers.

IV. The Supreme Court Decision

In an opinion well worth the wait, the Supreme Court reversed and upended the lower courts' long-standing experiment with the professional-speech doctrine. Laudably, the Court's opinion, written by Justice Clarence Thomas, begins by squarely confronting the doctrinal elephant in the room: Like the Ninth Circuit, the Supreme Court acknowledges that the Licensed Notice was a content-based regulation of speech, given that it compelled individuals to engage in speech of a particular content. Unlike the Ninth Circuit however, the Supreme Court was not bound by any precedent establishing a professional speech exception to ordinary First Amendment doctrine.

Addressing the professional-speech question on a clean slate, the Court began (as it has in so many other cases) by reiterating the doctrinal rule forbidding content-based restrictions on speech. The Court also emphasized that exceptions to that rule

[74] Brief of Amicus Curiae Public Citizen, Inc., in Support of Respondents at 16, NIFLA v. Becerra, 138 S. Ct. 2361 (2018) (No. 16-1140).

[75] Brief for the Cato Institute as Amicus Curiae in Support of Petitioners at 3–6, NIFLA v. Becerra, 138 S. Ct. 2361 (2018) (No. 16-1140).

[76] Brief of Amicus Curiae Institute for Justice in Support of Petitioners at 3–4, NIFLA v. Becerra, 138 S. Ct. 2361 (2018) (No. 16-1140).

cannot be *created*—they can only be *recognized* as already existing based on "persuasive evidence . . . of a long (if heretofore unrecognized) tradition to that effect."[77] While this evidentiary requirement is longstanding, the Supreme Court's restatement of the principle here matters, if only because lower courts have sometimes been reluctant to heed the Court's repeated warnings on this point.[78]

In the face of this evidentiary burden, the professional-speech doctrine fared less well than it had in the lower courts. The Supreme Court not only found no historical support for the doctrine, it determined that the doctrine itself posed a serious threat to speech rights generally. Looking first to its own precedents, the Court could identify only two situations in which it had upheld restrictions on the speech of "professionals": Commercial advertisement by those professionals, and restrictions on professional conduct that nonetheless involved speech.

The first category is epitomized by *Zauderer v. Office of Disciplinary Counsel of the Supreme Court of Ohio*.[79] But the Court noted *Zauderer* involved not only commercial advertising but required only the disclosure of "purely factual and uncontroversial information" about the services being advertised.[80] That was far afield from the factual information required by the Licensed Notice, which was both controversial (given that it was about abortion) and not descriptive of the services the centers themselves offered.

The Court's refusal to consider *Zauderer* as embodying a general rule for "professional speech" seems indisputable, particularly because the Court has considered any number of restrictions on professionals' commercial speech and has consistently treated them as restrictions on commercial speech rather than as restrictions on professionals. Just as with any other commercial-speech restriction,

---

[77] NIFLA, 138 S. Ct. at 2372 (internal quotations omitted).

[78] Compare United States v. Stevens, 559 U.S. 460, 472 (2010) (cautioning that courts do not have "a freewheeling authority to declare new categories of speech outside the scope of the First Amendment") with Pickup, 740 F.3d at 1221 (9th Cir. 2014) (O'Scannlain, J., dissenting from denial of rehearing en banc) (arguing that the creation of a "professional speech" exception was an exercise of exactly that sort of freewheeling authority).

[79] 471 U.S. 626 (1985).

[80] NIFLA, 138 S. Ct. at 2372 (citing Zauderer, 471 U.S. at 651).

the Court has demanded evidence to justify them, upholding some[81] and rejecting others.[82] These cases fit well into the Court's overall treatment of commercial speech restrictions (of which the modern Court is generally, if not universally, skeptical). It would be odd, then, if these cases were instead an implicit recognition of a broad exemption from First Amendment scrutiny for restrictions on so-called professional speech.

The second category of cases involving "professional" speech, the Court clarified, are regulations of professional *conduct* with an incidental effect on the professional's speech.[83] "While drawing the line between speech and conduct can be difficult," the Court acknowledged, "this Court's precedents have long drawn it."[84]

The primary precedent on speech/conduct confronting the Court in *NIFLA* was *Planned Parenthood of Southeastern Pa. v. Casey*.[85] In that case, the Court rejected some provisions of a Pennsylvania abortion law, but upheld (with little analysis) an "informed consent" requirement that prohibited doctors from providing abortions without first providing a variety of information to the patient. This information ranged from the probable gestational age of the child to information about state-created print-outs detailing assistance programs available to new mothers.[86]

The Court's *NIFLA* opinion dispensed quickly with *Casey*: That case was about obtaining informed consent before performing a medical procedure, while the notice required in *NIFLA* was not connected to any medical procedure whatsoever.[87] As discussed more fully in the next section, this leaves the substantive question of how the First Amendment interacts with informed-consent requirements deeply unsettled. But for purposes of resolving *NIFLA*, the Court found things clear enough: That case was about informed consent

[81] E.g., Ohralik v. Ohio State Bar Ass'n, 436 U.S. 447, 456–57 (1978) (upholding restriction on in-person solicitation by lawyers based on record of long-standing prohibitions on the practice and dangers it posed to consumers).

[82] E.g., Edenfield v. Fane, 507 U.S. 761, 770–73 (1993) (declining to extend *Ohralik*'s holding to accountants without comparable record evidence).

[83] NIFLA, 138 S. Ct. at 2373.

[84] *Id.*

[85] 505 U.S. 833 (1992).

[86] *Id.* at 881.

[87] NIFLA, 138 S. Ct. at 2373.

to a medical procedure, and this case was about hanging unwanted signs in your office lobby.

Having found no support for professional speech in its own cases, the Court also rejected the professional-speech doctrine on its own merits, both because professional speech is important and because a First Amendment exemption for "professional speech" would grant governments new powers of unpredictable and uncontrollable scope.

First, the Court reaffirmed that the core purpose of the First Amendment is to safeguard an "uninhibited marketplace of ideas in which truth will ultimately prevail,"[88] and that so-called professionals have just as much role to play in this search for truth as any other.[89] On a certain level, this seems obvious—perhaps particularly to readers who are themselves professionals and therefore certain of the many important things they have to say. But the true import of this passage of the Court's opinion is the breadth of topics it finds at the heart of the First Amendment—topics ranging from "the ethics of assisted suicide" to "the wisdom of divorce" to "the amount of money that should be devoted to savings."[90] This, in keeping with modern precedent, is a complete rejection of the notion that the First Amendment can protect only "speech that is explicitly political."[91] Instead, the First Amendment protects speech that is *important*—and the measure of importance is not importance to the government or even to democracy. The measure of importance is whether speech is important to the speaker and to the listener. And by that metric, advice from professionals like doctors and lawyers falls at the very heart of the First Amendment.

Beyond the importance of professionals' speech, the Court also noted the danger of excluding "professionals" from the First Amendment, because no one knows quite who they are. The doctrine set forth by the Ninth Circuit in *NIFLA* would cover "doctors, lawyers, nurses, physical therapists, truck drivers, bartenders, barbers, and many others."[92] Giving states such a slippery tool to

---

[88] McCullen v. Coakley, 134 S. Ct. 2518, 2529 (2014) (quotation marks omitted).

[89] NIFLA, 138 S. Ct. at 2374–75.

[90] *Id.* at 2375.

[91] Robert Bork, Neutral Principles and Some First Amendment Problems, 47 Indiana L. J. 1, 20 (1971); accord Robert Post & Amanda Shanor, Adam Smith's First Amendment, 128 Harv. L. Rev. F. 165 (2015).

[92] NIFLA, 138 S. Ct. at 2375.

escape First Amendment scrutiny would invite exactly the kind of invidious discrimination against disfavored speakers that the First Amendment is meant to protect against.[93]

Again, the Court's position here is borne out by lived experience in the lower courts. As noted above, courts and government officials had seized upon the professional speech exception for exactly that purpose: In 2015, for example, the Oregon State Board of Examiners for Engineering and Land Surveyors assessed a $1,000 fine against a private citizen for submitting technical testimony at a public meeting without a license. His "reports, commentary, and testimony," the board ruled, were the acts of a "professional" and thus "clearly not protected speech."[94]

Having determined that no special "professional speech" rule governed, the Supreme Court made short work of both the Licensed and the Unlicensed Notice requirements. The Licensed Notice would fail even intermediate scrutiny because it was "wildly under-inclusive," applying only to a tiny slice of clinics that provided services to pregnant women. Additionally, the state had failed to provide evidence that less-restrictive alternatives (like having the government provide this information to women directly instead of conscripting unwilling clinics as its messengers) would be ineffective.[95]

The Court then found that the Unlicensed Notice would similarly fail any level of scrutiny. While the state asserted an interest in ensuring that crisis-pregnancy centers did not deceive women into thinking they were receiving medical care from licensed professionals, it had failed to adduce evidence (at least at the preliminary-injunction stage) that people were actually being deceived in the first place. And, in any event, the state's remedy—requiring its word-for-word disclosure at every facility, without regard to how clear that facility was in communicating its unlicensed status in the first place—was both unnecessarily burdensome and strangely under-inclusive. Among other things, the FACT Act covered facilities that provided pregnancy tests

---

[93] *Id.* (cleaned up).

[94] Final Order by Default at 16–17, In the Matter of Dale La Forest, Case No. 2697 (Aug. 14, 2015), available at http://ij.org/wp-content/uploads/2017/04/OR-Math-La-Forest-Default-Order-IJ083240xA6322-1.pdf.

[95] NIFLA, 138 S. Ct. at 2375–76.

but not other unlicensed facilities that could just as easily fool people into thinking they provided licensed medical care.[96]

Beyond the Court's controlling opinion, two other justices filed opinions of their own. First, Justice Anthony Kennedy (joined by Chief Justice John Roberts and Justices Samuel Alito and Neil Gorsuch) wrote a concurring opinion underscoring the dangerous viewpoint discrimination that might lurk at the heart of the challenged law. While careful to note that the record was insufficiently developed to draw any firm conclusions, Justice Kennedy noted that it certainly appeared from the face of the law that California sought to conscript a particular subset of people (pro-life pregnancy centers) into conveying a message directly at odds with their core beliefs (specifically, information about state-subsidized abortions). Far removed from any actual concerns about deception or consumer confusion, Justice Kennedy noted that such a law would represent a serious threat to "freedom of thought and belief" that could not be tolerated in a free society.[97]

Finally, in dissent, Justice Stephen Breyer (joined by Justices Ruth Bader Ginsburg, Sonia Sotomayor, and Elena Kagan) decried the majority opinion for imperiling a wide array of "economic and social legislation" that, in his view, must escape judicial scrutiny at the risk of reviving *Lochner v. New York*.[98] This is not the first time that Justice Breyer has invoked the ghost of *Lochner* to warn against the dangers of scrutinizing restrictions on speech too closely,[99] but the argument here bears examination.

Perhaps the most telling difference between the dissent and the majority opinion in *NIFLA* rests in their disparate treatment of *Casey*. Recall that the majority distinguishes *Casey* on the grounds that *Casey* involved informed consent to a medical procedure and that California's law here was attendant on no such medical procedure.

---

[96] *Id.*

[97] *Id.* at 2379 (Kennedy, J., concurring). We suspect that Justice Thomas agreed with all this, but of course if he had joined his brethren here, there would have been two majority opinions.

[98] *Id.* at 2381 (Breyer, J., dissenting).

[99] E.g., Sorrell v. IMS Health, Inc., 564 U.S. 552, 585 (2011) (Breyer, J., dissenting); cf. *id.* at 567 (noting that while "the Constitution does not enact Mr. Herbert Spencer's Social Statics[, i]t does enact the First Amendment" (citations and quotation marks omitted)).

Justice Breyer sharply disagrees, noting that the state's interest in disclosure should be equally strong:

> No one doubts that choosing an abortion is a medical procedure that involves certain health risks. But the same is true of carrying a child to term and giving birth.... Nationwide, childbirth is 14 times more likely than abortion to result in the woman's death. Health considerations do not favor disclosure of alternatives and risks associated with the latter but not those associated with the former.[100]

The dissent, of course, is not incorrect: Just as abortion comes with potential health implications, so too does carrying a child to term. But that hardly goes far enough. Having sex in the first place has health implications, only some of which are pregnancy-related. Actually having small children has health implications, ranging from lost sleep to the ever-present danger of stepping on toys in the middle of the night.[101] The state's interest in informing us of these potential consequences, then, seems equally strong at any point from puberty to death.

This interest, though, tells us nothing about the First Amendment scrutiny required of any regulation in this area. That is because the initial inquiry in a First Amendment case is not into the government's interest but instead (as the majority in *NIFLA* notes) into what the government is regulating: speech or conduct. That is, the first question is whether the law at issue is one "abridging the freedom of speech."[102] If it is, the First Amendment applies.

Any other test runs the risk of leaving government officials as the final arbiters of what people must (or must not) hear at any particular point in their lives. And that would result in people's ability to engage in conversations about vital life decisions being left up to, in essence, the vicissitudes of geography. Government officials in Alabama will surely have a different view of how best to balance the various health risks surrounding sex and pregnancy than do officials in California. If the democratic process can freely regulate

[100] NIFLA, 138 S. Ct. at 2386 (Breyer, J., dissenting).

[101] See Sonali Kohli, The Science of Why Stepping on Legos Makes You Want to Die, Quartz, Mar. 20, 2015, https://qz.com/366858/legos-are-so-painful-to-step-on -because-of-physics.

[102] U.S. Const. amend. I.

conversations on such weighty topics, we could expect extremely different conversations to be permitted (or required) in each place. But fundamentally, the First Amendment is meant to ensure that government officials with different ideologies cannot control the conversation; only the individuals actually having it can do so.

This does not mean, of course, that governments may not conduct public-information campaigns, regulate misleading commercial speech, or require certain factual disclosures. It simply means that individual Americans must retain the basic right to decide what they want to say and who they want to listen to—a right that cannot be overridden simply because government officials want to make sure we hear the things they want us to hear.

V. Implications for Other Cases, Future Litigation

The impact of the Supreme Court's decision in *NIFLA* will be seismic. As discussed above, the professional-speech exception to the First Amendment had spread widely throughout the lower courts. Indeed, while it is true that no opinion of the Supreme Court had ever endorsed the doctrine, it is equally true that no appellate court had ever rejected it. Courts had disagreed about the scope and nature of the doctrine,[103] but no court had squarely rejected it as the Supreme Court now has. This marks a major change in the law as applied by lower courts.

It does not presage the invalidation of professional licensing as a whole. Most state licensing laws will have no First Amendment applications at all.[104] The First Amendment question, again, boils down to whether the application of a statute or regulation is triggered by *communicating a message*, and most professional regulations will not be. Financial advisers take money from their clients to invest on their behalf; doctors perform surgeries; lawyers prepare and file binding legal documents. Even some regulations of "speech" in the colloquial sense will be regulations of "conduct" under this test. Consider a doctor writing a prescription: The doctor of course writes words on a piece of paper to write a prescription, but the government regulation

[103] Compare King v. Governor of N.J., 776 F.3d 216 (3d Cir. 2014) with Pickup v. Brown, 740 F.3d 1208 (9th Cir. 2014).

[104] This does not, of course, necessarily mean such laws are constitutional. See St. Joseph Abbey v. Castille, 712 F.3d 215 (5th Cir. 2013).

of that act has nothing to do with the message communicated and everything to do with the *legal effect* of the prescription (that is, giving the recipient the legal right to access a controlled substance). In other words, there is a difference between a law preventing a doctor from *saying* "you would benefit from using this substance" and a law preventing a doctor from in effect *giving a patient* that substance.

It is also worth noting that there is a difference between *prophylactic* restrictions on speech and laws that punish speech that actually causes harm.[105] Recognizing that the First Amendment protects professional advice does not mean an end to actions for malpractice. Instead of resulting in the wholesale elimination of these regulations, *NIFLA* will shift the focus to a question of whether particular *applications* of the regulations are infringements on speech rather than restrictions on conduct. And these laws are already being drawn. Just a week before *NIFLA* was handed down, the Rhode Island Supreme Court announced oral argument in a set of three cases exploring the boundaries of the state's unauthorized practice of law rule.[106] These cases will give that court one of the earliest chances to construe *NIFLA*, as it explores whether the state's rules allow punishment of a notary who discusses the substance of legal documents during a real-estate closing.

But *NIFLA* also has implications for the economy far beyond the regulation of traditional professionals like lawyers or doctors. The Supreme Court's elimination of the professional-speech doctrine will mean a sharp reduction in the government's ability to prohibit people from conveying information in the name of economic regulation. This will have enormous implications for the regulation and continued growth of modern technologies, as more and more people earn their living not from their physical conduct but from the information they can provide.

---

[105] See, e.g., United States v. Alvarez, 567 U.S. 709, 718–19 (2012) (noting that false statements that create a "legally cognizable harm" can be punished consistent with the First Amendment); cf. Paul M. Sherman, Occupational Speech and the First Amendment, 128 Harv. L. Rev. F. 183, 195–96 (2015) (noting that actions for medical and legal malpractice predate both licensing requirements and the First Amendment itself and therefore presumably are not barred by the First Amendment).

[106] See In re William E. Paplauskas, Jr., No. 2018-161-M.P. (June 18, 2018); In re Daniel S. Balkun and Balkun Title & Closing, Inc., No. 2018-162-M.P. (June 18, 2018); In re SouthCoast Title and Escrow, Inc., No. 2018-163-M.P. (June 18, 2018).

Take Vizaline, LLC—a Mississippi startup that uses a computer algorithm to translate publicly available legal descriptions of property (called "metes and bounds") into a line drawing of the property line overlaid onto a satellite image of the area. The service provides an easy way for human beings to visualize abstract legal descriptions, and it is particularly useful for banks making loans on small properties whose cash value does not justify hiring a land surveyor to draw a map.[107] The service drew no complaints from its customers, but it did draw a lawsuit from the state's Board of Licensure for Professional Engineers and Surveyors, which argued that the software constituted the unlicensed practice of surveying and demanded that Vizaline disgorge all the money it earned in the state by satisfying its uncomplaining customers. If occupational licensing were indeed exempt from First Amendment scrutiny, companies like Vizaline could be swept out of business by their pre-internet competitors. In the wake of *NIFLA*, however, states' ability to constrain the flow of this sort of information will be sharply curtailed.

The Court's opinion in *NIFLA* also leaves some unsettled questions, largely about the scope of the government's power to demand disclosures tied to someone's underlying conduct—an uncertainty that rests largely with the Court's relatively brief treatment of *Casey*. *Casey*'s somewhat gnomic reasoning has long puzzled lower courts dealing with medicine-related speech restrictions,[108] and *NIFLA* gives little guidance as to what, exactly, *Casey* continues to mean. Some commentators have suggested that *Casey* is indeed a compelled-speech case and that it can be reconciled with the doctrine on the grounds that an informed-consent requirement is an "easy case" that would satisfy even strict scrutiny under the First Amendment.[109] There is some appeal to this view. After all, there

[107] See generally Institute for Justice, Mississippi Mapping, https://ij.org/case/mississippi-mapping.

[108] Compare Tex. Med. Providers Performing Abortion Servs. v. Lakey, 667 F.3d 570, 575–76 (5th Cir. 2012) (finding that *Casey* establishes a standard of review for abortion-related informed-consent requirements that is "the antithesis of strict scrutiny") with Stuart v. Camnitz, 774 F.3d 238, 249 (4th Cir. 2014) ("The single paragraph in *Casey* does not assert that physicians forfeit their First Amendment rights in the procedures surrounding abortions, nor does it announce the proper level of scrutiny to be applied to abortion regulations that compel speech to the extraordinary extent present here.")

[109] Rodney A. Smolla, Professional Speech and the First Amendment, 119 W. Va. L. Rev. 67, 81 (2016).

seems an extremely compelling interest in ensuring that doctors don't perform tonsillectomies without first telling the patient that the surgery involves removing their tonsils.

The Court's *NIFLA* opinion, though, seems to suggest that *Casey* does not require First Amendment scrutiny at all because informed consent is simply a restriction on the professional *conduct* of performing the underlying medical procedure. This, too, has something to recommend it. The Court's modern free-speech analysis is largely focused on what *triggers* the application of a particular law. If "the conduct triggering coverage under [a] statute consists of communicating a message," then the statute is a restriction on speech subject to First Amendment scrutiny.[110] Under that view (perhaps) the Court is suggesting that the regulation in *Casey* functioned solely as a regulation of the conduct of performing an abortion—that is, that it was the functional equivalent of a regulation that simply said "it is illegal to perform an abortion without the patient's informed consent." This leaves wholly unanswered, though, how much information a patient needs to have to give "informed consent" to any given procedure—and how willing courts will be to police the boundaries of such requirements.

Conclusion

For years, federal appellate courts have disregarded the admonitions of the U.S. Supreme Court and accorded second-class status to the speech and advice of people who talk for a living. The *NIFLA* decision instructs them, in no uncertain terms, to stop. This major shift in the federal courts' approach to occupational speech will have sweeping effects on the ability of entrepreneurs and others to convey their knowledge and opinions to a willing audience—and a concomitant effect on the ability of government officials to control what information can be shared. Whatever one's feelings on the crisis-pregnancy centers at the heart of this case, that is an outcome worth celebrating.

[110] Holder v. Humanitarian Law Project, 561 U.S. 1, 28 (2010).

Regulation of Political Apparel in Polling Places: Why the Supreme Court's *Mansky* Opinion Did Not Go Far Enough

*Rodney A. Smolla**

I. Introduction

In *Minnesota Voters Alliance v. Mansky*, the Supreme Court struck down a Minnesota law prohibiting voters from wearing various political messages on buttons or clothing inside a polling place on Election Day.[1] In an opinion written by Chief Justice John Roberts, the Court held that Minnesota's sweeping ban on political expression violated the First Amendment. The vote was 7–2, with Justice Sonia Sotomayor, joined by Justice Stephen Breyer, dissenting.

The Minnesota law was breathtaking in its sweep, and, for that reason, easy pickings. Minnesota's law was "uncommonly silly"[2] and undoubtedly unconstitutional. The Supreme Court was absolutely right in striking it down. Yet the opinion in *Mansky* was markedly reserved, filled with hedging caveats and provisos.

Chief Justice Roberts has emerged as one of the Court's true First Amendment zealots. His opinions are often fired by eloquent passion for freedom of speech. In *United States v. Stevens*, for example, he wrote for the Court in striking down a ban on graphic depictions of animal cruelty, rejecting the position that First Amendment protection should extend only to "categories of speech that survive an ad hoc balancing of relative social costs and benefits."[3] Rather, he wrote, the "First Amendment itself reflects a judgment by the American people

---

* Dean and Professor of Law, Widener University Delaware Law School.

[1] Minn. Voters All. v. Mansky, 138 S. Ct. 1876 (2018).

[2] See Griswold v. Connecticut, 381 U.S. 479, 527 (1965) (Stewart, J., dissenting) ("I think this is an uncommonly silly law.").

[3] United States v. Stevens, 559 U.S. 460, 470 (2010).

that the benefits of its restrictions on the Government outweigh the costs."[4] His opinion emphatically declared, "Our Constitution forecloses any attempt to revise that judgment simply on the basis that some speech is not worth it."[5] Even more striking was his opinion in *Snyder v. Phelps*, upholding the mean-spirited and deeply offensive homophobic military funeral picketing by the Westboro Baptist Church, in which he concluded:

> Speech is powerful. It can stir people to action, move them to tears of both joy and sorrow, and—as it did here—inflict great pain. On the facts before us, we cannot react to that pain by punishing the speaker. As a Nation we have chosen a different course—to protect even hurtful speech on public issues to ensure that we do not stifle public debate. That choice requires that we shield Westboro from tort liability for its picketing in this case.[6]

None of this First Amendment fire was visible in *Mansky*, however. To the contrary, the chief justice went out of his way to leave open the possibility that less extreme restrictions on polling place apparel and accessories might be upheld.

While the outcome of the case was laudable, the hedging and trimming in the Court's opinion may do much future mischief. First Amendment jurisprudence and the vibrancy of our democratic process would have been better served by a more robust condemnation of the paternalistic impulse of states to control what people wear when they cast a vote.

This article describes the *Mansky* holding, exposes the Court's hints and innuendos suggesting that narrower voting apparel laws might be upheld, explores the roots of the Court's reticence to condemn more broadly bans on what people wear to vote, and critiques the Court for not acting more aggressively to curb such laws.

II. The Court's Holding

A. The Minnesota Ban

Minnesota's law contained three prohibitions on expressive activity in and around polling places on Election Day. All three were part

---

[4] *Id.*

[5] *Id.*

[6] Snyder v. Phelps, 562 U.S. 443, 460–61 (2011).

of a statute bearing the title "Election day prohibitions," and a subsection entitled "Soliciting near polling places."[7]

The first prohibition declared, "A person may not display campaign material, post signs, ask, solicit, or in any manner try to induce or persuade a voter within a polling place or within 100 feet of the building in which a polling place is situated, or anywhere on the public property on which a polling place is situated, on primary or election day to vote for or refrain from voting for a candidate or ballot question."[8] This provision, prohibiting campaign workers and others from attempting to influence voters as they arrive to vote, was not challenged in *Mansky*. It was indistinguishable from a similar Tennessee law previously upheld by the Supreme Court in 1992, in *Burson v. Freeman*.[9]

The second prohibition declared, "A person may not provide political badges, political buttons, or other political insignia to be worn at or about the polling place on the day of a primary or election."[10] This sentence was not the focus of the litigation in *Mansky*, but it might have been. If a voter has a right to wear a button or T-shirt displaying messages such as "National Rifle Association" or "Black Lives Matter," then surely there is a corresponding right by others to provide a button or T-shirt bearing those messages to a voter. The second prohibition was not formally challenged by the litigants in *Mansky*, however, nor did the Court remark on it. Its fate will await another day.

Minnesota's third prohibition, the "political apparel" restriction, declared, "A political badge, political button, or other political insignia may not be worn at or about the polling place on primary or election day."[11] Beneficently, the statute contained a carve-out reciting, "Nothing in this subdivision prohibits the distribution of 'I VOTED' stickers." Only this third political apparel provision was challenged in *Mansky*.

Persons wearing such political contraband to the polling place on Election Day were law-violators, but not big-time criminals. Trafficking in or possessing illegal political buttons was not exactly like dealing cocaine. Election officials were instructed to first approach

---

[7] Minn. Stat. § 211B.11(1) (Supp. 2017).

[8] *Id.*

[9] 504 U.S. 191 (1992).

[10] Minn. Stat. § 211B.11(1) (Supp. 2017).

[11] *Id.*

the offending voter and ask the voter to conceal or remove the illegal message.[12] A voter who refuses to remove or conceal the offending message must still then be allowed to vote. The election official, however, is to make it "clear that the incident 'will be recorded and referred to appropriate authorities.'" This is something akin to a middle schooler being admonished that an incident will go on his or her permanent record.

Though no one in Minnesota could go to jail for wearing a banned message, legal consequences could ensue. Violators were subjected to an administrative process before the Minnesota Office of Administrative Hearings, which had the power to issue a reprimand or impose a civil penalty.[13] A Minnesota county attorney with nothing better to do could also charge the violator with a petty misdemeanor, carrying up to a $300 fine.

For the challengers who brought the litigation in *Mansky*, it surely was not so much the penalty as the principle that supplied the rub. The challengers were led by the Minnesota Voters Alliance, a nonprofit seeking better government through election reforms, its executive director, Andrew Cilek, and Susan Jeffers, an election judge. Among the messages the challengers sought to wear to the polling place were buttons saying "Please I.D. Me" and a "Tea Party Patriots" shirt. Andrew Cilek appeared to draw the greatest hassle from election officials. In addition to wearing a "Please I.D. Me" button, he had the temerity to wear a T-shirt with the words "Don't Tread on Me" and a "Tea Party Patriots" logo. Cilek was twice turned away from the polls altogether (something which was not supposed to happen). When Cilek was finally allowed to vote, an election official recorded the incident.[14]

B. The Reach of the Minnesota Ban

In First Amendment challenges to government restriction on expression, the parties often begin with a threshold spar over exactly what is and what is not prohibited by the restriction. Governments will typically try to make the restriction appear narrow, and no big deal. Minnesota tried this, seeking to save itself in *Mansky* by limiting

[12] Mansky, 138 S. Ct. at 1883.
[13] Minn. Stat. §§ 211B.32, 211B.35(2) (2014).
[14] Mansky, 138 S. Ct. at 1884.

the meaning of its political apparel ban. The effort backfired. The more talking Minnesota did, the more trouble it made for itself.

The Minnesota secretary of state distributed a guideline policy, providing that the apparel ban included, but was not limited to:

- Any item including the name of a political party in Minnesota, such as the Republican, [Democratic–Farmer–Labor], Independence, Green or Libertarian parties;
- Any item including the name of a candidate at any election;
- Any item in support of or opposition to a ballot question at any election;
- Issue oriented material designed to influence or impact voting (including specifically the "Please I.D. Me" buttons);
- Material promoting a group with recognizable political views (such as the Tea Party, MoveOn.org, and so on).[15]

The first three examples were clear enough, as the Court saw them. They banned the names of political parties, the names of candidates, and messaging expressing support or opposition to a ballot question.[16] Whether or not these prohibitions violated the First Amendment, at least the substantive reach of the prohibitions was easy to understand. (As later explained, the Court strongly hinted that had the Minnesota law been limited to these examples, it would not have been struck down.)

As to the other two examples, Minnesota had some explaining to do, and the more it explained, the worse things got. Both the statute and the guidelines used the word "political" in a manner that the Court described as "unmoored."[17] The dictionary definition of "political" is expansive, encompassing "anything 'of or relating to government, a government, or the conduct of government affairs.'"[18] As the Court lamented, under this definition the mere wearing of a button that said "Vote!" could qualify.[19]

While Minnesota tried to confine the meaning of "political" to electoral choices facing the voter on Election Day, the Court did not

[15] *Id.* at 1884.

[16] *Id.* at 1889.

[17] *Id.* at 1888.

[18] *Id.* (quoting Webster's Third New International Dictionary 1755 (2002)).

[19] *Id.* at 1888.

buy the state's effort. Minnesota argued that the ban only reached "'words and symbols that an objectively reasonable observer would perceive as conveying a message about the electoral choices at issue in [the] polling place.'"[20] The Court pointed out, however, that the statutory language banned "campaign material," and then, over and above that, also banned "political" material. And at oral argument, the counsel for Minnesota conceded that the law expanded "'the scope of what is prohibited from campaign speech to additional political speech.'"[21] This was a candid concession, but not one that helped the state's cause.

The fourth of the five guidelines provided by the state, explaining that the law banned "[I]ssue oriented materials designed to influence or impact voting," proved particularly problematic. The word "issue" appeared to encompass any subject "on which a political candidate or party has taken a stance."[22] The reason that "Please I.D. Me" buttons were not allowed, even though *no ballot questions dealt with voter identification*, for example, was that Republican candidates for governor and secretary of state *had* taken positions on voter-identification laws. Minnesota conceded at oral argument that a button stating "#MeToo" would be banned if a candidate for office had brought up issues relating to sexual harassment and assault. The Court suggested that even the message "Support Our Troops" could be banned if a candidate or party had engaged on issues of military funding or aid to veterans.[23]

Moving from bad to worse, the final exemplar offered by Minnesota, banning messages "promoting a group with recognizable political views," drove the chief justice to the heights of apoplectic sarcasm. Noting that any number of groups might take positions on issues of public concern, from the American Civil Liberties Union, the AARP, the World Wildlife Fund, to Ben & Jerry's, the potential sweep of this aspect of the ban clearly pushed the Court over the edge. (The chief justice did not mention the Cato Institute—but that was mere oversight.)

Conjuring the political stir over the policy of the Boy Scouts to exclude members based on sexual orientation, the Court suggested

20 *Id.* at 1888–89 (quoting Brief for Respondents at 13).
21 *Id.* at 1889 (quoting Transcript of Oral Arg. at 50).
22 *Id.* at 1889.
23 *Id.* at 1890.

that a Scout leader stopping to vote on his way to a troop meeting might have been asked to cover his uniform.[24] The most unkindest cut of all.

C. *The Forum Status of Polling Places*

The Court began its substantive First Amendment analysis by assessing the public forum status of a polling place, beginning with an overview primer on public-forum law. "Generally speaking, our cases recognize three types of government-controlled spaces: traditional public forums, designated public forums, and nonpublic forums. In a traditional public forum—parks, streets, sidewalks, and the like—the government may impose reasonable time, place, and manner restrictions on private speech, but restrictions based on content must satisfy strict scrutiny, and those based on viewpoint are prohibited."[25] Identical standards "apply in designated public forums—spaces that have 'not traditionally been regarded as a public forum' but which the government has 'intentionally opened up for that purpose.'"[26] In "a nonpublic forum, on the other hand—a space that 'is not by tradition or designation a forum for public communication'—the government has much more flexibility to craft rules limiting speech."[27] "The government may reserve such a forum 'for its intended purposes, communicative or otherwise, as long as the regulation on speech is reasonable and not an effort to suppress expression merely because public officials oppose the speaker's view.'"[28]

The Court proceeded to hold that a polling place is a nonpublic forum. "It is, at least on Election Day, government-controlled property set aside for the sole purpose of voting."[29] The First Amendment standards governing speech regulation in a nonpublic forum are quite lax. Provided the government does not engage in viewpoint discrimination, restrictions on expression in a nonpublic forum need only be "'reasonable in light of the purpose served by

[24] *Id.*

[25] *Id.* at 1885.

[26] *Id.* (internal citation omitted).

[27] *Id.* (quoting Perry Educ. Assn. v. Perry Local Educators' Ass'n., 460 U.S. 37, 46 (1983)).

[28] *Id.*

[29] *Id.* at 1886.

the forum.'"[30] The Minnesota law was neutral as to viewpoint—it would bar both a "Trump" button and a "Clinton" button, or both an "All Lives Matter" and a "Black Lives Matter" T-shirt. This meant the law need only be reasonable in relation to the purpose of the forum, a test that in most cases is not easy to flunk. But Minnesota flunked it.

D. Striking Down the Ban as Unreasonable

The Court struck down the Minnesota ban, insisting that the state must "draw a reasonable line" and must be able to "articulate some sensible basis for distinguishing what may come in from what must stay out."[31]

Given the manifold sweep and mushy subjectivity of the Minnesota ban, the better question is not why the Court struck the law down as why the vote was only 7–2 and not unanimous. Since the mere engagement by a political candidate or a political party on an issue was enough to push that issue out-of-bounds for voting-place apparel, Minnesota's law required election officials to keep tabs on what candidates and parties stood for in order to keep tab on what messages could be worn. This alone was enough to do in the rule. "A rule whose fair enforcement requires an election judge to maintain a mental index of the platforms and positions of every candidate and party on the ballot is not reasonable."[32]

The picking and choosing necessary to determine who or what was in or out when it came to other organizations and messages was equally unsavory. The Court's opinion mocking these choices was close to parody. "All Lives Matter" was *probably* out, "The National Rifle Association" was *definitely* out, but a "Rainbow Flag" was in *unless* a candidate's campaign position or a ballot issue somehow dealt with gay rights.[33] Or consider my personal favorite: a shirt simply displaying the text of the Second Amendment would be banned, but a shirt displaying the text of the First Amendment would not.[34] Go figure.

[30] *Id.* (quoting Cornelius v. NAACP Legal Defense & Educ. Fund, Inc., 473 U.S. 788, 806 (1985))

[31] *Id.* at 1888.

[32] *Id.* at 1889.

[33] *Id.* at 1891.

[34] *Id.*

With all these infirmities, it is easy enough to see why the Court wisely sought to put the law out of its misery. As noted, it was easy pickings, and hard to see it any other way.

This might seem uncharitable to Justices Sotomayor and Breyer, who perhaps *did* see it another way. But not really. Even Justice Sotomayor's opinion did not attempt to defend the Minnesota ban on the merits as constitutionally permissible, *assuming* the Minnesota ban actually meant what the chief justice's opinion for the Court said it meant. The dissent merely argued that the Court should have certified the definition of the law to the Minnesota Supreme Court, to give that court the chance to render a narrowing construction consistent with First Amendment standards, thereby obviating "the hypothetical line-drawing problems" that she believed animated the decision of the majority.[35]

III. *Mansky's* Limits

Justice Sotomayor's dissenting lament that Minnesota should have been given a chance to save itself carries significant clues and cues. Her point presupposes that Minnesota *could* save itself—that a more narrowly crafted ban would not have been struck down as unconstitutional, even under the principles articulated by the *Mansky* majority. There are numerous indications in the majority opinion suggesting that she is correct. As I state in my closing critique, I am not enamored of this assessment on its merits, but as prediction, it is probably sound.

Recall that in the majority opinion, the principal fault line was the divide between what I will label political "campaign" speech and "political issue" or "political organization" speech. Minnesota kept trying to narrow the interpretation of its own law to mere campaign speech, such as speech backing a particular candidate or an issue directly in play on a pending ballot, while the Court kept insisting that, on the record before it, the law was not so limited.

---

[35] *Id*. at 1893 (Sotomayor, J., dissenting) ("I agree with the Court that casting a vote is a weighty civic act and that States may reasonably take steps to ensure that partisan discord not follow the voter up to the voting booth, including by prohibit[ing] certain apparel [in polling places] because of the message it conveys. . . . I disagree, however, with the Court's decision to declare Minnesota's political apparel ban unconstitutional on its face because, in its view, the ban is not capable of reasoned application . . . when the Court has not first afforded the Minnesota state courts a reasonable opportunity to pass upon and construe the statute.") (cleaned up).

Did this signal that if Minnesota's attempt at narrowing had been credible, the result would have been different? Would the Court approve a law prohibiting speech within the confines of a polling place urging the election or rejection of a candidate or specific ballot measure? The most revealing tea leaves may be gathered from the very end of the opinion, where the Court wrote, "That is not to say that Minnesota has set upon an impossible task."[36]

I take this as code reminiscent of the lyric from the group Solid Base: "This is how you do it." Upon suggesting the task of limiting political apparel was not impossible, the Court immediately cited laws from two of Minnesota's sister states, California and Texas. The laws of both focused on naming the names of candidates and naming specific ballot measures before the voters, laws the Court described as "proscribing displays (including apparel) in more lucid terms."[37]

"Lucid," like probably constitutional. The Court immediately invoked the stock disclaimer, cautioning that it was not purporting to decide issues not before it: "We do not suggest that such provisions set the outer limit of what a State may proscribe, and do not pass on the constitutionality of laws that are not before us. But we do hold that if a State wishes to set its polling places apart as areas free of partisan discord, it must employ a more discernible approach than the one Minnesota has offered here." As in, "Dude, can you take a hint?"

I can take one, and if I were a betting man—oh, I am!—I would bet that as matters currently stand, the California and Texas laws, and others of their ilk, are short odds to prevail in any constitutional challenge.

Yes, I'm a betting man—and I tend to pull for underdogs. In the next two sections, I first opine on why I think the Court was so cautious. I follow with an argument attempting to improve my odds—explaining why the Court should be open to establishing heartier

---

[36] *Id.* at 1891.

[37] *Id.* (citing, Cal. Elec. Code Ann. § 319.5 (West Cum. Supp. 2018) (prohibiting "the visible display . . . of information that advocates for or against any candidate or measure," including the "display of a candidate's name, likeness, or logo," the "display of a ballot measure's number, title, subject, or logo," and "[b]uttons, hats," or "shirts" containing such information); Tex. Elec. Code Ann. § 61.010(a) (West 2010) (prohibiting the wearing of "a badge, insignia, emblem, or other similar communicative device relating to a candidate, measure, or political party appearing on the ballot, or to the conduct of the election.").

First Amendment principles striking down *all* restrictions on the wearing of merely passive voter apparel inside a polling place, provided that voters keep quietly to themselves while standing in line.

IV. Overreacting to History

The Court in *Mansky* was overly influenced by the sorry realities of American voting practices in the 19th century. Fortunately, widespread reform measures were enacted to address the abuses that were rampant in those times. One set of those reforms, designed to keep political activists at bay from voters within a 100-foot buffer of the polling place, was approved in 1992 in *Burson*. The Court relied on perfectly fine history, and *Burson* upheld a perfectly fine law. But neither the abuses of the distant past nor the rationales of *Burson* should be enough to justify blanket bans on political voting apparel. Reforms of the sort approved in *Burson* solved the problem. Political-apparel bans, in contrast, are overkill, attacking a problem that does not exist, at great sacrifice to core free-speech values.

The Court's historical account was elegantly and efficiently told. In a nutshell, in the olden days, casting a vote was a venture into a carnival-like, no-holds-barred, coercive, corrupt, and largely lawless space. Think the bar scenes in *Star Wars* or *Westworld*. Creep me and freak me out. Voters did not come to a polling place in which governmentally approved ballots were available, but rather showed up with privately prepared ballots, often "party tickets," preselecting their choices.[38] No secret ballots yet existed, and voters approaching the "voting window" ran through a gauntlet of political seduction, jeers, and cheers. "Crowds would gather to heckle and harass voters who appeared to be supporting the other side."[39]

These shenanigans, deeply antithetical to democratic values, led to reforms adopting the secret, or "Australian" ballot, and state enactments calculated to place at bay the bizarre bazar of hawkers, hustlers, and heavies that formed the gauntlet separating the voter from the voting booth. "Between 1888 and 1896, nearly every State adopted the secret ballot."[40] But providing for a secret ballot was not enough to improve the system. Something had to be done to shelter voters

[38] *Id.* at 1882–83.

[39] *Id.*

[40] *Id.* at 1883.

from the gauntlet of harassment and pressure they were forced to endure while entering the polling place. To that end, "States enacted 'viewpoint-neutral restrictions on election-day speech' in the immediate vicinity of the polls."[41] By 1900, 34 of 45 states had such restrictions, and today, "all 50 States and the District of Columbia have laws curbing various forms of speech in and around polling places on Election Day."[42]

This sordid history drove the Supreme Court's decision in *Burson*, which upheld a Tennessee law imposing a 100-foot campaign-free zone around polling place entrances. The four justices in the plurality in *Burson* treated the spaces immediately outside polling places as public forums. Yet they ruled that, even applying the strict scrutiny standard applicable to the content-based regulation of speech in public forums, the Tennessee law was justified by the compelling state interests in curbing Election Day abuses. Justice Antonin Scalia supplied the fifth vote, in a concurring opinion that argued that the spaces outside polling places were not public forums. Employing the more pliant "reasonableness" standard applicable to regulations in nonpublic forums, Justice Scalia also voted to sustain the Tennessee law.[43]

As the Court in *Mansky* summarized *Burson*, the *Burson* "analysis emphasized the problems of fraud, voter intimidation, confusion, and general disorder that had plagued polling places in the past."[44] It was against this sleazy historical backdrop that *Burson* upheld Tennessee's 100-foot buffer zone. The Court in *Mansky* explained, *Burson* was "supported by overwhelming consensus among the States and 'common sense,' that a campaign-free zone outside the polls was 'necessary' to secure the advantages of the secret ballot and protect the right to vote."[45] The plurality in *Burson* reasoned, "[t]he State of Tennessee has decided that [the] last 15 seconds before its citizens enter the polling place should be their own, as free from interference as possible."[46]

Burson focused on the gauntlet outside polling places. *Mansky* focused on the space inside the polling place doors. The Court in *Mansky* held that the interior of the polling place was a nonpublic forum.

---

[41] *Id.* (quoting Burson, 504 U.S. at 214–15 (Scalia, J., concurring in judgment)).

[42] *Id.* at 1883.

[43] Burson, 504 U.S. at 214–16 (Scalia, J., concurring in judgment).

[44] Mansky, 138 S. Ct. at 1886 (citing Burson, 504 U.S. at 200–04 (plurality opinion)).

[45] *Id.* (citing Burson, 504 U.S. at 200, 206–08, 211 (plurality opinion)).

[46] Burson, 504 U.S. at 210.

That holding in itself was not especially problematic. It would have been a stretch to treat the inside of a polling place as a traditional or designated public forum.

Where the Court went wrong, however, was in imbuing the inside of the polling place with almost mystical qualities. The Court treated the interior of the polling place as a *reflective space*, not a *debating* space. The critical passage in Chief Justice Roberts's *Mansky* opinion thus stated:

> In any event, we see no basis for rejecting Minnesota's determination that some forms of advocacy should be excluded from the polling place, to set it aside as "an island of calm in which voters can peacefully contemplate their choices." . . . Casting a vote is a weighty civic act, akin to a jury's return of a verdict, or a representative's vote on a piece of legislation. It is a time for choosing, not campaigning. The State may reasonably decide that the interior of the polling place should reflect that distinction.[47]

While the Court in *Mansky* struck down Minnesota's law, the passage above reflected the Court's general sympathy for what Minnesota sought to achieve. The Court's quarrel was not with the end the state sought to achieve, but its means in attempting to achieve it. The Court was careful to advise that its ruling ought not be read to imply the unconstitutionality of all restrictions on messaging inside a polling place and hinted that highly partisan messages directed to the election or defeat of a particular candidate could survive First Amendment challenge. "Minnesota, like other States, has sought to strike the balance in a way that affords the voter the opportunity to exercise his civic duty in a setting removed from the clamor and din of electioneering," the Court observed.[48] "While that choice is generally worthy of our respect, Minnesota has not supported its good intentions with a law capable of reasoned application."[49]

V. Critique—Why the Court Did Not Go Far Enough

A. The Rule Should Be: All Passive Speech Allowed, but Quiet in the Room

I believe the Court's hints that it would approve more narrowly confined restrictions on what voters may wear to polling places is

---

[47] Mansky, 138 S. Ct. at 1887 (internal citation omitted).

[48] *Id*. at 1892.

[49] *Id*.

ominous and ill-considered. If and when the Court actually takes up a case posing those issues, I hope the Court gives the issue fresh consideration and does not consider itself bound by its dicta in *Mansky*. Specifically, my hope is that the Court will reconsider the propriety of this unfortunate remark: "Thus, in light of the special purpose of the polling place itself, Minnesota may choose to prohibit certain apparel there because of the message it conveys, so that voters may focus on the important decisions immediately at hand."[50]

The constitutional rule that the Court *should* adopt in future cases is quite simple: Voters should be permitted to wear any buttons or clothing they please, expressing any political position whatsoever inside a polling place on Election Day. The First Amendment should be construed to entitle a voter to wear buttons or apparel within a polling place urging the election or defeat of any candidate or the approval or rejection of any ballot measure. The *only* license governments should have to control expressive activity within the polling place is to demand political silence while inside the polling place. Governments may reasonably insist that, once inside the 100-foot perimeter approved in *Burson* and inside the actual polling place facility addressed in *Mansky*, voters must refrain from *actively* speaking on political issues or addressing others in an attempt to persuade or proselytize. The mere *passive* wearing of political messages on a voter's person, however, should be deemed protected by the First Amendment and immunized from punishment.

In stating that voters should be able to wear passively any political message they please inside the polling place, I really mean any message that would be protected if worn in a public forum. Speech that might subject a person to some legal liability in the general marketplace, such as incitement, a true threat, obscenity, defamation, a violation of intellectual property rights, and so on, is not constitutionally protected in any context, inside or outside a polling place. But as long as the message would be protected by the First Amendment in a public forum—on the sidewalks and streets as the voter approaches the polling place—the voter should be allowed to wear the message inside the polling place while politely maintaining political quiet in the room.

Even if the inside of a polling place is a nonpublic forum, the regulation of passive, nondisruptive self-expression by voters is

---

[50] *Id.* at 1888.

unreasonable in relation to the function and purpose of the voting place. Two interrelated rationales support this claim.

B. *Political Speech Worn on the Person Is of the Highest Constitutional Value*

The wearing of political messages *on the person of the voter on Election Day* should be understood to occupy a place at the very pinnacle of the expression protected by the First Amendment. No speech matters more than speech advocating candidates or causes on Election Day. No expression of that speech is more personal, intimate, fulfilling, and meaningful *to the speaker* than speech expressed on the *speaker's person*.

Modern First Amendment doctrine extends robust protection to a wide range of speech that is not "political."[51] Even so, political speech is always treated as being at the very core of the First Amendment's purpose and protection.[52] "Whatever differences may exist about interpretations of the First Amendment, there is practically universal agreement that a major purpose of that Amendment was to protect the free discussion of governmental affairs."[53] Countless "cases have often noted the close connection between our Nation's commitment to self-government and the rights protected by the First Amendment."[54]

[51] W. Va. State Bd. of Educ. v. Barnette, 319 U.S. 624, 642 (1943) ("If there is any fixed star in our constitutional constellation, it is that no official, high or petty, can prescribe what shall be orthodox in politics, nationalism, religion, or other matters of opinion.").

[52] As the Supreme Court recognized in a case I argued there, political speech is "at the core of what the First Amendment is designed to protect." Virginia v. Black, 538 U.S. 343, 365 (2003) (plurality opinion).

[53] Landmark Commc'ns, Inc. v. Virginia, 435 U.S. 829, 838 (1978) (cleaned up).

[54] Knox v. SEIU, Local 1000, 567 U.S. 298, 308-09 (2012) (citing Brown v. Hartlage, 456 U.S. 45, 52 (1982)) ("At the core of the First Amendment are certain basic conceptions about the manner in which political discussion in a representative democracy should proceed."); Buckley v. Valeo, 424 U.S. 1, 93, n. 127 (1976) (per curiam) ("[T]he central purpose of the Speech and Press Clauses was to assure a society in which 'uninhibited, robust, and wide-open' public debate concerning matters of public interest would thrive, for only in such a society can a healthy representative democracy flourish."); Cox v. Louisiana, 379 U.S. 536, 552 (1965); ("Maintenance of the opportunity for free political discussion is a basic tenet of our constitutional democracy."); Whitney v. California, 274 U.S. 357, 375 (1927) (Brandeis, J., concurring); Patterson v. Colorado ex rel. Att'y Gen. of Colo., 205 U.S. 454, 465 (1907) (Harlan, J., dissenting).

The importance of a political message *to the speaker* is especially heightened when the speaker is personally identified with the message. Such unification of speech and speaker is the quintessential embodiment of the American right to speak one's mind just because it *is* one's mind. The value is both personal and collective. As Justice Louis Brandeis wrote, "freedom to think as you will and to speak as you think are means indispensable to the discovery and spread of political truth."[55] That is why a political sign posted on one's own home window,[56] or expression on one's own car,[57] has special First Amendment respect. The Supreme Court's decision in *Ladue v. Gilleo*,[58] striking down a ban on residential political signs, invoked Aristotle to make this essential point:

> Displaying a sign from one's own residence often carries a message quite distinct from placing the same sign someplace else, or conveying the same text or picture by other means. Precisely because of their location, such signs provide information about the identity of the "speaker." As an early and eminent student of rhetoric observed, the identity of the speaker is an important component of many attempts to persuade.[59]

If special veneration for political speech identified with the speaker is deserved for a sign posted at a residence, surely it is deserving of even more reverence when expressed on the physical person of the speaker.

There is a heavy-handed orthodoxy being imposed by a requirement that a voter cover up the voter's messages upon entering the polling place. The government ought not force voters to accept and internalize that somehow their continued passive self-expression on

---

[55] Whitney, 274 U.S. at 375 (Brandeis, J., concurring).

[56] City of Ladue v. Gilleo, 512 U.S. 43, 56 (1994).

[57] Wooley v. Maynard, 430 U.S. 705, 715 (1977) (upholding the right of a New Hampshire citizen to block out the motto "Live Free or Die" on his license plate, because the state could not force citizens to "use their private property as a 'mobile billboard' for the State's ideological message.").

[58] 512 U.S. at 59.

[59] *Id.* at 56 (citing Aristotle 2, Rhetoric, Book 1, ch. 2, in 8 Great Books of the Western World, Encyclopedia Brittanica 595 (M. Adler ed., 2d ed. 1990) ("We believe good men more fully and more readily than others: this is true generally whatever the question is, and absolutely true where exact certainty is impossible and opinions are divided.")).

political matters is dirty or undignified once they walk inside the polling place. The government has no right to treat the voting place as if the voter is walking into some kind of civic church. Perhaps some voters feel that they should remove their buttons on entering the polling place, out of some sense of respect for the polling place's deliberative dignity. That is just fine—but surely not *all* voters feel that way, and the government ought not paternalistically impose its sensibilities on all who come to vote absent some palpable demonstration that such expression causes genuine harm.

C. Passive Speech Poses No Reasonable Threat to the "Weighty Civic Act" of Voting

This leads to the second rationale for declaring restrictions on voter apparel unconstitutional. The harms the government seeks to prevent are chimerical. The risk that mere passive political expression visible to other voters as they stand in line to cast ballots will induce fraud, coercion, disorder, or chaos is fanciful, unrealistic, and paternalistic.

In the open spaces of society, the default rule is that speech is not censored merely because it may offend some viewers. The classic First Amendment principle is that the viewer should simply avert his or her eyes. "In most circumstances, 'the Constitution does not permit the government to decide which types of otherwise protected speech are sufficiently offensive to require protection for the unwilling listener or viewer.'"[60] To the contrary, "the burden normally falls upon the viewer to avoid further bombardment of [his] sensibilities simply by averting [his] eyes."[61] The authority of government, "consonant with the Constitution, to shut off discourse solely to protect others from hearing it is, in other words, dependent upon a showing that substantial privacy interests are being invaded in an essentially intolerable manner."[62] Quietly standing in line with persons expressing contrary political views is not suffering an invasion of privacy in an "essentially intolerable manner."

During campaign seasons, voters are constantly exposed to political messages with which they disagree. That exposure escalates as an election approaches, reaching its crescendo on final approach to

---

[60] Snyder, 562 U.S. at 459 (quoting Erznoznik v. Jacksonville, 422 U.S. 205, 210–11 (1975)).

[61] Erznoznik, 422 U.S. at 210–11 (internal citation omitted).

[62] Cohen v. California, 403 U.S. 15, 21 (1971).

Election Day. "Many are those who must endure speech they do not like, but that is a necessary cost of freedom."[63] Voters are adults. They can handle it. Modern First Amendment law is grounded in a deep skepticism of government paternalism.[64] Voters ought not be treated as precious fragile snowflakes. "The First Amendment confirms the freedom to think for ourselves."[65]

Against the backdrop of the saturation of political messages common in society in the lead-up to an election, the notion that somehow a final glimpse of a "Trump" or "Clinton" button inside the voting place worn by a fellow voter, or spotting someone wearing a National Rifle Association or Black Lives Matter T-shirt, will somehow cause such fear and trembling as to disrupt the integrity of the civic act of voting, is entirely unreasonable. The paranoid speculation that last-minute exposure to the passive political messaging of others might persuade or dissuade a voter in the exercise of a ballot choice is hardly a cogent justification for censorship. "[T]he fear that speech might persuade provides no lawful basis for quieting it."[66]

Quietude inside the polling place, and the ultimate privacy of the voting booth itself, are enough to ensure that voters have ample opportunity for pressure-free deliberation and reflection in casting their ballots. Restrictions beyond that should be treated as unreasonable under the First Amendment.

The Court in *Mansky* took note of this distinction between passive, nondisruptive expression and active engagement, noting that in other contexts the Supreme Court had occasionally discussed the nondisruptive nature of passive expression. The Court thus conceded that "our decisions have noted the 'nondisruptive' nature of expressive apparel in more mundane settings."[67] The Court cited as examples its decision involving the wearing of T-Shirts or buttons in airports,[68] and more famously, its landmark decision upholding

---

[63] Sorrell v. IMS Health Inc., 564 U.S. 552, 575 (2011).

[64] Va. State Bd. of Pharmacy v. Va. Citizens Consumer Council, Inc., 425 U.S. 748, 770 (1976) ("There is, of course, an alternative to this highly paternalistic approach.").

[65] Citizens United v. FEC, 558 U.S. 310, 356 (2010).

[66] Sorrell, 564 U.S. at 576.

[67] Mansky, 138 S. Ct. at 1887.

[68] Bd. of Airport Comm'rs of Los Angeles v. Jews for Jesus, Inc., 482 U.S. 569, 576 (1987) (characterizing as nondisruptive "the wearing of a T-shirt or button that contains a political message" in an airport).

the right of a middle-school child, Mary Beth Tinker, to wear a black armband to school to protest the Vietnam War.[69] The Court distinguished those "more mundane settings," however, from the polling place on Election Day, a place that the Court appeared to imbue with a sort of civic sacredness, as if the voter in walking into the polling place was entering a temple of democracy:

> But those observations do not speak to the unique context of a polling place on Election Day. Members of the public are brought together at that place, at the end of what may have been a divisive election season, to reach considered decisions about their government and laws. The State may reasonably take steps to ensure that partisan discord not follow the voter up to the voting booth, and distract from a sense of shared civic obligation at the moment it counts the most. That interest may be thwarted by displays that do not raise significant concerns in other situations.[70]

The passage above may indicate that the Court has already made up its mind on this matter, and that the argument I am advancing here has already lost. I hope that is not the case, and that the Court will be open to reconsideration.

The notion that the *act of voting* should be private and reflective is perfectly sound. And as a technical matter, the notion that the physical interior of a polling place is a nonpublic forum, and not a public forum like the outside streets and sidewalks, is sound as well. But the idea that the space inside the polling place *before* the voter gets inside the voting booth must be sanitized and cleansed of all passive political messages worn on the person of the voter simply goes too far. Voters waiting in line are not captive audiences in any meaningful sense. The Supreme Court has warned against expansion of "captive audience" principles.[71] To treat waiting in line with other voters who are wearing political messages contrary to one's own as the sort of coercive invasion of privacy sufficient to trigger authentic captive audience concerns is entirely implausible.

---

[69] Tinker v. Des Moines Indep. Cmty Sch. Dist., 393 U.S. 503, 508 (1969) (students wearing black armbands to protest the Vietnam War engaged in "silent, passive expression of opinion, unaccompanied by any disorder or disturbance").

[70] Mansky, 138 S. Ct. at 1888.

[71] Snyder, 562 U.S. at 459 ("As a general matter, we have applied the captive audience doctrine only sparingly to protect unwilling listeners from protected speech.").

Near the close of the opinion in *Mansky*, the Court observed that "Minnesota, like other States, has sought to strike the balance in a way that affords the voter the opportunity to exercise his civic duty in a setting removed from the clamor and din of electioneering." But the quiet wearing of buttons and T-shirts bearing political messages inside the polling place cannot be fairly characterized as "the *clamor and din* of electioneering."[72] As long as there is quiet and order as people stand in line, there is no clamor, there is no din.

The Court characterized casting a vote as a "weighty civic act," a characterization also endorsed in Justice Sotomayor's dissent.[73] The casting of a vote is indeed a weighty civic act. But the weight of the act is fully protected by ensconcing the voter in the privacy and quiet of the voting booth. Any voter knows full well that as he or she casts a vote for one candidate or cause, a voter in an adjacent booth may be casting a vote exactly the opposite. Standing in line with those fellow citizens, their views made quietly and passively visible, will be no shock to any voter who has paid any attention to political contests in the days and weeks leading to the election, or in the walk or drive to the polling place. The notion that standing in the quiet *public* company of fellow citizens passively expressing differing views just prior to entering the polling booth somehow diminishes the solemnity or deliberative dignity of the *private* exercise of the final "weighty civic act" of voting inside the booth defies common sense. The First Amendment stands against aggrandizing paternalistic regulations indulging in assumptions that voters are so hair-trigger hypersensitive that they need shelter from such passive political messaging.

VI. Conclusion

There are plenty of laws on the books to preserve order or to prevent voter intimidation or fraud. The First Amendment poses no bar to their enforcement. But American voters are not so squeamish, frail, or fragile as to be intimidated or defrauded by a fellow voter's T-shirt or button. Nor are they so hot-tempered that they will be reflexively

[72] Mansky, 138 S. Ct. at 1892.

[73] *Id.* at 1887; *id.* at 1893 (Sotomayor, J., dissenting) ("I agree with the Court that '[c]asting a vote is a weighty civic act' and that 'State[s] may reasonably take steps to ensure that partisan discord not follow the voter up to the voting booth,' including by 'prohibit[ing] certain apparel [in polling places] because of the message it conveys.'").

driven to fisticuffs or undignified outbursts at the mere sight of the very opposing views to which they have been unrelentingly exposed in the weeks and hours and minutes leading up to their vote. Yes, voting is a weighty civic act that should be exercised in an atmosphere of decorum and dignity. Yet there is nothing inherently undignified in the expression of a political message. In America, we call that democracy.[74]

[74] See Rodney Smolla, Symposium: Nothing Undignified about Political Messaging—In America, We Call that Democracy," SCOTUSblog, Jan. 23, 2018, http://www.scotusblog.com/2018/01/symposium-nothing-undignified-political-messaging-america-call-democracy.

Betting on Federalism: *Murphy v. NCAA* and the Future of Sports Gambling

*Mark Brnovich**

"Money won is twice as sweet as money earned."

—Eddie Felson, *The Color of Money*

I. Introduction

"Supreme Court Ruling Favors Sports Betting."[1] So reported the *New York Times* the day the Court decided *Murphy v. National Collegiate Athletic Association*, a decision striking down a federal law that generally prohibited states from legalizing sports gambling.[2] The *Washington Post* and *Los Angeles Times* also focused on the sports betting implications of the decision[3]—and reasonably so: Sports gambling is a big business already, and it will likely grow bigger still after *Murphy*. But whether *Murphy* will actually result in the widespread legalization of sports gambling is difficult to predict. Sports betting policy will likely unfold on a state-by-state basis, amid a legal, cultural, and technological landscape that has changed in important ways in the decades since the statute at issue was enacted. More importantly, *Murphy*'s meaning extends far beyond sports gambling, with implications for a wide range of federal laws that curtail state authority. And therein may lie *Murphy*'s real significance: On a host of issues, it promises to

---

* Mark Brnovich is Attorney General of Arizona. Thanks also to Andrew G. Pappas, Assistant Solicitor General of Arizona, and Esther J. Winne, Legal Policy Adviser for the Arizona Attorney General.

[1] Adam Liptak & Kevin Draper, Supreme Court Ruling Favors Sports Betting, N.Y. Times, May 14, 2018, https://nyti.ms/2Ikgtyh.

[2] Murphy v. Nat'l Collegiate Athletic Ass'n [NCAA], 138 S. Ct. 1461 (2018).

[3] Robert Barnes, Justices Rule that States Can Authorize Sports Betting, Wash. Post, May 15, 2018, https://wapo.st/2uEmdKf; David G. Savage, Supreme Court Tosses Ban on Sports Betting, L.A. Times, May 15, 2018, https://lat.ms/2GrSjf2.

produce the kind of federal-state tension on which our federal system thrives. That federalism, in turn, helps secure our liberties.

II. Factual and Legal Background

At issue in *Murphy* was the Professional and Amateur Sports Protection Act (PASPA), which generally forbids states to "authorize" sports betting.[4] Congress enacted PASPA in 1992, after a century or so of shifting attitudes about gambling. As described in greater detail below, gambling was largely illegal throughout the United States by the late 19th century, but those prohibitions began to be relaxed by the 1930s, and state lotteries quickly mushroomed in the 1960s and 1970s. In 1988, Congress enacted the Indian Gaming Regulatory Act, spurring the development of casinos on Indian lands across the country and later the advent of legalized casino gambling by many states. But casino *sports* gambling remained illegal outside Nevada. By the early 1990s, it appeared that might change too, "and this sparked federal efforts to stem the tide."[5] The result was PASPA, promoted on the ground that it would "protect young people" and "safeguard the integrity of sports."[6]

The law's core provision forbids a state or any of its subdivisions "'to sponsor, operate, advertise, promote, license, or authorize by law or compact . . . a lottery, sweepstakes, or other betting, gambling, or wagering scheme based . . . on' competitive sporting events."[7] A second provision "makes it 'unlawful' for 'a person to sponsor, operate, advertise, or promote' those same gambling schemes" if "done 'pursuant to the law or compact of a governmental entity.'"[8] But rather than make sports gambling a federal crime, PASPA authorizes the U.S. attorney general, as well as professional and amateur sports organizations, to sue to enjoin violations.

When PASPA was adopted, Nevada allowed sports gambling in casinos, while three other states—Delaware, Montana, and Oregon—hosted sports lotteries or allowed sports pools. PASPA expressly grandfathered in these activities, while a separate provision allowed New Jersey to legalize sports gambling in Atlantic City as long as it did so by the

---

[4] Murphy, 138 S. Ct. at 1468 (citing 28 U.S.C. § 3702(1)).

[5] *Id.* at 1470.

[6] *Id.*

[7] *Id.* (quoting 28 U.S.C. § 3702(1)).

[8] *Id.* (quoting 28 U.S.C. § 3702(2)).

beginning of 1994.[9] It didn't, but in 2011, Garden State voters amended the state's constitution to allow the legislature to authorize sports gambling.[10] The legislature enacted such a law the next year.[11] The major professional sports leagues and NCAA sued in federal court to enjoin the law on the ground that it violated PASPA. Relying on the doctrine that Congress may not "commandeer" a state's exercise of its lawmaking power—that the federal government can't force states to enforce federal law—New Jersey "argued . . . that PASPA unconstitutionally infringed the State's sovereign authority to end its sports gambling ban."[12]

The Supreme Court first articulated this anti-commandeering rule in *New York v. United States,* a "pioneering case" that "concerned a federal law that required a State, under certain circumstances, either to 'take title' to low-level radioactive waste or to 'regulat[e] according to the instructions of Congress.'"[13] The Court held the law was unconstitutional because the Constitution does not authorize Congress to impose obligations on state governments to achieve federal objectives.[14] The Court "traced this rule to the basic structure of government established under the Constitution," which empowers Congress "to regulate individuals, not States."[15] "Where a federal interest is sufficiently strong to cause Congress to legislate," the Court in *New York* explained, "it must do so directly; it may not conscript state governments as its agents."[16]

Five years later, in *Printz v. United States,* "the Court applied the same principles" to strike down "a federal statute requiring state and local law enforcement officers to perform background checks and related tasks in connection with applications for handgun licenses."[17] The Court held that the federal government may not "command [any of] the States' officers, or those of their political subdivisions, to administer or enforce a federal regulatory program."[18]

---

[9] *Id.* at 1471 (citing 28 U.S.C. § § 3704(a)(1)-(2), 3704(a)(3)).

[10] See N.J. Const. art. IV, § 7, ¶(2)(D), (F).

[11] 2011 N.J. Laws 1723.

[12] Murphy, 138 S. Ct. at 1471 (citing NCAA v. Christie, 926 F. Supp. 2d 551, 561 (D.N.J. 2013)).

[13] Murphy, 138 S. Ct. at 1476 (quoting New York, 505 U.S. 144, 175 (1992)).

[14] New York, 505 U.S. at 176.

[15] Murphy, 138 S. Ct. at 1476 (quoting New York, 505 U.S. at 166).

[16] New York, 505 U.S. at 178.

[17] Murphy, 138 S. Ct. at 1477 (citing Printz v. United States, 521 U.S. 898 (1997)).

[18] Printz, 521 U.S. at 935.

New Jersey argued that these principles also applied to PASPA's anti-authorization provision: By telling the state that it could not authorize sports gambling, Congress was attempting to "commandeer the [state's] legislative processes."[19] The district court disagreed, and the U.S. Court of Appeals for the Third Circuit affirmed. "The panel thought it significant that PASPA does not impose any *affirmative command*" and "did not interpret PASPA as prohibiting the *repeal* of laws outlawing sports gambling."[20]

New Jersey unsuccessfully sought review by the U.S. Supreme Court.[21] Opposing the state's petition for certiorari, the federal government argued "that PASPA does not require New Jersey 'to leave in place the state-law prohibitions against sports gambling that it had chosen to adopt prior to PASPA's enactment. To the contrary, New Jersey is free to repeal those prohibitions in whole or in part.'"[22]

In 2014, the New Jersey legislature did just that, partially repealing its sports betting laws. Specifically, the 2014 law "repeal[ed] the provisions of state law prohibiting sports gambling insofar as they concerned the 'placement and acceptance of wagers' on sporting events by persons 21 years of age or older at a horseracing track or a casino or gambling house in Atlantic City," and "specified that the repeal was effective only as to wagers on sporting events not involving a New Jersey college team or a collegiate sporting event taking place in the State."[23]

The same plaintiffs filed a new suit and won before the district court and, eventually, the Third Circuit sitting en banc. Abandoning some of its prior reasoning as "facile," the en banc court found that the new law "constitutes an authorization"—and thus violates PASPA—"because it 'selectively remove[s] a prohibition on sports wagering in a manner that permissively channels wagering activity to particular locations or operators.'"[24] The court did not say whether a complete repeal would have been permissible.

[19] New York, 505 U.S. at 161 (quoting Hodel v. Va. State Surface Mining & Reclamation Ass'n, Inc., 452 U.S. 264, 288 (1981)).

[20] Murphy, 138 S. Ct. at 1471–72 (emphases added) (citing NCAA v. Christie, 730 F.3d 208, 231–32 (3d Cir. 2013)).

[21] *Id.* at 1472.

[22] *Id.*

[23] *Id.*

[24] *Id.* (quoting NCAA v. Governor of N.J., 832 F.3d 389, 401 (3d Cir. 2016) (en banc)).

The Supreme Court granted review and reversed. Writing for a 7–2 Court, Justice Samuel Alito began by analyzing what constitutes an "authorization" for PASPA purposes: whether "any state law that has the effect of permitting sports gambling . . . amounts to an authorization" (as New Jersey argued), or whether authorization instead requires some kind of "affirmative action" to "empower" entities to "conduct sports gambling operations" (as the leagues contended).[25] The Court sided with New Jersey's interpretation but determined that "the competing definitions offered by the parties lead to the same conclusion": "The repeal of a state law banning sports gambling not only 'permits' sports gambling . . . it also gives those now free to conduct a sports betting operation the 'right or authority to act'; it 'empowers' them."[26]

Under either definition, the Court held, PASPA's anti-authorization provision violates the Constitution's anti-commandeering principle, which expresses "a fundamental structural decision incorporated into the Constitution" to "withhold from Congress the power to issue orders directly to the States."[27] The Constitution both limits and preserves state sovereignty, and it does so both directly and implicitly. One such limitation is the Supremacy Clause, which "means that when federal and state law conflict, federal law prevails and state law is preempted."[28] But while Congress's enumerated legislative powers are "sizeable," "they are not unlimited": the Constitution confers on Congress "only certain enumerated powers," reserving "all other legislative power . . . for the States."[29] Importantly, the power the Constitution "confers upon Congress [is] the power to regulate individuals, not States."[30] "In this respect, the Constitution represented a sharp break from the Articles of Confederation," under which "'Congress lacked the authority in most respects to govern the people directly.'"[31] And indeed, "conspicuously absent from the list of powers given to Congress is the power to issue direct orders to the governments of the States."[32]

[25] Murphy, 138 S. Ct. at 1473.
[26] Id. at 1474.
[27] Id. at 1475.
[28] Id. at 1476.
[29] Id.
[30] Id. at 1479 (quoting New York, 505 U.S. at 166).
[31] Id. at 1476 (quoting New York, 505 U.S. at 163).
[32] Id.

Here's the jurisprudential sequence in other words: In *New York*, the Court struck down "a federal law that required a State, under certain circumstances, either to 'take title' to low-level radioactive waste or to 'regulat[e] according to the instructions of Congress";[33] and in *Printz*, the Court held unconstitutional "a federal statute requiring state and local law enforcement officers to perform background checks and related tasks in connection with applications for handgun licenses."[34] Now, in *Murphy*, the Court extended *New York* and *Printz*'s logic to conclude the PASPA provision prohibiting states to authorize sports gambling also violates the anti-commandeering rule. "That provision unequivocally dictates what a state legislature may and may not do . . . as if federal officers were installed in state legislative chambers and were armed with the authority to stop legislators from voting on any offending proposals."[35]

The Court rejected the "empty" distinction between federal laws that "command[] 'affirmative' action as opposed to imposing a prohibition," because "[t]he basic principle—that Congress cannot issue direct orders to state legislatures—applies in either event."[36] Justice Alito also found no prior decision in which the Court upheld a law in which Congress "commandeered the legislative process" by "direct[ing] the States either to enact or to refrain from enacting a regulation of the conduct of activities occurring within their borders."[37]

The Court also concluded that PASPA's anti-authorization provision wasn't a preemption provision. To preempt state law, the Court explained, the PASPA provision would have to "represent the exercise of a power conferred on Congress by the Constitution" and "must be best read as one that regulates private actors."[38] All three types of preemption—"conflict," "express," and "field"—"work in the same way": "Congress enacts a law that imposes restrictions or confers rights on private actors; a state law confers rights or imposes restrictions that conflict with the federal law; and therefore the federal law

---

[33] Murphy, 138 S. Ct. at 1476. (citing New York, 505 U.S. at 175).

[34] *Id.* at 1477 (citing Printz, 521 U.S. at 898).

[35] *Id.* at 1478.

[36] *Id.*

[37] *Id.* at 1479.

[38] *Id.*

takes precedence and the state law is preempted."[39] PASPA's anti-authorization provision doesn't fit the bill, "because there is no way in which [it] . . . can be understood as a regulation of private actors": it neither confers federal rights nor imposes federal restrictions on private actors wanting to conduct sports gambling operations.[40] Instead, the provision is "a direct command to the States," which "is exactly what the anticommandeering rule does not allow."[41]

The Court thus invalidated PASPA's anti-authorization provision.[42] But the Court did not end its analysis there. Instead, it went on to consider whether it could affirm the Third Circuit's decision on the ground that New Jersey's 2014 law violates PASPA's prohibition on States' "licens[ing]" sports gambling.[43] The Court held that it could not, because "that provision suffers from the same defect as the prohibition of state authorization": "[i]t issues a direct order to the state legislature."[44]

Finally, the Court considered whether the anti-authorization provision's invalidity "dooms the remainder of PASPA," or whether that provision could be severed from the rest of the statute.[45] To decide the question, the Court asked whether Congress would have enacted each of PASPA's remaining provisions without the anti-authorization in place. The Court answered *no*, and thus invalidated the statute as a whole.[46]

This severability analysis divided the Court far more than the commandeering question. Justice Clarence Thomas concurred in the Court's opinion but wrote separately to urge the Court to reconsider its severability precedents and to dispute the dissent's assumption that "Congress can prohibit sports gambling that does not cross state lines."[47] Justice Stephen Breyer joined the majority in all but the severability analysis, and there instead joined in part

[39] Murphy, 138 S. Ct. at 1480.

[40] *Id.* at 1481.

[41] *Id.*

[42] *Id.*

[43] *Id.*

[44] *Id.* at 1481–82.

[45] *Id.*

[46] *Id.* at 1482–85. The severability aspect of this case may prove to be as significant as the federalism ruling.

[47] *Id.* at 1485–87 (Thomas, J., concurring).

Justice Ruth Bader Ginsburg's "dissent."[48] While framed as a dissent, Justice Ginsburg's opinion, also joined in full by Justice Sonia Sotomayor, assumes that PASPA's anti-authorization provision violates the anti-commandeering rule.[49] Thus no justice actually disagreed with the majority's core holding.

III. Sports Gambling Past, Present, and Future

The direct policy implications of any Supreme Court action might ordinarily be the simplest to spot. For example, if a warrantless search is struck down, we can expect similarly situated law enforcement to obtain a warrant next time. Here, curiously, the direct policy impact on permissible sports gaming is more difficult to read as a result of the nation's yo-yoing appetite for gambling. Are we all sports gamblers now?

Murphy's most immediate result, of course, was that it cleared the way for New Jersey to legalize sports gambling. New Jersey promptly did just that,[50] and in the first few weeks that sports betting was legal there, gamblers placed more than $16 million in wagers.[51] As for other states, more than 20, including Arizona, joined an amicus brief urging the Supreme Court to strike down PASPA as unconstitutional. Whether other states will actually join New Jersey in legalizing sports gambling is difficult to predict, but gambling is as old as America itself,[52] and attitudes about gambling have changed dramatically over time.

Lotteries were used in the early days of the American colonies to raise funds. The first recorded "American" lottery took place in 1612, when the Virginia Company raised 29,000 pounds for the benefit of the Jamestown settlement.[53] Later, Ben Franklin himself ran an early

---

[48] Murphy, 138 S. Ct. at 1488–91 (Ginsburg, J., dissenting).

[49] *Id.* at 1489; see also *id.* at 1490 ("In PASPA, *shorn of the prohibition on modifying or repealing state law*, Congress permissibly exercised its authority to regulate commerce by instructing States and private parties to refrain from operating sports-gambling schemes." (emphasis added)).

[50] N.J. P.L. 2018, ch. 33 (2018), Assembly No. 4111.

[51] Samantha Marcus, N.J. Sports Betting Took $16M in Wagers in Opening Weeks. Here's What We Bet On, NJ.com, July 12, 2018, https://bit.ly/2Awo7St.

[52] In fact, gambling is quite a bit older than America. According to ancient mythology, Zeus, Hades, and Poseidon split heaven, hell, and the sea with the throw of dice. In ancient Egypt, depictions of gambling date back to 3500 B.C., and a gaming board was found in King Tut's tomb. Biblical scriptures describe Roman soldiers casting lots for Christ's clothes. And Chinese playing cards have been found from the 12th century.

[53] Nat'l Gambling Impact Study Comm'n, Lotteries (1999), http://govinfo.library .unt.edu/ngisc/research/lotteries.html (last visited Aug. 15, 2018).

version of the lottery in Philadelphia.[54] By the mid-18th century lotteries were used in all 13 American colonies for both community and private purposes, including to finance construction at private universities like Harvard and Yale.[55] The Continental Congress even authorized a lottery in a failed effort to fund the Continental Army during the Revolutionary War.[56]

In the 19th century, however, American attitudes toward gambling began to change. In addition to ongoing concerns about the moral decadence associated with gambling, stories of corruption and cheating spread, which lead to a backlash against the pastime. One of the most famous examples of this corruption took place in 1823. In that year, Congress had authorized a Grand National Lottery to fund the beautification of Washington, D.C. But when the time came for the prize to be paid, the organizer of the contest ran off with the proceeds and the lucky winner was left to fight his way through the court system to get it back.[57] As gambling, particularly state-sponsored lotteries, fell out of favor with the American public, there was a corresponding shift in state laws about wagering. By the beginning of the 20th century, most states had eliminated state-sponsored lotteries.

Throughout the early history of the United States, the federal government and courts had left regulation of gambling to the states as part of their authority to regulate for the health, safety, and morals of their citizens. That deference was so significant that states were permitted to host lotteries across state lines. For example, Louisiana used a lottery to raise money after the devastation of the Civil War and accepted payment from individuals outside the state via the U.S. Postal Service. According to historical accounts, only seven percent of the lottery revenue came from inside the state.[58]

---

[54] Benjamin Franklin, Scheme of the First Philadelphia Lottery, Pa. Gazette, December 5, 1747, reprinted in Franklin Papers, Nat'l Archives: Founders Online, https://founders.archive.gov/documents/Franklin/01-03-02-0097 (last visited Aug. 15, 2018).

[55] Nat'l Gambling Impact Study Comm'n, *supra* note 53.

[56] Image 1 of United States Lottery (Nov. 18, 1776), in Documents from the Continental Congress and the Constitutional Convention, 1774-89 (Library of Congress), https://www.loc.gov/resource/bdsdcc.01701/?st=text; see also William N. Thomson, Gambling in America: An Encyclopedia of History Issues, and Society, at x, xxvi (2001).

[57] Mark Jacob & Stephan Benzkofer, 10 Things You Might Not Know about the Lottery, Chicago Tribune, Aug. 22, 2014, https://trib.in/2O06SuE.

[58] History of Lotteries, La. Lottery Corp., https://louisianalottery.com/history-of-lotteries (last visited Aug. 15, 2018).

But after the D.C. debacle, opposition to lotteries grew widespread. And in 1895, Congress enacted the Federal Lottery Act, which prohibited the transportation of lottery tickets across state lines. In 1903, the Supreme Court narrowly upheld the act by a 5-4 decision, in *Champion v. Ames*, declaring that transferring lottery tickets across state lines was subject to the Commerce Clause.[59] The Court's close vote is both a sign of the monumental change in Commerce Clause jurisprudence over the last century and the significant deference the Court traditionally afforded the states with regulation of gambling.

For several decades, legalized gambling remained out of favor with the majority of Americans. It was not until 1964 that the state of New Hampshire established the country's first modern state-run lottery.[60] And that enactment only took place after a 10-year effort on the part of lottery proponents.[61] Once New Hampshire opened the gates, however, a number of states followed and instituted their own state-sponsored lotteries.

Like the rest of the rollercoaster history of gambling, American attitudes toward *sports* gambling also shifted over time—including over the 26 years that PASPA was in effect. But the basic philosophical divide over whether sports gambling should be legal remains. Advocates of legalizing sports gambling argue that wagering is already taking place and that when it is conducted in an illegal space (as it commonly is), it poses dangers for those who participate.[62] Proponents thus argue that states should fully legalize sports gambling, so they can regulate it and profit from it.

---

[59] 188 U.S. 321 (1903) (also known as "Lottery Case").

[60] Danny Lewis, Queen Elizabeth I Held England's First Official Lottery 450 Years Ago, Smithsonian.com, Jan. 13, 2016, https://bit.ly/2M8BZ6Q.

[61] History, N.H. Lottery Comm'n, www.nhlottery.com/about-us/history.aspx (last visited Aug. 15, 2018).

[62] According to the National Gambling Impact Study Commission, 20 years ago when Americans legally spent about $2.8 billion in Nevada each year on sports betting, they were placing $80–380 billion in *illegal* sports wagers. Nat'l Gambling Impact Study Comm'n, Final Report, June 18, 1999, https://bit.ly/2Oy5Hnf. More recently, in 2017, gamblers spent around $4.9 billion placing legal bets with Nevada bookies. According to industry experts, this is less than four percent of the total amount wagered, which makes the amount Americans bet illegally on sports around $123 billion per year—more than 20 times greater than the legal, regulated, sports-betting market. See Michelle Minton, Competitive Enterprise Inst., Legalizing Sports Betting in the United States, 1 (2018), https://cei.org/content/legalizing-sports-betting-united-states.

These advocates get it at least partially right. There is no doubt that states can profit from the legalization of sports wagering. But it's an open question how large a sports-betting profit states could turn. In 2017, customers bet $4.9 billion in Nevada sportsbooks. However, out of every dollar bet, the books kept just over five cents.[63] And the books made only $1.1 million off the 2018 Super Bowl, one of the smallest wins in the history of legal betting on the game.[64] A state's profit will also depend partly on what kind of sports gambling the state permits. Nevada allows its residents to gamble online, but not all states may be interested in opening the door that wide. For example, states may choose to restrict sports gambling to casinos or limit the sports eligible for wagers. Additionally, Nevada already has established itself as the epicenter for gambling, and it could take other states decades to match the wagers that are placed there. For this reason, the profits may be smaller than states expect and, consequently, profit may play a less significant role in a state's decision to legalize sports betting.

Opponents of legalized sports wagering continue to raise the same concerns they have outlined for years—that it serves as a regressive tax, that it legalizes bad behavior, and that it threatens the integrity of sporting events. And there may be some truth to their concerns. If America's history of gambling is any gauge, it is clear that legalizing gambling doesn't eliminate fraud or corruption associated with the pastime. The reality is that where gambling exists, associated social costs will likely follow, including criminal activity and negative impacts on families.[65] It is estimated that two million Americans suffer from a compulsive gambling disorder, and anyone who wagers may run the risk of falling into debt, which can lead to a host of other problems.[66]

At the same time, well-regulated gambling may offer a way to mitigate many of these concerns and provide a fairly safe arena for individual gamblers. These concerns apply to all forms of gambling,

[63] UNLV Center for Gaming Research (2018), Nevada Sports Betting Totals: 1984–2017, http://gaming.unlv.edu/reports/NV_sportsbetting.pdf.

[64] Matt Bonesteel, Las Vegas Sportsbooks Post Smallest Super Bowl Win Since 2011, Thanks to Eagles Win, Wash. Post, Feb. 6, 2018, https://wapo.st/2Lkki89.

[65] Mark Brnovich & Tom Gede, Internet Gaming: Is It Too Late to Reboot?, 12 Engage 34 (2011), https://bit.ly/2M9FIRo. *Engage* has since been renamed the *Federalist Society Review*.

[66] Daniel Bortz, Gambling Addicts Seduced by Growing Casino Accessibility, U.S. News & World Rep., Mar. 28, 2013, https://bit.ly/2LR9TQC.

much of which is already legal in states and on Indian lands. And important as it is to safeguard the integrity of professional and amateur sports, the truth is that sports betting already happens every day, some of it legally in Nevada casinos. As of today, we haven't seen these activities have a significant impact on the integrity of sports.

While the basic philosophical arguments over sports gambling have not changed since 1992, gambling itself has changed drastically in the 26 years since PASPA was enacted. Many of those changes are the result of significant technological advances. When Congress enacted PASPA, sportsbooks were operated telephonically or in person. Since then, sports wagering has become possible online and now through mobile smartphones. As a result, some of the practical complications that might have limited participation in sports betting during the 1990s have been completely eliminated. Individuals interested in sports gambling can place wagers from their own couches with daily fantasy sports providers such as DraftKings or FanDuel. Further, with the explosion of social leagues like Fantasy Football, interest in sports betting has increased dramatically in recent years. According to polls cited recently in a comprehensive Competitive Enterprise Institute report, in 2008, one in six Americans admitted to gambling on professional sports each year; by 2016, that number had increased to one in three.[67]

And it's not just the technology that has evolved; public opinion is evolving as well. In late 2017, a poll was released showing that for the first time in history, a majority of Americans approved of legalizing sports betting.[68] At the time, 55 percent of respondents approved of legalizing professional sports betting. This was a complete flip from a 1993 sampling taken shortly after PASPA was enacted, when 56 percent of Americans disapproved of legalizing professional-sports betting.[69]

History has shown us that a change in American attitudes toward gambling often results in a change in American laws regarding gambling, so it is unsurprising that there has also been a drastic change in the state regulation of gambling over the last two decades.

[67] Minton, *supra* note 62, at 6.

[68] Rick Maese & Emily Guskin, Poll: For the First Time, Majority of Americans Approve of Legalizing Sports Betting, Wash. Post, July 17, 2018, https://wapo.st/2n1IOvX.

[69] *Id.*

Today, all states but Hawaii and Utah have legalized gambling in some form. Although just over 30 states had a state-sponsored lottery when PAPSA went into effect, lotteries now exist in 44 states as well as several territories.[70] Nearly the same number of states allow some form of casino-style gambling. The spread of tribal gaming, now permitted in 30 states or territories, has also contributed avenues for legalized gambling. Where tribal gaming is permitted, a specific compact with the state controls the type of gambling that is allowed on tribal lands. With the Supreme Court's decision in *Murphy*, sports betting is now eligible to be added to each compact if the state and tribe agree to its inclusion.

What does all of this mean? It means that it is still anyone's guess what is going to happen now that the Supreme Court has invalidated the law that effectively banned legal sports wagering anywhere outside Nevada. As noted, New Jersey legalized sports betting within weeks after *Murphy* was decided. Delaware actually beat New Jersey to the punch, becoming the first state to start accepting bets outside Nevada.[71] Approximately two dozen other states have pending legislation or proposals to begin building a regulatory structure for sports wagering within their borders. This, combined with the legal and cultural shifts in favor of gambling, suggests that Nevada's monopoly over sports wagering may be coming to an end. On the other hand, opposition to legalized sports betting remains deep for both moral and practical reasons. Additionally, history has taught us that sports wagering requires an effective regulatory structure to ensure the integrity of the games, protect the players, and keep criminal elements from infiltrating the industry. But erecting an effective regulatory structure, especially in today's fractured political environment, is no easy feat.

IV. Other Federalism Implications

Murphy's impact beyond sports gambling is potentially very broad, implicating a wide range of issues where Congress and the states are at odds. One of those issues is immigration and the possibility, as some commentators have suggested, that *Murphy* may "confer on

[70] Minton, *supra* note 62, at 2.

[71] Rick Maese, Delaware Is the First New State to Bet on Sports Gambling, But It Might Not Pay Off, Wash. Post, June 5, 2018, https://wapo.st/2Jc2Lxz.

states a new immunity from federal laws that try to prohibit states from conferring benefits like university seats and drivers' licenses on state residents."[72] Federal law provides that "an alien who is not [otherwise qualified by the statute] is not eligible for any State or local public benefit [as defined in the statute]."[73] "This federal law not only looks like a 'direct' regulation of state and local governments," according to one commentator, "but also does not contain any defense that any private party could easily raise in litigation."[74] As *Murphy* makes clear, the power the Constitution "confers upon Congress [is] the power to regulate individuals, not States."[75]

Murphy may have additional immigration-related implications for so-called sanctuary cities.[76] The statute "at the heart of the current federal effort to enjoin and penalize"[77] those cities, 8 U.S.C. § 1373, provides that, a "local government entity or official may not prohibit, or in any way restrict, any government entity or official from sending to, or receiving from, the Immigration and Naturalization Service information regarding the citizenship or immigration status, lawful or unlawful, of any individual."[78] As some commentators have suggested, this arguably "qualifies as an 'order' to state and local officials, and—like PASPA," may "undermine[] states' control over their governmental machinery and partially transfer[] it to the federal government."[79]

Applying this logic, a Pennsylvania federal district court recently held that Section 1373 violates the Tenth Amendment.[80] The court's opinion begins with *Hamlet* and *Coriolanus*, sails on toward Scylla and Charybdis, and 30 pages later gets to Philadelphia's claim for a declaratory judgment that it was complying with Section 1373

---

[72] Rick Hills, Murphy v. NCAA's Escape from Baseline Hell, PrawfsBlog, May 16, 2018, https://bit.ly/2McsNy7.

[73] *Id.* (quoting 8 U.S.C. § 1621(a)).

[74] *Id.*

[75] Murphy, 138 S. Ct. at 1479 (quoting New York, 505 U.S. at 166).

[76] See, e.g., Ilya Somin, Broader Implications of the Supreme Court's Sports Gambling Decision, The Volokh Conspiracy, May 16, 2018, https://bit.ly/2Oy7Y1L.

[77] Garrett Epps, The Supreme Court Says Congress Can't Make States Dance to Its Tune, The Atlantic, May 14, 2018, https://bit.ly/2LIS7zU.

[78] 8 U.S.C. § 1373(a).

[79] Somin, *supra* note 76.

[80] City of Phila. v. Sessions, 309 F. Supp. 3d 289 (E.D. Pa. 2018).

"as constitutionally construed."[81] The court found that the two paragraphs of Section 1373 that applied to the city "by their plain terms prevent 'Federal, State, or local government entit[ies] or official[s] from' engaging in certain activities," and thus "closely parallel the anti-authorization condition in PASPA."[82] Just as the PASPA provision "'dictates what a state legislature may and may not do,'" the court reasoned, the pertinent provisions of Section 1373 "do the same, by prohibiting certain conduct of government entities or officials."[83] The court therefore held that those provisions were unconstitutional, and that Philadelphia did not need to comply with them.[84]

Similarly, in the lawsuit brought by the Trump administration against California in *United States v. California*, a federal district court held that Section 1373 did not preempt a California law that prohibits state law enforcement agencies from sharing certain information for immigration enforcement purposes.[85] Although the district court ultimately concluded that the California law and Section 1373 did not conflict—and, therefore, the state law was not preempted—it agreed with the analysis of the district court in Pennsylvania that, in light of *Murphy*, "the constitutionality of Section 1373 [is] highly suspect."[86]

On the other hand, as one Ninth Circuit judge recently noted in dissent, "none of [the principles behind the anticommandeering rule] supports attempts to frustrate the carrying out of national programs and policies (like immigration) by prohibiting communications between national and state or local officials."[87]

[81] *Id.* at 329.

[82] *Id.*

[83] *Id.* (quoting Murphy, 138 S. Ct. at 1478).

[84] *Id.* at *344.

[85] No. 18-264, 2018 WL 3301414, at *13–*17 (E.D. Cal. July 5, 2018) (analyzing, among other laws, Cal. Gov't Code § 7284.6(a)(1)(C) & (D)). Similar to the court in the Philadelphia case, the court here noted (in dictum) that "Section 1373 does just what *Murphy* proscribes: it tells States they may not prohibit (i.e., through legislation) the sharing of information regarding immigration status with the INS or other government entities." *Id.* at *13.

[86] *Id.* at *14.

[87] City of San Francisco v. Trump, No. 17-17478, 2018 WL 3637911, at *14n.7 (9th Cir. Aug. 1, 2018) (Fernandez, J., dissenting) (citing New York, 179 F.3d at 35). The majority of the panel case concluded, under separation-of-powers principles and the Constitution's Spending Clause, that the executive branch may not withhold all federal grants from sanctuary jurisdictions in the absence of congressional authorization. The court did not discuss the constitutionality of Section 1373.

Murphy may also have implications for federal limits on state taxation. A professor who calls *Murphy* "the most important federalism decision since *NFIB v. Sebelius*"[88]—the 2012 decision upholding most of the Affordable Care Act—has argued that *Murphy* may doom not only Section 1373 but also "a whole host of federal statutes [that] limit the tax authorities of states and their subdivisions" by directly forbidding states to tax certain persons or things.[89] This may actually *"undersell[]"* the point.[90] Roughly 110 federal laws limit state taxing authority—some with "major economic impact"—that might be "jeopardized if we take seriously the claim in *Murphy* that Congress 'may not order a state legislature to refrain from enacting a law.'"[91]

Some of those laws are indeed framed in the same kinds of prohibitory terms as PASPA's anti-authorization provision. One statute, for example, provides that "[n]o State . . . may impose or assess a tax on or with respect to the generation or transmission of electricity which . . . results, either directly or indirectly in a greater tax burden on electricity which is generated and transmitted in interstate commerce than on electricity which is generated and transmitted in intrastate commerce."[92] Is this so different from Congress forbidding a state to authorize sports betting? Another law says that "[n]o State may impose an income tax on any retirement income of an individual who is not a resident or domiciliary of such State."[93] Does this confer rights on such "an individual" or is that framing just a subterfuge to evade the anti-commandeering doctrine? A third statute says, "[s]tocks and obligations of the United States government are exempt from taxation by a State or a political subdivision of a State."[94] As one commentator notes, this is "phrased as an exemption rather than a prohibition, but per Justice Alito [in *Murphy*], 'it is a mistake to be confused by the way in which a preemption provision is phrased.'"[95]

---

[88] Daniel Hemel, Murphy's Law and Economics, Medium.com, May 15, 2018, https://bit.ly/2v9iTae.

[89] Daniel Hemel, Justice Alito, State Tax Hero?, Medium.com, May 15, 2018, https://bit.ly/2MdWz5P.

[90] Brian Galle, Murphy's (Misguided) Law, Medium.com, May 15, 2018, https://bit.ly/2AvYtNM (emphasis added).

[91] *Id.*

[92] Hemel, Justice Alito, State Tax Hero?, *supra* note 89 (citing 15 U.S.C. § 391).

[93] *Id.* (citing 4 U.S.C. § 114).

[94] *Id.* (citing 31 U.S.C. § 3124).

[95] Hemel, Justice Alito, State Tax Hero?, *supra* note 89.

These laws and others may well be vulnerable after *Murphy*. But where such a challenge might emerge—and whether a political constituency could coalesce to sustain it—is hard to say. Although possible, it is difficult in any event to imagine courts' invalidating scores of congressional limits on state taxation. Perhaps *Murphy* "*could* have far-reaching consequences" but won't, because "those consequences are largely unintended,"[96] or maybe the Supreme Court will "eventually disavow[] most of *Murphy* or limit[] it to its facts."[97] Time will tell.

V. Why Federalism Matters

What seems clear already is that *Murphy* will add to the dynamic tension at the heart of our federal system, and "[i]n the tension between federal and state power lies the promise of liberty" for all Americans.[98] "[F]ederalism was the unique contribution of the Framers to political science and political theory."[99] As the Court in *Murphy* explained, "[w]hen the original States declared their independence, they claimed the powers inherent in sovereignty—in the words of the Declaration of Independence, the authority 'to do all . . . Acts and Things which Independent States may of right do.'"[100] The states surrendered some but not all of these powers to the new federal government, retaining "'a residuary and inviolable sovereignty,'" which "our Constitution preserves . . . in two ways."[101] First, the text and structure of the Constitution reserve to the states "a substantial portion of the Nation's primary sovereignty, together with the dignity and essential attributes inhering in that status."[102] Second, and particularly relevant in *Murphy*, "the constitutional design secures the founding generation's rejection of the concept of a central government that would act upon and through the States in favor of a

---

[96] Michael Dorf, The Political Stakes of Commandeering in Murphy v. NCAA, Dorf on Law, May 16, 2018, https://bit.ly/2OBQAJt (emphasis added).

[97] Galle, *supra* note 86.

[98] Gregory v. Ashcroft, 501 U.S. 452, 459 (1991).

[99] United States v. Lopez, 514 U.S. 549, 575 (1995) (Kennedy, J., concurring).

[100] Murphy, 138 S. Ct. at 1475 (quoting The Declaration of Independence para. 32 (U.S. 1776)).

[101] Alden v. Maine, 527 U.S. 706, 714–15 (1999) (quoting The Federalist No. 39 (James Madison)).

[102] *Id.* at 714.

system in which the State and Federal Governments would exercise concurrent authority over the people."[103]

This choice was in part a product of the Framers' experience under the Articles of Confederation. Under that system, "Congress lacked the authority in most respects to govern the people directly."[104] Instead, it "acted with powers, greatly restricted, only upon the States."[105] That experience "persuaded . . . [the Framers] that using the States as the instruments of federal governance was both ineffectual and provocative of federal-state conflict."[106]

At the Constitutional Convention, two competing proposals for the new government emerged—the Virginia Plan, under which "Congress would exercise legislative authority directly upon the individuals, without employing the States as intermediaries," and the New Jersey Plan, under which "Congress would continue to require the approval of the States before legislating, as it had under the Articles of Confederation."[107] Edmund Randolph objected to the New Jersey Plan on the grounds that it might require the federal government to coerce the states, and "[c]oercion [is] *impracticable, expensive, cruel to individuals.*"[108] James Madison raised similar practical concerns. In the end, "the Framers explicitly chose a Constitution that confers upon Congress the power to regulate individuals, not States."[109]

In this, as Chief Justice Salmon P. Chase explained a century and a half ago, "the preservation of the States, and the maintenance of their governments, are as much within the design and care of the Constitution as the preservation of the Union and the maintenance of the National government."[110] This "[d]ual sovereignty is a defining feature of our Nation's constitutional blueprint."[111]

---

[103] *Id.* (quoting Printz, 521 U.S. at 919–20) (internal quotation marks omitted).

[104] New York, 505 U.S. at 163.

[105] Lane Cty. v. Oregon, 7 Wall. 71, 76 (1869).

[106] Printz, 521 U.S. at 919 (citing The Federalist No. 15 (Hamilton)).

[107] New York, 505 U.S. at 164.

[108] *Id.* (quoting 1 Records of the Federal Convention of 1787, at 255–56 (Max Farrand, ed., 1911)).

[109] *Id.* at 166.

[110] Texas v. White, 74 U.S. 700, 725 (1869).

[111] Fed. Mar. Comm'n v. S.C. State Ports Auth., 535 U.S. 743, 751 (2002).

And it has both practical and philosophic dimensions. Yes, the federal structure helps keep the federal and state governments in their lanes and serves "to ensure that States function as political entities in their own right."[112] Moreover, "[s]tate sovereignty is not just an end in itself,"[113] and "[f]ederalism is more than an exercise in setting the boundary between different institutions of government for their own integrity."[114] Instead—and this was the Framers' key insight—"federalism secures to citizens the liberties that derive from the diffusion of sovereign power."[115]

As Justice Anthony Kennedy put it, the Framers understood that "freedom was enhanced by the creation of two governments, not one."[116] As Justice Antonin Scalia wrote in *Printz* quoting Kennedy:

> The great innovation of this design was that "our citizens would have two political capacities, one state and one federal, each protected from incursion by the other"—"a legal system unprecedented in form and design, establishing two orders of government, each with its own direct relationship, its own privity, its own set of mutual rights and obligations to the people who sustain it and are governed by it."[117]

Or, as Madison explained it, America's "compound republic" creates a "double security [for] the rights of the people. The different governments will control each other, at the same time that each will be controlled by itself."[118]

This federalist system protects political liberties.[119] It "assures a decentralized government that will be more sensitive to the diverse needs of a heterogenous society; it increases opportunity for citizen involvement in democratic processes; it allows for more innovation and experimentation in government; and it makes government

[112] Bond v. United States, 564 U.S. 211, 221 (2011).

[113] New York, 505 U.S. at 181.

[114] Bond, 564 U.S. at 221.

[115] New York, 505 U.S. at 181 (quoting Coleman v. Thompson, 501 U.S. 722, 759 (1991) (Blackmun, J., dissenting)).

[116] Lopez, 514 U.S. at 576 (Kennedy, J., concurring).

[117] Printz, 521 U.S. at 920 (quoting U.S. Term Limits, Inc. v. Thornton, 514 U.S. 779, 838 (1995) (Kennedy, J., concurring)).

[118] The Federalist No. 51 (James Madison).

[119] Bond, 564 U.S. at 221.

more responsive by putting the States in competition for a mobile citizenry."[120]

Federalism also protects individual liberty. "It allows States to respond, through the enactment of positive law, to the initiative of those who seek a voice in shaping the destiny of their own times without having to rely solely upon the political processes that control a remote central power."[121] To borrow Justice Louis Brandeis's memorable (if misunderstood) phrase, it allows states to act as laboratories of democracy.[122] "By denying any one government complete jurisdiction over all the concerns of public life, federalism protects the liberty of the individual from arbitrary power."[123] "Just as the separation and independence of the coordinate branches of the Federal Government serve to prevent the accumulation of excessive power in any one branch, a healthy balance of power between the States and the Federal Government will reduce the risk of tyranny and abuse from either front."[124]

The anti-commandeering rule implicit in the Constitution and reaffirmed in *Murphy* is one of these "structural protections of liberty."[125] And it has still other advantages, as the Court in *Murphy, Printz,* and *New York* noted. It promotes political accountability for one, by showing voters who deserves credit or blame for a given regulation—the states or the federal government. It also "prevents Congress from shifting the costs of regulation to the States"; it requires Congress to weigh the benefits and costs of a given program and then, if Congress chooses to enact the program, to fund it.[126] And *Murphy* makes explicit what *Printz* and *New York* implied: the

---

[120] Gregory, 501 U.S. at 458.

[121] Bond, 564 U.S. at 221.

[122] New State Ice Co. v. Liebmann, 285 U.S. 262, 311 (1932) (Brandeis, J., dissenting). Professor Michael Greve notes that "Brandeis's famous dictum had almost nothing to do with federalism and everything to do with his commitment to scientific socialism," a "substantive view" that "continues to inhibit a truly experimental federalist politics." Michael S. Greve, Laboratories of Democracy: Anatomy of a Metaphor, Am. Enterprise Inst. Federalist Outlook, Mar. 31, 2001, http://www.aei.org/publication/laboratories-of-democracy.

[123] Bond, 564 U.S. at 222.

[124] Gregory, 501 U.S. at 458.

[125] Murphy, 138 S. Ct. at 1477 (quoting Printz, 521 U.S. at 921).

[126] *Id.*

anti-commandeering rule applies with equal force whether Congress affirmatively directs a state to act or prohibits a state from doing so.

Exactly what *Murphy* portends for one federal law or another is, as noted, difficult to predict. What seems clearer is that as that question plays out in Congress, state legislatures, and the courts, the healthy tensions it produces will only add to the vitality of our federal structure and, along with it, help secure the people's liberty. That such conflict could inure to citizens' benefit might seem counterintuitive. But that, after all, is the Newtonian logic of our constitutional structure, which divides power among "opposite and rival interests" so that "each may be a check on the other," and individual interests "may be a sentinel over the public rights."[127] *Murphy* may well help stoke rivalries between the states and the federal government on a whole host of issues, from sanctuary cities and taxation (as discussed earlier), to medical marijuana, guns, environmental mandates, and a wide swath of other matters where state and federal interests often diverge. Those rivalries will help ensure that the states and the federal government remain effective checks on one another, and that neither will usurp the rights of the people.

VI. Conclusion

Murphy reaffirms a principle at the foundation of our constitutional structure—that Congress may not issue direct orders to states or otherwise operate the machinery of state government. At least in the near term, the decision allows each state to decide for itself whether to legalize sports gambling, and the states will decide that question in different ways. More broadly, *Murphy* will likely introduce new questions about the balance of power between Congress and the states. All of this is good for federalism—and a healthy federalism is a win for all Americans.

---

[127] The Federalist No. 51 (James Madison).

The History of Internet Sales Taxes from 1789 to the Present Day: *South Dakota v. Wayfair*

*Joseph Bishop-Henchman**

On June 21, 2018, the U.S. Supreme Court ruled that South Dakota can require collection of its sales tax on sales to its residents by out-of-state internet retailers.[1] The 5-4 decision overruled two earlier precedents, *National Bellas Hess, Inc. v. Illinois Department of Revenue* (1967) and *Quill Corp. v. North Dakota* (1992), which had both held that only businesses with a physical presence in a state can be required to collect that state's sales tax.[2] The new rule, articulated in *Wayfair*, is that a state sales tax can be constitutionally collected so long as it does not discriminate against or place excessive burdens on those engaging in interstate commerce. South Dakota's law, with built-in protections for taxpayers and limitations on its authority, passed constitutional muster.

In one sense, the *Wayfair* case is unremarkable. Most observers had predicted the outcome as inevitable. The four dissenting justices did not bother to defend the old physical presence rule, writing that "*Bellas Hess* was wrongly decided, for many of the reasons given by the Court," disagreeing only that Congress should fix the problem

---

* Executive vice president and general counsel at the Tax Foundation. The Tax Foundation brief in support of neither party that Bishop-Henchman authored in *Wayfair* was cited twice by the Court. He has also testified to Congress seven times and to states dozens of times on these issues since 2010.

[1] South Dakota v. Wayfair, Inc., 138 S. Ct. 2080 (2018). Technically, the tax being collected is the state's use tax, a tax imposed at an identical rate as the sales tax on any purchase by a resident where sales tax has not otherwise been collected. Every state with a sales tax has a use tax, and their nondiscriminatory imposition was upheld in Henneford v. Silas Mason Co., Inc., 300 U.S. 577 (1937). To avoid pedantry I refer to them simply as sales taxes.

[2] See National Bellas Hess, Inc. v. Department of Revenue of Ill., 386 U.S. 753 (1967); Quill Corp. v. North Dakota, 504 U.S. 298 (1992).

rather than the Court.[3] News coverage was an almost whimsical oh-well-it-was-good-while-it-lasted-but-now-we-have-to-pay-tax-on-the-stuff-we-buy-online.[4] The largest online retailer, Amazon.com, had collected sales taxes nationwide since 2014, and shortly after the decision, rival Overstock.com said it would do so as well.[5] In the weeks after the decision, states began preparing laws identical to South Dakota's, with several announcing plans to return any additional revenue in the form of cuts to other taxes.

But in another sense, *Wayfair* is the most significant case of this Supreme Court term. E-commerce now represents 11 percent of all retail sales, growing by 15 percent each year. Forty *amicus* briefs were filed in the case, with groups normally allied on other issues finding themselves on opposing sides.[6] The attorney line to attend oral arguments in the case was the second longest of the term, behind only *Janus*.[7] The lineup of the justices was unusual: Justices Anthony

---

[3] Wayfair, 138 S. Ct. at 2101 (Roberts, C.J., dissenting).

[4] A somewhat-related law still remains in force: the Internet Tax Freedom Act (ITFA), a two-sentence bill passed by Congress as a temporary three-year measure in 1998, extended several times, and ultimately made permanent in 2016. ITFA bans new state or local taxes on internet access, and multiple or discriminatory taxes on internet commerce. Accordingly it expressly bans taxes that apply to internet sales but not offline sales.

[5] See, e.g., James Brumley, For Most Online Retailers, the Online Sales Tax Decision Is Non-Story, InvestorPlace, Jun. 23, 2018, https://finance.yahoo.com/news/most-online -retailers-online-sales-201634136.html; Corinne Ruff, Overstock to Collect Sales Tax Following SCOTUS Decision, Retail Dive, Jun. 26, 2018, https://www.retaildive.com /news/overstock-to-collect-sales-tax-following-scotus-decision/526547.

[6] Briefs supporting South Dakota included ones submitted by scholars Alex Brill and Alan Viard of the American Enterprise Institute; the city of Little Rock, Arkansas; trade associations for wholesalers, retailers, and shopping centers; 41 states and D.C., including many Republican-controlled states; Senators Heidi Heitkamp (D-ND), Lamar Alexander (R-TN), Richard Durbin (D-IL), and Mike Enzi (R-WY); and 60 tax and law professors of all ideological stripes. Briefs supporting Wayfair included ones submitted by New Hampshire and Montana; trade associations for catalog mailers and auctioneers; Etsy; practitioner group Tax Executives Institute; the National Tax-payers Union; the Competitive Enterprise Institute; and the Cato Institute. The Tax Foundation filed a brief in support of neither party, asking the Court to uphold South Dakota's law but to provide guidance stating that particular features of that law meant it did not burden interstate commerce.

[7] Discussion between the author and the marshal of the Court Apr. 17, 2018. Tax counsels for L.L. Bean win the most tenacious award, having slept out overnight in freezing cold (in their employer's gear) to be first in the public line (not counting paid line-standers). Non-lawyers who arrived after 5 a.m. did not get to see the oral argument.

Kennedy, Clarence Thomas, Ruth Bader Ginsburg, Samuel Alito, and Neil Gorsuch making up the majority, and Chief Justice John Roberts and Justices Stephen Breyer, Sonia Sotomayor, and Elena Kagan dissenting. It ended up being Justice Kennedy's final majority opinion, and his influence was felt on the decision. More than just about a South Dakota law, the case involved weighty and long unsettled questions such as due process limitations on jurisdiction, the proper roles of Congress and the courts in enforcing limitations on state actions taxing or regulating interstate commerce, the standard by which the Supreme Court should overrule prior decisions, the thorny question of state regulations that impact producers in other states, and how (or whether) to tax activities that happen everywhere and nowhere in the cloud or on the internet.

Wayfair may prove to be the first case where the Supreme Court truly confronted the need to pair, on one hand, constitutional and legal systems that define protections and obligations based on physical presence within geographic lines, and on the other, economic activities that are increasingly borderless, instantaneous, and nonphysical. As with all good constitutional stories, it starts in 1789.

Halting a Trade War, 1789 Edition

On September 17, 1787, the draft Constitution was approved by the Constitutional Convention, and it ultimately took effect on March 4, 1789, following state ratifications. The Convention had originally been called to consider amendments to the Articles of Confederation, which had governed, or more accurately failed to govern, the country since 1781.

The biggest shortcomings of the national government under the Articles of Confederation were its inability to raise revenue except through requests to the states and its requirement that all legislation be approved unanimously by each state.[8] "Attempted requisitions were regarded by the sovereign states as voluntary contributions or alms and were generally ignored. The payment of taxes came finally to be regarded as a romantically honorable act, or even as a sort of amiable and

---

[8] See Jared Walczak, How Failed Tax Policy Led to the Constitutional Convention, Tax Foundation, Sept. 16, 2016, https://taxfoundation.org/how-failed-tax-policy-led -constitutional-convention.

quixotic manifestation of eccentricity."[9] Attempts from 1783 through 1786 to enact federal taxes failed to achieve unanimous support, and the United States government quickly started going broke.

Another major shortcoming was that the Articles of Confederation neither prohibited trade wars between the states nor empowered the national government to stop them. States with ports taxed commerce bound for interior states, tariff wars proliferated, and the national economy was imperiled. New York imposed special entrance and clearance fees on all vessels heading to or from New Jersey or Connecticut. New Jersey retaliated by imposing a tax of 30 shillings a month on a lighthouse that New York City had purchased in Sandy Hook, New Jersey. Fisher Ames wrote, "The king of New York levied imposts upon New Jersey and Connecticut, and the nobles of Virginia bore with impatience their tributary dependence upon Baltimore and Philadelphia. Our discontents were fermenting into civil war."[10] Writing in 1824, U.S. Supreme Court Justice William Johnson described these actions as "destructive to the harmony of the states, and fatal to their commercial interests abroad. This was the immediate cause that led to the forming of a convention."[11]

James Madison orchestrated the Annapolis Convention in 1786 to attempt to halt this trade war, but only five states showed up. He then became determined to fix the issue in what became the Constitution by empowering the national government to restrain state actions that harm interstate commerce:

> [T]he desire of the commercial States to collect, in any form, an indirect revenue from their uncommercial neighbors, must appear not less impolitic than it is unfair; since it would stimulate the injured party, by resentment as well as interest, to resort to less convenient channels for their foreign trade. But the mild voice of reason, pleading the cause of an enlarged and permanent interest, is but too often drowned,

[9] Randolph Paul, Taxation in the United States 5 (1954).

[10] Allan Nevins, The American States During and After the Revolution, 1775–1789 at 555–57 (1927).

[11] Gibbons v. Ogden, 22 U.S. 1, 224 (Johnson, J., concurring). One biographer of Chief Justice John Marshall believes that Johnson's opinion was written in large part by Marshall himself, going "even further than the Court's opinion and express[ing] what was almost certainly Marshall's own view of the federal government's [exclusive] power." Joel Richard Paul, Without Precedent: Chief Justice John Marshall and His Times 370 (2018).

before public bodies as well as individuals, by the clamors
of an impatient avidity for immediate and immoderate
gain. The necessity of a superintending authority over the
reciprocal trade of confederated States has been illustrated.[12]

The Constitution thus contains several restrictions on states' ability to tax or burden interstate activity. Justice Joseph Story, praising these provisions in his *Commentaries* in 1833, wrote that "there is . . . wisdom and policy in restraining the states themselves from the exercise of [taxation] injuriously to the interests of each other. A petty warfare of regulation is thus prevented, which would rouse resentments, and create dissensions, to the ruin of the harmony and amity of the states."[13] The Import-Export Clause prohibits states from imposing taxes on imports beyond what is needed for inspection duties.[14] The Tonnage Clause prohibits state charges on shipping freight.[15] The Privileges and Immunities Clause protects the right of citizens to cross state lines in pursuit of an honest living.[16] And then there's the Commerce Clause.

---

[12] The Federalist No. 42 (James Madison).

[13] Joseph Story, Commentaries on the Constitution 2 (1833), at § 1013.

[14] U.S. Const. art. I, § 10, cl. 2 ("No State shall, without the Consent of the Congress, lay any Imposts or Duties on Imports or Exports, except what may be absolutely necessary for executing its inspection Laws: and the net Produce of all Duties and Imposts, laid by any State on Imports or Exports, shall be for the Use of the Treasury of the United States; and all such Laws shall be subject to the Revision and Controul of the Congress."). See, e.g., Michelin Corp. v. Wages, 423 U.S. 276, 286 (1976) (stating that the Import-Export Clause prohibits import taxes that "create special protective tariffs or particular preferences for certain domestic goods."). Justice Clarence Thomas, a critic of dormant commerce clause jurisprudence, nonetheless argues that taxes that discriminate against nonresidents should be invalidated by the courts under the Import-Export Clause. See Camps Newfound/Owatanna, Inc. v. Town of Harrison, 520 U.S. 564, 610 (1997) (Thomas, J., dissenting) ("That the expansion effected by today's decision finds some support in the morass of our negative Commerce Clause case law only serves to highlight the need to abandon that failed jurisprudence and to consider restoring the original Import-Export Clause check on discriminatory state taxation to what appears to be its proper role.").

[15] U.S. Const. art. I, § 10, cl. 3 ("No State shall, without the Consent of Congress, lay any Duty of Tonnage . . .").

[16] U.S. Const. art. IV, § 2, cl. 1 ("The Citizens of each State shall be entitled to all Privileges and Immunities of Citizens in the several States."). See, e.g., United Bldg. & Constr. Trades v. Mayor of Camden, 465 U.S. 208, 219 (1984) (identifying "pursuit of a common calling" as a privilege of citizenship protected by the Constitution); Saenz v. Roe, 526 U.S. 489 (1999) (invalidating a law that did not restrict state travel per se but discouraged the crossing of state lines with a punitive and discriminatory law);

The Other Commerce Clause: From Complete Bar to
Complete Auto

Readers of the *Cato Supreme Court Review* are familiar with the Commerce Clause. Over the course of cases from *McCullough* to *Schechter Poultry* to *Jones & Laughlin* to *Darby Lumber* to *Wickard* to *Lopez* to *Raich*, the Supreme Court transformed Congress's power to "regulate commerce . . . among the several States" into a federal power to regulate even non-commerce within one state, if it affects or could potentially affect interstate markets. Much of what the federal government does, for good or for ill, is thanks to this broad reading of the Commerce Clause.

Forget all that, for this is about a different Commerce Clause, sometimes called the dormant Commerce Clause or the negative Commerce Clause. The dormant Commerce Clause is a restriction on state laws that discriminate against interstate commerce, which is inferred by the grant of the power to regulate interstate commerce to the federal government. The "dormant" term comes from Chief Justice Marshall's majority opinion in *Gibbons v. Ogden*, where he explained that because the power to regulate interstate commerce was exclusively federal, it "must be placed in the hands of agents or lie dormant."[17] States can pass laws that affect or even regulate interstate commerce, but they are invalid if they discriminate against interstate commerce or excessively burden it.

Gibbons involved a stereotypical application of this doctrine. In 1808, New York granted a 30-year monopoly to Robert Livingston and Robert Fulton, giving them exclusive navigation rights for all boats for all bodies of water in New York state, including approaches to neighboring states. Aaron Ogden began a ferry service between Elizabethtown, New Jersey, and New York City with a license from this monopoly, doing business with Thomas Gibbons. The partnership went sour. Gibbons then obtained a federal license under a 1793 coastal trade law and began running a rival ferry on the same

---

id. at 511–12 (Rehnquist, J., dissenting) ("The right to travel clearly embraces the right to go from one place to another, and prohibits States from impeding the free passage of citizens); Erwin Chemerinsky, Constitutional Law 450 (2d ed. 2002) ("The vast majority of cases under the [Article IV] privileges and immunities clause involve states discriminating against out-of-staters with regard to their ability to earn a livelihood.").

17 Gibbons, 22 U.S. at 189. See also Willson v. Black Bird Creek Marsh Co., 27 U.S. 245, 252 (1829) (describing "the power to regulate commerce in its dormant state").

route, captained by Cornelius Vanderbilt. Ogden sued to enforce the monopoly, and New York state courts enjoined Gibbons from operating his ferry. In the U.S. Supreme Court, Gibbons's lawyer, Daniel Webster, argued that Congress had sole power of interstate commerce and the New York monopoly was void there.

The Supreme Court ruled in favor of Gibbons, finding that the ferry was interstate commerce and that the license granted under the federal 1793 law pre-empted any state license. That Congress had not specifically acted in this instance was to no avail; the Commerce Clause, the Court said, was written *"to regulate commerce;* to rescue it from the embarrassing and destructive consequences, resulting from the legislation of so many different States, and to place it under the protection of a uniform law."[18] That Congress did not act did not mean that states could.

So strong was the concern over states' misuse of their power, that the rule for a century and a half was that states could not tax interstate commerce at all. Unimportant and noncontroversial U.S. Supreme Court opinions contained language that would be shocking to us today, such as "[a] State is . . . precluded from taking any action which may fairly be deemed to have the effect of impeding the free flow of trade between States" or "[n]o State has the right to lay a tax on interstate commerce in any form."[19]

This complete bar eroded as the rise of multistate corporations created concern that an out-of-state company could "exploit" in-state markets without paying taxes to support in-state government services. The rule also became untenable as more and more economic activity became interstate. Few people today never buy or sell anything from someone in another state. These economic changes, together with the Supreme Court's defining the constitutional term "commerce among the several States" to encompass nearly all economic activity, and a federal government that has taken on many new areas of action and regulation, have led to a greatly expanded scope for the federal government and a narrowed exclusive scope for the states. A complete ban on taxation of anyone engaged in interstate commerce would greatly hobble state taxation.

---

[18] Gibbons, 22 U.S. at 11 (emphasis in original).

[19] Freeman v. Hewitt, 329 U.S. 249, 252-53 (1946); Leloup v. Port of Mobile, 127 U.S. 640, 648 (1888).

That something had to change became apparent in the 1950s, when the Court treated economically identical taxes differently based on "magic words" in the statute. The Court invalidated a license tax imposed on the in-state gross receipts of an out-of-state company, but upheld a franchise tax on an out-of-state company's "going concern value," measured by in-state gross receipts.[20] Justices and scholars became dissatisfied with a legal test that simply rewarded draftsmanship while missing the important question: "whether the challenged tax produced results forbidden by the commerce clause."[21]

Consequently, the Court abandoned its formal rule in the *Complete Auto* case of 1977, instead ruling that states may tax interstate commerce if the tax meets a four-part test: nexus, fair apportionment, nondiscrimination, and fairly related.[22]

Substantial Nexus

Substantial nexus is a sufficient connection between the state and the taxpayer. We'll come back to it.

Fair Apportionment

Fair apportionment means that the state cannot tax beyond its fair share of interstate commerce. It is determined by internal consistency: if every jurisdiction had the same tax, would it result in more than 100 percent of the business's income being subject to tax?[23]

What percent of a company's income can one state subject to its taxation? If all states can tax 100 percent of a company's income, that would lead to double taxation. Before the 20th century, most corporations were chartered by one state and therefore did not legally exist in other states. The rise of multistate corporations, and state corporate income taxes, gave rise to the need to apportion income among several states.

---

[20] See Complete Auto Transit, Inc. v. Brady, 430 U.S. 274, 284 (1977) (comparing Ry. Express Agency v. Virginia, 347 U.S. 359 (1954) (Railway Express I) and Ry. Express Agency v. Virginia, 358 U.S. 434 (1959) (Railway Express II)).

[21] *Id.* at 285.

[22] *Id.* at 279.

[23] See Container Corp. v. Franchise Tax Bd., 463 U.S. 159, 169 (1983) (applying the internal consistency test).

In 1957, a three-factor apportionment formula was developed as the Uniform Division of Income for Tax Purposes Act (UDITPA), equally weighing sales, property, and payroll. If a company has 25 percent of its sales in State A, 100 percent of its property in State A, and 75 percent of its payroll in State A, then State A can subject two-thirds of that company's income to its corporate tax (25 plus 100 plus 75, divided by 3, is 66.66). Only three states adopted UDITPA, most preferring to game apportionment rules to benefit favored (in-state) companies.

After a series of decisions where the Supreme Court upheld state power to tax businesses based on the presence of door-to-door sales-people and independent contractors, Congress passed a temporary restriction on new state laws on those areas (still on the books today) and set up a committee to recommend permanent legislation.[24] The Willis Commission, as it was called, spent the early 1960s holding hearings and recommending a uniform state income tax base and an evenly weighted two-factor apportionment formula (property and payroll). Sales was not included in the formula in the view that the purpose of the corporate income tax is to pay for government services it uses, which is where its property and payroll are, not its sales.

States were alarmed by the Willis Commission's proposed formula, and successfully pressured Congress to withdraw the bill in return for states adopting the UDITPA formula. By 1970, most states had done so and Congress dropped the proposals. Since then, however, states have again begun gaming apportionment formulas, competing with each other to weigh the sales factor more heavily. Half the states today have a sales-factor-only formula, which benefits in-state companies.[25] The Supreme Court upheld the single sales-factor formula in 1978 as compliant with internal consistency, and further held in 1987 that gross receipts taxes need not be apportioned as they are inherently apportioned.[26]

---

[24] See Northwestern Cement Co. v. Minnesota, 358 U.S. 450 (1959), overruled by Interstate Income Act of 1959, P.L. 86-272, codified at 15 U.S.C. §§ 381–384; Scripto v. Carson, 362 U.S. 207 (1960).

[25] UDITPA is probably better called DITPA nowadays.

[26] See Moorman Mfg. Co. v. Bair, 437 U.S. 267 (1978); Tyler Pipe Co. v. Washington, 483 U.S. 232 (1987).

Nondiscrimination

A state cannot tax out-of-state activity or taxpayers while exempting similar in-state activity or taxpayers. Justice Anthony Kennedy, drawing on writings by Madison and Hamilton, wrote in 1994, "The central rationale for the rule against discrimination is to prohibit state or municipal laws whose object is local economic protectionism, laws that would excite those jealousies and retaliatory measures the Constitution was designed to prevent."[27]

States have tried to enact pretty much every permutation of discriminatory taxation, and the Supreme Court has been vigilant about stopping them all. It disallowed a New York tax solely on out-of-state activity that left identical in-state activity untaxed;[28] a Louisiana tax on all activity but where in-state activity receives significant credits;[29] a New York tax on out-of-state activity simultaneous with an exemption for in-state activity;[30] a Hawaii tax on all activity that exempted in-state activity;[31] a Pennsylvania fee on all activity coupled with reduced taxes on in-state activity;[32] an Ohio tax credit for all activity that was disallowed for out-of-state taxpayers;[33] a Massachusetts tax on all activity with the revenue distributed to in-state taxpayers only;[34] a Maine tax exemption given only to taxpayers engaged in in-state activity;[35] and a Maryland tax on all activity with a partial credit for out-of-state activity and a full credit given for in-state activity only.[36]

Several of these cases featured dissents from Justices Thomas and Antonin Scalia, as they disagreed with the whole notion of the dormant Commerce Clause. Justice Thomas has described it as an

---

[27] C&A Carbone, Inc. v. Town of Clarkstown, N.Y., 511 U.S. 383 (1994) (quoting The Federalist No. 22, at 143–145 (A. Hamilton) (C. Rossiter ed. 1961); James Madison, Vices of the Political System of the United States, in 2 Writings of James Madison 362–63 (G. Hunt ed. 1901)).

[28] See Boston Stock Exchange v. State Tax Comm'n, 429 U.S. 318 (1977).

[29] See Maryland v. Louisiana (1981), 451 U.S. 725 (1981).

[30] See Westinghouse Elec. Co. v. Tully, 466 U.S. 388 (1984).

[31] See Bacchus Imports, Ltd. v. Dias, 468 U.S. 263 (1984).

[32] See Am. Trucking Ass'n v. Scheiner, 483 U.S. 266 (1987).

[33] See New Energy Co. v. Limbach, 486 U.S. 269 (1988).

[34] See West Lynn Creamery, Inc. v. Healy, 512 U.S. 186 (1994).

[35] See Camps Newfound/Owatanna, Inc. v. Town of Harrison, 520 U.S. 564 (1997).

[36] See Comptroller of Treasury of Maryland v. Wynne, 135 S. Ct. 1787 (2015).

"exercise of judicial power in an area for which there is no textual basis," in order to reach "what intuitively seemed to be a desirable result and in some cases arguably was the constitutionally correct result."[37] Justice Scalia, sharing the objection over the textual basis for the doctrine, added that the dormant Commerce Clause results in judges doing things beyond "interpreting a legal text, discerning a legal tradition, or even applying a stable body of precedents. It instead requires us to balance the needs of commerce against the needs of state governments. That is a task for legislators, not judges." Scalia ultimately decided to "vote to set aside a tax under the negative Commerce Clause if (but only if) it discriminates on its face against interstate commerce or cannot be distinguished from a tax this Court has already held unconstitutional."[38]

Justices Scalia and Thomas were therefore automatic votes to sustain most state tax laws from challenge. In *Wayfair*, Justice Thomas was consequently part of the majority, rejecting Wayfair's effort to strike down the South Dakota law. He was joined by Justice Scalia's successor on the bench, Justice Neil Gorsuch, who cryptically expressed discomfort with the dormant Commerce Clause doctrine:

> The Commerce Clause is found in Article I and authorizes *Congress* to regulate interstate commerce. Meanwhile our dormant commerce cases suggest Article III *courts* may invalidate state laws that offend no congressional statute. Whether and how much of this can be squared with the text of the Commerce Clause, justified by *stare decisis*, or defended as misbranded products of federalism or antidiscrimination imperatives flowing from Article IV's Privileges and Immunities Clause are questions for another day.[39]

This author has suggested that Congress could address this objection by codifying the *Complete Auto* standard into federal law, thereby giving judges a statutory basis for enforcing the dormant Commerce Clause doctrine.[40] Congress has codified limits on state tax authority

[37] Camps/Newfound/Owatanna, 520 U.S. at 618 (Thomas, J., dissenting).

[38] Wynne, 135 S. Ct. at 1810–11 (Scalia, J., dissenting).

[39] Wayfair, 138 S. Ct. at 2100–01 (Gorsuch, J., concurring).

[40] See Joseph Henchman, The Limits of State Tax Powers: A Modest Reply to Justice Scalia, Tax Foundation, May 27, 2015, https://taxfoundation.org/limits-state-tax-powers-modest-reply-justice-scalia (suggesting federal codification of the *Complete Auto* test); Joseph Bishop-Henchman, Post-Wayfair Options for Congress, Written Testimony to

in particular circumstances, such as with discriminatory taxation of federal employees, interstate travel, or railroad property.

Fairly Related

The state tax must be fairly related to services provided to the taxpayer. The Court has subsequently interpreted this to mean "reasonably related to services received by the taxpayer," with a tax's excessiveness a legislative matter instead of a judicial one.[41]

In *Wayfair*, the Court majority observed that a state law that "regulat[es] even-handedly to effectuate a legitimate local public interest . . . will be upheld unless the burden imposed on such commerce is clearly excessive in relation to the putative local benefits," citing a balancing test from *Pike v. Bruce Church, Inc.*[42]

Do You Have Substantial Nexus?

To return to the topic of substantial nexus—a sufficient connection between the state and the taxpayer—a running issue is whether and how it is different from due process. The Court conflated nexus and due process jurisdiction in *Bellas Hess*, separated them in *Quill*, and now leaves open the question of to what extent states may constitutionally regulate out-of-state actors.

Civil Procedure 101: Due Process from Pennoyer to International Shoe

On Ninth Street in Columbia, Missouri, a town of 96,000 (including 33,000 students) and home of the annual Ragtime and Jazz Festival, Richard King opened a small cabaret club, The Blue Note, in 1980. By 1996 business was good and King decided to set up a website for the club. Shortly thereafter, he learned that the Bensusan Restaurant Co. of Manhattan had filed a lawsuit against him, in New York federal court, for violating its "The Blue Note" trademark registered in 1985. King's only contact with New York was that his website could be accessed from that state.[43]

---

the U.S. House Committee on the Judiciary, Jul. 24, 2018, https://taxfoundation.org /post-wayfair-options-congress (suggesting federal codification of the *Complete Auto* test and the *Wayfair* checklist).

41 Commonwealth Edison Co. v. Montana, 453 U.S. 609, 627 (1981) ("The simple fact is that the appropriate level or rate of taxation is essentially a matter for legislative, and not judicial, resolution.").

42 Wayfair, 138 S. Ct. at 2091 (quoting Pike v. Bruce Church, Inc., 397 U.S. 137, 142 (1970)).

43 See Bensusan Rest. Corp. v. King, 126 F.3d 25, 26 (2d Cir. 1997).

Courts have long been sympathetic to people like King, who face the expense and worry of defending (often meritless) lawsuits in a faraway place. The U.S. Constitution's Due Process clause has been held to protect such individuals "against the burdens of litigating in a distant or inconvenient forum" by ensuring that states do not "reach out beyond the limits imposed on them . . . in a federal system."[44] That principle—that it is unfair to be sued in a state where one has virtually no connections—is generally undisputed. The problem arises in drawing the line separating "virtually no connections" from "sufficient minimum contacts."

The historical line was physical presence. Looking at the Due Process Clause, the Court in *Pennoyer v. Neff* explained that "proceedings in a court of justice to determine the personal rights and obligations of parties over whom that court has no jurisdiction do not constitute due process of law."[45] Unless a defendant appeared in person, enforcing a judgment against him was considered so unfair that it violated the U.S. Constitution. If there was such a judgment, other states could refuse to enforce it as an abuse of power. At the dawn of the 20th century, scholar Thomas M. Cooley summarized the rule in his *Constitutional Limitations* (1903): "No state has authority to invade the jurisdiction of another, and by service of process compel parties there resident or being to submit their controversies to the determination of its courts."

The physical presence requirement for personal jurisdiction was first significantly challenged by the rise of interstate property ownership and motorist accidents caused by out-of-state drivers. States could seize (attach) the in-state property of an out-of-state defendant pending the outcome of the case, provided the state gave notice to the owner. While those "in rem" actions—as well as divorce actions, which were treated similarly—were within the confines of the physical presence rule, it allowed states to reach defendants who lived outside the state. Courts also developed the concept of implied consent to allow states to reach outside their borders to prosecute nonresident motorists who inflicted damages or injury within the state. By driving on the state's roads, a motorist was held to have automatically consented to jurisdiction over any lawsuits that might

---

[44] World-Wide Volkswagen v. Woodson, 444 U.S. 286, 292 (1980).

[45] Pennoyer v. Neff, 95 U.S. 714, 733 (1878).

arise from the driving, although he had to receive notice of the lawsuit.[46]

The physical presence rule was stretched the most in suits involving corporate defendants, because corporations are a legal fiction and their physical existence is intangible. Some states required that corporations appoint an agent to receive service of process, and if a corporation was "present" without such an appointment, a state official was designated to receive service of process on its behalf. Determining presence became the critical question. "Under both the presence theory and the implied consent theory, the first question to be asked was whether the corporation was 'doing business' within the state. . . . '[D]oing business' gradually came to be a test in and of itself."[47]

In 1945, in *International Shoe v. Washington*, the Court abandoned the physical presence rule in favor of defendant-specific multifactor fairness inquiry. The case (and its progeny) look at a company's conduct in the state, evaluating whether there are "minimum contacts" with the jurisdiction such that a lawsuit involving the nonpresent defendant does not offend "traditional notions of fair play and substantial justice."[48]

As applied today, out-of-state corporate defendants with continuous and systematic activity in the state, or even single or occasional acts, can be required to answer a lawsuit based on that specific activity ("specific jurisdiction"). However, the Court over the past decade has worked to narrow the extent of potential personal jurisdiction, holding (over consistent objections from Justice Sonia Sotomayor) that out-of-state corporate defendants cannot be forced to answer general lawsuits unrelated to their in-state activity ("general jurisdiction") in a state that is not "fairly regarded as home," where they do not have continuous and systematic business contacts.[49]

Is this standard the right one? It's still not a requirement for in-state presence of people or property but the standard is less broad

[46] See, e.g., Hess v. Pawloski, 274 U.S. 352, 355 (1927).

[47] Jack H. Friedenthal, Arthur R. Miller, & John E. Sexton, Civil Procedure: Cases and Materials, at 74 (8th Ed. 2001, John J. Cound, ed.).

[48] International Shoe Co. v. Washington, 326 U.S. 310, 316 (1945).

[49] Goodyear Dunlop Tires Operations, S.A. v. Brown, 564 U.S. 915–24 (2011); See also Daimler AG v. Bauman, 134 S. Ct. 746 (2014); BNSF Railway Co. v. Tyrrell, 137 S. Ct. 1549 (2017); Bristol-Myers Squibb Co. v. Superior Court, 137 S. Ct. 1773 (2017).

than it used to be. Future expansive cases of internet taxation may therefore raise due process as a viable objection.[50]

National Bellas Hess

In the 1960s, Illinois sought to require catalog mailer National Bellas Hess to collect Illinois sales tax on its sales to Illinois residents. The company was headquartered in Missouri, and while it sent catalogs and deliveries to Illinois by mail, it had no salespeople or property in the state, nor did it advertise in the state. It did not sell only in Illinois, but in every state in the country.

In 1967, the Court struck down the Illinois attempt, stating that "the Constitution requires some definite link, some minimum connection, between a state and the person, property or transaction it seeks to tax."[51] The Court concluded that was missing in this case, and that a state cannot impose a tax collection requirement on a company "whose only connection with customers in the State is by common carrier or the United States mail."[52] The Court further described the danger it was avoiding:

> And if the power of Illinois to impose use tax burdens upon National were upheld, the resulting impediments upon the free conduct of its interstate business would be neither imaginary nor remote. For if Illinois can impose such burdens, so can every other State, and so, indeed, can every municipality, every school district, and every other political subdivision throughout the Nation with power to impose sales and use taxes. The many variations in rates of tax, in allowable exemptions, and in administrative and record-keeping requirements could entangle National's interstate business in a virtual welter of complicated obligations to local jurisdictions with no legitimate claim to impose "a fair share of the cost of the local government."

---

[50] The Cato Institute's *Wayfair* brief sought to raise this Due Process issue immediately. See Trevor Burrus & Matthew Larosiere, South Dakota v. Wayfair: A Taxing Decision, Cato at Liberty, Jun. 21, 2018, https://www.cato.org/blog/south-dakota-v-wayfair-taxing-decision. The Court's opinion acknowledged the point but left it for another day, given that a due process objection had not been raised and *Wayfair's* in-state activities were considerable.

[51] Bellas Hess, 386 U.S. at 756 (cleaned up).

[52] *Id.* at 758.

> The very purpose of the Commerce Clause was to ensure a national economy free from such unjustifiable local entanglements. Under the Constitution, this is a domain where Congress alone has the power of regulation and control.[53]

Three justices dissented, detailing National Bellas Hess's "large-scale, systematic, continuous solicitation and exploitation of the Illinois consumer market" and observing that it therefore "enjoys the benefits of, and profits from the facilities nurtured by, the State of Illinois as fully as if it were a retail store or maintained salesmen therein."[54] Perhaps some interstate catalog activity should be excused from use tax collection obligations "because of its sporadic or minor nature," the dissenters conceded, but they found no Commerce Clause or Due Process Clause violation.[55]

Quill

Ten years later (1977), having articulated the nexus requirement in *Complete Auto*, the Court had to define it. *Complete Auto* did not cite *Bellas Hess*, and *Bellas Hess* itself was unclear whether physical presence was a requirement of the Due Process Clause or the Commerce Clause. In a case involving magazine sales but no other presence, the Court did quickly reject a California attempt to enact a "slightest presence" nexus standard, three weeks after *Complete Auto*.[56] So was *Bellas Hess* still good law?

As the 1980s rolled on, academics criticized *Bellas Hess* as arcane, formalistic, and outmoded. "The economic, social, and commercial landscape upon which Bellas Hess was premised no longer exists, save perhaps in the fertile imaginations of attorneys representing mail order interests. . . . The burgeoning technological advances of the 1970s and 1980s have created revolutionary communications abilities and marketing methods which were undreamed of in 1967."[57] In 1987, the Court ruled that an out-of-state company's independent contractors in a state created nexus for that company,

---

[53] *Id.* at 759.

[54] *Id.* at 762 (Fortas, J., dissenting).

[55] *Id.* at 763 (Fortas, J., dissenting).

[56] Nat'l Geographic v. Cal. Bd. of Equalization, 430 U.S. 551 (1977).

[57] State v. Quill Corp., 470 N.W.2d 203, 208 (N.D. 1991).

reaffirming a 1960 decision predating *Bellas Hess*.[58] State courts began disregarding the *Quill* decision and authorities hoped that the rise of new technologies would relax the Court's concern about the burdens of tax collection. North Dakota decided to give it a shot.

Seeking an unsympathetic defendant, North Dakota sent a deficiency notice to office supply catalog company Quill Corporation, directing them to collect the state's sales and use tax. The company had some $1 million in sales to 3,000 customers in North Dakota but no property or employees in the state; all deliveries were made by mail or common carrier. North Dakota was one of 34 states that had enacted tax obligations on nonpresent companies, up from 11 at the time of *Bellas Hess*.

The 8-1 decision in *Quill* arrested that trend, with Justice John Paul Stevens's opinion for the Court giving several reasons for its decision, finding that the company could not be forced to collect North Dakota's sales tax.

First, the Court emphasized the nexus requirement of *Complete Auto*. By requiring a connection between a taxing state and a company, nexus "ensure[s] that state taxation does not unduly burden interstate commerce."[59] In North Dakota, any company that advertised three times in ways that reached residents of the state became obligated to collect taxes for the state, and the Court described that obligation as a burden on interstate commerce.

Second, the Court discussed "the continuing value of a bright-line rule."[60] The physical presence rule "firmly establishes the boundaries of legitimate state authority to impose a duty to collect sales and use taxes and reduces litigation concerning those taxes."[61] Justice Scalia separately wrote that the only litigation that seemed to arise in 25 years of applying *Bellas Hess* were state efforts to overrule it: "Concern that reaffirmance of *Bellas Hess* will lead to a flurry of litigation over the meaning of 'physical presence,' . . . seems to me contradicted by 25 years of experience under the decision."[62]

---

[58] See Scripto, Inc. v. Carson, 362 U.S. 207 (1960). *Quill* described these two cases as the "furthest extension" of nexus. See Quill, 504 U.S. at 306.

[59] Quill, 504 U.S. at 313.

[60] *Id.* at 317.

[61] *Id.* at 315.

[62] *Id.* at 321 (Scalia, J., concurring).

Third, the Court expressed concern about disrupting settled expectations.[63] "A bright-line rule in the area of sales and use taxes also encourages settled expectations and, in doing so, fosters investment by businesses and individuals."[64] Justices Scalia, Kennedy, and Thomas wrote a separate opinion basing their decision on a refusal to upset those expectations: "Having affirmatively suggested that the 'physical presence' rule could be reconciled with our new jurisprudence, we ought not visit economic hardship upon those who took us at our word."[65]

The Court also clarified that the physical presence rule is grounded in the Commerce Clause, not the Due Process Clause. "The requirements of due process are met irrespective of a corporation's lack of physical presence in the taxing State."[66] While the Quill Corp. had sufficient minimum contacts to be within the *jurisdiction* of the state under the Due Process Clause, its lack of physical presence was insufficient nexus to be within the *taxing power* of the state under the Commerce Clause.

Because the rule is grounded in the Commerce Clause, the Court noted that Congress has the power to alter it. "No matter how we evaluate the burdens that use taxes impose on interstate commerce, Congress remains free to disagree with our conclusion."[67] Justice Scalia was even more direct: "Congress has the final say over regulation of interstate commerce, and it can change the rule of *Bellas Hess*

---

[63] It is state tax lawyer lore that North Dakota was going to win the case until its attorney general, Nicholas Spaeth, was asked at oral argument by Justice Sandra Day O'Connor whether overruling *Bellas Hess* would result in multiyear retroactive collection. His colleagues, including then-State Tax Commissioner, now-Senator Heidi Heitkamp (D-ND), had urged him to unequivocally foreclose any retroactive collection authority. Spaeth instead replied, "It might." Multistate Tax Commission attorney Alan Friedman, who assisted the case, coordinated a number of states to file a supplemental brief foreclosing retroactive collection, but Spaeth vetoed it and it was not filed. See Billy Hamilton, Remembrance of Things Not So Past: The Story Behind the Quill Decision, 59 State Tax Notes 807 (2011). The Supreme Court has not definitively spoken on the extent of permissible retroactive state tax collection under the Due Process Clause. See Joseph Henchman & Kavya Rajasekar, The Bounds of Retroactive State Taxes, Tax Foundation, Feb. 9, 2017, https://goo.gl/7LWSGn.

[64] Quill, 504 U.S. at 316.

[65] *Id.* at 321 (Scalia, J., concurring).

[66] *Id.* at 308.

[67] *Id.* at 318.

by simply saying so."[68] That would not be the case with the Due Process Clause, which Congress cannot override.[69]

Justice Byron White dissented, calling physical presence "anachronistic," "artificial," and not premised on "economic reality."[70] He favored abandoning all nexus inquiry beyond the minimum contacts rule of personal jurisdiction. White had been in the *Bellas Hess* majority; his change of heart arose primarily out of a sense of injustice at the fact that some sales escape taxation, and the erroneous belief that technological change has made keeping track of thousands of tax laws, rates, and exemptions no longer burdensome. Citing the states' legal briefs as expert authority, White asserted that "the costs of compliance . . . , in light of today's modern computer and software technology, appear to be nominal."[71] Although White indicated some concern about retroactive collection of taxes if the physical presence rule was abandoned, he did not even address the likelihood that multiple states will seek to tax the same companies and the same sales.

25 Years of Nothing: How *Wayfair* Happened

Attempts to Meet Quill's *Challenge and Reduce State Compliance Burdens*

Frustrated by congressional inaction in overruling *Quill*, states set up the Streamlined Sales & Use Tax Agreement (SSUTA) in 1999 to "(1) significantly reduce, if not eliminate, the current compliance and administrative burdens imposed upon remote sellers; and (2) preserve state and local sovereignty."[72] As one scholar observed, "If a more uniform sales and use tax regime were in place, or if the specter of thousands of local jurisdictions were removed, the commerce clause nexus standard would approach

---

[68] *Id.* at 320 (Scalia, J., concurring).

[69] See *id.* at 313 ("Thus, the 'substantial nexus' requirement is not, like due process' 'minimum contacts' requirement, a proxy for notice, but rather a means for limiting state burdens on interstate commerce.").

[70] *Id.* at 321 (White, J., concurring in part and dissenting in part).

[71] *Id.* at 332.

[72] Brian S. Masterson, Note, Collecting Sales and Use Tax on Electronic Commerce: E-Confusion or E-Collection, 79 N.C. L. Rev. 203, 226 (2000).

the due process standard, and the physical presence test would be obviated."[73]

Twenty-three states are members of Streamlined.[74] Joining means committing to centralizing state-level sales tax administration, conforming to uniform definitions of products, providing sellers with rate lookup software, and forgoing fractional rates on favored products. SSUTA has been less successful than it could be, due to the nonparticipation by most states, including the large states of Arizona, California, Florida, Illinois, Massachusetts, New York, and Texas. Some states refuse to join to maintain idiosyncratic sales tax practices, such as Maryland's "rounding rule," requiring vendors to round remainders of four and above up, rather than the more common practice of rounding up only remainders of five and above, or Chicago's decision to tax sales of bottled water, soda, non-soda drinks, restaurant meals, candy, and groceries all at different tax rates.[75]

A series of proposed federal bills sought to (1) allow states to collect sales tax from remote sellers while (2) requiring states to simplify their tax systems. The level of simplifications required steadily improved as the bills evolved, from the earlier Main Street Fairness Act to the Marketplace Equity Act to the Marketplace Fairness Act (MFA) to the Remote Transactions Parity Act (RTPA). The MFA was approved by the Senate in a 69 to 27 vote in May 2013, but did not come to a vote in the House.[76] RTPA, with protections against interstate audits, was nearly included in 2018 omnibus budget legislation in an effort by Rep. Kristi Noem (R-SD) to act before the *Wayfair* decision was announced. The chairman of the House Judiciary Committee, Rep. Bob Goodlatte (R-VA), opposed both bills and refused to

[73] John A. Swain, State Sales and Use Tax Jurisdiction: An Economic Nexus Standard for the Twenty-First Century, 38 Ga. L. Rev. 343, 363–64 (2003).

[74] Arkansas, Georgia, Indiana, Iowa, Kansas, Kentucky, Michigan, Minnesota, Nebraska, Nevada, New Jersey, North Carolina, North Dakota, Ohio, Oklahoma, Rhode Island, South Dakota, Utah, Vermont, Washington, West Virginia, Wisconsin, and Wyoming. See Streamlined Sales Tax Governing Board, Inc., http://www.streamlinedsalestax.org (last visited Aug. 9, 2018).

[75] See, e.g., How Does Avatax Handle Rounding in Maryland?, Avalara, Aug. 5, 2016, https://goo.gl/YdyA1W; Tax List, City of Chicago, https://goo.gl/28y3Mj (last visited Aug. 9, 2018).

[76] See Joseph Henchman, The Marketplace Fairness Act: A Primer, Tax Foundation, Jul. 2014, https://taxfoundation.org/marketplace-fairness-act-primer.

hold hearings or votes on them. Supporters included state officials and brick-and-mortar retailers who face competition that need not collect sales taxes.

Goodlatte did, however, put forward a proposal based on the International Fuel Tax Agreement (IFTA). Under IFTA, truckers pay fuel taxes to a central clearinghouse, which then divvies up the money up among states based on total miles traveled. Truckers therefore don't have an incentive to fill up in low-tax states nor do they need to comply with dozens of different state fuel tax forms. Goodlatte's proposal, which never got even as far as draft legislation, envisioned internet retailers collecting a sales tax at the rate of their state of origin,[77] with the revenue remitted via a voluntary clearinghouse to the state where the product was delivered. If enacted, it would transform the sales tax on consumers into a leaky tax on businesses, with sellers facing strong incentives to locate in no-sales-tax states or foreign jurisdictions.

Failed Attempts to Expand Quill's *Nexus Standard to Protect Taxpayers*

Quill's physical presence rule only applied to sales taxes. There's really no reason it should have been limited to just that tax; if the principle of physical presence is constitutionally derived, it should apply to business taxes as well.

The conceptual argument for physical presence is stronger for business and individual taxes: a major justification for taxes is the "benefit principle," the idea that people owe taxes as a way of paying for services used where they reside. Sales taxes should thus be owed where residents buy their goods and services, corporate income taxes should be owed where the corporation has property and employees, and individual income taxes owed where people reside and work. Internationally, jurisdiction to tax business is defined by permanent establishment, a concept very similar to physical presence.

No luck, however: the Supreme Court consistently refused to hear cases seeking to expand *Quill* in this regard. A credit card company was forced to pay a West Virginia business tax despite having no

---

[77] "Origin" is a difficult-to-define term for a corporation, as it can be state of headquarters, state of incorporation, state where distribution facilities are located, state where most business takes place, or perhaps nowhere at all.

property or employees in the state.[78] A Delaware company, holding and leasing out intellectual property for the popular Toys 'R' Us chain—and thus taking advantage of Delaware's lack of tax on such transactions—was forced to pay South Carolina business tax on the basis of having accounts receivable (customers) in the state.[79] KFC's royalty arm was forced to pay Iowa business tax on the basis of franchised restaurants in the state.[80] A nonresident company was forced to pay Kentucky's business tax because it was a member of a partnership that did business in the state.[81] General Motors was forced to pay Seattle's business tax on the basis of its wholesale contracts with dealers and its advertising, despite having no property or employees in the city.[82] A New Jersey company had to pay Washington business tax based on the periodic presence of salespeople who did not work permanently in the state.[83] A Tennessee attempt to collect business taxes on the basis that the physical credit cards they provided in-state customers constituted in-state property was rejected by the state court, but the Supreme Court declined to hear the state's appeal.[84] States with gross receipts taxes, like Ohio and Washington, have been particularly assertive of expansive nexus.

Bloomberg Tax's annual hefty volume, *Survey of State Tax Departments* (now over 500 pages), consists of state tax departments explaining what sorts of activities will result in tax nexus within a state.[85] Four states declined to answer at all (New York, Ohio, Oklahoma, and South Carolina). A further seven states unhelpfully said their

[78] Tax Comm'r of West Virginia v. MBNA America Bank, 640 S.E.2d 226 (W.V. 2006), cert. denied, 551 U.S. 1141 (2007).

[79] Geoffrey Inc. v. South Carolina Tax Comm'n, 437 S.E.2d 13 (S.C. 1993), cert. denied, 510 U.S. 992 (1993).

[80] KFC Corp. v. Iowa Dep't of Revenue, 792 N.W.2d 308 (Iowa 2010), cert. denied, 565 U.S. 817 (2011).

[81] Ky. Dep't of Revenue v. Asworth, LLC, No. 2007-CA-002549-MR (Ky. Ct. App. Feb 5, 2010), cert. denied, 562 U.S. 1200 (2011).

[82] General Motors Corp. v. City of Seattle, 25 P.3d 1022 (Wash. Ct. App. 2001), review denied, 84 P.3d 1230 (Wash. 2001), cert. denied, 535 U.S. 1056 (2002).

[83] Lamtec Corp. v. Dep't of Revenue of Washington, 246 P.3d 788 (Wash. 2011), cert. denied, 565 U.S. 816 (2011).

[84] J.C. Penney Nat'l Bank v. Comm'r of Revenue, 19 S.W.3d 831 (Tenn. Ct. App. 1999), cert. denied, 531 U.S. 927 (2000).

[85] See Bloomberg Tax, Survey of State Tax Departments (2018), https://www.bna.com/state-tax-survey.

answers cannot be relied upon as guidance by taxpayers (Alabama, Florida, Georgia, Indiana, Iowa, Massachusetts, and New Mexico). The remaining states provide a variety of bewildering and mostly inconsistent rules for when activity creates a tax obligation. Does attending a trade show or a seminar create nexus in the state hosting it? Does having one nonsales telecommuting employee in the state create nexus? Does shipping in a returnable container versus a common carrier create nexus? Does placing an internet browser cookie on someone's computer create nexus in that someone's state? Does downloading an app in a hub airport while waiting between two interstate flights create nexus in the state of that hub airport? Once established, how long does nexus last? It is not just that we have different answers for different states, but also that many states supply vague or indeterminate nonanswers to many of these questions.

A proposed federal law, the Business Activity Tax Simplification Act (BATSA), would establish a stronger nexus standard than just physical presence. Under BATSA, a business would only be subject to tax burdens in a state where they have property or employees for at least 15 days in a year. It would address taxation in instances of fleeting physical presence, such as an incident where New Jersey seized a truck of merchandise the instant it crossed into the state, demanding that the owning and now-physically-present company remit $46,200 in tax payments.[86] (The company paid.) State governments strongly oppose BATSA, as it would reduce state business tax collections by several billion dollars annually.[87]

Another proposed federal law, the Mobile Workforce State Income Tax Simplification Act, would establish a stronger nexus standard than just physical presence for individual income taxes. Mobile Workforce would limit states from imposing or collecting individual

[86] See Joseph Henchman, BATSA Hearing: Shaken Down on the New Jersey State Line, Tax Foundation, Feb. 21, 2008, https://taxfoundation.org/batsa-hearing-shaken-down-new-jersey-state-line.

[87] See, e.g., Joseph Henchman, Thoughts on the BATSA Hearing, Tax Foundation, Jun. 25, 2008, https://taxfoundation.org/thoughts-batsa-hearing. Judiciary Committee Chairman Rep. John Conyers (D-MI) echoed this point, asking the witnesses what he is supposed to tell Gov. Jennifer Granholm (D-MI) when the BATSA bill might reduce that state's revenues by $400 million. My answer would be that it is money Michigan probably shouldn't be collecting in the first place, and a tax reform based on broad bases and low rates (as opposed to Michigan's current narrow bases and high rates) would improve the state's fiscal situation and business climate.

income tax on those who are in the state for fewer than 30 days. Most states technically require such payments when someone is in the state for even a day, and even require withholding to be set up in advance. Since all states provide a credit for taxes paid to another state, today people fill out 20 or 30 tax returns for a net national wash. Most everyone, except New York officials and state tax administrators, support this legislation and it has bipartisan cosponsorship. State tax administrators instead urge states to voluntarily adopt a more convoluted model, which no state has.[88] The bill excludes entertainers and athletes from its protections, which it shouldn't.

Successful Attempts to Use Quill's *Nexus Standard to Expand State Tax Power*

Even though a corporation's physical presence is difficult to ascertain, corporations being intangible pieces of paper (often in Delaware) through which people act, the physical presence rule was sometimes described as an effective bright-line limitation on state tax power. This author was one such person, worried that the drift toward economic nexus standards in the business tax context would be unlikely to limit state tax overreaching if applied more broadly.[89]

But states discovered ways to turn the *Quill* shield into a sword. Prior to the *Wayfair* decision, 31 states had found a way to pass a law requiring tax collection by out-of-state internet sellers.

New York's "click-through nexus" law was mimicked by 21 other states.[90] The law includes in its definition of physical presence any person who is paid by an out-of-state company for referral links to the out-of-state company's website, if the out-of-state company has sales of at least $10,000 per year in the state. So if Amazon.com paid someone

---

[88] See, e.g., Buckingham, Doolittle & Burroughs, LLC, MTC Proposes Measures to Simplify State Income Tax Withholding for Mobile Employees, Apr. 21, 2001, https://www.bdblaw.com/mtc-proposes-measures-to-simplify-state-income-tax-withholding-for-mobile-employees.

[89] See Joseph Henchman, Why the Quill Physical Presence Rule Shouldn't Go the Way of Personal Jurisdiction, 46 State Tax Notes 387 (2007).

[90] N.Y. Tax Law § 1101(b)(8)(vi). Similar laws were adopted by Arkansas, California, Colorado, Connecticut, Georgia, Illinois, Kansas, Louisiana, Maine, Michigan, Minnesota, Missouri, Nevada, New Jersey, North Carolina, Ohio, Pennsylvania, Rhode Island, Tennessee, Vermont, and Washington. Idaho enacted a version while *Wayfair* was being considered, in March 2018.

commissions for items purchased thanks to links from someone's website, Amazon.com had nexus with New York despite the lack of any other physical presence in the state. This statute was upheld by state courts, finding that contracts with in-state nonemployees who solicit customers for compensation constitutes substantial nexus.[91] While these statutes provide for an ability to rebut the presumption that solicitation occurred, rebutting such presumption would inherently be futile, as it is hard to prove what has not been done by individuals on the internet.

Colorado's "notice and reporting" law was mimicked by nine other states.[92] The law requires that out-of-state internet retailers (1) provide Colorado purchasers a "transactional notice" at the time of purchase, informing them that the purchase may be subject to Colorado's use tax; (2) provide an "annual purchase summary" with the dates, amounts, and categories of purchases of all Colorado purchasers with purchases over $500; and (3) file with the Colorado Department of Revenue an annual report listing their customers' names, addresses, and total purchases. Reporting requirements under these notice-and-reporting statutes are deliberately cumbersome so as to compel collection. A panel of the Tenth Circuit, which included then-Judge Gorsuch, upheld the Colorado statute after concluding that *Quill*'s holding applied to sales and use tax collection and not to the imposition of regulatory requirements.[93] One version of the law was struck down on First Amendment grounds.[94] However, the Supreme

---

[91] Overstock.com, Inc. v. New York State Dep't of Taxation & Fin., 987 N.E.2d 621, 626 (N.Y. 2013), cert. denied 571 U.S. 1071 (2013) ("Active in-state solicitation that produces a significant amount of revenue qualifies as more than a 'slightest presence.'").

[92] Colo. Rev. Stat. § 39-21-112(3.5). Similar laws were adopted by Alabama, Kentucky, Louisiana, Oklahoma, Pennsylvania, Rhode Island, Tennessee, Vermont, and Washington.

[93] See Direct Marketing Association v. Brohl, 814 F.3d 1129 (10th Cir. 2016).

[94] A North Carolina revenue ruling similar to the Colorado statute was struck down on these grounds. See Amazon.com LLC v. Lay, 758 F. Supp. 2d 1154 (W.D. Wash. 2010). The ACLU joined with Amazon.com to challenge this, noting the danger of unnecessarily requiring disclosure of purchases such as the movie *Lolita* or the book *How to Leave Your Husband*, or even the name of the website as some websites sell embarrassing things. The court held that the First Amendment forbids state tax collectors from knowing what taxpayers are buying. *Id.* at 1170 ("Citizens are entitled to receive information and ideas through books, films and other expressive materials anonymously.").

Court declined to hear an appeal from both Colorado and federal judge rulings that the law was constitutional.[95]

Three states passed regulations requiring sales tax collection by out-of-state entities that engage in an enumerated list of activities.[96] While none of the activities by themselves constitutes physical presence, the thinking is that they cumulatively constitute substantial nexus.

Massachusetts and Ohio pursued "cookie nexus" enactments that define the placement of website cookies on the computers of in-state users as physical presence in the state.[97] Cookie nexus essentially gives a state the power to tax any seller on the planet if one of their residents accesses the vendor's website or downloads its app. Advertising in a state has historically not created nexus, or even personal jurisdiction, and the Massachusetts and Ohio provisions create obligations solely for the online equivalent of advertising, cookies, and apps.

Overruling Quill

In March 2015, Justice Kennedy asked for an opportunity to overrule *Quill*.[98] The case was *DMA v. Brohl*, a unanimous decision reversing the Tenth Circuit and holding that federal courts could hear a challenge to Colorado's notice-and-reporting law.[99] Kennedy's four-page concurring opinion described *Bellas Hess* as a doctrinal aberration, regretted that *Quill* did not revisit the physical presence rule in light of *Complete Auto*, and acknowledged state revenue losses from the inability to collect sales taxes on remote sales.

---

[95] See Direct Marketing Ass'n v. Brohl, 2016 WL 9735793 (D. Colo. Nov. 1, 2016), cert. denied 137 S. Ct. 591 (U.S. Dec. 12, 2016); Direct Marketing Ass'n v. Brohl, 814 F.3d 1129 (10th Cir. 2016), cert. denied 137 S. Ct. 593 (U.S. Dec. 12, 2016).

[96] Ala. Admin. Code r. 810-6-2.90.03; Miss. Code R. § 35.IV.3.09; Tenn. Comp. R. & Regs. 1320-05-01-.129.

[97] Reg. 830, 830 Mass. Code Regs. 64H.1.7 (withdrawn); Ohio Rev. Code § 5741.01(I) (2)(i).

[98] See Direct Marketing Ass'n v. Brohl, 135 S. Ct. 1124, 1134 (Kennedy, J., concurring).

[99] See *id.*, reversing Direct Marketing Ass'n v. Brohl, 735 F.3d 904 (10th Cir. 2013). The Tenth Circuit had held that the challenge was barred by the Tax Injunction Act, a federal law that limits federal courts' ability to "enjoin, suspend, or restrain the assessment, levy, or collection of any tax under State law where a plain, speedy, and efficient remedy may be had in the courts of such State." 28 U.S.C. § 1341.

South Dakota answered the challenge.[100] Its law, S.B. 106, required sales tax collection by out-of-state sellers if they have a minimum of $100,000 in sales or 200 transactions per year in the state. This *de minimis* threshold, or safe harbor, has the effect of excluding those sellers with incidental sales into the state and where establishing collection mechanisms might outstrip the business's incremental revenue from selling into South Dakota. South Dakota's statute also has a provision barring retroactive collection. South Dakota passed the law with unanimous votes and it was signed into law on March 22, 2016, to take effect on May 1, 2016.

South Dakota was well-chosen as the state to bring the challenge. South Dakota is a full member of SSUTA. Unlike other states that decry the erosion of their sales tax base while exempting goods and services that total over half their economy, South Dakota taxes it all. South Dakota taxes groceries (taxed in full by only seven states of the 45 plus the District of Columbia with the tax), clothing (taxed in full by 39 states), nonprescription drugs (taxed by 35 states), personal services such as dry cleaning and haircuts (taxed in full by only four states), real estate transactions (taxed by only three states), legal transactions (taxed by only three states), accounting services (taxed by only three states), and even lobbying services (taxed by only six states). Internet sales are the only thing South Dakota does not tax, because it could not under *Quill.* And while there are local sales taxes in South Dakota, the state keeps it simple in requiring them to adhere to the state base of transactions and only at uniform rates. Finally, South Dakota has no state individual income or corporate income tax; sales and property taxes are essentially its only taxes and make up three-quarters of total South Dakota state and local tax revenue.

The case moved quickly. On April 28, 2016, South Dakota notified four companies of the pending effective date. Three of the companies (Wayfair, Overstock.com, and Newegg) refused to collect, citing

---

[100] The South Dakota law had been developed by attorney Eric Citron; presented to and then approved in January 2016 by the State and Local Taxation Task Force of the National Conference of State Legislatures, a forum for state legislators, state fiscal officers, the business community, and other interested parties; and championed by South Dakota State Senator Deb Peters (R). See Maria Koklanaris, EXCLUSIVE: SD's Counsel on Wayfair's Road to High Court, Law360, May 4, 2018, https://www.law360.com/articles/1040455/exclusive-sd-s-counsel-on-wayfair-s-road-to-high-court.

Quill, and sued. By the law's own terms, its enforcement was suspended until the conclusion of legal proceedings. On January 17, 2017, a federal court declined to entertain jurisdiction, considering it a state tax matter.[101] On March 6, 2017, a South Dakota Sixth Judicial Circuit judge ruled in favor of Wayfair, citing *Quill.* The South Dakota Supreme Court heard oral argument on August 29, 2017, and issued its opinion shortly thereafter, affirming the trial court.[102] The petition for writ of certiorari followed on October 2, 2017, and was granted on January 12, 2018.[103] Oral argument was heard on April 17 and the decision handed down on June 21.

Oral argument left some supporters of the South Dakota law worried. Justice Ginsburg lobbed softballs at the state's attorney, but Justice Thomas stayed characteristically silent and Justice Kennedy stayed unusually silent. Kennedy chimed in only to observe that no one was arguing that the physical presence standard was correct.

The eventual dissenters consumed most of the questioning time. Justice Sotomayor began the state's argument time with a rapid-fire series of questions indicating her discomfort with the law.[104] Justice Breyer expressed frustration with the incomplete record and with how the Court might possibly resolve the case.[105] Chief Justice Roberts asked pointedly whether Congress might be better equipped to resolve the nexus standard. Justice Kagan asked tough questions of both sides.

Justice Kennedy delivered the opinion for the five-justice majority. After reciting the history of the dormant Commerce Clause, he summarized the doctrine: "First, state regulations may not discriminate against interstate commerce; and second, States may not impose

[101] See South Dakota v. Wayfair, Inc., 229 F. Supp. 3d 1026 (D. S.D. 2017).

[102] See State v. Wayfair, Inc., 901 N.W.2d 754 (S.D. 2017), aff'g State v. Wayfair, Inc., 2017 WL 4358293 (S.D. Cir. Mar. 6, 2017). South Dakota has no intermediate appeals court.

[103] 138 S. Ct. 735 (2018). The author, who was married on September 23, 2017, apologizes to his husband for spending part of their honeymoon working on an amicus brief in support of this petition.

[104] See Transcript of Oral Arg. at 3–5, South Dakota v. Wayfair, 138 S. Ct. 2080 (2018) (No. 17–494).

[105] *Id.* at 15 (Justice Breyer: "[T]he reason I'm asking like this is because I read through these briefs. When I read your briefs, I thought absolutely right. And then I read the other briefs, and I thought absolutely right. And you cannot both be absolutely right.").

undue burdens on interstate commerce."[106] He recited the *Complete Auto* test as the formulation of that doctrine, and then noted the emergence of the physical presence rule in *Bellas Hess* and its reaffirmance in *Quill.*

The opinion then gives three reasons for deeming *Quill* flawed. First, physical presence is not a necessary interpretation of substantial nexus from *Complete Auto.* Kennedy writes that "[t]he physical presence rule is a poor proxy for the compliance costs faced by companies that do business in multiple States," comparing a company with a salesperson in each state that must therefore collect tax in each state with a company with 500 people in one central location and a website accessible in every state that need only collect in one state. Second, the *Quill* rule creates market distortions between brick-and-mortar and online retailers—"a judicially created tax shelter," in the Court's words—and an incentive to avoid physical presence in multiple states purely for tax avoidance reasons.[107] Third, the physical presence standard is arbitrary and formalistic, rather than looking at the substance of a law's compliance burdens or discriminatory effect.

The Court acknowledged substantial reliance on its earlier decisions, conducting a *stare decisis* analysis. Against this reliance the Court listed the need to correct an error depriving states from exercising lawful powers, the strong growth of e-commerce and consequent growth in the states' revenue shortfalls from being unable to tax online sellers, and the variety of state laws working to "embroil courts in technical and arbitrary disputes about what counts as physical presence."[108]

The Court also acknowledged burdens associated with tax compliance but expressed hope that software and other systems will be able to reduce these costs. The Court noted that South Dakota, as a SSUTA member, had done much to make compliance easier. If not, the Court stated, Congress could act to address these problems through legislation. Finally, small sellers seeking relief from future state laws that impose excessive burdens on them "may still do so under other theories."[109]

[106] Wayfair, 138 S. Ct. at 2084.

[107] The Court cited Wayfair's website, which stated "One of the best things about buying through Wayfair is that we do not have to charge sales tax." *Id.* at 2096.

[108] *Id.* at 2098.

[109] *Id.* at 2099. This could be a reference to the Due Process Clause, other parts of the *Complete Auto* test, or the *Pike* balancing test. The Due Process question of to what

The Court then stated that "the physical presence rule of *Quill* is unsound and incorrect," and overruled *Quill* and *Bellas Hess*.[110] The Court concludes that the statute's standard of $100,000 in sales or 200 transactions can only be met if "the seller availed itself of the substantial privilege of carrying on business in South Dakota. And respondents are large, national companies that undoubtedly maintain an extensive virtual presence. Thus, the substantial nexus requirement of *Complete Auto* is satisfied in this case."[111]

The decision did not end there, and experts since have debated whether what follows is *dicta* or precedent. The Court remands the South Dakota law for further consideration. But first, it offers a checklist of why the law might just be constitutional:

> That said, South Dakota's tax system includes several features that appear designed to prevent discrimination against or undue burdens upon interstate commerce. First, the Act applies a safe harbor to those who transact only limited business in South Dakota. Second, the Act ensures that no obligation to remit the sales tax may be applied retroactively. S. B. 106, § 5. Third, South Dakota is one of more than 20 States that have adopted the Streamlined Sales and Use Tax Agreement. This system standardizes taxes to reduce administrative and compliance costs: It requires a single, state level tax administration, uniform definitions of products and services, simplified tax rate structures, and other uniform rules. It also provides sellers access to sales tax administration software paid for by the State. Sellers who choose to use such software are immune from audit liability.[112]

Justice Thomas concurred to write that he should have joined the *Quill* dissent in 1992.[113] Justice Gorsuch concurred, joining the majority in full and adding that he questions Commerce Clause doctrine.[114]

---

extent a state can regulate an out-of-state entity—raised by the Cato Institute in its amicus brief—is therefore left for another day. *Pike* compares the benefits to the state and burdens on the interstate business for a law otherwise valid under the Commerce Clause. The *Pike* test is very deferential to the state and therefore tough for a taxpayer to win.

[110] *Id.*

[111] *Id.*

[112] *Id.* at 2099–2100.

[113] *Id.* at 2100 (Thomas, J., concurring).

[114] *Id.* at 2100 (Gorsuch, J., concurring).

Chief Justice Roberts, writing for the four dissenters, acknowledged that *Bellas Hess* was wrongly decided but urged that any change to the physical presence rule be undertaken by Congress.[115] Unlike in other contexts where only the Supreme Court can reverse a previous decision, Commerce Clause decisions by the Court can be changed by Congress. Roberts also took issue with the Court's sense of urgency, pointing out that states are already able to collect the vast majority of potential online sales tax revenue. He worried that the burden of getting it wrong will fall squarely on small sellers, another reason for Congress to draw where the line should be instead of the Court.

What Happens Next

States may now tax internet sales with some confidence, so long as the tax complies with jurisdiction to tax or regulate under the Due Process Clause, with the Internet Tax Freedom Act, with the *Complete Auto* test, with the *Wayfair* checklist, and with the *Pike* balancing test.[116] As of August 1, 2018, 10 states[117] have internet sales taxes complying with all those items, including the boxes of the *Wayfair* checklist:

1. *Safe harbor:* exclude "those who transact only limited business" in the state. (South Dakota's is $100,000 in sales or 200 transactions.)

---

[115] *Id.* at 2101 (Roberts, C.J., dissenting).

[116] Put another way, a state may tax interstate commerce if (1) it has personal jurisdiction over the person, either through (1a) in-state presence, (1b) an out-of-state person with systematic and continuous contacts in the case relating to the issue involved, or (1c) an out-of-state person whose activities are such that the state can rightly be regarded as home; (2) and the tax is neither (2a) on internet access or (2b) a multiple or discriminatory tax on internet commerce; and (3a) the person has substantial nexus in the state, which can be met with a (3a1) safe harbor excluding *de minimis* activity and (3a2) a ban on retroactivity and tax system and minimized burdens and simplifications for easy compliance, which may include (3a3) single state-level administration for all sales taxes in the state, (3a4) uniform definitions of products and services, (3a5) a simplified rate structure, (3a6) access to sales tax administration software, and (3a7) liability immunity for sellers who make errors while relying on the software, (3b) the tax is nondiscriminatory, not taxing out-of-state activity or taxpayers while exempting similar in-state activity or taxpayers, (3c) the tax is fairly apportioned, such that if every state adopted such a tax it would not result in multiple taxation, and (3d) the tax is fairly related to services received by the taxpayer; and (4) the tax otherwise does not impose burdens on interstate commerce clearly excessive in relation to the putative local benefits.

[117] Georgia, Indiana, Iowa, Kentucky, New Jersey, North Dakota, South Dakota, Utah, Vermont, and Wyoming.

2. *No retroactive collection.*
3. *Single state-level administration* of all sales taxes in the state.
4. *Uniform definitions* of products and services.
5. *Simplified tax rate structures.* (South Dakota requires the same tax base between state and local sales tax and no partial tax rates for certain items.)
6. *Software:* Access to sales tax administration software is provided by the state.
7. *Immunity:* Sellers who use the software are not liable for errors derived from relying on it.

An additional 13 states have completed items 3 through 7 of the *Wayfair* checklist automatically through SSUTA membership but have not yet passed enabling legislation to make them compliant with items 1 and 2 of the *Wayfair* checklist.[118]

Of the remaining 22 states plus the District of Columbia with a sales tax, significant state actions would be required before remote seller sales tax collection could proceed without it being an excessive burden on interstate commerce. This list includes large states such as Arizona, California, Florida, Illinois, Massachusetts, New York, Pennsylvania, and Texas. These states have so far resisted any sales tax simplifications or adherence to uniform rules. They are therefore risks for attempting to collect taxes without first improving their sales taxes as envisioned by *Wayfair*.

Alabama was considered by many experts in likely danger of pursuing retroactive collection, but its state Department of Revenue announced on July 3 that it would seek to collect only from October 1, 2018, prospectively. Two states have promulgated revenue rules currently seeking collection prior to the date of the *Wayfair* decision: Mississippi (transactions after December 1, 2017) and Tennessee (transactions after July 1, 2017). Comments by officials of both states suggest they will abandon these efforts to instead pursue legislation similar to South Dakota's. Several states have recently passed effective dates: Hawaii (January 1, 2018, recently revised to July 1, 2018[119]), Kentucky (July 1, 2018), Minnesota (June 21, 2018),

---

[118] Arkansas, Kansas, Michigan, Minnesota, Nebraska, Nevada, North Carolina, Ohio, Oklahoma, Rhode Island, Washington, West Virginia, and Wisconsin.

[119] Hawaiian officials changed their position after they were pointedly asked if they wanted to be the state to ruin it for all the other states, by collecting retroactively and thereby inviting a congressional response.

Oklahoma (July 1, 2018), and Pennsylvania (March 1, 2018). No other state has announced retroactive collection although the vast majority of states have yet to adopt enabling legislation that would specify effective dates. Minnesota's $10,000 *de minimis* threshold, however, might be the subject of the next lawsuit.

It is worth noting that many states are likely to use the *Wayfair* decision as an opportunity to reform their state tax systems. Alabama, Arizona, Colorado, and Louisiana impose significant compliance costs on their retailers, and the need to comply with *Wayfair* may enable them to overcome internal resistance to a better sales tax system. Several states, such as Missouri and Utah, have proposed that the additional revenue from internet sales tax be used to cut other taxes.

One open question is marketplaces: websites such as eBay or Etsy that provide a platform for sellers. These websites may act on their own initiative to provide their sellers with means to collect sales taxes. However, six states (Alabama, Connecticut, Minnesota, Oklahoma, Pennsylvania, and Washington) have enacted laws requiring marketplaces to collect for their sellers. There are potentially unintended consequences from changing the "merchant of record," as some of these laws do, and a danger of reaching offline hosts for gatherings of sellers such as swap meets and farmers' markets.

Another open question is local sales taxes, which are levied in 38 states. South Dakota's law did not explicitly authorize online sellers to collect local sales taxes. Arizona, Colorado, and Louisiana even permit local sales taxes to have a different base of taxable transactions than the state sales tax.[120] Nationally, a total of 10,708 jurisdictions in the United States impose a sales tax, ranging by state on the high end from 1,277 in Missouri, 1,153 in Texas, 908 in Iowa, and 800 in Alabama, to just one each in the states of Connecticut, Indiana, Kentucky, Maine, Maryland, Massachusetts, and Michigan.[121] Nearly all states require that all sales taxes in the state be collected by one entity, eliminating the need for sellers to comply with multiple filing. The two that don't, Colorado and Louisiana,

[120] See Jared Walczak & Scott Drenkard, State and Local Sales Tax Rates 2018, Tax Foundation, Feb. 13, 2018, https://taxfoundation.org/state-and-local-sales-tax-rates-2018.

[121] Email to author from Tricia Schafer-Petrecz, Pub. Relations & Soc. Media Lead, Vertex, Inc.

will either need to fix their system or likely forgo collection of those local taxes.

On July 24, 2018, just over a month after the *Wayfair* decision, U.S. House Judiciary Chairman Goodlatte held a hearing on post-*Wayfair* options for Congress.[122] Eight witnesses testified, but few legislators showed up to hear them. The ideas offered included codifying the *Wayfair* checklist so as to ensure states follow it, re-enacting the physical presence rule, passing BATSA, passing legislation limiting applicability of state regulations beyond their borders, enacting a multiyear moratorium on state *Wayfair*-enabling legislation, and doing nothing at all. States that had been urging passage of the Marketplace Fairness Act or the Remote Transactions Parity Act now invoke federalism and urge Congress to let them be.[123] Internet sellers, previously lobbying against congressional action or insisting on origin-sourcing solutions, now want a federal law codifying meaningful simplifications.[124] The smart money is, as usual, on Congress not passing anything. If anything passes, a ban on retroactive collection seemed to get the broadest consensus of support.[125]

There are those who look at this case and see only the sales tax they will now have to pay on their online purchases. Some may be mad, some may be indifferent, but the payments will happen and internet commerce will continue to grow.

There are those who look at this case and see states now able to collect owed taxes from scofflaw businesses who had taken advantage of an arcane judicial tax break. They are obviously pleased, if a

---

[122] Examining the *Wayfair* Decision and Its Ramifications for Consumers and Small Businesses, Hearing Before the H. Jud. Comm., 115th Cong. (2018), available at https://judiciary.house.gov/hearing/examining-the-wayfair-decision-and-its-ramifications-for-consumers-and-small-businesses.

[123] *Id.* (statement of Utah State Sen. Curt Bramble) ("I'm here today to ask Congress, and you Mr. Chair to continue doing what this committee and Congress has done thus far, and that is, nothing—to not act.").

[124] *Id.* (written statement of Steve DelBianco, President, NetChoice), http://netchoice.org/wp-content/uploads/2018-07-24-NetChoice-testimony-House-Judiciary-hearing-on-Wayfair.pdf (listing 20 proposed simplifications to be codified in federal law).

[125] On July 13, 2018, Wells Fargo announced a $481 million earnings restatement to account for potentially increased assertions of state business tax economic nexus following the *Wayfair* decision. See Andrea Muse, Wells Fargo Adjusts Income Tax Reserves Following Wayfair, State Tax Notes, Jul. 17, 2018, https://www.taxnotes.com/editors-pick/wells-fargo-adjusts-income-tax-reserves-following-wayfair.

little worried that some state might go too far and invite Congress to clamp down and rescind some of this authority.

There are those who look at this case and see a Commerce Clause that was meant to restrain states from enacting discriminatory or burdensome taxes, with physical presence a bizarre and ineffective proxy for this standard when it comes to sales taxes on a state's own residents. They are glad to see it go, if a little worried that economic nexus may spread further to where it doesn't belong, to business taxes or international taxes.

There are those who look at this case and see state politicians hungrily raising taxes on one of the most innovative business sectors, dumping the collection duties on out-of-state businesses with no ability to object, and poised to export more tax burdens in an Articles of Confederation redux. They are not happy about *Wayfair*, but nor were they happy with the status quo prior as states found ways to abuse the physical presence rule. As they vigilantly watch state enactments and wait for the passage of BATSA and Mobile Workforce and other preemption legislation, they can be reassured that at least Justice Thomas didn't win the day and *Wayfair* reaffirmed the judicial role in limiting state power under the Commerce Clause.

There are those who look at this case and see a state passing a regulation on out-of-state entities, asserting that its state law has power beyond its borders. *Wayfair* is just the latest of a series of disappointments for them, which stretch back to *International Shoe*'s ruling that selling into a state can sometimes mean obeying that state's laws, or even further back. But they can take solace in three things. First, South Dakota's *Wayfair* collection regulation is entirely related to its tax authority over its own residents, making it hard to expand easily to new and wild contexts. Second, any regulations have to apply equally within the state, or else be struck down as discriminatory. That doesn't preclude all petty tyrannies but it does stop many. Third, such laws still must be enforced, which itself is a limitation on extraterritorial regulation. South Dakota can seize merchandise at the state line, but it will need voluntary compliance, Customs cooperation, or China's acquiescence enforcing a tax deficiency judgment if a seller in that country won't collect South Dakota's sales tax.

There are those who look at this case and worry how, on one hand, a legal and regulatory system premised on employers and employees, wages and benefits, getting services if you're inside this border and not if you're not, will survive a collision with, on the other hand, an app-based, cloud-based, borderless, org-chart-less, instantaneous, everywhere-and-nowhere economy. For such people, they can take solace that consumption taxes like the sales tax might be the last tax standing. Businesses will pay nothing if their physical presence is in the cloud, income and payroll taxes get a lot harder to collect if everyone is their own app-based boss, and property taxes become more voluntary as mobility and technology mean people can do their job while living anywhere. But people still must buy stuff and pay their use tax. Governments might just have to be more responsive to those residents to keep tax revenues flowing.

We probably have a long time before we must truly confront these questions. Most people still work near their home, buy in their state, and sell where they can be. But there is admittedly a danger of waiting too long to act, as taxi companies and newspapers and Borders bookstores did. It is a testament to the Framers of the Constitution that their solutions to their problems remain relevant for us today. *Wayfair* revisited an application of a constitutional principle on how to collect one tax from residents of a state, but it left intact the timeless idea that parochial state interests do not get to burden interstate commerce. At least until the next case.

"Officers" in the Supreme Court: *Lucia v. SEC*

*Jennifer L. Mascott**

In 2013, an adjudicator determined that Raymond Lucia and his investment companies should pay a $300,000 fine for violating securities laws.[1] Even more crippling, the adjudicator determined that for having provided erroneous information regarding the retirement earnings his prospective investors would receive, Mr. Lucia should be barred for life from providing the investor-related services that had formed the basis of his livelihood.[2]

One might assume that an adjudicator with the power to levy such a fine and order a man to quit his chosen profession was a judge—in particular, an Article III judge, as we call judges in the federal system.[3] Indeed, Mr. Lucia referred to his adjudicator as "Judge."[4]

But the adjudicator in Mr. Lucia's case was an administrative law judge (ALJ) ensconced within the Securities and Exchange Commission (SEC). And the SEC itself, as represented by its commissioners, had the ultimate authority to approve or disapprove the ALJ's initial determination before the ruling became effective.

* Assistant professor of law, Antonin Scalia Law School, George Mason University. I filed an amicus brief in *Lucia v. SEC* based on my study of the original public meaning of the Appointments Clause, the constitutional provision at issue in this case. See Jennifer L. Mascott, Who Are "Officers of the United States"?, 70 Stan. L. Rev. 443 (2018). Thanks to Evan Bernick for excellent comments and suggestions on an earlier draft of this article and to Walter Olson, Meggan DeWitt, and Ilya Shapiro for excellent and substantial editing work on the article.

[1] See Lucia v. SEC, 138 S. Ct. 2044, 2049–50 (2018); Raymond J. Lucia Cos. v. SEC, 832 F.3d 277, 282–83 (D.C. Cir. 2016).

[2] See Lucia, 138 S. Ct. at 2049–50.

[3] See U.S. Const. art. III, § 1 ("The judicial Power of the United States, shall be vested in one supreme Court, and in such inferior Courts as the Congress may from time to time ordain and establish.").

[4] See Lucia, 138 S. Ct. at 2050 (referring to "Judge Elliot").

This is the same SEC under whose authority, rules, and regulations the charges against Mr. Lucia were brought in the first place.[5]

The Constitution sharply distinguishes Article III judges from officials of the executive branch. It imbues them with independence and separates them from the political branches where decisions are made with an eye toward popular support and the next election. It accords them lifetime salary and tenure protection but subjects them to the rigorous vetting of presidential appointment and confirmation by the Senate—a process that typically involves a public hearing and thorough review of the prospective judge's prior writings and financial and employment records. At least in some cases, it further checks their discretion through the mechanism of a civil jury trial.

Executive officials, in contrast, are constitutionally held accountable to the public by way of elected officials and in particular the president, who is empowered both to appoint them and to oversee their actions.[6] Although Congress also plays a vital oversight role in appropriations and legislation, executive officials are ultimately accountable to the people primarily to the extent that the elected president must take responsibility for their actions. The Constitution ties responsibility for executive actors to the president by giving him or his appointed department heads responsibility for the selection of all "officers" of the executive branch, as provided in Article II, section 2, clause 2 of the Constitution—the Appointments Clause.

The adjudicator in Lucia's case, however, had come to his post by a different route. He had been selected not by the SEC's presidentially appointed commissioners, but by the staff of the agency.[7] And the Appointments Clause in relevant part provides that officers of the federal government are to be appointed only by the president, "Courts of Law," or "Heads of Departments."[8] In this case, the latter

---

[5] See *id.* at 2049–50.

[6] See U.S. Const. art. II, § 1, cl. 1 ("The executive Power shall be vested in a President of the United States."); *id.*, § 2, cl. 2 ("[H]e shall nominate, and . . . appoint . . . [all] Officers of the United States."); *id.* art. II, § 3 ("[H]e shall take Care that the Laws be faithfully executed.").

[7] See Lucia, 138 S. Ct. at 2051.

[8] U.S. Const. art. II, § 2, cl. 2 ("[The President] shall nominate, and by and with the Advice and Consent of the Senate, shall appoint Ambassadors, other public Ministers and Consuls, Judges of the supreme Court, and all other Officers of the United States, whose Appointments are not herein otherwise provided for, and which shall be established by Law: but the Congress may by Law vest the Appointment of such inferior

would mean the SEC commissioners. His appointment was therefore not valid, Lucia argued.

Here was the legal sticking point: Where and when was the ALJ an "Officer[] of the United States," in the language of the clause, as opposed to just an ordinary federal employee, regarding whose hiring the Appointments Clause had nothing distinctive to say? As it happened, whether and when ALJs were officers remained an open legal question. The Court had last taken up the scope of the Appointments Clause close to 30 years earlier in a case involving Tax Court special trial judges, a class of adjudicative actors with powers and duties similar, but not precisely identical, to those at the SEC.[9]

In the end, Lucia won his claim by a vote of 7-2 in a set of four opinions explained in depth below.[10] In a narrow and fact-bound opinion by Justice Elena Kagan, six members of the Court found the SEC's ALJs to be "officers" because of the extensive factual similarities between their responsibilities and those of the Tax Court special trial judges that the Court had labeled "officers" in 1991. The opinion took no major steps toward further defining the phrase "Officers of the United States" for future cases. Two of the six justices joining the majority opinion would have gone further and applied the original public meaning of the Appointments Clause in a broad way for future cases. Justice Stephen Breyer, the seventh vote for Lucia, ruled for him on statutory grounds, expressing discomfort about classifying ALJs as Article II "officers" based on independence concerns elaborated in more detail below. And two justices dissented, concluding that the ALJs are mere federal "employees," beyond the reach of the Appointments Clause entirely.

Officers, as they think proper, in the President alone, in the Courts of Law, or in the Heads of Departments.").

[9] A separate Appointments Clause issue that is important but not directly relevant to the *Lucia* case is how to draw the line between principal officers, who must be appointed through presidential nomination subject to Senate advice and consent, and "inferior officers," who may be appointed either in that fashion or by the president alone, by a department head, or by a court of law. See U.S. Const. art. II, § 2, cl. 2 (. . . "but the Congress may by Law vest the Appointment of such inferior Officers, as they think proper, in the President alone, in the Courts of Law, or in the Heads of Departments"). No party to the *Lucia* litigation contended that SEC ALJs are principal officers, so the question instead was whether they should count as inferior officers or as government employees.

[10] See *Lucia,* 138 S. Ct. at 2048.

Lurking alongside the *Lucia* case—but not part of the justices' decision—are important questions of both policy and constitutional significance. Over the years, recognizing that ALJs preside over important cases imposing significant consequences on regulated parties, Congress accorded ALJs statutory protections to try to mimic the independence safeguards of Article III judges.[11] Are any of these statutory protections in conflict with the designation of ALJs as Article II "officers"? First, for example, Congress restricted the removal of ALJs by providing that ALJs may be fired only for "good cause" as "established and determined by the Merit Systems Protection Board."[12] The government in *Lucia* contended that these tenure rules may be in tension with the "executive power" vested in the president by Article II, section 1[13]—the flip side of the appointments power, the removal power is a powerful mechanism of constitutional accountability.[14] Second, Congress had provided for merit-based competitive selection of numerous executive officials, and prior to the *Lucia* decision, ALJs had been hired subject to those provisions.[15] Do such restrictions on executive branch selection of officers improperly constrict department head authority under the Appointments Clause?

Before I address those questions, here is more on the background of the *Lucia* case and how it arrived at the Court.

I. Factual Background

The 2010 Dodd-Frank Act[16] gave SEC enforcement actions a broader reach, and litigants subject to stringent civil penalties by SEC adjudicators responded by challenging the agency with increased vigor. One of these litigants was Raymond Lucia.

---

[11] *Id.* at 2060 (Breyer, J., concurring in the judgment in part and dissenting in part) (describing these provisions). See generally Brief of Administrative Law Scholars as Amici Curiae Supporting Neither Party, Lucia v. SEC, 138 S. Ct. 2044 (2018) (No. 17-130).

[12] 5 U.S.C. § 7521(a). See also 5 C.F.R. § 930.204(a) (2018) (granting SEC ALJs "a career appointment").

[13] See U.S. Const. art. II, § 1, cl. 1; Brief for Respondent SEC Supporting Petitioners at 39–55, Lucia v. SEC, 138 S. Ct. 2044 (2018) (No. 17-130) (merits brief).

[14] See, e.g., Free Enter. Fund v. Public Co. Accounting Oversight Bd., 561 U.S. 477, 483 (2010).

[15] See Brief of Administrative Law Scholars, *supra* note 11, at 8–10.

[16] Dodd-Frank Wall Street Reform and Consumer Protection Act, Pub. L. No. 111-203, 124 Stat. 1376 (2010) (codified as amended in scattered sections of the U.S. Code).

An SEC ALJ issued an initial decision hitting him with $300,000 in civil penalties and a lifetime bar from his SEC-related profession.[17] The commission next remanded the case for the ALJ to issue further findings of fact on several charges that the ALJ's initial decision had left unaddressed. Following a "revised initial decision," the commission considered the case again and ultimately imposed sanctions identical to those initially imposed by the ALJ.[18] The SEC routinely gives less close review to ALJ initial decisions than it provided in this case.[19] But even when the SEC chooses not to review an initial decision, the commission still must issue an order to make that decision final,[20] at which point "the initial decision is deemed the action of the Commission."[21]

Lucia eventually brought his case to the D.C. Circuit, contending that the ALJ was an officer under Supreme Court precedent, and the ALJ's appointment by staff therefore was invalid.[22] If ALJs are "officers," the Appointments Clause requires their appointment by the president or a department head[23]—here, the SEC commissioners.[24]

So, what do we know about the meaning of the word "officer" in the Appointments Clause? Well, as administrative law scholars Gary Lawson and Jerry Mashaw have observed, until recently we didn't know much.[25] In its 1976 decision in *Buckley v. Valeo*, the Supreme Court determined generally that officers are those with "significant authority"—that is, those who "exercis[e] responsibility

---

[17] See Lucia, 138 S. Ct. at 2050.

[18] See Raymond J. Lucia Cos., 832 F.3d at 283, aff'd by an equally divided court, 868 F.3d 1021 (D.C. Cir. 2017) (en banc), rev'd, Lucia v. SEC, 138 S. Ct. 2044 (2018).

[19] See Brief for Petitioners at 4, Lucia v. SEC, 138 S. Ct. 2044 (2018) (No. 17-130).

[20] 17 C.F.R. § 201.360(d)(2) (2018).

[21] Lucia, 138 S. Ct. at 2049 (quoting 15 U.S.C. § 78d-1(c)).

[22] See Raymond J. Lucia Cos., 832 F.3d at 283–89.

[23] See Jennifer L. Mascott, Constitutionally Conforming Agency Adjudication, 2 Loy. U. Chi. J. Reg. Compliance 22, 27–33 (2017) (explaining that under the original meaning of the Constitution, the executive department head or the president—not a court of law—must appoint executive branch "officers").

[24] See Free Enter. Fund, 561 U.S. at 511–13 (concluding that the commissioners are the SEC's department head).

[25] See Jennifer L. Mascott, Who Are "Officers of the United States"?, 70 Stan. L. Rev. 443, 451–53 & n.34 (2018) (discussing the relevant literature).

under the public laws of the Nation."[26] In 1991, the Court in *Freytag v. Commissioner* filled in the lines just a little bit more by suggesting that elements like discretionary authority and the handling of important issues indicate officer status. The *Freytag* Court also thought it was indicative of officer status that the special trial judges (STJs) at issue in that case "perform[ed] more than ministerial tasks" such as taking testimony, conducting trials, ruling on evidence admissibility, and holding authority to enforce discovery orders.[27]

The U.S. Court of Appeals for the D.C. Circuit nonetheless had interpreted some language in the alternative in *Freytag* to suggest that one additional mandatory characteristic of constitutional "officers" is that they issue final decisions for their agency. In *Freytag* the Supreme Court had said that "[e]ven if" the STJs' duties "were not as significant" as the Court had concluded they were, the STJs would be officers in any event because they issued final decisions in a certain subset of cases.[28]

In 2000, the D.C. Circuit had occasion to apply *Freytag's* holding in an Appointments Clause challenge involving administrative law judges within the Federal Deposit Insurance Corporation (FDIC). In that case, *Landry v. FDIC*, the court interpreted *Freytag's* language-in-the-alternative to mean the FDIC ALJs were not officers because unlike the *Freytag* STJs, the FDIC adjudicators did not issue final decisions for their agency in any class of cases.[29] The D.C. Circuit reached an analogous determination in August 2016 in *Lucia's* case, contending that the *Freytag* Court must have seen final decisionmaking authority as critical to its officer holding because otherwise the Court would not have taken the time to discuss the limited class of cases where STJs exercised such authority.[30]

In December 2016, the U.S. Court of Appeals for the Tenth Circuit split from the D.C. Circuit's interpretation and held that the SEC's ALJs are officers even though they typically issue only "initial decisions."[31] In contrast to the D.C. Circuit, the Tenth Circuit

---

[26] 424 U.S. 1, 126, 131 (1976) (per curiam).

[27] 501 U.S. 868, 881–82 (1991).

[28] See *id.* at 882.

[29] See Landry v. FDIC, 204 F.3d 1125, 1133–34 (D.C. Cir. 2000).

[30] See Raymond J. Lucia Cos., 832 F.3d at 284–85.

[31] Bandimere v. SEC, 844 F.3d 1168 (10th Cir. 2016); 17 C.F.R. § 201.360.

concluded that final decisionmaking authority was not dispositive to the Court's holding in *Freytag,* citing *Freytag's* explanation that a focus on such authority obscured the independent officer-level significance of the STJ's remaining duties.[32] To further buttress its holding that the SEC ALJs are officers, the Tenth Circuit cited a lengthy list of officials found to be officers by the Supreme Court over a period of approximately 150 years, including officials of as low a level as administrative clerks.

In 2017, Lucia persuaded the D.C. Circuit to sit en banc to reconsider its "officer" standard and address the newly developed circuit split. The SEC heartily defended the D.C. Circuit's past precedent,[33] however, and the en banc D.C. Circuit court split evenly, issuing a 5–5 judgment that essentially reaffirmed the original panel decision.[34] Lucia predictably petitioned for certiorari review in the Supreme Court.

Then the plot thickened. When the time came for the government to submit its brief in opposition to review, it instead filed a brief *supporting* review.[35] Although this position may have seemed surprising to some, it essentially brought the Justice Department's position on interrelated Article II issues into greater consistency. The very same day that the en banc D.C. Circuit was hearing the *Lucia* litigation, it also heard arguments in *PHH v. CFPB,* in which the Trump administration had argued that Article II oversight authority gave it the power to remove individual agency heads from the putatively independent Consumer Financial Protection Bureau (CFPB) on the ground that to "take Care" that the laws are faithfully executed the president must have authority to oversee executive branch officials.[36] During the doubleheader en banc arguments that day it was striking to see the Justice Department step in to the CFPB case to assert an executive power of *removal* but leave the SEC to argue for itself that

[32] Bandimere, 844 F.3d at 1172–73.

[33] See Landry, 204 F.3d at 1125.

[34] Raymond J. Lucia Cos., Inc. v. SEC, 868 F.3d 1021, 1021 (D.C. Cir. 2017) (en banc); D.C. Cir. R. 35(d).

[35] Brief for Respondent SEC, Lucia v. SEC, 138 S. Ct. 2044 (2018) (No. 17-130) (cert-stage brief).

[36] See, e.g., Brief for the United States as Amicus Curiae, PHH Corp. v. CFPB, 881 F.3d 75 (D.C. Cir. 2018) (No. 15-1177).

there was no requirement of presidential authority over key administrative *appointments*.[37]

The solicitor general's cert-stage brief in favor of Supreme Court review of *Lucia* went on record in support of the Appointments Clause as a key constitutional accountability mechanism over the selection of executive officials. Also maintaining consistency with the office's *PHH* position, the SG's brief went on to ask the Court to clarify the contours of statutory executive removal authority over ALJs,[38] an invitation the Court was to turn down with its narrow ultimate opinion.[39] But the SG's discussion of removal in its cert-stage and merits *Lucia* briefs set the stage for what will almost certainly be future challenges arguing that the open-ended-as-currently-applied, triple for-cause tenure protections for ALJs at independent agencies are a bridge too far.[40]

Because both of the original parties in *Lucia* were now in agreement on the core constitutional question of whether SEC ALJs were officers, Chief Justice John Roberts appointed amicus curiae to argue in favor of the judgment below. Somewhat unexpectedly, rather than trying just to beef up the D.C. Circuit's longstanding arguments for non-officer ALJ status based on its interpretation of *Freytag*, amicus also sought to reach back into Founding-era history to support the non-officer position.

The court-appointed amicus contended that *as a historical matter,* the class of constitutional "officers" includes only those "who have the authority, in their own name, to bind[] the government or third

---

[37] See generally Jennifer Mascott, D.C. Circuit's Double-Header on Article II, 36 Yale J. on Reg.: Notice & Comment, May 26, 2017, http://yalejreg.com/nc/d-c-circuits-double-header-on-article-ii-by-jennifer-mascott.

[38] See Brief for Respondent SEC, *supra* note 35, at 18–21 (cert-stage). Contentions that the tenure protections for ALJs improperly restrict the president's executive oversight authority also formed a significant portion of the Cato Institute's arguments as amicus in *Lucia*. See Brief for the Cato Institute as Amicus Curiae Supporting Petitioners at 10–17, Lucia v. SEC, 138 S. Ct. 2044 (2018) (No. 17-130).

[39] See Lucia v. SEC, 138 S.Ct. at 2050 n.1.

[40] See Brief for Respondent SEC Supporting Petitioners, *supra* note 13, at 39–55, (merits brief); Brief for Respondent SEC, *supra* note 35, at 20 (cert-stage brief) (detailing the up to three levels of tenure protection for SEC ALJs through (1) the good cause limitations on firing ALJs themselves, (2) the Supreme Court's assumption that commissioners of independent agencies like the SEC enjoy tenure protections, and (3) the tenure protections of members of the Merit Systems Protection Board who must determine that good cause exists to fire ALJs).

parties for the benefit of the public."[41] Amicus based this argument principally on the historical example of deputy federal marshals and deputy customs collectors, who were on record as existing as early as 1789 and were not appointed as Article II officers. This particular argument had never before been raised in defense of the government's non-officer treatment of ALJs.

If amicus's understanding of this Founding-era history were correct, it might have provided powerful new evidence in support of a narrow conception of Article II officer status.[42] But historical evidence suggests the deputy marshals and customs officials were not appointed independently as Article II officers because they were viewed simply as agents, or shadows, of the principal marshals and customs officials who bore personal liability for their deputies' actions.[43] In other words, the deputy officials were not seen as truly independent entities at all—either as employees *or* "officers" separate and apart from the principal officials for whom they served as agents.[44] Moreover, as further described below, amicus's officer test overlooked evidence of the original public meaning of

---

[41] Brief for Court-Appointed Amicus Curiae Supporting the Judgment Below at 2, Lucia v. SEC, 138 S. Ct. 2044 (2018) (No. 17-130) (internal quotation omitted) (alteration in original).

[42] That said, it is unclear that even amicus's binding-order-in-her-own-name "officer" test would have excluded as many officials from the reach of the Appointments Clause as amicus seemed to suggest. For example, the SEC ALJs arguably would still be officers under this test as they made final decisions constraining third parties while presiding over formal agency adjudication. See Jennifer Mascott, Missing History in the Court-Appointed Amicus Brief in *Lucia v. SEC*, 36 Yale J. on Reg.: Notice & Comment (Mar. 28, 2018), http://yalejreg.com/nc/missing-history-in-the-court-appointed-amicus-brief-in-lucia-v-sec/ (discussing ALJ-issued subpoenas and other disciplinary authority). Also, the Pacific Legal Foundation appears to have identified a lower-level Food and Drug Administration official who has been promulgating agency rules in her own name without an Article II appointment. See Todd Gaziano & Tommy Berry, Career Civil Servants Illegitimately Rule America, Wall St. J., Feb. 28, 2018, https://on.wsj.com/2GioaD3.

[43] See Mascott, *supra* note 25, at 517–22; Aditya Bamzai, The Attorney General and Early Appointments Clause Practice, 93 Notre Dame L. Rev. 1501, 1503–04 (2018).

[44] See, e.g., Alexander Hamilton, U.S. Sec'y of the Treasury, List of Civil Officers of the United States, Except Judges, with Their Emoluments, for the Year Ending October 1, 1792 (1793), in 1 American State Papers; Miscellaneous 57, 59–60 (Walter Lowrie & Walter S. Franklin eds., 1834) (omitting any reference to deputy marshals on a list "of the persons holding civil officers or employments under the United States" despite including the list of 16 federal marshals).

the text of the Appointments Clause[45] as well as the early practice of Article II appointments of individuals with tasks as ministerial as recordkeeping—clerks who did not issue binding orders of any kind, much less binding orders *"in their own name."*

So what story, then, does history actually tell?

II. History of the Appointments Clause

In the *Stanford Law Review* earlier this year, I published a lengthy study on 18th-century officers and the original meaning of the phrase "Officers of the United States."[46] Substantial Founding-era evidence suggests that if the Court ever were to take a fresh look at the Appointments Clause's original meaning, it would find that the Clause applies to a much larger portion of the federal government than those appointed as "officers" under current practice.[47] Examination of the constitutional text, thousands of 18th-century uses of the term "officer," and early practice indicates that the original meaning of "Officers of the United States" included every federal civil official with ongoing responsibility to carry out a statutory duty.[48] SEC ALJs carry out tasks that Congress has assigned to the SEC.[49] Therefore, the SEC's ALJs would be constitutional officers under this standard as well as under the Court's modern Appointments Clause jurisprudence.

The original meaning of officer "would likely extend to thousands of officials not currently appointed as Article II officers, such as tax collectors, disaster relief officials, customs officials, and administrative judges."[50] This conclusion might sound destabilizing,

---

[45] See generally Mascott, *supra* note 25, at 465–507 (analyzing the original public meaning of the Article II phrase "Officers of the United States").

[46] See generally Mascott, *supra* note 25. The material in Part II of this article is substantially derived from this Stanford Law Review article as well as from the amicus brief that I filed in *Lucia*. Almost all of the passages in the Part II introduction and sections II.A-B of this article are taken verbatim from my *Lucia* brief, which presented a detailed summary of the historical evidence from the Stanford article. A version of this section previously appeared in the Stanford Law Review at 70 Stan. L. Rev. 443 (2018). When possible and appropriate, please cite to that version. For information visit: stanfordlawreview.org.

[47] See Mascott, *supra* note 25, at 545–58, 564.

[48] See *id.* at 453–54 ("[T]he most likely original public meaning of 'officer' is one whom the government entrusts with ongoing responsibility to perform a statutory duty of any level of importance.").

[49] See 15 U.S.C. § 78d-1(a); 17 C.F.R. §§ 200.14, 200.30-9 (2018).

[50] Mascott, *supra* note 25, at 443.

but significant portions of the civil-service hiring system might be brought into alignment with Article II if executive department heads provided final sign-off on job candidates vetted through merit-based selection procedures. The key component to constitutional appointments is that the president or the head of a department must sit atop an officer selection system for which he or she maintains responsibility. Article II requires a chain of accountability[51] in hiring decisions from the lowest-ranking officer up to the department head and, ultimately, the elected president.

A. Original Public Meaning of the Appointments Clause

The Appointments Clause requires that all "Officers of the United States" be appointed by the president with Senate advice and consent, the president alone, "Heads of Departments," or "Courts of Law."[52] This Article II limitation on the number of actors authorized to make final decisions in selecting officers helps to ensure that the public knows the identity of the official who bears ultimate responsibility for each officer appointment.[53]

Concerns about transparency, accountability, and excellence in government service existed from the Founding. The Framers selected the mechanism of the Appointments Clause to safeguard these core values—believing that transparency in officer appointments would hold the elected executive and his or her department heads accountable for selecting well-qualified personnel.[54] Proper interpretation of which officials are encompassed by the phrase "Officers of the United States" is a fundamental component of correctly, and completely, implementing the Appointments Clause's democratic accountability protections.

[51] Cf. Dina Mishra, An Executive-Power Non-delegation Doctrine for the Private Administration of Federal Law, 68 Vand. L. Rev. 1509, 1569–70 (2015) (discussing the concept of a "chain of accountability" related to removal restrictions).

[52] U.S. Const. art. II, § 2, cl. 2.

[53] Mascott, *supra* note 25, at 447.

[54] See, e.g., The Federalist No. 76 (Alexander Hamilton) (observing that individual responsibility for governmental appointments "will naturally beget a livelier sense of duty, and a more exact regard to reputation" than appointments determined by an "assembly of men"); 1 The Records of the Federal Convention of 1787, at 70 (Max Farrand ed., 1911) (Mr. Wilson: "If appointments of Officers are made by a sing. Ex [single Executive] he is responsible for the propriety of the same."); Mascott, *supra* note 25, at 456–58 & n.58, 552–53 & n.663, 558–59 (Part IV.B.1).

Substantial 18th-century evidence indicates that the original pub-lic meaning of the phrase was broad, encompassing every federal civil official "with ongoing responsibility for a federal statutory duty."[55] An official's governmental duty did not have to rise to any minimal level of significance for the official to come within Appoint-ments Clause requirements. Nor did the term "officer" necessarily relate to an official's power to exercise discretion or engage in final decisionmaking—in contrast to the suggestions of contemporary case law. Officials with duties as nondiscretionary as recordkeeping were considered officers. In contrast to the contemporary classifica-tion of federal officials as either employees or officers, the Founders more likely would have considered workers not rising to the level of officer to be "attendants" or "servants."

1. Methodology

My historical study of federal officers relied on two distinct tech-niques: (1) corpus linguistics-style analysis of documents from the Founding era to identify the original meaning of the phrase "Officers of the United States," and (2) detailed study of appointment practices enacted by the First Congress.[56] Corpus linguistics interpretive anal-ysis involves the adaptation of empirically based big-data techniques to statutory and constitutional interpretation.[57] One key insight from the field is that examination of *every use* of a term in a wide variety of Founding-era documents can yield a more complete, impartial un-derstanding of the word than cherry-picking a handful of statements to support one's preferred interpretation.[58]

This analysis suggested first that "Officers of the United States" was not a term of art setting aside a particularly important class of officers. Rather, the modifier "of the United States" denotes that the clause applies to federal, and not state, officers. The 18th-century

[55] Mascott, *supra* note 25, at 454, 465.

[56] *Id.* at 443.

[57] See generally James C. Phillips et al., Corpus Linguistics & Original Public Mean-ing: A New Tool to Make Originalism More Empirical, 126 Yale L.J.F. 21, 27–29 (2016); see also Mascott, *supra* note 25 at 466–68.

[58] See, e.g., Randy E. Barnett, New Evidence of the Original Meaning of the Commerce Clause, 55 Ark. L. Rev. 847, 856–57 (2003); see also Mascott, *supra* note 25, at 469–70 (explaining the "officer" study's corpus linguistics-style methodology in greater depth).

meaning of officer in turn encompassed all officials "with ongoing responsibility to perform a statutory duty."[59] Early federal officials carrying out statutory duties were considered officers even where the statute creating the duty did not specify which officer had to perform it.

2. The constitutional text and drafting history

Even though the Constitution includes no definition of "Officers of the United States," the president's authority to nominate judges, certain diplomatic officers, and "all other Officers of the United States" suggests the phrase encompasses a larger group than just diplomats and judges.[60] This suggestion is further confirmed by the clause's subsequent reference to a class of "inferior Officers."[61] The Constitution's two additional references to "Officers of the United States" merely describe consequences that derive from Article II officer status—such as the possibility of facing impeachment and the requirement of commissioning by the president.

The Constitution uses some formulation of the terms "office(s)" and "officer(s)" 30 additional times.[62] These references do not explicitly indicate what level of authority constitutional officers hold—although the Necessary and Proper Clause may hold some clues. That clause authorizes Congress to "make all Laws which shall be necessary and proper for carrying into Execution the foregoing Powers, and all other Powers vested by this Constitution in the Government of the United States, or in any Department or Officer thereof."[63] This provision could be read as permitting the authority to exercise federal power to reside only in the federal government itself or its departments or "Officer[s]"—not a lower-level non-officer class.

Even though the constitutional text itself does not make clear the precise dividing line between the level of authority held by officers

---

[59] See Mascott, *supra* note 25, at 454.

[60] See U.S. Const. art. II, § 2, cl. 2 ("[The President] . . . shall appoint Ambassadors, other public Ministers and Consuls, Judges of the supreme Court, and all other Officers of the United States . . . "); Mascott, *supra* note 25, at 470.

[61] See U.S. Const. art. II, § 2, cl. 2 (". . . but the Congress may by Law vest the Appointment of such inferior Officers, as they think proper . . .").

[62] See Mascott, *supra* note 25, at 470–71 n.139 (discussing this evidence and the "Necessary and Proper Clause" textual analysis).

[63] U.S. Const. art. I, § 8, cl. 18.

and any less important non-officer group, the text—in conjunction with significant external Founding-era evidence—indicates that the phrase "Officers of the United States" was not a new term of art for especially important officials.[64] For example, intratextual analysis[65] of the Constitution's repeated uses of the modifying phrase "of the United States" and the Appointments Clause's drafting history suggest that "Officers *of the United States*" just connotes a broad class of federal officers spanning multiple branches of the government, as distinct from purely executive officers. The earliest drafts of the Constitution apparently authorized the president to appoint only executive officers, as they gave legislators the authority to appoint non-executive officers such as judges. Appointments Clause drafts transformed from referencing just "officers" to including the full phrase "Officers of the United States" at the same near-final stage of the drafting process at which the president acquired the authority to appoint non-executive "Judges of the supreme Court" and ambassadors.[66]

Several other constitutional uses of the phrase "of the United States" similarly refer to the federal, as opposed to the state, level of government. For example, Article II, section 2, clause 1 establishes the president as "Commander in Chief of the Army and Navy of the United States, and of the Militia of the several States." The Oaths Clause requires "executive and judicial Officers, both of the United States and of the several States, [to] be bound by Oath or Affirmation, to support this Constitution." And Article IV, section 3, clause 2 instructs that "nothing in this Constitution shall be so construed as to Prejudice any Claims of the United States, or of any particular State." Each of these clauses' references to "of the United States" juxtaposed with a parallel reference to state-level government underscores the phrase's use as a modifier setting aside a federal-level category.[67]

The earliest written uses of the full phrase "Officers of the United States" confirm this analysis. Examination of every use of the phrase in the journals of the Continental Congress and a database of early

---

[64] Mascott, *supra* note 25, at 471–79 (Part II.A.2).

[65] See generally, Akhil Reed Amar, Intratextualism, 112 Harv. L. Rev. 747 (1999) (describing "intratextualism" as a technique for interpreting the Constitution).

[66] See Mascott, *supra* note 25, at 472–73.

[67] See *id.* at 473–74 et seq.

newspaper records showed the phrase arising as early as 1778 in descriptions of *continental,* as opposed to state-level, military officers. For example, a 1782 War Office report suggested that the government should not pay a military officer "as an officer of the United States" for the time period that he had served as a military officer "of a particular State." And the minutes from a February 1778 session of the Continental Congress described continental-level civil and military officers as "officer[s] of the United States."[68]

3. Founding-era dictionaries and commentaries

If "Officers of the United States" is not a term of art for especially important officials, the late 18th-century meaning of the standalone term "officer" is relevant for determining the authority level of federal officials under the Appointments Clause. A survey of 10 Founding-era dictionaries indicated that a civil "officer" generally was defined as a "man employed by the public(k)"; "office" typically was defined as a "public employment" or a "public charge."[69]

Eighteenth-century legal dictionaries also connected the concepts of "duty" and "office." For example, Matthew Bacon reported that "'the Word *Officium* principally implies a Duty, and . . . the Charge of such Duty'" and observed that one "'is not the less a Public Officer, where his Authority is confined to narrow Limits; because it is the Duty of his Office, and the Nature of that Duty, which makes him a Public Officer, and not the Extent of his Authority.'"[70] Bacon's analysis also suggests that officer status was not connected with holding discretion or binding authority. He describes a class of "'Ministerial Offices'" including positions that "'required only the Skill of Writing after a Copy,'" and chirographers who kept records of court-imposed fines.[71]

Nathan Bailey's popular Founding-era dictionary used the words "officer(s)" and "office(s)" more than 500 times to define other terms, characterizing as "officers" many assistants, recordkeepers,

---

[68] See *id.* at 477–79 & nn. 175, 176 (discussing the evidence described in this paragraph).

[69] See *id.* at 484, 486–87.

[70] See *id.* at 488–89 (quoting 3 Matthew Bacon, A New Abridgment of the Law *718–19 (4th ed. 1778)).

[71] See *id.* at 489 (quoting Bacon, *supra* note 70, at *734).

and other public officials engaged in menial tasks.[72] For example, a sword-bearer was "an officer who carries the sword of state before a magistrate." A "Swabber" was "an inferior officer on board a ship of war, whose office it is to take care that the ship be kept clean." A "sewer" was "an officer who comes in before the meat of a King or Nobleman, and places it upon the table." A "Gauger" was "an officer employed in gaging," or measuring the contents of a vessel. And a Chafe-Wax was "an Officer belonging to the Lord Chancellor, who fits the wax for [the] sealing of writs."

These dictionaries would have influenced the late 18th-century American understanding of the term "officer." The Framers intentionally rejected the British approach for creating offices and appointing officers, but no evidence suggests the Constitution imported an altered meaning of the word "officer" itself. One complaint underlying the colonists' war for independence was that the king had "erected a multitude of New Offices, and sent hither swarms of Officers to harrass our people."[73] Under British practice, the king had power to both create and fill public offices. The Framers rejected this potential for abuse, cleanly separating the authority to establish new offices from the power to name officers to fill them.[74] This structural safeguard promoted accountability and transparency through its broad applicability to lower-level, ministerial officials under the original meaning of the term "officer."

4. Founding-era debates and analysis

Farrand's records of the constitutional drafting debates, the Federalist Papers, and the Borden collection of Anti-Federalist essays contain hundreds of references to the terms "officer(s)" and "office(s)." Examination of the context of these references, as well as every mention of "Officers of the United States" in Elliot's records of the ratification debates, strongly suggests that "officer" had a very broad scope in the late 18th century. Following are several

---

[72] See *id.* at 485, 490. The dictionary definitions discussed in this paragraph and many other definitions of menial "officer" positions are detailed on pages 490–92 of Mascott, *supra* note 25.

[73] The Declaration of Independence para. 12 (U.S. 1776); Mascott, *supra* note 25, at 492.

[74] Hanah Metchis Volokh, The Two Appointments Clauses: Statutory Qualifications for Federal Officers, 10 U. Pa. J. Const. L. 745, 769 (2008).

illustrative examples.[75] During the North Carolina ratification debate, Archibald Maclaine described "inferior officers of the United States" as petty officers who maintained "trifling" duties.[76] Joseph Taylor observed that if the Constitution were adopted, "we shall have a large number of officers in North Carolina under the appointment of Congress" because, for example, there would be "a great number of tax-gatherers."[77] During the drafting debates, Gouverneur Morris observed that the executive would have the duty to appoint "ministerial officers of the administration of public affairs." Later in the drafting process, James Wilson observed that the appointing power would encompass even "tide-waiter[s]," a position that Samuel Johnson's dictionary described as an "officer who watches the landing of goods at the customhouse."[78]

The Anti-Federalist essayist with the pseudonym "Federal Farmer" expressed concern that federal taxation powers would lead to "many thousand officers solely created by, and dependent upon the union."[79] James Madison disagreed and believed the federal government would have relatively few officers in comparison to the states.[80] But this is because James Madison had concluded that state officers might collect taxes for the federal government and that the federal government's "few and defined" powers would cause its officers to be "exceed[ed] beyond all proportion," by officers carrying out the states' "numerous and indefinite"

---

[75] See Mascott, *supra* note 25, at 494–504 (detailing the examples discussed in this paragraph and the next as well as additional supporting evidence and potential counter-examples).

[76] The Debates in the Several State Conventions, on the Adoption of the Federal Constitution 43–44 (Jonathan Elliot ed., 2d ed. 1836) (statement of Mr. Maclaine).

[77] Anti-Federalist No. 66: "From North Carolina"; Debate during North Carolina Ratifying Convention, in The Anti-Federalist Papers 262, 262 (Bill Bailey ed., n.d.), https://www.thefederalistpapers.org/wp-content/uploads/2012/11/The-Anti-Federalist-Papers-Special-Edition.pdf.

[78] See Tidewaiter, 2 Samuel Johnson, A Dictionary of the English Language (6th ed. 1785).

[79] See Anti-Federalist No. 41–43 (Part I): The Quantity of Power the Union Must Possess Is One Thing; The Mode of Exercising the Powers Given Is Quite a Different Consideration (Federal Farmer XVII) (1788), in The Anti-Federalist Papers, *supra* note 77, at 148, 149.

[80] See Mascott, *supra* note 25, at 502.

powers.[81] Madison nonetheless understood the term "officer" itself to have a broad scope, embracing many levels of officials including "justices of peace, officers of militia, [and] ministerial officers of justice."[82]

This broad understanding of the meaning of "officer" extended back to the preconstitutional period under the Continental Congress.[83] For example, a 1778 resolution regarding military hospitals characterized "apothecaries, mates, stewards, [and] matrons" as "officers." These individuals had nondiscretionary duties far below the level that contemporary courts have considered mandatory for "officer" status. A 1775 Continental Congress committee report indicated that the role of mates and apothecaries was to "visit and attend the sick." The 1775 report also characterized clerks and storekeepers as "officers," observing that storekeepers were "[t]o receive and deliver the bedding and other necessaries by order of the [hospital] director" and clerks were "[t]o keep accounts for the director and store keepers."

B. Early Appointment Practices

The early appointment practices throughout the First Congress by and large confirm the public meaning interpretation of Article II "officers" as officials responsible for an ongoing statutory duty.[84] The only categories of civil executive officials in ongoing positions cleanly excluded from Article II appointment practices were (1) officials akin to "servants" or "attendants" and (2) several categories of deputy officials treated just as shadows of the primary officers who could face personal legal liability for their deputies' acts. These categories of deputies have no general modern analog. The Founding-era deputies who instead acted as aides or seconds-in-command, without a similar technical liability relationship to their primary officers, were selected in compliance with the Appointments Clause.

---

[81] See *id.* at 502 & nn.327, 329; The Federalist No. 45 (James Madison).

[82] See Mascott, *supra* note 25, at 502 & n.329 (internal quotation omitted).

[83] See *id.* at 537–45 (describing the examples discussed in this paragraph, among other evidence, but also explaining that the actual appointment methods used to fill a number of these positions appeared to be in some tension with the description of them as "office[s]").

[84] See *id.* at 507–45 (Part III) (detailing the evidence from early practice).

Officials as varied as internal revenue inspectors and supervisors, lighthouse keepers and superintendents, ship masters and first, second, and third mates on revenue cutters (although not "mariners" and "boys"), customs collectors, surveyors, and naval officers also were selected in compliance with the Appointments Clause.[85] Early Article II officers who provide some of the starkest evidence contradicting modern lower-court determinations that Article II status involves discretion are the recordkeeping clerks treated as officers from the time of the First Congress.[86] These clerks had responsibilities as menial as transcribing treasury books, copying account statements, counting money, and keeping records of the certificates given to ships authorized to import goods.

Contrary to the suggestion of some modern judicial opinions that Congress can determine "officer" status based on whether it chooses to directly tie statutory duties to a particular official, the original meaning of "officer" encompassed every official who happened to carry out a statutory task—whether Congress had explicitly assigned it to that individual or not. For example, the clerks who kept statutory records were considered officers even when the statutes simply mandated executive recordkeeping as a general matter without specifically assigning clerks to the job.[87] Analogously, today if Congress were to authorize an agency to promulgate rules, every official participating in that task would be an "officer" under the statutory duty standard.

In contrast, messengers and office-keepers did not carry out legislative tasks authorized or required by Congress, so they were not "officers" and Congress consequently did not need to establish their positions "by Law."[88] Individuals in these positions served more as assistants and carried out nonstatutorily required tasks like arranging newspapers, preserving printed copies of statutory records, and preparing items for mail delivery.

---

[85] See *id.* at 523, 528 n.508, 531, 533. But see *id.* at 528–30 & n.508, 531 (explaining possible counter-examples like certain officials in the military, the Territories, and the National Bank).

[86] See, e.g., Tucker v. Comm'r, 676 F.3d 1129, 1133 (D.C. Cir. 2012); Mascott, *supra* note 25, at 510–15 (Part III.A).

[87] See *id.* at 507–08, 514–15 & n.414.

[88] See U.S. Const. art. II, § 2 (requiring that Congress establish the appointments for officers "by Law"); Mascott, *supra* note 25, at 459, 509–10.

Initially, seemingly inconsistent with the clerk-messenger dividing line, Congress waited 10 years to submit lower-level customs officials like weighers, measurers, gaugers, and inspectors to appointment by their department head, the treasury secretary. But numerous Founding-era writings described these individuals as "officers."[89] And by 1799 Congress had statutorily required the treasury secretary to approve appointments of both inspectors and the weighers, measurers, and gaugers who had the nondiscretionary statutory task of measuring the quantities of goods being imported.[90] An 1843 attorney general opinion expressly clarified that customs inspectors are Article II officers and the 1799 provision mandating treasury secretary appointment of customs officials was constitutionally required.[91]

C. Brief History of the Appointments Clause in the Courts

Despite the apparent contemporary perception of Article II "officers" as comprising a small group, arguably the history of the Supreme Court's judgments in Appointments Clause cases is largely consistent with a broad conception of "officer."[92] Several cases bear mention.

As an initial matter, in 1823 Chief Justice John Marshall espoused what was essentially the statutory duty standard for "officer" status in an opinion he drafted while presiding in circuit court. In *United States v. Maurice*, he wrote, "An office is defined to be 'a public charge or employment,' and he who performs the duties of the office, is an officer. If employed on the part of the United States, he is an officer of the United States."[93] The only category of public employment that Marshall excluded from "officer" status was that of government contractor.[94]

---

[89] See *id.* at 524–26.

[90] See Act of Mar. 2, 1799, ch. 22, § 21, 1 Stat. 627, 642 (amended 1811).

[91] See Appointment & Removal of Inspectors of Customs, 4 Op. Att'y Gen. 162, 164–65 (1843).

[92] See Mascott, *supra* note 25, at 463–65. See also *id.* at 463 n.99 (discussing the analysis of a 1996 Office of Legal Counsel memo canvassing the jurisprudence on Article II "officer" status, see Constitutional Separation of Powers between the President and Cong., 20 Op. O.L.C. 124, 139–48 (1996)).

[93] 26 F. Cas. 1211, 1214 (C.C.D. Va. 1823).

[94] See *id.* ("Although an office is 'an employment,' it does not follow that every employment is an office. A man may certainly be employed under a contract, express or implied to do an act, or perform a service, without becoming an officer. But if a duty

Across decades of Supreme Court opinions—as the Tenth Circuit noted in 2016—the Court has described numerous governmental positions as offices, including a number of positions that might seem relatively insignificant.[95] For example, in 1839 the Court clarified that a district court clerk responsible for "keep[ing] the records of the Court, and receiv[ing] the fees provided by law for his services" was an Article II officer. In 1877 the Court observed that an assistant-surgeon in the navy medical corps held an office. And in 1886 the Court observed that cadet engineers studying at the Naval Academy were constitutional officers.[96]

In 1878, the Court indicated in *United States v. Germaine* that "thousands of clerks in the Departments of the Treasury, Interior, and the others" were constitutional officers.[97] This further confirms the notion of Article II officer status for the earliest recordkeeping clerks. The Court's analysis in *Germaine* bears further discussion, however. The opinion provides some color for the Court's understanding of officer status by reiterating that the term "embraces the ideas of tenure, duration, emolument, and duties."[98] Further, the Court emphasized the dispositive significance of duties being "continuing and permanent," not "occasional and intermittent."[99] Because the civil surgeon in this particular case had intermittent duties and was hired only to make periodic examinations of

---

be a continuing one . . . if those duties continue, though the person be changed; it seems very difficult to distinguish such a charge or employment from an office, or the person who performs the duties from an officer."). Without exploring whether such a characteristic is necessary for "officer" status, in a subsequent passage of the opinion Marshall describes the relevant official's duties as "important" and says they would need to be performed by an officer unless "performed by contract." See *id.*

[95] Bandimere v. SEC, 844 F3d. 1168, 1173–74 (10th Cir. 2016).

[96] Ex parte Hennen, 38 U.S. 230, 257–58 (1839); United States v. Moore, 95 U.S. 760, 761–63 (1877) (observing that the position "has every ingredient of an office" without clarifying further what those ingredients are); United States v. Perkins, 116 U.S. 483, 483–84 (1886).

[97] See United States v. Germaine, 99 U.S. 508, 510–11 (1878) (describing these clerks' appointments by the heads of departments, authorized by Article II to appoint "inferior officers").

[98] See *id.* at 511. See also E. Garrett West, Clarifying the Employee-Officer Distinction in Appointments Clause Jurisprudence, 127 Yale L.J. Forum 42 (2017) (discussing *Germaine* and other earlier 19th-century Supreme Court cases that espouse similar reasoning, as well as providing a contrasting take on Marshall's reasoning in *Maurice*).

[99] Germaine, 99 U.S. at 511–12.

pension applicants—more like a government contractor providing services—the Court concluded he was not an Article II officer.[100]

It is worth lingering for a moment on this reasoning from *Germaine* because in recent years the opinion has been misunderstood—and even mistakenly characterized by the Court. In 2010 in *Free Enterprise Fund v. Public Company Accounting Oversight Board*, the Supreme Court relied on *Germaine* to suggest that at least 90 percent of full-time government workers are non-officer civil servants.[101] But that was a badly mistaken description of the relevant proposition in *Germaine*. Indeed, the Court in *Germaine* did say that one "may be an agent or employé working for the government and paid by it, as nine-tenths of the persons rendering service to the government undoubtedly are, without thereby becoming its officers."[102] But *Germaine* was all about non-officers hired by the government for intermittent services, channeling *Maurice*'s reasoning from a half-century earlier—not a case about a supposed large class of non-officer continuing government employees.

It is unclear when the perception first arose that the merit-based civil service is at odds with Article II officer status.[103] In 1871, the attorney general issued an opinion addressing the constitutionality of merit-based selection procedures for Article II officer clerks.[104] Ultimately the opinion concluded that if a department head were required to hire the one top-ranked candidate from a merit-based selection process, such a constraint would impermissibly restrict department head appointment authority. But the opinion suggested such procedures might be constitutional if they instead preserved a sufficiently broad range of multiple top-ranked candidates from which the department head could choose. Or that merit-based considerations may be appropriate to provide just a *recommendation* to

---

[100] See *id.* at 508, 512.

[101] See Free Enter. Fund, 561 U.S. at 506 & n.9. See also Lucia v. SEC, 138 S. Ct. at 2065 (Sotomayor, J., dissenting) (citing *Free Enterprise Fund* for this same interpretation of *Germaine*).

[102] Germaine, 99 U.S. at 509.

[103] Justice Breyer conveyed this perception during the *Lucia* oral argument. See Transcript of Oral Arg. at 16–17, Lucia v. SEC, 138 S. Ct. 2044 (2018) (No. 17-130) (tying together a determination whether ALJs are "officers" with the future existence of "the merit civil service at the higher levels").

[104] See Civil-Serv. Comm'n, 13 Op. Att'y Gen. 516 (1871).

the appointing official, who then would not be "bound to abide by it, if satisfied that the appointment of another would best serve the public interests." The opinion said it was unclear exactly how many potential candidates, and how much discretion, a constitutional appointment process would entail.

What is striking about the attorney general's opinion, however, is that merit-based selection procedures were under consideration for government officials thought to be Article II officers—suggesting that at least as of the late 19th century, merit-based selection requirements and Article II officer appointments were thought to be potentially compatible.[105] It was not necessarily one or the other.

Article II authorizes Congress to establish positions "by Law,"[106] and there is some thought that this congressional officer-creation power carries with it a measure of authority to impose qualifications on who may fill an office.[107] Perhaps some type of merit-based officer selection system could be one permissible form of such a qualification, at least in a limited form. Of course, a department head must have the final say in officer selection and have a meaningful range of candidates from which to choose. Also, the individuals helping the department head to carry out the objective merit-based selection procedures would themselves need to be properly appointed, at least under the original meaning of the Appointments Clause. But if every individual involved in objective, merit-based officer hiring were properly appointed, perhaps Article II would permit at least certain inferior officers to be subject to a minimal threshold qualification requirement, or to a merit-based advisory system in which appointing officials had the benefit of information gleaned from objective merit-based vetting of potential candidates based on certain predetermined criteria.[108] Viewing at least some kind of merit-based officer qualifications as compatible with Article II officer status may make it more feasible, or likely, that Congress would be open

---

[105] See *id.* at 518–19 (referencing clerks and marshals).

[106] U.S. Const. art. II, § 2, cl. 2.

[107] See Mascott, *supra* note 25, at 551.

[108] See Civil-Serv. Comm'n, 13 Op. Att'y Gen. 516, 520, 523–24 (Attorney General Amos Akerman: "I see no constitutional objection to an examining board, rendering no imperative judgments, but only aiding the appointing power with information. A legal obligation to follow the judgment of such a board is inconsistent with the constitutional independence of the appointing power.").

to applying the democratic accountability protections of department head appointment to a larger proportion of government officials in compliance with the original meaning of Article II.[109]

Finally, despite the Court's apparent misinterpretation of *Germaine* in *Free Enterprise Fund*, even the Court's modern cases leading up to *Lucia* could be interpreted as consistent, to a degree, with a historic understanding of Article II. In *Buckley*, the Court held that the very high-level Federal Election Commissioners held sufficiently "significant authority" to qualify as officers. And then in *Freytag*, the Court found that special trial judges had sufficient discretionary involvement with significant matters that they were Article II officers. In contrast to how these cases have been interpreted in the lower courts, they did not necessarily mandate that every officer have discretion or "significant authority."[110] Rather, those cases found that the relevant government positions before the Court satisfied sufficient, but perhaps not necessary, conditions for Article II officer status.

III. The Supreme Court Opinions in *Lucia*

The Supreme Court's consideration of *Lucia* this spring met with a lot of hype. Part of the intensity stemmed from concerns within the administrative law community that application of political appointment procedures to ALJs would undermine values of independence typically associated with judicial decisionmakers.[111]

Some of the excitement surrounding the case was due simply to the solicitor general's new litigating position in the Supreme Court. But reactions to the SG's new litigation strategy were intensified by the SG's decision to move beyond challenging the ALJ appointment process to question the proper scope of ALJ removal as well.[112]

---

[109] See Mascott, *supra* note 25, at 551–65 (explaining the relevant considerations in reforming the civil-service system to ensure more officials are selected consistent with the chain of democratic accountability protections inherent in Article II).

[110] See Brief of Professor Jennifer L. Mascott as Amicus Curiae Supporting Petitioners at 7, Lucia v. SEC, 138 S. Ct. 2044 (2018) (No. 17-130).

[111] See generally, e.g., Brief of Administrative Law Scholars as Amici Curiae Supporting Neither Party, *supra* note 11; Brief of Constitutional and Administrative Law Scholars as Amici Curiae Supporting Affirmance, Lucia v. SEC, 138 S. Ct. 2044 (2018) (No. 17-130).

[112] See Brief for Respondent SEC Supporting Petitioners, *supra* note 13, at 45–55 (merits brief).

At the height of the *Lucia* frenzy, some commentators even suggested that the SG may have planted removal questions in the *Lucia* case to intentionally lay the groundwork for a Court decision that could support the presidential firing of Special Counsel Robert Mueller.[113] Such support would have been hard to derive from any decision in *Lucia*, however, even one with great breadth, as the SG's removal challenge involved the proper interpretation of a statutory provision relevant to disciplinary action *only* for ALJs.[114] Further, the SG did not ask for the Court to find the statutory ALJ tenure protections entirely unconstitutional. Rather, he requested that the Court give them a clarifying construction.[115]

In the end, *Lucia* went out with a whimper—at least as far as the actual holding in the case is concerned. The Court held 7-2 for the government and Mr. Lucia, concluding that the SEC's ALJs are Article II officers.[116] But the Court decided the case on about as narrow a basis as possible. The Court did not address the removal issues raised by the government.[117] It did not do much at all to further clarify the elements that make a government official an officer, declining either to further explain the meaning of "significant authority"

---

[113] See, e.g., Cary Coglianese, "Good Cause" Does Not Mean Anything Goes, The Regulatory Review Blog (Apr. 18, 2018), https://www.theregreview.org/2018/04/18/coglianese-good-cause-not-anything-goes (addressing these arguments).

[114] See 5 U.S.C. § 7521(a); Jennifer Mascott, The Government and the Appointments Clause—Just the Facts, 36 Yale J. on Reg.: Notice & Comment (Apr. 23, 2018), http://yalejreg.com/nc/the-government-and-the-appointments-clause-just-the-facts.

[115] See Brief for Respondent SEC Supporting Petitioners, *supra* note 13, at 12–13 (merits brief) (suggesting that the Court should construe "'good cause' for removing an ALJ . . . to include an ALJ's misconduct or failure to follow lawful directives or to perform adequately" and suggesting that the Court should interpret the statutory role for the Merit Systems Protection Board in ALJ removals to consist only of "determining whether evidence exists to support the agency's view that 'good cause' . . . exists").

[116] See Lucia, 138 S. Ct. at 2048.

[117] See *id.* at 2050 n.1. The Court indicated that it would prefer to wait to address those removal issues—if at all—until the issues receive full briefing in the lower courts. The parties had not litigated the statutory removal protections for ALJs in the courts below, and the majority opinion noted that the Supreme Court "ordinarily await[s] thorough lower court opinions to guide [its] analysis of the merits" of an issue. See *id.* (internal quotation omitted). This statement may be like waving a red flag in front of regulated parties facing ALJs in administrative hearings who may be ready and willing to file claims that can give the Court the kind of record on removal that it lacked in *Lucia*.

or return to a historically grounded concept of "officer."[118] It did not even give much guidance about how its holding is to be implemented on remand.

Instead, it took the approach of the minimalist interpretation of its decisions in *Buckley* and *Freytag* described above. It determined just that the administrative law judges before it were officers without clarifying exactly which of the characteristics of the ALJs might be mandatory for officer status moving forward.

Here, in more depth, is what the Court said.

A. Majority Opinion

Observers at the *Lucia* oral argument on April 23, 2018, may have predicted that a narrow holding was coming. Multiple justices seemed genuinely unsure about the proper way to define the concept of "officer" in Article II. Justice Sonia Sotomayor felt the history of the meaning of the term based on early practice was unclear.[119] Justice Breyer told the litigants that he really did not know what to do in the case because of the potential consequences of finding ALJs are officers.[120] And Justice Samuel Alito offered perhaps the most piercing question to the government in the current tense special counsel climate, asking whether federal law enforcement officials would fall within the category of appointed "officers" under the government's conception of the term.[121] Justice Kagan, the eventual author of the majority opinion, cut through the complexity, stating that the *Lucia* ALJs and *Freytag* STJs shared nine out of their "top 10 attributes" and asking the Court-appointed amicus why that did not resolve the case.[122]

Two months later, in the *Lucia* opinion, Justice Kagan wrote that the "adjudicative officials" found to be officers in *Freytag* "are near-carbon copies of the [SEC's] ALJs." Thus the Court's *Freytag* analysis "(sans any more detailed legal criteria) necessarily decides this

---

[118] See *id.* at 2051 (declining to "elaborate on *Buckley*'s 'significant authority' test").

[119] See Transcript, *supra* note 103, at 23–24 (Sotomayor: "You know, a U.S. marshal was – deputy wasn't an officer but a – and customs inspectors weren't officers, but shipmasters were. All of this seems a little bit difficult to quantify.").

[120] See *id.* at 16–17.

[121] See *id.* at 26–29.

[122] See *id.* at 37.

case."[123] With this sentence, the Court may have been waving lower courts away from treating each ALJ characteristic described in the opinion as mandatory for Article II status across the board. Perhaps fending off future D.C. Circuit-style fossilizations of fact-bound characteristics, like the *Landry* overemphasis on occasional final decisionmaking authority, the majority here underscored that it simply found the ALJs' characteristics to be over the "officer" threshold under a very fact-bound application of *Freytag*.

The ALJ characteristics shared with STJs that collectively cross the "officer" threshold include the following: The SEC ALJs "hold a continuing office established by law." And they exercise "significant discretion when carrying out . . . important functions" encompassing "the authority needed to ensure fair and orderly adversarial hearings." In particular, they take testimony, receive evidence, examine witnesses, and may take prehearing depositions. They conduct trials during which "they administer oaths, rule on motions, and generally regulat[e] the course of a hearing, as well as the conduct of parties and counsel." They "rule on the admissibility of evidence" and "thus critically shape the administrative record." Also, they "have the power to enforce compliance with discovery orders" through the ability to "punish all [c]ontemptuous conduct . . . by means as severe as excluding the offender from the hearing."[124]

Justice Kagan noted that in at least one respect, the SEC ALJs even surpass the *Freytag* STJs in the extent of their authority. The ALJs have a "more autonomous role" when they issue their decisions. In major cases, "a regular Tax Court judge must always review an STJ's opinion," but "the SEC can decide against reviewing an ALJ decision at all." When the commission "declines review (and issues an order saying so), the ALJ's decision itself becomes final and is deemed the action of the Commission."[125]

Fascinatingly, earlier in the opinion when Justice Kagan first described the SEC ALJs' "extensive powers," she went even further and characterized the ALJs as "exercis[ing] authority comparable to that of a federal district judge conducting a bench trial."[126] With that

---

[123] Lucia, 138 S. Ct. at 2052.

[124] *Id.* at 2053 (internal quotations omitted).

[125] *Id.* at 2053–54 (internal quotations omitted).

[126] *Id.* at 2049 (internal quotations omitted).

description, Justice Kagan, perhaps unintentionally, picked up on the theme that had lurked beneath the surface of the entire Supreme Court litigation—that the question whether agency adjudicators should be subject to electorally accountable executive appointments can be hard to untangle because ALJs' modern traits often make them seem more like officials in the judicial branch.

Even though the majority opinion indicated that the Court was not establishing new legal criteria for officer status, the opinion nonetheless specified that certain criteria definitively are *irrelevant* to officer status. First, the Court noted that it is irrelevant to officer status which specific compliance enforcement powers an official holds. Second, the particular level of deference that an agency awards to ALJ factfinding generally is irrelevant to the Article II analysis.[127]

One additional insight that the *Lucia* opinion provides is emphasis, or at least reaffirmation, of the Article II officer requirement that an official's responsibilities be "continuing."[128] When courts have evaluated officer status in recent years, they have tended to focus more on the level of importance, or significance, of an official's duties rather than highlighting the ongoing duty aspect of officer status emphasized in the 19th-century opinions. The Court here turned attention back to the 19th-century century *Germaine* language that centrally emphasized this requirement. It is unclear exactly why the *Lucia* majority decided to shine a spotlight on the continuing nature of officer status front and center in this opinion since that element was not contested here. Perhaps the Court's emphasis will lay the basis for the Court to impose greater limits on the officer category going forward, an approach that could have special significance as more and more government duties are privatized.[129] Or, perhaps the Court was just trying to clean up its characterization of *Germaine* in *Free Enterprise Fund* and restore the understanding of *Germaine* as a case about workers-for-hire rather than the civil service.

The Court in the end, however, left many follow-on questions unaddressed. First, how many governmental positions fall within its reach?

---

[127] See *id.* at 2054–55.

[128] See *id.* at 2051.

[129] See generally Dep't of Trans. v. Ass'n of Amer. Railroads, 135 S. Ct. 1225, 1234–40 (Alito, J., concurring) ("[O]ne way the Government can regulate without accountability is by passing off a Government operation as an independent private concern.").

The Court was careful not to say, explaining that "maybe one day we will see a need to refine or enhance the test *Buckley* set out so concisely. But that day is not this one."[130] Despite the very factbound nature of the Court's judgment, ALJs who preside over "adversarial hearings"[131] in agencies other than the SEC likely have duties that are sufficiently indistinguishable from the *Lucia* ALJ that they should now be considered officers. But the question whether adjudicators in nonadversarial or informal proceedings must be treated as officers as a constitutional matter may very well be the subject of future litigation.

In addition to declining to update the *Buckley* test, the Court also declined to definitively resolve what sorts of remedies should be available in instances in which previous hearings had been held by improperly appointed ALJs. The majority opinion did specify that on remand in this specific litigation, Mr. Lucia must receive a "new hearing before a properly appointed official" who is *someone other than* the ALJ who previously heard his case.[132] But the Court said the presence of a new decisionmaker may not always be required, if, for example, a substitute decisionmaker is unavailable. That complication could occur if "the Appointments Clause problem [were to be] with the Commission itself, so that there is no substitute decisionmaker," in which case "the rule of necessity would presumably kick in and allow the Commission to do the rehearing." Finally, the Court also said it saw "no reason to address" whether the SEC's "order 'ratif[ying]' the prior appointments of its ALJs" was constitutionally adequate. The Court noted that the SEC could find ways around reliance on the ratification order either by "decid[ing] to conduct Lucia's rehearing itself" or "assign[ing] the hearing to an ALJ who has received a constitutional appointment independent of the ratification."[133]

B. *The Separate Writings and the Dissent*

Justice Clarence Thomas, joined by Justice Neil Gorsuch, joined the Court's opinion in full but also wrote separately in concurrence.

---

130 Lucia, 138 S. Ct. at 2052.

131 Cf. *id.* at 2048 (comparing the SEC ALJs to STJs "in conducting adversarial inquiries").

132 *Id.* at 2055 & n.5 (internal quotations omitted).

133 *Id.* at 2055 & n.6.

They observed the challenges of applying the majority's factbound opinion moving forward.[134] Instead they would have further clarified the proper definition of "officer" by applying the term's original public meaning, which they described as "encompass[ing] all federal civil officials with responsibility for an ongoing statutory duty." This included even those officers with "ministerial statutory duties" like recordkeepers and clerks. Justices Thomas and Gorsuch emphasized the Appointments Clause's attempt to "strike[] a balance between efficiency and accountability" with its inferior officer appointment mechanism. The Article II clause "maintains clear lines of accountability—encouraging good appointments and giving the public someone to blame for bad ones" by "specifying only a limited number of actors who can appoint inferior officers without Senate confirmation."[135]

Justice Breyer joined the majority only in the judgment. Instead of finding that the *Lucia* ALJ was unlawfully appointed as a *constitutional* matter, he would have found that the SEC's ALJ appointments constituted a *statutory* violation.[136] He noted that the Administrative Procedure Act requires *agencies* to appoint their ALJs—and the commission did not satisfy that mandate here, leaving ALJ appointments up to staff. Justice Breyer explicitly declined to decide the constitutional "officer" status of ALJs out of concern that the ALJs' Article II status may open up their "statutory 'for cause' removal protections" to constitutional concerns.

Justice Sotomayor dissented, joined by Justice Ruth Bader Ginsburg.[137] She noted that the Court's "significant authority" jurisprudence "offers little guidance on who qualifies as an 'Officer of the United States.'" She would try to offer further clarity by holding "that one requisite component of 'significant authority' is the ability to make final, binding decisions on behalf of the Government." This test would "[c]onfirm[] that final decisionmaking authority is

---

[134] See *id.* at 2056 (Thomas, J., concurring) ("Moving forward, . . . this Court will not be able to decide every Appointments Clause case by comparing it to *Freytag*.").

[135] *Id.* at 2055–56 (internal quotations omitted).

[136] See *id.* at 2057–58 (Breyer, J., concurring in the judgment in part and dissenting in part). See also Jennifer Nou, The SEC's Improper Subdelegation (Statutory, not Constitutional), 36 Yale J. on Reg.: Notice & Comment, Apr. 11, 2018, http://yalejreg.com/nc/the-secs-improper-subdelegation-statutory-not-constitutional.

[137] *Lucia*, 138 S. Ct. at 2064–67 (Sotomayor, J., dissenting).

a prerequisite to officer status" and that any official who merely "investigates, advises, or recommends" is not an Article II "officer."

IV. Conclusion: The Road Ahead

Despite *Lucia*'s narrowness, it took only a few weeks for tremors to be felt within the agency adjudication system. On July 10, the president issued an executive order to implement *Lucia*.[138] But the order, as is the president's prerogative in oversight of the executive branch, extends beyond the technical four corners of the *Lucia* ruling.

The parties in *Lucia* challenged only the role of SEC staff in making the final appointment of ALJs; they had not challenged the initial evaluation of ALJ candidates through statutory and regulatory competitive service, merit-based procedures.[139] Nonetheless, the executive order notes "doubt regarding the constitutionality" of using "competitive examination and competitive service selection procedures" to limit the discretion of agency heads who must appoint ALJs under Article II in light of *Lucia*.[140] Therefore, the order places "the position of ALJ in the excepted service" to "mitigate concerns about undue limitations on the selection of ALJs, reduce the likelihood of successful Appointments Clause challenges, and forestall litigation in which such concerns have been or might be raised." The executive order preserves merit-based consideration of ALJ candidates in that it calls on agencies to assess "critical qualities" and

[138] See generally Exec. Order No. 13,843, 83 Fed. Reg. 32,755 (July 10, 2018), https://bit.ly/2AV9CHX.

[139] See Lucia, 138 S. Ct. at 2051 (addressing only the constitutionality of the final ALJ selection by staff). As background, ALJs at agencies like the SEC typically have undergone competitive service selection to enter the ALJ system and then received an initial appointment at the Social Security Administration (SSA), which has hundreds of ALJs and is often the starting point for newly hired ALJs. Often ALJs at agencies like the SEC have been transferred to their current agency from this initial SSA assignment. Cf. Emily Bremer, A Shared Power to Appoint ALJs?, 36 Yale J. on Reg.: Notice & Comment, (Apr. 4, 2018), http://yalejreg.com/nc/a-shared-power-to-appoint-aljs/.

[140] See Exec. Order, *supra* note 138, at 32,755 ("Regardless of whether [competitive service selection] procedures would violate the Appointments Clause as applied to certain ALJs, there are sound policy reasons to take steps to eliminate doubt regarding the constitutionality of th[is] method of appointing officials who discharge such significant duties and exercise such significant discretion."). See also Mascott, *supra* note 110, at 33-34 (questioning the extent to which "competitive-based selection of ALJs may remain permissible").

hire ALJs based on considerations "such as work ethic, judgment, and ability to meet the particular needs of the agency" but leaves evaluation of those criteria more within the discretion of the agencies themselves. [141]

In addition, the executive order touches on tenure protections for ALJs. Action by Congress is necessary to comprehensively address ALJ removal issues as ALJ tenure protections are statutory. But, outside of what is "required by statute," the executive order provides that "Civil Service Rules and Regulations shall not apply" to ALJ removals, to Schedule A, C, or D positions, or to "positions excepted from the competitive service by statute."[142]

Litigants and lower courts have already begun incorporating lessons from *Lucia* as well. For example, on July 31, 2018, the U.S. Court of Appeals for the Sixth Circuit vacated penalties imposed by the Federal Mine Safety and Health Review Commission that had initially been imposed by an ALJ not appointed as an "inferior officer."[143] Because the commission's ALJs have responsibilities "commensurate with their SEC counterparts," the court concluded that they are "inferior officers" who had been improperly hired by the commission's chief ALJ.[144] And then in litigation with a more attenuated connection to *Lucia*, a military detainee challenged the structural constitutionality of his military commission proceeding on Appointments Clause grounds, contending that the "convening authority who purported to refer Appellee's case for trial . . . was never appointed in the manner required by the Appointments Clause."[145]

Over the next few months it will be intriguing to watch for the potential torrent of litigation filed to address the numerous questions the Court left open in *Lucia*. By answering only the precise question

---

[141] Exec. Order, *supra* note 138, at 32,755.

[142] See *id.* at 32,756 (establishing ALJs as Schedule E positions); *id.* at 32,757.

[143] Jones Brothers, Inc. v. Secretary of Labor, No. 17-3483, 2018 WL 3629059, at *2 (6th Cir. July 31, 2018).

[144] See *id.* at *5, *7.

[145] See Appellee's Combined Motion for Leave to File and Motion to Dismiss Because the Military Commission Lacked Subject-Matter Jurisdiction at 2–3, United States v. Al-Rahim Hussein Al-Nashiri, No. 18-002 (U.S. Ct. of Military Comm'n Rev. July 13, 2018), https://www.justsecurity.org/wp-content/uploads/2018/07/Appellees-Corrected-MTD-Lack-of-SMJ.pdf (citing *Lucia*).

needed to resolve the specific Appointments Clause issue in *Lucia*, the Court in a sense moved itself out of the central role in the interpretation and application of Appointments Clause restraints. The executive branch has already stepped in to play its role in guiding practice within administrative agencies and in adapting regulations to the executive's understanding of the contours of the clause. Perhaps Congress will follow suit and take up the mantle of more comprehensive civil-service reform.

Looking Ahead: October Term 2018

Erin E. Murphy[*]

Ordinarily after a term of the magnitude of October Term (OT) 2017, there isn't all that much of consequence to say about the term ahead, as blockbuster terms tend to be followed by quiet ones. And in one sense, that certainly looks to be true this year. Although the Supreme Court has 38 cases on its docket before the new term starts (as compared to 29 at this point last year), you have to squint pretty hard to come up with even one as headline-grabbing as the more than half dozen genuine blockbusters the Court decided last year. But, of course, last term also ended with one of the most potentially significant developments in recent years for the future of the Court: the retirement of Justice Anthony Kennedy. While any change in its makeup inevitably has a profound impact on the Court, this one will be no butterfly effect. Justice Kennedy has been the crucial swing vote on some of the biggest issues of the day for (at least) the past decade, including a few that the Court declined to resolve last term.

If you're looking for predictions about how Justice Kennedy's replacement will affect the Court, or an evaluation of Judge Brett Kavanaugh's qualifications or jurisprudential philosophy, this is not the place to find them. Instead, I will offer only this humble observation: It's going to take a heck of a lot more than one term to answer that question. That said, although the cases the Court has granted so far for OT 2018 may not reach the epic levels of the cases it confronted in OT 2017, there are at least a few that have the potential to offer us invaluable insight into how the Court's newest member will approach cross-cutting issues such as *stare decisis*, agency deference, separation of powers, and federalism. While the

* Erin E. Murphy is a partner in the Washington office of Kirkland & Ellis, LLP, specializing in Supreme Court and appellate litigation. She has argued four cases before the Supreme Court and briefed dozens more. The author wishes to thank Nicholas M. Gallagher for his invaluable contributions to this article. The views expressed are solely those of the author, not of Kirkland & Ellis or its clients.

rest of the world fixated on the future of *Roe v. Wade*, the Court quietly granted certiorari to decide whether to overrule three of its lesser-known—at least beyond nerdy Court-watcher circles—precedents. And while doomsayers prognosticate (or enthusiasts anticipate) the imminent resurrection of *Lochner*, the Court has its eyes set on a very different early 20th century doctrine that has fallen into desuetude.

Notably, many of the bigger cases the Court is set to consider this coming term do not necessarily divide neatly along ideological lines. One of the precedents the Court will consider whether to overrule was recently called into question by the strange bedfellows of Justices Clarence Thomas and Ruth Bader Ginsburg. Another has produced the interesting dynamic over the years where the Court's more conservative members push to open federal courts to constitutional claims that some of its more liberal members have been content to leave to the state courts. And the Court will consider whether to revive the long-dormant nondelegation doctrine, typically championed by more conservative circles, in the context of a challenge to federal sex offender registration rules, hardly a conservative cause du jour.

As of this writing, we know only about half of the cases the Court will consider next term. By term's end, the Court could once again be facing partisan gerrymandering, the intersection between LGBT rights and religious liberty, the Second Amendment, and any number of the various challenges to the Trump administration that are working their way through the lower courts. And much may be gleaned simply from watching what the Court does and does not agree to take, as that itself may suggest how strong the forces of instrumentalism remain. In short, we may not be in for another blockbuster term at this point, but if we watch carefully, we may learn quite a bit in the year to come about what the Court's latest changes in membership portend.

Chevron

The Court will kick things off on its First Monday with *Weyerhaeuser Company v. U.S. Fish and Wildlife Service*, otherwise know as the "dusky gopher frog" case. The dusky gopher frog is an endangered species that used to inhabit Mississippi, Alabama, and Louisiana, but is now found only in Mississippi. Its claim to fame appears to be that, "[i]f you pick up a gopher frog and hold it, the frog will play dead and even cover its eyes; if you hold the frog long enough, it will pe[e]k at you and then pretend to be dead again."[1] Charming or creepy? You decide. In 2012, the Fish and Wildlife Service (FWS) decided to designate 1,544 acres of privately owned property in Louisiana "critical habitat" for the frog—even though no dusky gopher frog has been spotted there for more than half a century. In fact, the property concededly lacks two of the three features that, by FWS's own telling, are essential to the frog's survival, which presumably explains why there are no dusky gopher frogs to be found there these days. Nonetheless, FWS forged ahead with the designation, even though it acknowledged that it would cost the landowners up to $34 million in lost development value.

According to the landowners, the absence of any dusky gopher frogs on their property poses a considerable problem for the agency under the text of the Endangered Species Act. The act defines "critical habitat" as areas "occupied by the species," or areas that are unoccupied but "essential for the conservation of the species."[2] In the landowners' view (embraced by Judge Priscilla Owen in her dissent from the panel decision below), "an area cannot be 'essential for the conservation of the species' if it is uninhabitable by the species and there is no reasonable probability that it will become habitable by the species."[3] The panel majority disagreed, concluding that the agency's conclusion that the property is "essential" to the conservation of the dusky gopher frog is entitled to *Chevron* deference. The panel also concluded that the agency's decision not to exclude the property from its designation on economic impact grounds—that is, under its power to "tak[e] into consideration the economic impact" of a critical habitat designation and exclude an area if "the benefits of such exclusion outweigh the benefits of" designation[4]—was not reviewable at all. After the full court denied rehearing en banc by a narrow 8-6 margin, with Judge Edith Jones writing for all six dissenters, the Supreme Court agreed to take up the case.

While *Weyerhaeuser* is at one level a run-of-the-mill statutory interpretation case, these days there is always more at stake when agency

[1] Markle Interests, L.L.C. v. U.S. Fish & Wildlife Serv., 827 F.3d 452, 458 n.2 (5th Cir. 2016).

[2] 16 U.S.C. § 1532(5)(A)(i)–(ii).

[3] Markle, 827 F.3d at 486 (Owen, J., dissenting).

[4] 16 U.S.C. § 1533(b)(2).

deference is involved given the ever-increasing criticism some of the justices have heaped upon *Chevron*. The chief justice warned in *City of Arlington v. FCC* that "the danger posed by the growing power of the administrative state cannot be dismissed."[5] Justice Thomas lamented in *Michigan v. EPA* that "*Chevron* deference precludes judges from exercising [independent] judgment, forcing them to abandon what they believe is the best reading of an ambiguous statute in favor of an agency's construction."[6] And then-Judge Neil Gorsuch openly suggested in his now-famous concurrence in *Gutierrez-Brizuela v. Lynch* that *Chevron* should be reconsidered, characterizing the doctrine as "permit[ting] executive bureaucracies to swallow huge amounts of core judicial and legislative power and concentrate federal power in a way that seems more than a little difficult to square with the Constitution of the framers' design."[7] Suffice it to say, if the justices see an opportunity to curtail agency deference, at least some of them are likely to take it.

This case has opportunities galore. The first question in the case squarely implicates the dividing line between *Chevron* step one and step two, which is an appealing avenue by which those justices who are not ready to throw *Chevron* out entirely can chip away at it. After all, the easiest way to cut back on *Chevron* deference is to make it harder to demonstrate that a statute is ambiguous, and thus trigger deference. Here, the landowners and their *amici* have offered the Court any number of ways to do so, invoking statutory context, legislative history, constitutional avoidance, the so-called "major questions" canon, and more. The second question, whether the agency's economic impact determination is subject to judicial review, turns on whether it qualifies under the Administrative Procedure Act as "agency action . . . committed to agency discretion by law."[8] Unsurprisingly, here too the landowners and their *amici* have encouraged the Court to embrace a narrow reading that would make this provision universally harder for agencies to invoke. For those with a keen interest in the future of the administrative state—or the future of the dusky gopher frog—this is definitely a case worth watching.

[5] 569 U.S. 290, 315 (2013) (Roberts, C.J., dissenting).

[6] 135 S. Ct. 2699, 2712 (2015) (Thomas, J., concurring).

[7] 834 F.3d 1142, 1149 (10th Cir. 2016) (Gorsuch, J., concurring).

[8] 5 U.S.C. § 701(a)(2).

The Nondelegation Doctrine

As Cass Sunstein famously quipped, the nondelegation doctrine "has had one good year, and 211 bad ones (and counting)."[9] That good year was 1935—the year of *A.L.A. Schechter Poultry Corporation v. United States*[10] and *Panama Refining Company v. Ryan*.[11] Since then, the Supreme Court has largely declined to enforce, and indeed steadily undermined, the notion that the Constitution imposes meaningful limits on what Congress may delegate to the executive branch. Even the rise of modern originalist jurisprudence has not reversed this trend. It was Justice Antonin Scalia, after all, who wrote the majority opinion in *Whitman v. American Trucking Associations*,[12] which gave us the "intelligible principle" rule, under which a principle has to be about as intelligible as Dadaist art to pass constitutional muster. But the Court surprised many this spring by agreeing to take up a splitless nondelegation question on which it had denied certiorari more than a dozen times over the past decade. The Court probably didn't take that step just to put the final nail in the nondelegation doctrine's coffin.

Gundy v. United States is certainly not the most obvious candidate for the revitalization of this long-dormant doctrine. The nondelegation doctrine is often championed by conservatives as a potential mechanism for placing meaningful constraints on the administrative state. The two cases in which it was successfully invoked challenged New Deal-era economic regulations—and nondelegation claims are often pressed (albeit often unsuccessfully) in cases challenging exceedingly broad delegations of law-making power to the legion of federal agencies tasked with regulating everything that can even conceivably be said to implicate commerce. *Gundy* arises in a very different context, and one perhaps a bit less appealing to the doctrine's champions: the Sex Offender Registration and Notification Act, better known as SORNA.

If ever there were an unconstitutional delegation of law-making power to the executive branch, SORNA would seem to be it. Through SORNA, Congress created a new federal registration requirement

---

[9] Cass R. Sunstein, Nondelegation Canons, 67 U. Chi. L. Rev. 315, 322 (2000).

[10] 295 U.S. 495 (1935).

[11] 293 U.S. 388 (1935).

[12] 531 U.S. 457 (2001).

for sex offenders, but then declined to resolve the seemingly critical question of whether this new requirement should apply to individuals who were convicted of a sex offense before SORNA was enacted. Instead, Congress left it to the attorney general "to specify the applicability of [its] requirements . . . to sex offenders convicted before the enactment of this chapter"—and provided exactly zero guidance as to how he should go about doing so.[13] To be sure, an argument could be made that the statute was not intended to give the attorney general discretion to decide *whether* to apply its requirements retroactively, but instead was intended to give discretion only to determine *how* to do so (for example, how quickly and how far back). But the government made exactly that argument six years ago in *Reynolds v. United States*, the statutory interpretation precursor to *Gundy*, only to have it rejected by a lopsided majority of the Court as inconsistent with the text of the statute.[14] In a dissent joined by Justice Ginsburg, the ever-prescient Justice Scalia observed, "it is not entirely clear to me that Congress can constitutionally leave it to the Attorney General to decide—with no statutory standard whatever governing his discretion—whether a criminal statute will or will not apply to certain individuals."[15] Apparently, it is not entirely clear to at least four of the Court's current members either.

Gundy will be a very interesting case to watch. It certainly has the potential to be resolved on narrow grounds, as the power to extend criminal prohibitions is so significant, and the absence of any principle to guide the exercise of that power so stark, that the Court arguably need do nothing more than confirm the nondelegation doctrine's existence to conclude that SORNA violates it. Of course, even that would be consequential when dealing with a doctrine that has not been enforced by the Court since before most of the current justices were born. But there are undoubtedly at least a few justices who may be interested in doing something more.

Most notably, then—Judge Gorsuch made a powerful argument—in a case involving another provision of SORNA, proving that he has no qualms about context—that the nondelegation doctrine is an essential

---

[13] 34 U.S.C. § 20913(d).

[14] 565 U.S. 432 (2012).

[15] *Id.* at 450 (Scalia, J., dissenting).

structural safeguard of individual liberty.[16] As he put it, "[i]f the separation of powers means anything, it must mean that the prosecutor isn't allowed to define the crimes he gets to enforce."[17] Gorsuch also invoked the nondelegation doctrine in *Gutierrez-Brizuela* in support of his argument that *Chevron* and *Brand X* "seem[] more than a little difficult to square with the Constitution of the framers' design."[18] Suffice it to say, there is far more at stake in *Gundy* than SORNA. Of course, the justices understand that as well as the rest of us, which is precisely why the case has the potential to produce a classic Roberts Court narrow decision garnering broad consensus. That said, the opportunity to not only revive, but add real teeth to the nondelegation doctrine may prove more than some members of the Court can pass up.

The Takings Clause

At long last, the Supreme Court has granted certiorari to decide whether to overrule "the portion of *Williamson County Regional Planning Commission v. Hamilton Bank* that requires property owners to exhaust state court remedies to ripen federal takings claims."[19] Okay, maybe that's not quite as exciting to those of you who don't spend a lot of time working on takings cases, but Chief Justice William Rehnquist might have been pretty jazzed. In one of his very last opinions, he offered the characteristically humble admission that, while he had joined *Williamson County*, "further reflection and experience [led him] to think that [its] justifications . . . are suspect, while its impact on takings plaintiffs is dramatic."[20] Indeed. *Williamson County*'s fox-guarding-the-henhouse exhaustion requirement has proven among the more maddening of obstacles to vindicating a core constitutional right.

[16] United States v. Nichols, 784 F.3d 666, 675 (10th Cir. 2014) (Gorsuch, J., dissenting from denial of reh'g en banc).

[17] *Id.*

[18] Gutierrez-Brizuela v. Lynch, 834 F.3d 1142, 1149 (2016) (Gorsuch, J., concurring). In *Brand X*, the Supreme Court ruled that *Chevron* deference trumps lower-court precedents unless that court had held that the statute in question was "unambiguous" for *Chevron* purposes. Nat'l Cable & Telecomm. Ass'n v. Brand X Internet Svcs., 545 U.S. 967 (2005).

[19] Petition for Writ of Certiorari at i, Knick v. Township of Scott, No. 17-647 (U.S. filed Oct. 31, 2017).

[20] San Remo Hotel, LP v. City and County of San Francisco, 545 U.S. 323, 352 (2005) (Rehnquist, C.J., concurring).

Knick v. Township of Scott is not exactly your ordinary takings fare. You may be surprised to learn that it remains legal in most states to bury deceased loved ones in your backyard. Pennsylvania is one of them, and the practice of "backyard burials" apparently goes back several centuries in rural western-Pennsylvania Scott Township. About 10 year ago, the township claims to have discovered an ancient burial ground on Rose Mary Knick's 90-acre farmland. The township then enacted an ordinance declaring that all cemeteries must be kept open to the public during daylight hours, and declared Knick in violation when she declined to open her heretofore-private property to the public. Knick sued the township in state court, arguing that this state-mandated public easement over her private property was an unconstitutional taking. But after the township withdrew the notice of violation and stayed enforcement of the ordinance as to Knick, the state court refused to resolve her claim unless and until the township initiated a civil enforcement action against her.

Knick then turned to the federal courts, only to be rebuffed by the *Williamson County* rule. Under that 1985 decision, before bringing a federal takings claim in federal court, a property owner not only must demonstrate that the state has made a final decision to take her property, but also must seek (and be denied) just compensation in state court. Because the state court wouldn't allow Knick to litigate her takings claim until the township brings an enforcement action, the federal courts dismissed her effort to vindicate her property rights as unripe, concluding that she must first go seek just compensation for any taking in state court.

Knick is a classic illustration of how the *Williamson County* rule "all but guarantees that claimants will be unable to utilize the federal courts to enforce the Fifth Amendment's just compensation guarantee."[21] On the one hand, a federal court typically won't hear a takings claim if it has not been exhausted in state court. On the other hand, once a state court has considered and rejected the takings claim, the property owner is precluded from relitigating the claim in federal court. Indeed, that is exactly what the Court held in *San Remo Hotel, LP v. City and County of San Francisco*, prompting Chief Justice Rehnquist (joined by Justices Sandra Day O'Connor, Anthony Kennedy, and Thomas) to suggest that maybe it was time to give *Williamson County* another look.[22] Making matters worse, some state governments and

---

[21] *Id.* at 351.

[22] *Id.* at 348–52 (2005) (Rehnquist, C.J., concurring).

officials have even managed to remove state court takings claims to federal court, only to then get them dismissed by the federal court for failure to exhaust in state court. All of this led Justice Thomas (joined by Justice Kennedy) to opine a couple of terms ago that the *Williamson County* rule has "downgraded the protection afforded by the Takings Clause to second-class status."[23] (More on second-class rights to come.)

Odds are, the *Williamson County* rule's days are numbered. While the Court has occasionally granted certiorari in recent years to decide whether to overrule one of its precedents, only to befuddle Court-watchers with an apparent change of heart,[24] this rule has built up enough animosity over the years that it seems an unlikely candidate for begrudging reaffirmation. Indeed, perhaps because state courts have unsurprisingly proven less than entirely receptive to takings claims against the state, the Court has already taken to "attempt[ing] to ameliorate the effects of" the *Williamson County* rule by "recast[ing]" it "as a 'prudential' rather than jurisdictional requirement," which itself is a telling sign that several justices probably would not lament its demise.[25] The Court also declined to take up a second question presented in *Knick* that involved whether to narrow the rule, which does not bode well for its survival. So for those of us who often find ourselves frustrated by the dearth of federal court cases on key takings issues, there may finally be some light at the end of the tunnel.

State Sovereign Immunity

When the Supreme Court grants a case only to resolve it on narrow grounds that necessitate a remand, it's not uncommon for the case to find its way back a second time. Last year we saw the return of *Encino Motorcars, LLC v. Navarro,* and this year we will see the return of *Sturgeon v. Frost* (otherwise known as the Alaska hovercraft case). But *Franchise Tax Board of California v. Hyatt* will receive the rare distinction this term of making its third appearance before the Supreme Court.

This case arises out of a long-running tax dispute between Gilbert Hyatt and California's Franchise Tax Board. Hyatt lived in California

---

[23] Arrigoni Enterprises, LLC v. Town of Durham, 136 S. Ct. 1409, 1411 (2016) (Thomas, J., dissenting from denial of cert.).

[24] See, e.g., Kimble v. Marvel Enterprises, Inc., 135 S. Ct. 2501 (2015).

[25] Arrigoni Enterprises, 136 U.S. at 1411.

for 23 years, but after earning hundreds of millions of taxable dollars there, he filed a state tax return in 1992 claiming that he had moved to Nevada—a state that conveniently has no income tax. The Tax Board got wind that Hyatt may not actually have moved when he said he did, and it proceeded to undertake a rather comprehensive audit that (allegedly) involved, among other things, "peer[ing] through Hyatt's windows" and "rummag[ing] around in his garbage."[26] After the audit confirmed its suspicions, the Tax Board informed Hyatt that he owed the state $10 million in taxes, interest, and penalties. Hyatt responded not only by protesting the audit through administrative channels, but by suing the Tax Board, claiming that it committed various torts, including invasion of privacy, intentional infliction of emotional distress, and fraud, during the course of its audit. And he decided to bring his lawsuit in Nevada state court. The Tax Board tried to invoke sovereign immunity but was precluded from doing so by *Nevada v. Hall*, a 1979 case in which the Supreme Court held that states do not have sovereign immunity in the courts of other states.[27]

Hyatt made its first trip to the Supreme Court back in 2003, when a unanimous Court held that the Full Faith and Credit Clause did not require the Nevada courts to abide by a California statute that gives the Tax Board immunity from suit in the California courts.[28] The case then went back down to the state court, where, given the rare opportunity to stick it to tax collectors (and out-of-state tax collectors, no less), a Nevada jury awarded Hyatt a staggering $388 million in compensatory and punitive damages, to which the trial court judge tacked on $102 million in interest. The Nevada Supreme Court ultimately reversed the $52 million judgment on the invasion of privacy claim, but affirmed the $1 million judgment on the fraud claim, and remanded for a new trial on the emotional distress claim (on which the jury had awarded $85 million) after finding various evidentiary errors. The court also threw out the $250 million punitive damages award and took punitives off the table on remand.

At that point, the U.S. Supreme Court intervened again, this time granting certiorari to decide whether to overrule *Nevada v. Hall*, or, short of that, to decide whether California was at least entitled to

---

[26] Franchise Tax Bd. of Cal. v. Hyatt ("Hyatt II"), 136 S. Ct. 1277, 1284 (2016) (Roberts, C.J., dissenting).

[27] 440 U.S. 410 (1979).

[28] Hyatt v. Franchise Tax Bd., 538 U.S. 488 (2003).

the same immunities and protections in Nevada court that Nevada has extended to its *own* state entities.[29] After Justice Scalia's death left the Court with only eight members, it divided equally on the *Nevada v. Hall* question. But in a decision that smacked of compromise, a six-justice majority held that the Tax Board was at least entitled to invoke the $50,000 damages cap that would apply in a tort claim against a Nevada state entity.[30] On remand, the Nevada Supreme Court reduced the fraud judgment to $50,000. But it reversed course on the emotional distress claim, now claiming that the same evidentiary errors that previously led it to grant a new trial were actually harmless, and so awarded Hyatt $50,000 on that claim as well.

That brings us to *Hyatt III*, in which the Court has agreed once again to consider whether to overrule *Nevada v. Hall*, this time hopefully with a majority to resolve that question. Part of what makes that question such an interesting one is that both parties claim to be trying to vindicate state sovereignty. According to the Tax Board, allowing a state to be haled in to the courts of another state without its permission is an affront to the sovereignty to which states are entitled. Hyatt, on the other hand, maintains that it would be an affront to state sovereignty to demand that states grant immunity to their sister states, as sovereigns traditionally have the right to decide for themselves whether to grant immunity to other sovereigns in their courts. *Hyatt* also has the wonderful irony, pointed out by Justice Ginsburg in the last go-around,[31] of being the mirror image of *Hall*, as California itself was the state that helped convince the *Hall* Court that *Nevada* should be subject to suit in *California* state court. As of this writing, the Court is down a member once again, and given the outcome in *Hyatt II*, odds are it is a member whose vote will be necessary to reach a majority. But hopefully we will have a ninth justice soon enough to avoid the need for a *Hyatt IV*.

The Double Jeopardy Clause

Hyatt isn't the only case on the Court's docket this term involving state sovereignty—or the only such case in which *stare decisis* will feature. After 11 relists, the Court finally decided on its last

[29] The firm at which the author was employed at the time, Bancroft PLLC, represented the Tax Board in Hyatt II.

[30] Hyatt II, 136 S. Ct. at 1281–83.

[31] Transcript of Oral Arg. at 15, Hyatt II, 136 S. Ct. 1277 (No. 14-1175).

June orders list to grant certiorari in *Gamble v. United States* to decide whether to overrule the "separate sovereigns" (a.k.a. "dual sovereigns") exception to the Double Jeopardy Clause.

The Double Jeopardy Clause provides that "No person shall . . . be subject for the same offence to be twice put in jeopardy of life or limb."[32] While it's hard to see why the identity of the prosecutor makes a difference under that language, the Supreme Court has long held that the Double Jeopardy Clause does not prohibit the federal government and a state from prosecuting someone for the same crime. This so-called "separate sovereigns" exception is (at least according to Gamble) a bit of an anachronism. It originated at a time when the Court had held that the Double Jeopardy Clause did not apply to the states, and one of the Court's reasons for crafting the exception was its view that "[t]he Fifth Amendment . . . applies only to proceedings by the Federal Government."[33] Of course, that is no longer the case; the Court concluded decades ago that the Fourteenth Amendment incorporates the Double Jeopardy Clause against the states.[34] While that considerably undermined at least one of the justifications on which the Court had relied in crafting the separate-sovereigns exception, the Court has continued to adhere to its pre-incorporation precedents holding that successive state and federal prosecutions for the same crime do not offend the Double Jeopardy Clause, even as it cabined the scope of the separate-sovereigns doctrine in other contexts.[35] And the Court has denied review in numerous cases over the years that asked whether the separate-sovereigns exception should be overruled.

The separate-sovereigns doctrine found its way back to the Court's collective attention a few terms ago, when the Court was asked to decide whether Puerto Rico qualifies as a separate sovereign for purpose of the exception.[36] Puerto Rico couldn't convince

[32] U.S. Const., amend. V.

[33] Abbate v. United States, 359 U.S. 187, 194 (1959); see also Bartkus v. Illinois, 359 U.S. 121 (1959).

[34] See Benton v. Maryland, 395 U.S. 784, 787 (1969).

[35] See, e.g., Elkins v. United States, 364 U.S. 206 (1960) (overruling pre-incorporation precedent allowing federal officers to use evidence unlawfully obtained by state officers); Murphy v. Waterfront Comm'n, 378 U.S. 52 (1964) (overruling pre-incorporation precedent holding that one sovereign could use testimony unlawfully compelled by another).

[36] See Puerto Rico v. Sanchez Valle, 136 S. Ct. 1863 (2016).

the Court that it was entitled to this dignity, but the case did lead a few justices to question whether the exception even makes sense: The case prompted a concurrence from the strange bedfellows of Justices Ginsburg and Thomas, suggesting that the separate-sovereigns doctrine is inconsistent with the Double Jeopardy Clause and "bears fresh examination in an appropriate case."[37]

Terrance Gamble decided to take them up on the invitation. About a decade ago, Gamble was convicted of second-degree robbery, leaving him barred under both federal and state law from possessing a firearm. About three years ago, Gamble was pulled over for a faulty taillight, and, lo and behold, the officer found marijuana and a handgun in his car. Alabama proceeded to prosecute Gamble for drug possession and for being a felon in possession of a firearm. In the meantime, the federal government decided to prosecute him too, for the same incident and the same crime of being a felon in possession in a firearm. And while the state court sentenced Gamble to only one year in prison for the firearm offense, the federal court issued a sentence nearly four times as long. Fortunately for Gamble, he was savvy enough to preserve a double jeopardy challenge to the successive federal prosecution in his conditional guilty plea. And after spending several months on the Relist Watch alongside a few other petitions raising the same issue, he surprised everyone by garnering a grant rather than a dissent from denial. So it seems that Justices Ginsburg and Thomas aren't the only ones interested in revisiting a precedent that Justice Hugo Black described as "an affront to human dignity and . . . dangerous to human freedom."[38]

The Excessive Fines Clause

Speaking of incorporation, the Supreme Court doesn't see a lot of incorporation questions these days. With the exception of the Second Amendment, which wasn't incorporated until 2010—because most courts refused to acknowledge the right's existence for the better part of a century—most of the protections found in the Bill of Rights were incorporated against the states 50 years ago. There are a still a handful of stragglers, however, and the Court will soon confront one of them: the Eighth Amendment's Excessive Fines Clause.

[37] *Id.* at 1877 (Ginsburg, J., concurring).
[38] Abbate, 359 U.S. at 203 (Black, J., dissenting).

Enter Tyson Timbs. In 2012, Timbs received about $73,000 in life insurance after his father died. Timbs decided to splurge on a $42,000 Land Rover, which he then used to drive around Indiana and Ohio spending the rest of the money on drugs. As he candidly put it, "[u]nfortunately, I had a whole bunch of money, which isn't a good idea for a drug addict to have."[39] When the money ran out, Timbs took to small-time dealing to supply his habit—including, unbeknownst to him, to several undercover officers. After a series of controlled buys, Timbs was arrested. He pled guilty and was sentenced to a year of house arrest, five years of probation, and $1,200 in fines and costs. But that wasn't enough for the state of Indiana. Invoking its civil asset forfeiture law, the state came for his Land Rover too.

Although the state trial court found that Timbs had used the Land Rover to transport drugs, it concluded that forcing him to forfeit a $42,000 Land Rover would violate the Excessive Fines Clause, as the value of the vehicle (even taking into account a bit of depreciation for the 15,000 miles Timbs put on it) was grossly disproportionate to a drug offense that carried a maximum fine of $10,000. The state appellate court agreed, but the Indiana Supreme Court reversed, concluding that since the U.S. Supreme Court has never clearly held that the Excessive Fines Clause is incorporated against the states, the Indiana courts need not do so of their own accord. In reaching that conclusion, the court added to a "surprising amount of confusion as to whether the Excessive Fines Clause has been incorporated against the states."[40] Timbs sought certiorari, and Indiana tried to convince the Court that the case is a poor vehicle, as it were, but the Court took the case anyway, vehicle and all. (Literally: The case is captioned *Tyson Timbs and a 2012 Land Rover LR2 v. State of Indiana.*)

While the Court's last foray into incorporation proved quite contentious, this case seems unlikely to do the same. For one thing, it doesn't involve that most divisive of enumerated rights, the Second Amendment. And at least so far, it doesn't look like Timbs is hoping to use his case to revitalize the Privileges or Immunities Clause. That said, the case does implicate the growing concerns that have been expressed about whether modern civil forfeiture law is truly consistent

[39] Adam Liptak, He Sold Drugs for $225. Indiana Took His $42,000 Land Rover, N.Y. Times, June 25, 2018, https://www.nytimes.com/2018/06/25/us/politics/supreme-court-civil-asset-forfeiture.html.

[40] Reyes v. N. Tex. Tollway Auth., 830 F. Supp. 2d 194, 206 (N.D. Tex. 2011).

with the Constitution. Just last year, Justice Thomas penned a statement respecting the denial of certiorari in which he called for the Court to take a harder look at civil forfeiture law, highlighting its self-dealing nature, its potential for corruption, and the "egregious and well-chronicled abuses" it has produced.[41] This case doesn't present the Due Process Clause challenge Justice Thomas invited, but it does present an opportunity for the Court to impose at least one meaningful constraint on what "has in recent decades become [a] widespread and highly profitable" tool for cash-strapped states.[42]

Retaliatory Arrest Redux

If you can't manage to squeeze a second (or, better yet, third) petition out of the same case, presenting a question the Court recently declined to resolve can often be the next best thing. This term, the Court will have its third chance in the past six years to decide whether the existence of probable cause defeats a First Amendment retaliatory arrest claim.

The Court first granted certiorari to consider that question in *Reichle v. Howard,* but it ended up reserving the question and resolving the case on qualified immunity grounds.[43] Last year, the Court took the issue up again in *Lozman v. City of Riviera Beach,* the second of its cases involving famed floating house owner Fane Lozman, who successfully persuaded the Court in his first trip up that his abode did not qualify as a "vessel" for purposes of federal admiralty jurisdiction.[44] Apparently the City of Riviera Beach isn't wild about this self-proclaimed "persistent and tenacious underdog";[45] it arrested him roughly 15 seconds after he stood up to talk about government corruption at a city council meeting, thus prompting his First Amendment retaliatory arrest claim. But the Court ultimately decided *Lozman II* on exceedingly narrow grounds, concluding that the absence of probable cause need not be proven to pursue a First

[41] Leonard v. Texas, 137 S. Ct. 847, 848 (2017) (Thomas, J., statement respecting denial of cert.).

[42] *Id.*

[43] 566 U.S. 658 (2012).

[44] Lozman v. City of Riviera Beach ("Lozman I"), 568 U.S. 115 (2013).

[45] Adam Liptak, A Persistent Gadfly Wins Again in the Supreme Court, N.Y. Times, June 18, 2018, https://www.nytimes.com/2018/06/18/us/politics/a-persistent-gadfly-wins-again-in-the-supreme-court.html.

Amendment retaliatory arrest claim "[o]n facts like these," and leaving for another day what rule applies "in other contexts."[46] In other words, the Court decided that Lozman could pursue his claim—and didn't decide much else.

Fortunately, the Court had a third case waiting in the wings: *Nieves v. Bartlett*. *Nieves* is one of two cases on the Court's docket this term arising out of Alaska. The first involves hovercrafts; this one, extreme snowmobiling. Every spring, thousands of extreme skiers, snowmobilers, and spectators gather in the Hoodoo Mountains of Alaska for Arctic Man, a multiday festival featuring a high-speed ski and snowmobile race. Shockingly, this annual ritual also features a fair amount of alcohol consumption. Four years ago, two Alaska state troopers patrolling Arctic Man became suspicious that there might be some underage drinking going on at a campsite party Russell Bartlett was attending. Bartlett, who had admittedly had at least a few beers at that point, declined their invitation to talk. And when one of the troopers tried to question a few of the underage attendees, he loudly informed the minors that the troopers had no right to question them without a parent or guardian present.

At that point, Bartlett and one of the troopers got into a physical struggle; who started it appears to be a matter of some dispute, but it ultimately ended with Bartlett being arrested for disorderly conduct and resisting arrest. He was released the next morning, and the state dropped the charges about a year later, at which point Bartlett decided to bring (among other things) a First Amendment retaliatory arrest claim. The district court rejected his claim after concluding that there was probable cause for the arrest, but the U.S. Court of Appeals for the Ninth Circuit reversed, holding that probable cause doesn't bar a First Amendment retaliatory arrest claim. So this case squarely presents the question *Lozman* reserved: whether the existence of probable cause bars a First Amendment retaliatory arrest claim "in other contexts."

While there's nothing unusual about a near-unanimous Roberts Court resolving a case on narrow, fact-specific grounds, it's at least a little bit unusual for the Court to duck a question in one case, only to agree to take it up again just a few weeks later. After all, the Court certainly didn't jump at the chance to take up *Arlene's Flowers*—the case

---

[46] Lozman v. City of Riviera Beach (Lozman II), 138 S. Ct. 1945, 1955 (2018).

of the Washington florist who didn't want to create floral arrangements for a same-sex wedding—after narrowly resolving *Masterpiece Cakeshop*—the case of the Colorado baker—or to revisit partisan gerrymandering in North Carolina after kicking last term's Wisconsin challenge on standing grounds. Here, the Court's actions may reflect some tension between the justices' views about the probable cause issue and their views about the particular facts of Lozman's case, which suggested that the city really had formulated a plan to arrest Lozman in retaliation for being a vocal critic of and frequent litigator against the city. Indeed, perhaps what the justices were really uncomfortable with in *Lozman II* was Lozman's concession that the city had probable cause to arrest him. If so, that would not bode well for Bartlett, as his case comes to the Court on a pretty solid factual finding that, whatever exactly may have happened at Arctic Man 2014, the troopers had probable cause to arrest him. That leaves his case looking a lot more like the concern Justice Thomas voiced in his dissent in *Lozman II* arguing that probable cause should indeed categorically bar a First Amendment retaliatory-arrest claim—namely, an effort "to harass officers with the kind of suits that common-law courts deemed intolerable."[47] That may not be an option a majority of the Court is anxious to preserve.

Waiting in the Wings

The Court has all manner of petitions awaiting its return from summer recess, and it undoubtedly will have the opportunity to consider several hot-button issues before term's end. Here are a few of the highlights on the horizon.

Title VII

The Court will soon consider a pair of petitions presenting a question that has generated considerable heated debated in the lower courts over the past two years—namely, whether Title VII's prohibition on employment discrimination "because of . . . sex" includes discrimination on the basis of sexual orientation. A divided en banc Seventh Circuit said yes last year in *Hively v. Ivy Tech Community College of Indiana*—a case in which Judge Richard Posner garnered some decidedly unhelpful-to-his-side-of-the-cause attention for his

---

[47] *Id.* at 1958 (Thomas, J., dissenting).

concurrence opining that he "would prefer to see us acknowledge openly that today we, who are judges rather than members of Congress, are imposing on a half-century-old statute a meaning of 'sex discrimination' that the Congress that enacted it would not have accepted."[48] This year, a divided en banc Second Circuit reached the same result in *Zarda v. Altitude Express, Inc.,*[49] while a panel of the Eleventh Circuit found itself bound by 1979 circuit precedent to reach the opposite conclusion in *Bostock v. Clayton County Board of Commissioners.*[50] Petitions have been filed in both *Zarda* and *Bostock,* so the Court will soon have the opportunity to decide whether to wade into this thicket now, or to allow the issue to continue to percolate in the lower courts. Most likely, whether the Court takes one of these cases will depend largely on whether it is convinced that the Second and Seventh Circuit decisions are wrong. If so, then the Court may be more willing to take up the issue now; if not, the Court may be more inclined to wait this hot-button issue out a bit longer and see whether en banc proceedings resolve any conflict between the most recent decisions in this area and decades-old precedent like the one relied upon in *Bostock.*

Partisan Gerrymandering

Although the Court certainly didn't leave anyone with the impression this past term that it was itching to get its hands on another partisan gerrymandering case, this is one area in which the choice will not be entirely up to the Court. While *Gill v. Whitford* (the Wisconsin case) was pending, a two-judge majority of a three-judge district court in the Middle District of North Carolina issued a sweeping decision invalidating North Carolina's congressional map on partisan gerrymandering grounds, holding that the map violated not only the Equal Protection Clause and the First Amendment, but two provisions of the Elections Clause to boot.[51] The Supreme Court promptly issued an emergency stay (over the dissent of Justices Ginsburg and Sonia Sotomayor), and the Court ultimately vacated the decision and

---

[48] 853 F.3d 339, 357 (7th Cir. 2017) (en banc) (Posner, J., concurring).

[49] 883 F.3d 100 (2d Cir. 2018).

[50] 723 F. App'x 964 (11th Cir. 2018) (per curiam).

[51] Common Cause v. Rucho, 279 F. Supp. 3d 587 (M.D.N.C. 2018). Full disclosure: In addition to representing the Wisconsin state legislature in Gill, the author's firm also represents the North Carolina legislative defendants in this litigation.

remanded the case for reconsideration in light of *Gill*. As of this writing, remand proceedings remained ongoing in the district court, but odds of the court reversing course and siding with the legislature are not high. And if the court does invalidate North Carolina's map once again, the Supreme Court will be all but guaranteed to hear the case, as it has mandatory jurisdiction over redistricting cases and is exceedingly unlikely to summarily affirm a decision invaliding the state's map given the open question of whether partisan gerrymandering claims are even justiciable. So when all is said and done, the Court may not have kicked this can very far down the road. But the Court did manage to kick it just far enough that the next case will be decided by a Court that doesn't include Justice Kennedy, who authorized the controlling decision declining to resolve the justiciability question in *Vieth v. Jubelirer*.[52] Perhaps next time around we will finally get the long-awaited resolution of whether—and if so under what circumstances and what standard—partisan gerrymandering claims are justiciable.

The Establishment Clause

The Court's Establishment Clause jurisprudence has been fractured for some time, in ways that go far beyond the role of any one justice. This term, the Court may have an opportunity to bring some clarity to this murky area in *American Humanist Association v. Maryland-National Capital Park and Planning Commission*.[53] *American Humanist* is the latest in a series of cases about cross-shaped-memorials. In 1925, the American Legion erected a Latin-cross shaped memorial to the 49 residents of Prince George's County, Maryland, who died fighting in World War I. Their names were inscribed upon a 9' × 2' plaque along the bottom, with the American Legion crest prominently in the middle of the cross and martial virtues inscribed in bronze along the base. Like so many of the World War I memorials that can be found throughout the country, the memorial's design was chosen to evoke the cross-shaped gravemarkers that carpeted the battlefields of World War I and were later erected in American cemeteries throughout Europe. The state took possession of the Bladensburg

---

[52] 541 U.S. 267, 306–17 (2004) (Kennedy, J., concurring).

[53] Another disclosure: The author's firm submitted an amicus brief on behalf of the Veterans of Foreign Wars of the United States and the National WWI Museum and Memorial in support of the petitioners in this case.

Peace Cross in 1961 for traffic control reasons, and the memorial now sits in the middle of a park filled with other such memorials. But not for long if the Fourth Circuit has its way, as a two-judge majority held that the memorial violates the Establishment Clause because the Latin cross "only holds value as a symbol of death and resurrection *because* of its affiliation with the crucifixion of Jesus Christ."[54] As the majority acknowledged, its decision calls into question the constitutionality of every government-owned cross-shaped memorial in the country—including two memorials that have long stood at Arlington National Cemetery. Combined with the six-judge dissent from rehearing en banc, that is certainly likely to attract the attention of at least a few justices when the companion petitions in this case come before the Court this fall.

The Second Amendment

Last, but (at least for this author) certainly not least, the Court will undoubtedly have at least one opportunity this term to consider whether the time has finally come to jump back into the Second Amendment fray. The Court hasn't taken a Second Amendment case since it decided *McDonald v. City of Chicago* back in 2010—or really *District of Columbia v. Heller* itself in 2008, because *McDonald* was a Fourteenth Amendment case—much to the dismay of some of the justices[55] (as well as to your author, who worked on several of the petitions the Court denied, and to the Cato Institute, which has filed amicus briefs supporting several Second Amendment petitions). The conventional wisdom is that there is a chink in the *Heller* and *McDonald* armor, a hypothesis that may soon be put to the test with the addition of a new justice. The Fifth Circuit recently denied en banc by the narrowest of margins in *Mance v. Sessions*, a case involving a challenge to federal restrictions on interstate handgun transfers, with seven judges dissenting and three—Judges

[54] Am. Humanist Ass'n v. Md.-Nat'l Capital Park & Planning Comm'n, 874 F.3d 195, 207 (4th Cir. 2018).

[55] See, e.g., Silvester v. Becerra, 138 S. Ct. 945 (2018) (Thomas, J., dissenting from denial of certiorari); Peruta v. California, 137 S. Ct. 1995 (2017) (Thomas, J., joined by Gorsuch, J., dissenting from denial of certiorari); Friedman v. Highland Park, 136 S. Ct. 447 (2015) (Thomas, J., joined by Scalia, J., dissenting from denial of certiorari); Jackson v. City and County of San Francisco, 135 S. Ct. 2799 (2015) (Thomas, J., joined by Scalia, J., dissenting from denial of cert.).

Jennifer Elrod, Don Willett, and James Ho—each authoring a dissent joined by all of their dissenting colleagues.[56] Four days later, Judge Diarmuid O'Scannlain authored his second 2-1 opinion holding that the Second Amendment protects a right to carry a handgun outside the home, this time invalidating Hawaii's open carry ban (the state also prohibits concealed carry, which *Peruta v. San Diego* allows it to do).[57] *Young v. Hawaii* will undoubtedly have a stop in the en banc court—*Peruta* was taken en banc by the Ninth Circuit on its own initiative after San Diego declined to file a petition—but both cases (along with a few others) will likely find their way to the Court in the not-too-distant future. Time will tell whether Justice Kennedy's replacement makes any difference in the long-running efforts to resuscitate *McDonald*'s admonition that the Second Amendment is not "a second-class right."[58]

* * *

In sum, at the moment OT 2018 may appear a bit lackluster in comparison to the blockbuster OT 2017. But even setting aside the many grants undoubtedly yet to come, there is much worth watching closely this coming year. At best, we will get invaluable insight into how the Court's newest members approach *stare decisis* and core structural constitutional constraints. At worst, we will still learn whether you can use your hovercraft in Alaska, what constrains the state from trying to seize your Land Rover, and where to turn if the state mandates public access to your private cemetery.

---

[56] Mance v. Sessions, No. 15-10311, 2018 WL 3544988 (5th Cir. July 20, 2018).

[57] Young v. Hawaii, No. 12-17808, 2018 WL 3542985 (9th Cir. July 24, 2018).

[58] McDonald v. City of Chicago, 561 U.S. 742, 780 (2010) (plurality).

Contributors

Thomas C. Berg is the James L. Oberstar professor of law and public policy at the University of St. Thomas School of Law (Minnesota), where he teaches constitutional law, religious liberty, intellectual property, and the religious liberty appellate clinic. In the clinic he supervises students writing briefs in major religious liberty cases, drawing on his experience drafting more than 50 briefs on issues of religious liberty and free speech in the Supreme Court and lower courts. Berg is also among the nation's leading scholars of law and religion. He has written more than 50 book chapters and journal articles and dozens of shorter pieces on religious freedom, constitutional law, and the role of religion in law, politics and society. His work has been cited several times by the U.S. Supreme Court and federal courts of appeals. He is the author of several books, including a leading casebook, *Religion and the Constitution* (with Michael McConnell and Christopher Lund), and *The State and Religion in a Nutshell*, and is at work on a new book, *Protecting Religious Liberty in a Polarized Age*. His other chief scholarly interest is the relation of intellectual property rights, social justice, and human development; he is co-editor of a forthcoming book concerning moral and religious perspectives on biotechnology patents. He received a B.S. in journalism from Northwestern University, an M.A. in philosophy and politics from Oxford University (as a Rhodes Scholar), and both an M.A. in religious studies and a J.D. from the University of Chicago. In law school, Berg served as executive editor of the law review and won two prizes for legal scholarship and writing. After clerking for Judge Alvin Rubin of the U.S. Court of Appeals for the Fifth Circuit, Berg practiced law with Mayer, Brown and Platt doing commercial litigation, appellate litigation, and nonprofit institutions' legal work.

Joseph Bishop-Henchman is executive vice president at the Tax Foundation, where he analyzes state tax trends, constitutional issues, and tax law developments. Joe has testified or presented to officials in 36 states, testified before Congress six times, and has written over 75 major studies on tax policy. In 2010, he was identified in *State Tax Notes* as among four people who "will likely dominate the field in the next 10 years." His expertise has been cited by the *Economist*, *New York Times*, *Wall Street Journal*, *USA Today*, *Washington Post*, and many others. He is the author of a book on distinguishing taxes from fees and the co-author of books on tax policy in North Carolina, Nebraska, and Nevada. His article *Why the Quill Physical Presence Rule Shouldn't Go the Way of Personal Jurisdiction* has been cited as a "spirited defense" of keeping tax jurisdiction based on physical presence. Before joining the Tax Foundation in 2005, he worked in the historic 2003 California recall election as press/policy aide to gubernatorial candidate and former baseball commissioner Peter Ueberroth, helped organize rallies against wasteful spending and the curfew law in his native San Diego County, and interned with the Office of the D.C. Attorney General, Citizens Against Government Waste, and University of California outreach in California's Central Valley. He is admitted to practice law in New York, Maryland, D.C., and before the U.S. Supreme Court. He holds a law degree from George Washington University and a bachelor's degree in political science with a minor in public policy from the University of California, Berkeley.

Josh Blackman is Professor of Law at the South Texas College of Law Houston. He specializes in constitutional law, the U.S. Supreme Court, and the intersection of law and technology. Josh is the author of the critically acclaimed *Unprecedented: The Constitutional Challenge to Obamacare* (2013), as well as *Unraveled: Obamacare, Religious Liberty, and Executive Power* (2016). He has also co-authored, with Randy E. Barnett & Josh Blackman, the leading case book *Constitutional Law: Cases in Context* (3rd Edition, Wolters Kluwer 2017). Josh was selected by Forbes Magazine for the "30 Under 30" in Law and Policy, has testified before the House Judiciary Committee on the constitutionality of executive action on immigration, and is an adjunct scholar at the Cato Institute. Josh is the founder and President of the Harlan Institute, the founder of FantasySCOTUS, the Internet's Premier Supreme Court Fantasy League, and blogs at JoshBlackman.com. Josh leads the cutting edge of legal analytics as Director of Judicial Research at LexPredict. He is the author of over two dozen law review articles, and his commentary has appeared in the *New York Times*, *Wall Street*

Journal, Washington Post, USA Today, L.A. Times, and other national publications. Josh clerked for the Honorable Danny J. Boggs on the U.S. Court of Appeals for the Sixth Circuit and for the Honorable Kim R. Gibson on the U.S. District Court for the Western District of Pennsylvania. Josh is a graduate of the George Mason University School of Law.

Mark Brnovich was inaugurated as Arizona's Attorney General in 2015. He previously served as director of the Arizona Department of Gaming, as an assistant U.S. attorney for the District of Arizona, and as an assistant attorney general with the state. He has also been a judge pro tem of Maricopa County Superior Court, deputy Maricopa County attorney, command staff judge advocate in the U.S. Army National Guard, and director of the Center for Constitutional Government at the Goldwater Institute. Brnovich is known for restoring public confidence in the office of "Arizona's Top Cop," for assembling some of the nation's most talented public servants for his administration, and for his administration's efforts in the area of consumer protection. Since Brnovich has been attorney general, the office has helped return over $130 million to Arizona's consumers. More recently, he was recognized as a "Leader of the Year" in public safety for his work in the area of law enforcement and consumer protection and advocacy.

Trevor Burrus is a research fellow in the Cato Institute's Robert A. Levy Center for Constitutional Studies and Center for the Study of Science, as well as managing editor of the Cato Supreme Court Review. His research interests include constitutional law, civil and criminal law, legal and political philosophy, legal history, and the interface between science and public policy. His academic work has appeared in journals such as the *Harvard Journal of Law and Public Policy,* the *New York University Journal of Law and Liberty,* the *New York University Annual Survey of American Law,* the *Syracuse Law Review,* and many others. His popular writing has appeared in the *Washington Post, New York Times, USA Today, Forbes,* Huffington Post, and others. Burrus lectures regularly on behalf of the Federalist Society, the Institute for Humane Studies, the Foundation for Economics Education, and other organizations, and he frequently appears on major media outlets. He is also the co-host of *Free Thoughts,* a weekly podcast that covers topics in libertarian theory, history, and philosophy. He is the editor of *A Conspiracy against Obamacare* (2013) and *Deep Commitments: The Past, Present, and Future of Religious Liberty* (2017), and holds a B.A. in philosophy from the University of Colorado at Boulder and a J.D. from the University of Denver Sturm College of Law.

Lucian E. Dervan is associate professor of law and director of criminal justice studies at Belmont University College of Law in Nashville. He focuses on domestic and international criminal law and is the recipient of numerous awards for his teaching and scholarship. Dervan is the author of two books and dozens of book chapters and articles. He is also the founder and author of *The Plea Bargaining Blog* and a contributing editor to the *White Collar Crime Prof Blog* (a member of the Law Professor Blogs Network). In addition to his writings, he regularly lectures regarding criminal law and has been invited to speak before the U.S. House Judiciary Committee, the U.S. Sentencing Commission, and the International Criminal Tribunal for the former Yugoslavia. Professor Dervan currently serves as chair of the ABA Criminal Justice Section. He is also the chair of the ABA Global White Collar Crime Institute and a member of the International Criminal Justice Standards Task Force. He also serves on the advisory committee of the NACDL White Collar Criminal Defense College at Stetson and as a faculty member at the program. Prior to joining the academy, Professor Dervan served as a law clerk to the Honorable Phyllis A. Kravitch of the U.S. Court of Appeals for the Eleventh Circuit. He also practiced law with King & Spalding LLP and Ford & Harrison LLP. Professor Dervan received his J.D. with high honors from Emory University School of Law, where he was an Emory Scholar, served as an articles editor for the *Emory Law Journal*, and was elected a member of the Order of the Coif. He received his B.A. with Honors from Davidson College.

David F. Forte is professor of law at Cleveland State University, where he was the inaugural holder of the Charles R. Emrick, Jr. – Calfee Halter & Griswold Endowed Chair. Recently, he was the Garwood Visiting Professor at Princeton University in the Department of Politics and Visiting Fellow at the James Madison Program in American Ideals and Institutions. He also held the position of Consultor to the Pontifical Council for the Family under Pope St. John Paul II and

Pope Benedict XVI. During the Reagan administration, Forte served as chief counsel to the U.S. delegation to the United Nations and alternate delegate to the Security Council. He has authored a number of briefs before the U.S. Supreme Court and has frequently testified before Congress and consulted with the State Department on human rights and international affairs issues. He has given over 300 invited addresses and papers at more than 100 academic institutions. His work has been cited by the U.S. Supreme Court. Forte was a Bradley Scholar at the Heritage Foundation, and visiting scholar at the Liberty Fund. He has also been a Civil War re-enactor and a merit badge counselor for the Boy Scouts. His teaching competencies include constitutional law, the First Amendment, Islamic law, jurisprudence, natural law, international law, international human rights, the presidency, and constitutional history. He holds degrees from Harvard College, Manchester University, England, the University of Toronto, and Columbia University.

Philip Hamburger is the Maurice and Hilda Friedman Professor of Law at Columbia Law School and the president of the New Civil Liberties Alliance. He is a leading scholar of constitutional law and its history, whose work spans religious liberty, freedom of speech, academic censorship, judicial review, the office and duty of judges, administrative power, the early development of liberal thought, and other areas. His books are *Separation of Church and State* (2002); *Law and Judicial Duty* (2008); *Is Administrative Law Unlawful?* (2014); and *The Administrative Threat* (2017). Before going to Columbia, Hamburger was the John P. Wilson Professor at the University of Chicago Law School, where he directed the Bigelow Program and legal history program. Earlier, he was the Oswald Symyster Colclough Research Professor at George Washington University Law School and a professor at the University of Connecticut Law School. He has been a visiting professor at the University of Virginia Law School and Northwestern Law School, where he was the Jack N. Pritzker Distinguished Visiting Professor of Law. Earlier, he practiced law in Philadelphia, specializing in business and corporate tax. He received his J.D. from Yale Law School.

James Knight is a legal intern in the Cato Institute's Robert A. Levy Center for Constitutional Studies. He received his B.A. *magna cum* *laude* in political science and philosophy from Fordham University and is currently a J.D. candidate at Georgetown University Law Center. At Georgetown, he is a Bradley Fellow and a senior article editor on the *Georgetown Journal of Law and Public Policy*.

Jennifer L. Mascott is an assistant professor of law. She also previously served as faculty director of the Supreme Court and administrative law clinics at Scalia Law School at George Mason University's Antonin Scalia Law School. Mascott teaches administrative law and writes in the areas of administrative and constitutional law and statutory interpretation. Her scholarship has been cited by the Supreme Court and has been published or is forthcoming in the *Stanford Law Review, George Mason Law Review, George Washington Law Review, BYU Law Review,* and *Loyola Journal of Regulatory Compliance*. The well-known *Legal Theory Blog* has reviewed her work as "path breaking," and she is a permanent commentator at the *Yale Journal of Regulation's Notice and Comment* blog. Mascott is a public member of the Administrative Conference of the United States and a former law clerk to Supreme Court Justice Clarence Thomas and Judge Brett M. Kavanaugh of the U.S. Court of Appeals for the D.C. Circuit.

Robert McNamara serves as a senior attorney with the Institute for Justice. He joined the Institute in August 2006 and litigates cutting-edge constitutional cases protecting free speech, property rights, economic liberty, and other individual liberties in both federal and state courts. McNamara's work has resulted in court victories for property owners fighting eminent domain abuse, tour guides fighting unconstitutional restrictions on their speech, taxi drivers seeking the right to own their own business, and many others. He also litigates in defense of innovation and entrepreneurship in medical care and was co-counsel in *Flynn v. Holder*, IJ's landmark challenge to the federal prohibition on compensating bone marrow donors. McNamara's writing has been published by outlets including the *New York Times, Wall Street Journal, Washington Post,* and dozens more nationwide. His opinions and views on legal issues have been featured in radio and television programs ranging from NPR's *All Things Considered* to Fox News Channel's *Hannity & Colmes*. Robert is a graduate of Boston University and the New York University School of Law, where he was a founding member and editor-in-chief of the *NYU Journal of Law & Liberty*.

Erin E. Murphy is a partner in the Washington office of Kirkland & Ellis LLP. Her practice focuses on Supreme Court, appellate, and constitutional litigation. She has argued four cases before the Supreme Court, including successfully arguing *Gill v. Whitford*, *McCutcheon v. FEC*, and *Texas v. United States*. Erin has been recognized by the *National Law Journal* as one of the nation's "Outstanding Women Lawyers" and a "Rising Star." She has been ranked by *Chambers & Partners* as one of the nation's top appellate lawyers; has been recognized by *The Legal 500 U.S.* for her appellate work; has been listed in *The Best Lawyers in America* for appellate practice; and was one of 10 lawyers featured on LinkedIn's list of "Top Professionals 35 and Under." Erin's work before the Supreme Court has included briefing such high-profile cases as *NFIB v. Sebelius*, *Hughes v. Talen Energy Marketing*, and *ABC v. Aereo*. She also has a robust practice before the federal courts of appeals, where she has presented argument before most of the circuits on several important statutory and constitutional questions, including the scope of the Second Amendment, the Takings Clause, and the National Labor Relations Act. Erin is the co-chair of programming for the Edward Coke Appellate Inn of Court, has taught as an adjunct professor at Georgetown University, and frequently speaks on topics relating to the Supreme Court and appellate advocacy.

Walter Olson is a senior fellow at the Cato Institute's Robert A. Levy Center for Constitutional Studies and is known for his writing on the American legal system. His books include *The Rule of Lawyers*, on mass litigation, *The Excuse Factory*, on lawsuits in the workplace, and most recently *Schools for Misrule*, on the state of the law schools. His first book, *The Litigation Explosion*, was one of the most widely discussed general-audience books on law of its time. It led the *Washington Post* to dub him "intellectual guru of tort reform." Active on social media, he is known as the founder and principal writer of what is generally considered the oldest blog on law as well as one of the most popular, Overlawyered.com. He has advised many public officials from the White House to town councils and in 2015 was named by Gov. Larry Hogan to be co-chair of the Maryland Redistricting Reform

Commission, which issued its report recommendations later that year to acclaim across the state. Before joining Cato, Olson was a senior fellow at the Manhattan Institute and an editor at the magazine *Regulation*, then edited by future Supreme Court Justice Antonin Scalia. Olson's more than 400 broadcast appearances include all the major networks, NPR, the BBC, *The Diane Rehm Show*, and *Oprah*.

Roger Pilon is vice president for legal affairs at the Cato Institute, the founding director of Cato's Center for Constitutional Studies, the inaugural holder of Cato's B. Kenneth Simon Chair in Constitutional Studies, and the founding publisher of the *Cato Supreme Court Review*. Before joining Cato he held five senior posts in the Reagan administration at the Office of Personnel Management, the State Department, and the Justice Department, and was a National Fellow at Stanford's Hoover Institution. In 1989, the Bicentennial Commission presented him with its Benjamin Franklin Award for excellence in writing on the U.S. Constitution. In 2001, Columbia University's School of General Studies awarded him its Alumni Medal of Distinction. Pilon lectures and debates at universities and law schools across the country and testifies often before Congress. His writings have appeared in major academic and popular journals and he appears often on radio and TV. Pilon holds a B.A. from Columbia University, an M.A. and a Ph.D. from the University of Chicago, and a J.D. from the George Washington University School of Law.

Ilya Shapiro is a senior fellow in constitutional studies at the Cato Institute and editor-in-chief of the *Cato Supreme Court Review*. Before joining Cato, he was a special assistant/advisor to the Multi-National Force in Iraq on rule of law issues and practiced international, political, commercial, and antitrust litigation at Patton Boggs and Cleary Gottlieb. Shapiro is the co-author (with David H. Gans) of *Religious Liberties for Corporations? Hobby Lobby, the Affordable Care Act, and the Constitution* (2014). He has contributed to many academic, popular, and professional publications and regularly provides media commentary—including an appearance on the *Colbert Report*—and is a legal consultant to CBS News. Shapiro has testified before Congress and state legislatures and, as coordinator of Cato's amicus brief program, has filed more than 300 "friend of the court" briefs in the Supreme Court. He lectures regularly on behalf of the Federalist

Society, was an inaugural Washington Fellow at the National Review Institute and a Lincoln Fellow at the Claremont Institute, and has been an adjunct professor at the George Washington University Law School. In 2015 *National Law Journal* named him to its list of "rising stars" (40 under 40). Before entering private practice, Shapiro clerked for Judge E. Grady Jolly of the U.S. Court of Appeals for the Fifth Circuit. He holds an A.B. from Princeton, an M.Sc. from the London School of Economics, and a J.D. from the University of Chicago (where he became a Tony Patiño Fellow). Shapiro is a member of the bars of New York, D.C., and the U.S. Supreme Court.

Paul Sherman is a senior attorney with the Institute for Justice. He joined the Institute in July 2007 and litigates cutting-edge constitutional cases protecting the First Amendment, economic liberty, property rights, and other individual liberties in both federal and state courts. Sherman has extensive experience litigating First Amendment cases. He previously represented syndicated newspaper columnist John Rosemond in a successful First Amendment challenge to occupational licensing laws that threaten to silence ordinary parenting advice. Sherman also represented blogger Steve Cooksey in a First Amendment challenge to North Carolina's dietetics law. In addition to his work on occupational speech, Sherman has litigated numerous campaign finance cases. He served as co-counsel in *SpeechNow.org v. FEC*, which the Congressional Research Service described as representing one of "the most fundamental changes to campaign finance law in decades." Sherman has challenged government overreach by dental and veterinary licensing boards in Alabama, Connecticut, Georgia, and Maryland. He is a prolific media writer and his views on the First Amendment and constitutional law have appeared in the *New York Times, Washington Post, Wall Street Journal,* and other media outlets. Sherman received his law degree from the George Washington University Law School in 2006. Before coming to the Institute, he worked as the associate director of the Center for Competitive Politics.

Rodney A. Smolla is dean and professor of law at the Delaware Law School of Widener University, in Wilmington, Delaware. He is a nationally known scholar on matters relating to constitutional law, civil rights, freedom of speech, and mass media, particularly matters relating to libel and privacy. He is the author five multi-volume legal treatises, all published by Thomson Reuters, which are updated twice annually: *Law of Defamation*; *Smolla and Nimmer on Freedom of Speech*; *Rights and Liabilities in Media Content, Internet, Broadcast, and Print*; *Federal Civil Rights Acts*; and, *Law of Lawyer Advertising*. Smolla has published over 100 articles in law reviews and other publications. He has served as chairman of the Association of American Law Schools Section on Defamation and Privacy Law, as chairman of the Association of American Law Schools Section on Mass Communications Law, among other positions. In 2011, he was appointed by Governor Nikki Haley to serve on the South Carolina Commission of Higher Education. Smolla has been and remains an active litigator. In practice, he is particularly well-known for his representation of American and international clients on matters relating to defamation and invasion of privacy. He is admitted to the Illinois, Virginia, and Delaware bars, and has participated as counsel or co-counsel in many matters in state and federal courts throughout the nation. He is a frequent advocate on a wide variety of legal issues, and has presented oral argument in state and federal courts across the country, including the U.S. Supreme Court. He received his J.D. from Duke University.